W9-AJR-909

CAREER
OPPORTUNITIES
IN JOURNALISM

CAREER OPPORTUNITIES IN JOURNALISM

JENNIFER BOBROW BURNS

Foreword by
Janice Castro
Assistant Dean and Director of
Graduate Journalism Programs,
Medill School of Journalism,
Northwestern University

Checkmark Books®
An imprint of Infobase Publishing

Career Opportunities in Journalism

Checkmark Books
An imprint of Infobase Publishing
132 West 31st Street
New York NY 10001

ISBN-10: 0-8160-6420-2
ISBN-13: 978-0-8160-6420-5

Library of Congress Cataloging-in-Publication Data

Burns, Jennifer Bobrow.
  Career opportunities in journalism / Jennifer Bobrow Burns ; foreword by Janice Castro.
      p. cm
  Includes bibliographical references and index.
   ISBN 0-8160-6420-2 (pb : alk. paper)   ISBN 0-8160-6419-9 (hc : alk. paper)
  1. Journalism—Vocational guidance. I. Title.

PN4797.B87 2007
070.4023—dc22   2006025280

Checkmark Books are available at special discounts when purchased in bulk quantities for businesses, associations, institutions, or sales promotions. Please call our Special Sales Department in New York at (212) 967-8800 or (800) 322-8755.

You can find Facts On File on the World Wide Web at http://www.factsonfile.com

Cover design by Nora Wertz

Printed in the United States of America

VB Hermitage 10   9   8   7   6   5   4   3   2   1

This book is printed on acid-free paper.

CONTENTS

FOREWORD

If you have picked up this book, you probably are wondering what it is like to be a journalist. What skills do you need? What kind of education and training? What are the jobs like? What is the best place to work? How does one get started? What do you need to know?

The answers to most of those questions have changed during the dozen or so years since 1994, when the *Palo Alto Weekly* in northern California became the first newspaper to publish regularly on the Web, and *Time* became the first newsmagazine to post its contents online.

Suddenly, *Palo Alto Weekly* readers could check the news without leaving their living room computers, and *Time* readers could see the cover story on Sunday evening, then chat online with the editors. Until that point, there were sharp distinctions separating the media. People who wanted to work as broadcast news reporters had to learn how to use a microphone and tell a story to a camera. Newspaper reporters gathered information in their communities or on their beats and wrote it up for publication once a day. Magazine reporters generally had a week or more between editions and often had several days to interview their sources and take photographs. Reporters needed to know what kind of news was important, how to get the story, and how to verify the facts and write the story well. They needed to be ethical communicators, never distorting the facts or inventing them. They had to earn the trust of their readers with every story. That has not changed, but the world around them has.

Fast-forward to 2006. This is a remarkably exciting time to consider a career in journalism. Journalists in all media have opportunities to create new kinds of reporting, using new tools and formats to serve lively interactive audiences. There are no print-only or TV-only newsrooms anymore, or any jobs in journalism that are immune to change. When I began my career as a reporter at *Time* three decades ago, the world of journalism was rather settled in its ways. There was a right way to do everything, and the journalism mantra at big media companies was "if it ain't broke, don't fix it." Imagine hearing that as a young journalist whenever you proposed a new idea. That media world was static. But that world is gone. Today constant change is the rule, and daily innovation is not only welcome but needed. Got good ideas? Come on in.

Profound and rapid change is transforming the media landscape. Many independent news companies have been acquired by sprawling media conglomerates such as Time Warner. Time Warner itself was swallowed up by America Online in 2000. Knight Ridder, one of the world's most important newspaper chains, abruptly ceased to exist in 2006 when it was bought by the McClatchy company and broken up. At the same time, a raft of new online-only news organizations such as CNET in San Francisco and TheStreet.com in New York City provide robust reporting in specialized fields, while Yahoo!, Google, and other new kinds of companies serve a global news audience with headlines they collect from the journalism companies that actually report and produce the stories. Within just five years after the *Palo Alto Weekly* began publishing online in 1994, digital delivery of news became an accepted part of every journalism company's operations, gradually forcing journalism companies to learn how to change.

What does it take to succeed in this new journalism world? Hard work, hunger for information, and a willingness to learn new techniques on the fly. Reporters still need to know how to get the facts, verify them carefully, and beat the competition to the good stories. Writers still need to craft graceful and engaging stories. More than ever before, journalists need to operate in a transparent fashion and follow ethical information-gathering and reporting practices. But the age of "appointment journalism" (newspapers in the morning, network news at night) is over. People now expect to hear the latest news at all hours of day and night. When people want to know something right away, they no longer look for the latest copy of the newsmagazine or dig out a reference book; they "Google" it. The average CNN viewer is aged 60. Most Americans under the age of 40 no longer read a newspaper every day, but 50 million Americans still read the news online each day, much of it on newspaper Web sites. At the same time, personal publishing is growing explosively: An estimated 48 million Americans have published their own stories, comments, photographs, videos, or other content online.

Journalism no longer is a one-way conversation, nor do most news companies have the luxury of delivering the news once per day. At papers such as the *New York Times,* the *Washington Post,* the *Chicago Tribune,* and *USA Today,* editors operate "continuous news" desks around the clock. When the newspaper reporters and editors who have worked all day go home in the evening, another shift of print and online editors keeps on reporting and posting news to the Web site that in many cases is fresher than the newspaper that will land on doorsteps the next morning. ABC News and other networks post online updates between newscasts and offer podcasts, do-it-yourself news downloads, and other interactive services.

All of these companies employ reporters and editors, producers and copy editors, photographers and videographers, feature editors, photo editors, and many of the other traditional news positions described in the following chapters. But these journalists need new kinds of skills. These days, reporters must be able to tell their stories in multiple media. Print reporters learn how to deliver live updates on television and sometimes file breaking news directly to their Web sites or record podcasts on the run. Many reporters capture their interviews on digital recorders so that excerpts can be posted online as sidebars or special downloads. Reporters who never before were expected to be photographers now carry digital cameras as well as their notebooks. Photographers are asked to write sidebars or record commentary for the online photo-essay. Print journalists work alongside multimedia producers in the newsroom who are building photo-essays with sound, interactive maps, and searchable databases to accompany their print or broadcast stories. For many journalists, this means knowing more about their stories and understanding their communities and the interests of their readers and viewers more deeply.

Some of the best journalists working today defy neat categorization as writers or reporters or photographers. *New York Times* multimedia reporter Naka Nathaniel, for example, produces interactive video, Flash movies, photo-essays, and audio commentaries, often working in war zones and other global trouble spots with columnist Nicholas Kristof. A graduate of the University of Texas, Nathaniel majored in journalism and was studying computers in the early 1990s, which some of his journalism friends found strange at the time. A year later, he was one of the first *New York Times* online reporters.

War correspondents who formerly had to leave the combat zone in order to send back stories or exposed film now carry the means of publishing into the field with them. They haul in satellite phones, videophones, digital cameras, and laptops and beam their stories from areas as remote as the rugged mountainscapes of Afghanistan, where Pulitzer Prize–winning photographer Cheryl Diaz Meyer covered the U.S. battles against terrorists in late 2001. In addition to her pencils and notepads, Meyer recalled carrying two Nikon bodies, several lenses, eight camera batteries, 50 AA-batteries, several rechargers, 15 memory cards, a Macintosh G3 laptop, two laptop batteries, an AC power adapter, a DC power adapter, a power strip, and a variety of other attachments and devices. She added a gasoline-powered generator once she realized she would be working in

areas with no electricity. Meyer took a crash course in how to use all of that equipment just before heading for the war zone.

What are editors looking for in young journalists amid this kaleidoscopic blur of media change? Curiosity, persistence, and a keen sense of the listening and reading community are key, and so is imagination and common sense. Good reporters have always awakened eager to know what happened since they went to sleep and motivated to find out and tell their communities. Fine editors always have excelled at shaping graceful and engaging information important to the people who read their publications or watch their newscasts. Now they know that their audiences have multiple sources of information and new kinds of information-seeking habits. People will ask for content of particular interest by signing up for RSS feeds, podcasts, vodcasts, or e-newsletter updates. Inventive news editors serve their communities in new ways by paying attention to the way they live and using the new tools at their command. At the *Naples Daily News* in Florida, online editor Rob Curley offers SMS alerts delivered to cell phones that can notify parents that their child's soccer game has been canceled, a dazzling daily videocast, comments areas on all stories, reader reviews of entertainment, and even wake-up calls. The site sends readers e-mail reminders of school and other community events and provides a complete audio download of the morning's news that readers can listen to on their way to work. The Naples team is creating innovative journalism by developing new editorial products.

This new multimedia environment is full of opportunity for motivated journalists. Someone reading this book may start a little company that changes the way the rest of us get our news. Someone else may win a Pulitzer Prize or an Oscar, invent a new digital device that makes our lives easier, or write a book that will change the direction of public policy. What it takes is good ideas, boundless curiosity, and a willingness to keep on learning new ways to discover stories and deliver them and dig again.

Editors and producers have told me that they are looking for bright young journalists who can work in multimedia, who understand visual storytelling, and who know how to process video, words, sounds, and pictures for digital delivery. All of these hiring managers mention first the importance of good writing and reporting skills, solid news judgment, and a passion for journalism. Critical thinking is vital. How do you sniff out a fake? When is a photo too perfect? Editors also say that young journalists must be comfortable with computers and with learning new skills on the fly. They seek people who can deal with rapid change and who can multitask well. They are looking for people who are focused on excellence, who are thorough and fair and meticulous about accuracy. They look for character, people who know their communities and can reach out to them with interactive messages, and welcome community contributions online. They seek people who want to be part of journalism's multifaceted, evolving new landscape. They want people who can embrace the new world of communications and help to shape it. And at a time of such sweeping change, they say it is no longer enough to be trained in journalism's basic skills. To really succeed in today's journalism world, it is important to understand the business of media, to understand how to find new ways of serving the community and developing new editorial products. Cross-training is not just a requirement for triathletes, after all. It is the new mantra of 21st-century journalism.

—Professor Janice Castro
Northwestern University

INDUSTRY OUTLOOK

As long as the First Amendment promises us freedom of speech, journalists will be around to tell it like it is. The fact that the media brings the events of our communities, the nation, and all of the world into our homes each day is what makes us an informed society. We have opinions and choices because we are able to express them. While journalists will always face criticism and scrutiny for their ethics and methods, the news they discover enlightens us all.

Many journalists feel passionately drawn to their work early on their lives. From the child who uncovers where the local bully keeps his stolen stash of candy to the teen who cracks the fixed student body election for her high school paper, journalists are driven by a desire to find the truth. Although all are good communicators, their mediums will vary. Some tell their stories through words, while others use visual images, including video, photography, and electronic media; many use a combination. However, all journalists have compelling stories to tell and a responsibility to inform the public.

Journalism has come a long way since newspapers were produced on the printing press. The advent of radio, television, and the Internet have shaped media in ways that no one could have predicted, and now no one can remember how we got our news before. With all our multimedia options, as a society we have developed shorter attention spans. News is fleeting, to head onto the back burner as soon as a more compelling story arrives on the scene. Journalists strive to grab our attention, as well as accurately record our history.

Regardless of whether we read it, hear it, watch it, or click on it, news shapes our society. It analyzes the events that make up the past and looks to the impact they will have on our future. The classic method that is taught in high schools around the country of "who, what, when, where, why, and how" still captures the essence of telling a story. To move into the future, journalists must build on this model and continue to find new and interesting ways to share the news. At their best, with fairness, objectivity, and high ethical standards, journalists enable us to form opinions about the events going on in our lives. While history marches on, there will be journalists to record it and comment on its ups and downs.

This book focuses on several of the major areas in which journalists can work; many journalists work in a number of different mediums throughout their careers. While there are similarities between the areas, there are also differences in their structure, work environment, and responsibilities. Following is some information about each of these career categories as well as overall themes and trends facing them today.

Print

Newspapers   Although industry insiders fear the day will come when this could happen, the Internet has not yet rendered newspapers obsolete. In homes around the world, people open their front doors in the morning to find their favorite paper on their doorstep, still one of the major ways they get the news.

According to MSN Encarta, in the United States in 2000, about 1,500 daily newspapers printed a total of 56 million copies. Almost 7,600 weekly newspapers circulated in the United States during that year as well. Many of these papers are consolidating regularly, as large parent companies buy them up, combine, and downsize.

However, newspaper journalism still represents a classic example of the discipline. The hectic newsroom, the fast pace, and tight deadlines cannot be replicated elsewhere. For new journalists just starting out in the field, getting a newspaper job can be the ultimate place to start. As a fledgling reporter covering a police beat in a small town, one can dream of grandeur later to come.

Typically, reporters begin wherever they can find a job. This will often be at small weekly papers, though graduates of top programs may find themselves at dailies. The advantage of starting out small can be the opportunity to develop skills and grow as a writer, with access to editors and much responsibility due to a limited staff. However, one must be careful of staying too long and getting stuck in a limited niche. If you are lucky enough to begin at a larger daily, be aware that the competition will be fierce. Take every chance to distinguish yourself and try not to get lost in the shuffle. Internships remain an essential way to break in.

Newspapers are structured with reporters and photographers supervised by editors, who have worked their way up to select, correct, and sometimes still write the news. Editors report to publishers who are concerned with the business of running a newspaper—profitability and the bottom line. Newspaper journalists may struggle with the fine line of bringing in readers but maintaining fairness and truth in their writing.

Currently, prospects are competitive for newspaper jobs. As many papers launch companion Web sites, reporters and editors with computer skills will have a tremendous advantage. While the medium may change, writing and reporting skills cannot be replaced by machines. Just as copyediting and newspaper photography have been revolutionized by computer systems, so can reporting. Newspaper journalists in the future will adapt and build their capabilities.

Magazines   Unlike most newspapers that report general news on a daily basis, magazines are typically specialized. They appeal to specific interest groups, whether women over 40, people who like to travel or own dogs, or senior citizens. Other magazines may be specialized in the sense that they are news magazines, regional magazines, or financial magazines.

Most magazines are published on a weekly or monthly basis, offering an alternative from the frenetic pace of breaking news. While some reporters thrive on getting the scoop for a late breaking story, others prefer writing for magazines, where they have more time to develop their style. Magazine stories are often features that are carried through with details. Furthermore, some reporters and writers may handle investigative pieces over a period of several weeks or months.

Magazines are structured similarly to newspapers with reporters, editors, and publishers working together to reconcile content with financial success. They may also use more freelance writers to work on their articles. Some journalists move between magazines and newspapers throughout their careers, though finding ultimately that they have a preference for one or the other. Writers with special interest areas of their own may often find their niche in magazines.

Competition is also quite tight for magazine jobs, as many publications struggle to remain successful in their market. Internships in the field, published clips, and well-developed writing skills remain ways to start in the field. Furthermore, as Internet companion sites become more widespread, computer skills are also valuable. Some publications have articles that are "Web only" in addition to posting their printed content.

Broadcasting

Television   With 98 percent of American homes having at least one television set, television is a crucial way people get their news. Anchors and reporters become familiar friends who are invited into our houses each day.

Breaking into television news remains more competitive than other areas of journalism, but with different skill sets required. While investigative and writing skills will always be important, presentation skills and appearance also play a large role for on-air jobs. Yet, there are many other behind the scenes jobs that are essential to television news, such as those of producers, camerapeople, writers, and editors.

The news director typically runs the newsroom with a staff including a managing editor, assignment editor, producers, reporters, and camerapeople. As breaking news happens, teams must be ready to act and go on the scene at a moment's notice. Hours may be longer and even more unpredictable in broadcast news than other areas of journalism. Television special reports can air at any time around the clock when something newsworthy appears. While newspapers do not put out extra editions, television news programs will preempt other programming and work tirelessly to cover scandals, tragedies, and other events with the immediacy the public expects.

As with other areas of journalism, internships are essential for gaining experience that can lead to a first job. Broadcasting majors can help hone reporting and producing skills, as well as provide some on-air exposure.

Aspiring television reporters should expect to relocate in order to get their first break, often to small towns in tiny markets. Insiders say that in today's market, turnover is low, as is security, so one must be prepared to fight for his or her job. However, for those who dream of being on-air or part of an on-air production, the struggle is worthwhile. Jobs in television are available at commercial networks, which operate a variety of commercial stations, public television, and cable television.

Radio   Radio still remains an essential area of news journalism. While other forms of multimedia have taken over the one-time role of radio, people still depend on the radio for news and programming, especially in their cars. All news stations play news, traffic, and weather around the clock, and commercial stations also include some combination of those three.

Another area of radio that offers more diversity for journalists is public radio. National Public Radio (NPR) and its local affiliates offer programming that is more feature-oriented. Radio journalists in this setting have the opportunity to develop features or special interest programs, host programs, and conduct in-depth exploration of issues. Jobs are also competitive and difficult to come by. Degrees and areas of expertise are more important as options are fewer. Campus radio offers an ideal way to get involved with the field.

New Media

Many experts believe that the future of journalism lies with the Internet. Certainly, it has changed expectations about when and how we get our news. People have news Web sites up on their computers all day long, at home or at the office. If we log on at 3 A.M. we expect up-to-the-minute updates about the world. Since the Internet is a 24-hour, 7-day-a-week, 365-day-a-year medium, it truly defines breaking news.

The new media industry is still defining itself and its role in journalism today. Many sites are companions of newspaper, magazine, and television counterparts, providing additional and updated information on a constant basis.

Working in new media is not for the lazy. Breaking news must be handled instantly, and reporters, producers, and editors must thrive under constant deadline pressure.

Positions and job titles are as in flux as the industry itself. A title of producer may mean something different from one Web site to another. Employers are still in the process of defining jobs and their roles. Dual assignments are common, such as people writing, editing, and producing all at once.

New media journalism offers opportunity for great advancement and creativity for those with the right skill sets. Some reporters start at Web sites right out of school, while others move from print publications. The Internet may also become an area of opportunity for broadcast journalists, with BBC.com as one of the first sites to feature Web anchors. Computer and technical skills are a key component to success, as journalists work together with graphics experts to determine how to create content that is visually as well as verbally compelling and keeps people on their site. As newspapers and magazines shift to enhancing their Web sites, positions will continue to grow.

Strategic Communication

Another area for journalists to work is that of strategic communication. Businesses and nonprofit organizations must get their messages out to the public. They have products to sell, missions to promote, and programs to advertise. Journalists in strategic communication may work in advertising, public relations, or corporate communications. They are responsible for writing and communicating in a variety of ways.

Some journalists in strategic communication write advertising copy, newsletters, or speeches. They might be responsible for shaping their organization's image or communicating their positions. Like other journalists, they take information and choose their angle or goal. Then they use their writing skills to present it to the public. The job outlook for journalists in strategic communication is fair to good, as companies place increased importance on protecting their images.

Education

The responsibility of training future journalists is an important one. At the college level, many journalism professors have not only studied the discipline of journalism, but they have been active professionals in the field. Journalism professors have expertise in all journalistic mediums and often have also had distinguished careers in industry. Sometimes they teach as adjunct instructors in addition to holding other jobs at newspapers, magazines, and radio/television stations.

At the top journalism programs across the country, professors have been Pulitzer Prize–winning reporters and top rated news producers. Faculty may teach at the undergraduate or graduate level and also frequently work as advisers to campus newspapers, magazines, radio, or television stations. Most hold master's degrees in journalism, and some have doctorates, but their experience is often as important as their education.

Some high schools also have journalism programs and journalism teachers may work at the high school level. Here, they instruct students in the basics of writing and reporting, building the foundation for future study. They also serve as advisers to campus publications or media. In public schools, teacher certification is necessary, while most private schools do not have the same requirement.

Outlook for jobs in education is fair, with strong competition for full-time faculty positions at colleges and universities. Teachers at the secondary school level are more marketable if they also teach English, history, or communications courses.

Conclusion

No matter what type of journalism interests you the most, a competitive but exciting road lies ahead. Writing, reporting, and editing skills, coupled with a tenacious, persistent, analytical, and inquisitive nature, will be valuable regardless of what you choose. The best way to get a feel for the work is through internships and experience. Write features for your high school newspaper, photograph sports for your college yearbook, or cover an art opening for a local magazine. Campus and small local radio and television stations hire interns and volunteers to report and produce both on-air and behind the scenes. No market is too small, no town too boring, and no hours too long if you want to be a journalist. Go after your passion and your career will follow. Read on to forge your path.

ACKNOWLEDGMENTS

I would like to extend my appreciation to all those who participated in some way with the creation of this book. Without their help, this book would not have been possible.

First, I would like to thank Janice Castro, assistant dean; Director, Graduate Journalism Programs; and assistant professor at the Medill School of Journalism, Northwestern University. As an experienced journalist, as well as educator who is responsible for training future journalists at one of our country's top journalism schools, I am grateful that she agreed to write the foreword for this book, and I thank her for her hard work.

Furthermore, I am grateful to my editor, James Chambers, for both his flexibility and accessibility. Sarah Fogarty, project editor, and Vanessa Nittoli, associate editor, have also been very helpful.

Next, I would like to express my gratitude to the many people who took the time to speak to (or e-mail) me about their jobs or to provide information in any way. The insight they shared contributed invaluably to my research and helped to make the career profiles more interesting and realistic. In addition to those who prefer to remain anonymous, they include:

Heather Bobrow Finn, former editorial assistant, *Marie Claire* magazine; Judy Bolch, professor, Harte Chair in Journalism, Missouri School of Journalism; Pat Grandjean, senior editor, *Connecticut Magazine*; Hannah McCaughey, creative director, *Outside Magazine*; Jean Marie Hamilton, managing editor, *Mpls. St. Paul Magazine*; Jody Buffalo, senior beauty editor, *Shape* magazine; Polly Blitzer, correspondent, *InStyle* magazine; Anita Dosik, STC; Fran Silverman, freelance journalist; Yasi Jahed, editorial researcher, *Workforce Management* magazine; Deb Hopp, publisher, *Mpls. St. Paul Magazine*; Karla-Jean Zander, HR research manager, Inland Press Association; Aviv Blasbalg, sports copy editor, *Connecticut Post*; Jim Simon, associate professor, Department of English, Fairfield University; Matt Suess, photographer; Ann Visser, president, Journalism Education Association; Society for Technical Communication; Suzette Moyer, director of graphics and design, *Hartford Courant*; Wanda Nicholson, manager, Association of American Editorial Cartoonists; Mike Keefe, editorial cartoonist, *Denver Post*; Mark Mandle, AdAge Research; Rachel Benevento; Erika Miller; Meghan Collins, Washingtonpost.com; Shelley Hassman Kadish, reporter, WSHU; Stacey Woelfel, news director, KOMU-TV; Noreen Welle, RTNDA.

Finally, I would like to thank my family for their love and support: my parents, Ellen and Robert; my sister, Heather; and, especially, my wonderful daughter, Sophie.

HOW TO USE THIS BOOK

If you have a nose for news, innate curiosity, and a skill with written words, then journalism might be the field for you. The quest for information and thirst to dig deeper to uncover the facts drives journalists to present information to the public that helps them shape opinions, arguments, and an overall understanding about current events. Whether their medium is print, broadcast, or the Internet, journalists objectively tell a story, engaging their viewers and readers in the world around them.

As you can see from the Table of Contents, journalism job titles and work environments are quite diverse. This book is broken down into nine general categories. In several of these categories, you will see some of the same job titles. For example, you will see "Reporter" in the sections for newspapers, television, and radio. While the job differs somewhat based on the setting, you'll discover that a reporter has the same basic responsibilities regardless of where he or she works. As a journalist, you can choose the genre that appeals the most to you—the on-air excitement of broadcast journalism, the passion and sweat of toiling away late nights at a daily paper, the glossy glamour and broader deadlines of a magazine, or the cutting-edge, up-to-the-minute challenge of new media. Many journalists move throughout several of these areas during their career.

Because the field is so varied, no one book could possibly contain all the potential job titles to be found in journalism. There are many more positions to be found than the 77 listed by this book. Use this sampling as a starting point for further research into any and all titles and industries of interest.

The Career Profiles

Each of the 77 career profiles in this book describes a different job found in journalism. It contains useful information that can serve as an introduction to encourage further research into each specific profession and general field. The following sections are included in each career profile.

Career Profile Snapshots and Career Ladders

Each career profile begins with a snapshot of information that will be found in more detail by reading further. At a quick glance, you can get a general sense of basic duties, salary ranges, employment and advancement prospects, and education, training, and skill requirements. The best geographical location to find employment is also included here. In most fields, the locations listed are by no means the only options but are the areas with the highest concentration of jobs.

Opposite the career profile snapshot is a career ladder, containing three job titles. The profiled job will always be in the middle of the three in order to provide an idea of the typical career path. You will find that within journalism, a common career path often includes movement from smaller to larger markets within the same job title. However, advancing to take on a different role with management responsibility (such as a reporter becoming an editor or news director) frequently happens as well.

Position Description

The position descriptions offer an overview of the basic duties and responsibilities of each career that is profiled. The goal of the position descriptions is for you to come away with an understanding of what someone in this occupation actually does on a regular basis. Information is included such as daily tasks, types of projects, and how each job fits in with other professions in the field. They may contain insight into typical hours, work environments, and the types of activities involved. Furthermore, the position descriptions share any background information about the industry that is needed to understand the career profile.

Salaries

Salaries for journalists vary tremendously based on their work setting and size of their market. For example, a reporter at a small town weekly may earn $12,000 per year, while a seasoned journalist at the *New York Times* can earn more than $200,000. The sky can be the limit for those journalists who become syndicated columnists, celebrity anchors, or best-selling authors. However, as many in the field will tell you, salaries are not as high as they would like for most journalists working in the trenches.

There are many factors that contribute to the large salary disparity that journalists face. The size of the market is the biggest salary predictor. Newspapers and magazines with the largest circulation and television and radio stations with the largest viewer/listener market have the money to pay their staff more than small publications and networks. Geographic location often goes right along with market size as small towns have fewer opportunities. Another salary indicator is based on years of experience. A first-year beat reporter earns considerably less than a beat reporter who has made a 20-year career of covering city hall.

The salary information in this section is compiled from several sources, including the Bureau of Labor Statistics, professional associations, salary surveys, employees in the field, and others. Since salary information becomes outdated very quickly, make sure information is accurate by checking recent sources. As you read over the figures, you can also use salary calculators from sites such as http://www.salary.com to compare salaries based on region.

Employment Prospects

Employment prospects are variable and often are directly affected by the economy. As with the salary data, the projections in this section come from the Bureau of Labor Statistics, professional associations, and employees in the field. Be sure to check updated information about the careers that interest you as prospects are constantly changing. They also vary based on the size, budget, and location of the position, as well as by type of organization.

Advancement Prospects

This section covers the advancement prospects for the career being profiled. It may include next steps within the same type of organization, as well as possible moves to other types of organizations that can result in higher salaries or more responsibility. It also discusses any training or other requirements that might be needed for advancement.

Within journalism, you will find that advancement does not necessarily consist of moving to the next position up on the corporate ladder. More typically, journalists advance by moving from smaller markets to larger ones in the same position.

Education and Training

While some positions within journalism require specific educational backgrounds and degrees, others have more flexible requirements. This section includes the required credentials, as well as the credentials that may not be essential but are widely preferred for employment. It discusses helpful undergraduate majors, course work, and graduate degrees. It also covers any training needed such as certificates or internships.

Special Requirements

Some of the profiled careers have special requirements such as licensure or certification. They might require certain degrees from accredited programs or the passing of specific exams for entry. This section handles these important facts and provides resources such as the Web sites and phone numbers for organizations that offer additional information.

Experience, Skills, and Personality Traits

Each career that is profiled requires certain skills, experience, and personality traits in order to be entered. This section discusses necessary skills, such as computer programs, foreign languages, public speaking, or other learned expertise. It also highlights personality traits and innate abilities, such as flexibility, curiosity, or patience that will enable one to be successful in this field. The positions that are being profiled range from entry level to those that require 10 years or more of experience. This section lets you know about experience required as well.

Unions and Associations

Professional associations are an excellent way to gain valuable information about a career field as well as participate in its growth. This section lists associations that may be useful to those in each job.

Tips for Entry

Here you can find helpful tips to learn more about each career. The tips may include insider advice from professionals, useful Web sites, and books. It also may include suggestions relating to course work or internships and lets you know how to get involved. The information is geared at offering additional information that can help you learn more about each position and the field. Repeatedly, you will see tips that advise gaining experience through campus journalism and media internships.

Additional Resources

Beyond the career profiles, there are several appendixes that have practical information to be used in your exploration. Here you can find contact information and other concrete resources to help you learn more about each field. The appendixes in this book are as follows:

Related Educational Programs

Journalism can be an undergraduate major or a graduate field of study. While debate exists within the field as to how critical it is to study journalism as opposed to a well-rounded liberal arts curriculum, there is no denying that journalism coursework and training is very valuable. Included in this section are accredited journalism and communication programs (certified by the Accrediting Council on Education in Journalism and Mass Communications), additional journalism programs, photojournalism programs, and other certificate and training programs. They are arranged by state and provide addresses, telephone numbers, and Web sites.

Professional Associations

In this section, the associations that are mentioned in the career profiles are listed alphabetically by industry. They can be found nationwide and many have worldwide members. Each association is listed, along with its mailing address, telephone number, and Web site.

Industry Publications, Internships, Fellowships and Scholarships, Other Resources, and Job Listings

The Internet is one of the best ways to learn about different careers. Web sites that are in this section may provide job listings, industry information, or other helpful tips about journalism careers. As URLs get updated frequently, check each site to make sure the information is still current. If you find a site is no longer valid, try typing the name into a search engine such as Google or Yahoo to find an updated link.

Industry publications are also excellent ways to keep up on journalism. They can offer news about current events, networking contacts, job listings, and more. Most have online editions as well.

Bibliography

In order to learn more about the many careers represented in this book, a bibliography for further reading is provided. The bibliography is listed by many of the same categories that are included in the Table of Contents for easy organization. Most books should be easy to find through local libraries, bookstores, and sites such as http://www.amazon.com.

NEWSPAPERS

EXECUTIVE EDITOR

CAREER PROFILE

Duties: Leads all editorial operations for a newspaper; determines editorial policy, vision, goals, and strategy

Alternate Title(s): Editor in Chief, Editor

Salary Range: $60,000 to $200,000 and up

Employment Prospects: Fair

Advancement Prospects: Fair

Best Geographical Location(s): All

Prerequisites:

Education or Training—Bachelor's degree; journalism major, minor, or graduate degree may be needed

Experience—10 to 20 years of newspaper journalism experience

Special Skills and Personality Traits—Excellent writing, reporting, and editing skills; sound news judgment; good leadership and managerial skills; savvy business sense; flexibility and ability to work well under pressure

CAREER LADDER

```
┌─────────────────────────────────┐
│   Executive Editor, larger paper │
└─────────────────────────────────┘

┌─────────────────────────────────┐
│        Executive Editor          │
└─────────────────────────────────┘

┌─────────────────────────────────┐
│        Managing Editor           │
└─────────────────────────────────┘
```

Position Description

Executive Editors are the big kahunas of the newspaper world. For their papers, it is their vision that guides editorial policy, determines writing style, takes positions on issues, and, most importantly, decides what constitutes news. Each paper has a personality along with its news coverage; the Executive Editor cultivates this image and presents it to the public.

When coming on board, Executive Editors bring with them new and innovative ideas to enhance their newspapers. These ideas can include new sections, columns, features, or format. These fresh suggestions serve to breathe new life into the paper and grow its readership. It is a way for Executive Editors to make their mark and expand their paper's appeal.

Executive Editors oversee all editorial and/or news operations for their papers. In order for the paper to run smoothly, Executive Editors work very closely with their managing editors, who serve as their second in command. Their relationship is crucial to the success of the newsroom. While many of their responsibilities are the same, Executive Editors set the goals and formulate the editorial policy. Their managing editors carry them out on a daily basis, checking in to discuss progress. These tasks can include daily editorial meetings as well as direct supervision of staff.

In addition to working with managing editors, Executive Editors also maintain a close partnership with the newspaper's publisher. This relationship ensures that editorial vision is consistent with the business objectives. Both parties are invested in the paper's success, and they work together to increase sales, maximize opportunities, and meet challenges.

When anything is questionable—a tip, a fact, a source—it is brought to the Executive Editor to make a decision. He or she determines the position the paper will take. Always aware of legal and ethical concerns, Executive Editors rely on their judgment and experience to avert problems.

With the managing editors, Executive Editors also set the budget. They decide what funds will be allocated for staff, training, and special projects and assignments.

Tremendous responsibility rests on the shoulders of Executive Editors. While other senior staff can pass off controversy, the buck stops here. Any lapse in judgment by reporters, editors, photographers, or other staff members ultimately comes down to Executive Editors. They are held accountable for complaints, grievances, or lawsuits related to copy. They must be experienced leaders as well as journalists to handle these situations with finesse.

Furthermore, the Executive Editor is the face of the paper in the community. It is his or her role to represent the paper in public and to reach out to the community at large. Papers sponsor events, scholarship programs, and other philanthropic and civic-minded causes. The Executive Editor makes these decisions and is there on hand for announcements, to greet the people, and to launch these programs. Executive Editors must enjoy and thrive in this public role.

Additional duties may include:

- Working with noneditorial department heads in areas such as circulation, production, and advertising
- Approving layout and design
- Reviewing financial reports
- Overseeing controversial copy
- Writing editorial opinion pieces
- Representing their paper in the outside media
- Enforcing deadlines
- Participating in the operations board with other department heads
- Offering feedback to management such as the publisher and president

At smaller papers, Executive Editors may have more hands-on interaction with staff. They may run editorial meetings and suggest story ideas directly, rather than discussing their thoughts only with senior department heads. Also, they may read, review, or edit copy before it goes to print.

Executive Editors can easily work more than 60 hours per week, including nights and weekends. Many feel their newspapers are their babies and they do what they have to in order to make sure the work is done and each issue is perfect. Some travel may be required to represent the newspaper, especially at larger papers.

Salaries
Each year, the Inland Press Association conducts the Newspaper Industry Compensation Survey, which is the authoritative "industry standard" for newspaper industry compensation planning. In 2004 top editors earned an average of $105,158 per year as their base salary. Their total direct compensation, including bonuses and other commissions, was $125,345.

There can be an enormous salary range for Executive Editors depending on the size and circulation of the paper. The survey participants reported a range spanning a low in total direct compensation at $22,400 and a high at $640,000.

Employment Prospects
Employment prospects for Executive Editors are fair. As newspapers merge and consolidate, jobs have been diminishing in number. Since Executive Editor is such a high-level position, competition for top jobs is fierce. Most jobs are found through professional contacts and networking developed from years of experience in the field.

Advancement Prospects
Executive Editors are at the top of their game, and in order to advance, they go from smaller papers to larger ones. At larger papers, they can use their expertise to have greater impact and more responsibility.

In addition to their newspaper jobs, many Executive Editors also write articles/columns/opinion pieces for other publications. Furthermore, some also go on the lecture circuit, write books, or make other public appearances and contributions.

Education and Training
With high competition for jobs, Executive Editors need bachelor's degrees at a minimum. They have formal education in journalism through an undergraduate major or minor, or a graduate degree. A master's degree in journalism is helpful not only for providing tangible journalism training but also as a tool for networking and gaining related experience (through required internships) to start out. Liberal arts coursework is also valuable for the well-rounded knowledge base it offers, as well as exposure to reading and writing.

Executive Editors get much of their training from experience in the newsroom. Many of them were the editors in chief of their high school, college, or graduate school papers. Internships and other types of experience-based education are essential for breaking in. Furthermore, early involvement at the helm of a paper is good preparation for such a role later on.

Experience, Skills, and Personality Traits
Executive Editors are experienced leaders and journalists. Typically, they have between 10 and 20 years of experience, having put in their time and worked through the ranks of editing and reporting in a newsroom. They have the journalism skills of writing, reporting, and editing to understand what makes a good story. Also, they have the vision of what they want their paper to accomplish through its coverage. Along with this vision comes competitive drive to take their paper to the top.

Additionally, Executive Editors are good leaders. They direct and mentor their staff, knowing how to get the best from them. They can combine business savvy with journalism, understanding the dynamics of the newspaper business and how to increase sales without compromising editorial objectives.

It is also important for Executive Editors to have superior news judgment. They need to be able to handle great responsibility with knowledge of legal and ethical issues such as slander and libel. Executive Editors are decisive, protecting and defending their opinions and choices.

At the level of Executive Editor, it is assumed that one has experience and familiarity with a variety of newsroom operations. This includes some knowledge of layout, design, and production, as well as computer programs such as QuarkXPress and others. Knowledge of AP (Associated Press) style and excellent grasp of language are also implied.

Unions and Associations

Executive Editors may belong to a variety of professional associations including the American Society of Newspaper Editors, the Newspaper Guild, the World Editors Forum, and the Newspaper Association of America.

Tips for Entry

1. Gain experience! Get involved with your student or community paper as soon as possible. Be willing to start at the bottom but express interest early on in taking a leadership role eventually.
2. Explore educational programs in journalism. If your campus does not offer a journalism major, take any related writing or communications courses. Check out Web sites such as http://highschooljournalism.org and see Appendix I for a list of schools.
3. Visit your campus career center to find out about journalism resources. Put together a résumé, gather a portfolio of clips, and seek internship opportunities.
4. Arrange an informational interview with an Executive Editor from your local paper. As an alternative, try the editor in chief of a campus paper. Learn more about what the job entails and how different professionals worked their way up.
5. Look at the career information and internship listings offered on the Web site of the American Society of Newspaper Editors: http://www.asne.org/index.cfm?id=2.

MANAGING EDITOR

CAREER PROFILE

Duties: Manages the daily editorial operations of a newspaper, including staff leadership, story coverage, and overall vision and tone

Alternate Title(s): None

Salary Range: $40,000 to $200,000 and up

Employment Prospects: Fair

Advancement Prospects: Fair

Best Geographical Location(s): All

Prerequisites:

Education or Training—Minimum of a bachelor's degree; journalism major, minor, or graduate degree essential

Experience—Five to 15 years of prior newspaper work

Special Skills and Personality Traits—Ability to combine journalism with business savvy; excellent writing and editing skills; strong managerial and leadership skills; good organization

CAREER LADDER

```
┌─────────────────────────────────────┐
│  Managing Editor, larger paper or    │
│           Executive Editor            │
└─────────────────────────────────────┘

┌─────────────────────────────────────┐
│           Managing Editor             │
└─────────────────────────────────────┘

┌─────────────────────────────────────┐
│  Assistant Managing Editor; Deputy    │
│   Editor; News Editor; or Managing    │
│         Editor, smaller paper         │
└─────────────────────────────────────┘
```

Position Description

Managing Editors run the daily operations of a newspaper. Second in command to the executive editor, they carry out the vision set by this chief. As their title suggests, Managing Editors have a dual role as both managers and editors. It is the Managing Editor who is responsible for getting the paper out each day.

Managing Editors and executive editors work closely together and have many of the same responsibilities. Together, they determine the goals and direction for their paper. However, it is the Managing Editors who handle the nuts and bolts of newsroom responsibilities. They are on the front line with the staff getting the tangible tasks done.

A major role for Managing Editors involves supervising staff. They handle staff human resources issues such as hiring and terminating decisions and performance evaluations. In this way, they are directly involved in recruiting and retaining the talent for their newspaper. Managing Editors understand what makes a good reporter and try to create a staff of the best people to contribute to the paper's success. Furthermore, they decide on salaries and raises, as well as deal with staff grievances and problems. Managing Editors can also handle professional development such as training for the editorial staff.

Staff supervision also involves setting the editorial goals. Managing Editors run news meetings and ensure that the mix of stories covered by each issue is appropriate. They confirm that there is not overlap between departments and that goals are being met. Managing Editors coordinate between different bureaus (city, state, national, international), different topic areas (such as sports or features), and different newspaper departments (copy desk, photography). A number of senior editors and department heads report directly to the Managing Editor; at large papers this can easily be 10 to 15 people or more.

Additionally, Managing Editors often serve as clearinghouses through which ideas and information are filtered. Although they usually do not assign stories to reporters directly, they play a large part in what gets covered by telling their direct editorial reports (such as an assigning editor) to delegate assignments to specific people. Managing Editors may serve as mentors to more junior editors and reporters as they advise them on their work.

Major projects also fall to Managing Editors. They regularly brainstorm ideas and check progress to make sure special issues and topics are being covered in a timely fashion. Also, they look over controversial stories to make sure the tone and position is consistent with the newspaper's view.

In addition to serving as leaders to their staff, Managing Editors also interact with the public. They often deal with reader concerns such as complaints, ideas, and suggestions. While the executive editor is the one making inroads with the community, the Managing Editor serves as the voice of the paper to individuals who need their questions addressed.

Additional duties may include:

- Working on the budget with the executive editor
- Providing input on layout and design
- Setting policy
- Making editorial decisions
- Editing and checking final copy
- Writing editorial or position pieces
- Directing page makeup
- Determining both long- and short-term plans
- Deciding on front-page copy
- Working on production
- Making any changes to staff or organizational structure
- Creating production timetables

At smaller papers, Managing Editors often have more writing and editorial responsibility. Larger papers with sizable staffs enable Managing Editors to delegate work to other high-level editors, but with less staff that is not an option.

As news happens around the clock, Managing Editors work long hours to get their jobs done. Workweeks can be 60 hours or more. Even when they send their staff members home, they often toil away into the night to make sure the paper is ready to go out. However, most Managing Editors will tell you that they love their jobs. Their passion for truth, eye for detail, nose for information, skill for writing, and desire to manage leads the way. They have worked their way up to get where they are and they would not have it any other way.

Salaries

Salaries for Managing Editors can vary greatly depending on the size and location of their newspapers, as well as their level of experience. According to the Inland Press Association's annual Newspaper Industry Compensation Survey, the authoritative "industry standard" for newspaper industry compensation planning, in 2004 Managing Editors earned an average of $77,839 per year as their base salary. Their total direct compensation, including bonuses and other commissions, was $87,435.

The survey participants reported a wide range in salaries, spanning a low in total direct compensation of $18,820 and a high of $408,140. This reflects the differences between small and large newspapers.

Employment Prospects

Employment prospects for Managing Editors overall are fair. As trends lead toward newspaper mergers, the number of jobs has been diminishing. The greatest opportunities are for those candidates with significant experience and they are often found through networking.

However, unlike some specialized positions, all newspapers employ Managing Editors, which means that jobs are out there. Also, some newspapers may employ more than one Managing Editor. For example, different Managing Editors may handle news, features, sports, and staff issues such as hiring and budgeting.

Advancement Prospects

Managing Editors can advance in a number of ways, depending on their ultimate goals. Many Managing Editors who have moved up through the editorial ranks as assistant managing editors or deputy editors continue to seek out that role, going from smaller papers to larger ones. The job description, level of responsibility, and salary level for Managing Editors can differ greatly from small town papers to big city nationals.

Additionally, Managing Editors are in a position to advance to executive editor if they desire. They may move from Managing Editor at a large paper to executive editor at a midsize paper, or advance directly depending on their qualifications.

Education and Training

With a minimum of a bachelor's degree required, Managing Editors also need some formal education in journalism. Whether it was their undergraduate major, undergraduate minor, or graduate degree, journalism education provides the tangible skills to launch a career as a journalist at this level. In addition to journalism courses, a liberal arts curriculum is also valuable in teaching research and writing, as well as offering a well-rounded knowledge base.

As students, it is crucial for aspiring journalists to complete internships and put in their time doing newspaper work. Journalism programs often require these hands-on experiences.

Most Managing Editors do not have formal business training but say that they learned about management and leadership through training offered on the job.

Experience, Skills, and Personality Traits

To become a Managing Editor, one must be both an excellent journalist and an effective leader. There is no doubt that a Managing Editor is a journalist first. Writing, reporting, and editing skills are crucial, as well as significant newspaper experience. He or she has moved up the journalism ranks and has held a variety of positions at newspapers of varying sizes by the time of reaching this career point.

However, business and management savvy are equally important in this role. A journalist who is not interested in taking on this type of responsibility would be better off seeking a job as an assigning editor. Managing Editors must handle money, time, and resources, which are outside of the journalism realm. While some have specific business experience, most develop this expertise on the job. Either way, though, the interest in management has to be there.

Furthermore, Managing Editors need to enjoy high levels of responsibility. While final decisions are left to the executive editor, Managing Editors are often on the front lines, handling controversial issues. They need to be able to stay calm and exercise good judgment. Also, they need to know what constitutes news and what makes the most effective stories. Managing Editors must know their mission and their readers to make difficult decisions regarding content.

Managing Editors should be leaders and mentors. They need to enjoy supervising people and be skilled at it as well. Their strong communication skills enable them to work effectively with their staff, the management of the newspaper, and the general public and readers. The ability to work well under pressure and adhere to tight deadlines is essential.

Unions and Associations

Managing Editors may belong to a variety of professional associations, including the Associated Press Managing Editors, the American Society of Newspaper Editors, the Newspaper Guild, and the Newspaper Association of America.

Tips for Entry

1. Even if you are sure about journalism, you may not know if the role of Managing Editor is right for you. If you think it sounds interesting, try to work your way up to becoming Managing Editor at your student newspaper. This will give you a sampling of the combination of management and editorial responsibilities involved.

2. Learn how to do database research, a crucial skill for today's journalists. Find out more about electronic databases such as LexisNexis, at http://www.lexisnexis. com.

3. Take journalism courses to learn not only about reporting but also about the big picture of working at a newspaper. Design, graphics, and photography all play a major role in addition to words.

4. Check out the Associated Press Managing Editors, the professional association specifically for managing editors, at http://www.apme.com.

5. If you are a student, explore http://www.studentpress. org/, the Internet home of the National Scholastic Press Association and the Associated Collegiate Press. These associations help high school and college students improve their student publications and launch their careers in journalism.

COPY EDITOR

CAREER PROFILE

Duties: Reviews stories for a newspaper before they go to print, checking for correct grammar, punctuation, spelling, usage, and style; may perform layout to ensure stories will fit on page

Alternate Title(s): None

Salary Range: $25,000 to $45,000 and up

Employment Prospects: Good

Advancement Prospects: Good

Best Geographical Location(s): All

Prerequisites:

Education or Training—Bachelor's degree in journalism or related field

Experience—Entry level to three years or more

Special Skills and Personality Traits—Excellent command of language; close attention to detail; strong spelling, grammatical, and usage understanding; well-organized

CAREER LADDER

Copy Editor, larger paper; Copy Chief; or Reporter

Copy Editor

Copy Editor, smaller paper or Intern

Position Description

After a reporter finishes a story, that is just the beginning of seeing it to fruition on the page. The reporter usually submits his or her story to an editor who reviews it once. Then, it is on to the Copy Editor who will make it ready for publication. Essential to effective newsroom operations, Copy Editors are the last stop before stories go to print.

Copy Editors check stories for grammar, spelling, punctuation, and usage. Far more than proofreaders, they look for stylistic consistency and word choice that fits the tone of the paper. They are masters of semantics, knowing which word to use when and why. Furthermore, each paper has its own technical idiosyncrasies with regard to numbers, abbreviations, jargon, slang, and more. While most adhere firmly to AP (Associated Press) Style, they all add their own flavor. Copy Editors are experts in both AP Style and the style of their paper.

Because they are journalists themselves, Copy Editors understand what makes an effective feature or news story. They look to see proper organization—where is the lead?—and good flow. Sometimes they may need to rewrite portions of stories that do not work. So as not to create ten-

sion between Copy Editors and reporters, extensive changes must be cleared by an assigning or other editor and often are sent back to the writer directly.

Additionally, Copy Editors also check stories for glaring factual errors. While the assumption is that reporters have their facts correct, Copy Editors need to take note of any information that sounds questionable and clarify it. They also look out for libel or slander that could hurt the newspaper.

Another portion of the job of Copy Editors includes writing headlines and captions. This is another opportunity for them to flex their journalistic skills, as they summarize a story in a few words that are succinct, catchy, and stay true to its essence. The art of writing captions requires an accompaniment that adds to the photo at hand, rather than stating what is already apparent.

Most Copy Editors are also responsible for some page design and layout. News design is an art and Copy Editors understand the nuances of assembling dynamic pages. Copy Editors may organize photos, graphics, and text together. This arrangement is important as it can determine which stories are highlighted. At today's papers, most page design and layout is done electronically. Copy Editors may use specific computer programs for typesetting and pagination.

As Copy Editors work with each story, another issue for them to focus on is space. They pay attention to its size and the portion it is allotted on the page. Copy Editors frequently must "trim" stories, cutting off sentences or paragraphs to make it fit. On the other hand, they also may need to "pad" stories, adding several sentences to fill up blank space. The decisions Copy Editors make here are crucial. They are careful not to compromise the story, making sure it still achieves its goals and delivers its message.

Their duties may include:

- Preparing mock-up pages before submitting final copy
- Working on page A1 of the paper
- Designing special pages or sections
- Video editing
- Building online content
- Working with editors, reporters, and photographers
- Creating covers and section fronts
- Editing Web content
- Working on a variety of desks, including news, features, sports, local, or business

Copy Editors are usually part of the news desk, and they report to a copy chief. In the old days, before the advent of computers and modern technology, Copy Editors sat in a horseshoe configuration, and the editors were known as the "rim" while the copy chief was known as the "slot." Some copy desks are still organized this way, although now with everyone sitting at a computer. Several Copy Editors usually work together, depending on the size of the paper. They usually receive story assignments from the copy chief, but some papers operate with an in-box of work, while others assign specific pages to each Copy Editor. In that case, the Copy Editor is responsible for everything on that particular page, including photos, graphics, and text.

Hours for Copy Editors will vary depending on their particular shift. Since some stories will come in late at night or early morning, some Copy Editors work the evening shift (5 P.M. to 1 A.M.), while others will report to work at 6 a.m. At some papers, the Copy Editors rotate the night shifts, and they find that they enjoy more regular hours than other editors and reporters.

Salaries
According to the Inland Press Association's annual Newspaper Industry Compensation Survey, the authoritative "industry standard" for newspaper industry compensation planning, in 2004, entry-level Copy Editors earned an average of $30,615 per year as their base salary. Those Copy Editors at the next level of experience earned an average of $36,722. With considerable experience, Copy Editors may earn $45,000 per year and up.

Employment Prospects
Employment prospects are relatively good for Copy Editors. Even as newspapers merge, Copy Editors are needed to get the paper into its final publication stage. Positions as Copy Editors can be entry-level, and many journalists believe it is a good way to get into the field. However, even at the entry-level, candidates are expected to have prior experience through internships.

Aspiring Copy Editors, particularly those without prior full-time work experience, should expect to be geographically flexible. Opportunities may arise in small towns nationwide, and these papers are a great way to get a foot in the door of newspaper journalism.

Advancement Prospects
There are a number of different directions in which Copy Editors may go for advancement. If they fall in love with the fast pace and flow of the copy desk, they may work their way toward becoming copy chief. Another related position would be a news editor on the news desk. Other Copy Editors may look to become reporters or assigning editors.

Like other positions in journalism, advancement often occurs by moving from small papers to larger ones. Copy Editors may begin in small towns at weeklies and move to up to dailies and then larger cities. Additionally, as they advance, Copy Editors may also get better work shifts.

Education and Training
Copy Editors should have a bachelor's degree in journalism or a related field. The job requires a clear understanding of the structure of a news story; this background is gained through journalism coursework. Journalism training also teaches layout and page design skills. Some Copy Editors may have bachelor's degrees in liberal arts fields and master's degrees in journalism. Expertise in grammar, spelling, and usage comes from the reading and writing required at the college level.

Training comes both on the job and through internship experience. Many Copy Editors may know a little about pagination coming in but can expect to learn more once a newspaper employs them. However, the training they get from internships is crucial. Working for school or local papers to learn the basics of the copy desk is an invaluable and necessary supplement to academic education.

Experience, Skills, and Personality Traits
Copy Editors need an excellent command of the English language. They must be sticklers for correct punctuation, grammar, spelling, and usage. Additionally, their eye for detail and ability to find errors is superb. Copy Editors need to write well themselves (especially for catchy headlines and captions), as well as recognize good writing in others.

For the design aspect of their jobs, Copy Editors need to be creative. They need good visual skills and innovative ideas to make layout fresh and interesting. They should have excellent news judgment and know how to appropriately trim, pad, and place stories.

To go along with the design responsibilities, they should be familiar with related computer programs such as QuarkXPress, InDesign, Photoshop, and/or NewsEdit. Copy Editors also need a firm grasp of AP (Associated Press) Style, the format in which most newspapers are written.

Furthermore, Copy Editors must be able to work on tight deadlines. They can juggle many projects at once and thrive under pressure.

Unions and Associations

There are a variety of professional associations to which Copy Editors can belong. The American Copy Editors Society is the main association specifically for the profession, but they might also belong to the American Society of Newspaper Editors and others.

Tips for Entry

1. Check out http://www.theslot.com/copyeditors.html to learn more about the life of a Copy Editor.
2. Take a look at *Copy Editor* (http://www.copyeditor.com/copy/copy.asp), a leading newsletter for Copy Editors working in a variety of settings.
3. Consult the Detroit Free Press jobs page at http://www.freep.com/jobspage/index.htm to read descriptions of Copy Editor jobs.
4. The Web site of the American Copy Editors Society (http://www.copydesk.org) offers job listings, quizzes, and editing guidelines, among other resources important to Copy Editors.
5. The Journalism Education Association (http://www.jea.org/resources/curriculum/copyediting/copyediting.html) offers excellent copyediting resources including quizzes, copyediting symbols, and information about AP style.
6. Learn more about AP Style through resources gathered at http://journalism.okstate.edu/LPE/ap.html.

NEWS EDITOR

CAREER PROFILE

Duties: Runs the news desk for a newspaper; may be responsible for assigning, editing, coordinating, and reporting on news coverage

Alternate Title(s): None

Salary Range: $45,000 to $65,000 and up

Employment Prospects: Fair

Advancement Prospects: Fair

Best Geographical Location(s): All

Prerequisites:

Education or Training—Bachelor's degree in journalism or related field; master's degree is also valuable

Experience—Three to seven years

Special Skills and Personality Traits—Excellent writing, editing, and reporting skills; strong command of language including spelling, punctuation, grammar, and usage; good management skills; superb news judgment

CAREER LADDER

```
┌─────────────────────────────────┐
│        Managing Editor          │
└─────────────────────────────────┘

┌─────────────────────────────────┐
│          News Editor            │
└─────────────────────────────────┘

┌─────────────────────────────────┐
│   Assistant News Editor,        │
│   Copy Editor, Beat Reporter, or│
│   General Assignment Reporter   │
└─────────────────────────────────┘
```

Position Description

Newspapers are comprised of many departments, not all of which can be actually defined as news. However, by definition, the news will always be the most important part of the paper and the piece that makes it what it is. The news, including what is covered and how, is managed by the News Editor.

As managers of the news desk, News Editors lead news reporters on various desks (e.g., city, state) and beats (e.g., city hall). They help them to plan their coverage and discuss any pending issues or problems. It is part of their job to make sure that each beat is covered and that all news has an assigned reporter each day. News Editors are always on the pulse of breaking news, constantly checking the Internet and news wires. This way, they make sure that no vital news is missed on any given day.

Furthermore, News Editors work under especially tight deadline pressure. Since the news does not stop happening around the clock, they must always be on top of late-breaking stories. News Editors must often make quick decisions about coverage, and they often work long hours to accommodate breaking news. If something important has hap-

pened, they will stay as long as they need to in order to shift copy and fit it in.

News Editors also play a number of roles in the newsroom. As editors, they often line edit copy after reporters hand it in, checking for content, style, and structure, as well as questionable facts or libelous material.

Additionally, News Editors may also work on page design. They may piece together the news pages with copy, graphics, and photos to develop the appropriate balance. Pagination, the process of creating, numbering, and designing each page is also an important part of design.

Particularly at smaller papers, many News Editors also have some writing responsibility. Whether it is a regular column or beat area or a matter of reporting on breaking news as it happens, News Editors are experienced journalists who can handle this aspect of their job.

Other News Editors may also function as copy chiefs or assigning editors. Those who head copy departments manage the copy editors and the copy editing process. News Editors who work as assigning editors delegate story assignments to various reporters and freelancers.

Their duties may include:

- Hiring news reporters
- Developing news budgets
- Running daily news meetings
- Coordinating with the graphics department on matching visual images with stories
- Searching wire services for stories
- Executing spot news as it happens
- Working with other editors focusing on specific beats or regions
- Completing special projects
- Training new staff members
- Working with News Editors from other bureaus

Usually reporting to the managing editor, News Editors also work closely with senior staff. They may advise managing editors, assigning editors, and even executive editors about reporting assignments and editorial decisions affecting the news desk.

As supervisors, News Editors provide valuable feedback to the reporters and writers reporting to them. They help them to generate ideas and challenge them to go after the most in-depth and accurate coverage. News Editors may have staffs ranging in size from three to nine or more working directly for them. Their supervisory role is vital because it helps to set the tone and style of the news coverage.

News Editors can work among the longest or most irregular hours in the newsroom. Some are responsible for night shifts, while others face early morning into mid-afternoon. In spite of the tough workload, most News Editors feel passionate about their jobs. The quest for truth and information and the ability to bring it to the public can be exhilarating.

Salaries
Salaries for News Editors vary depending on the size and circulation of their paper. Averages tend to come in between $50,000 and $60,000. While News Editors coming in to their positions with little experience might earn in the low $20,000s, News Editors with significant experience (five years or more) can earn up to $100,000 and more.

Geographic location and the level of the position also affect salary. News Editors who are considered senior staff and who manage a large team are at the high end of the salary spectrum.

Employment Prospects
For News Editors, employment prospects are fair. With newspapers folding and consolidating, jobs are more competitive than ever. The best opportunities are for those with the right combination of education and experience. Candidates with bachelor's degrees in journalism and especially master's degrees will have an edge.

To make themselves marketable, News Editors need experience with copyediting and page design, as well as reporting. They should be willing to start out at smaller weekly papers in small towns before advancing to larger publications. Additional opportunities may come from editing online news portals.

Advancement Prospects
Advancement prospects are also fair for News Editors. Like other positions in journalism, advancement often occurs by moving from smaller papers to larger ones in bigger markets. News Editors may begin as copy editors or reporters before deciding on news editing as a goal. They gather together a portfolio of writing clips, as well as design experience, to find positions with more responsibility.

Education and Training
News Editors should have bachelor's degrees in journalism or a related field. Insiders recommend a combination of a journalism and liberal arts education to become the most well-rounded journalist possible. An undergraduate major or minor in journalism is common, as is a liberal arts major and a master's degree in journalism.

Training for News Editors comes on the job and through internships. Exposure to a newsroom is key, and internships provide hands-on experience. News Editors need training in writing, reporting, and editing, as well as some leadership and management.

Experience, Skills, and Personality Traits
Like other journalists, News Editors need a stellar command of language. For their editing responsibilities, they need a strong grasp of spelling, grammar, punctuation, usage, and AP (Associated Press) style. They must understand what makes an effective news story, as well as the tone and angle of their particular newspaper. News Editors use this knowledge in their own writing and to edit the writing of others.

News Editors also need to be successful leaders and managers. They must be able to challenge and motivate their staff to maintain high journalistic standards. Also, News Editors need good news judgment. Curious and aware, they are up to the minute with what is going on. Their ability to juggle multiple tasks and meet close deadlines is also important. News Editors often do not rest until they are certain all the news that can possibly be in each issue has made it in time.

Additionally, for the page design component of their work, News Editors should be familiar with QuarkXPress, Adobe Photoshop, and other computer programs for pagination and page design.

Unions and Associations
There are a variety of professional associations to which News Editors may belong. These include the American Society of

Newspaper Editors, the American Journalism Review, Investigative Reporters and Editors, and the Newspaper Guild.

Tips for Entry

1. Do you have a passion for news? Take in news in all types of formats: newspapers, online, television, and radio. Note differences in styles and tone.
2. Also, become aware of the different types of news coverage offered by competing newspapers in the same city. Compare and contrast their styles. What stands out to you about each one?
3. Take a look at job listings for News Editors on sites such as http://www.journalismjobs.com and http://www.JournalismNext.com.
4. Work as a campus editor for your school newspaper. This experience is good preparation for news editing.
5. Hone your writing skills by taking courses in English and communications.

FEATURES EDITOR

CAREER PROFILE

Duties: Manages the features component of a newspaper, including in-depth and human-interest stories

Alternate Title(s): Lifestyles Editor, Special Sections Editor, Arts and Entertainment Editor

Salary Range: $30,000 to $70,000 and up

Employment Prospects: Fair

Advancement Prospects: Fair

Best Geographical Location(s): All

Prerequisites:

Education or Training—Bachelor's degree in journalism or related field; master's degree also helpful

Experience—Three to seven years of newspaper experience

Special Skills and Personality Traits—Excellent writing, editing, and reporting skills; strong organizational skills; management and leadership ability; ability to work well under pressure and meet tight deadlines; interest in and knowledge of popular culture

CAREER LADDER

```
┌─────────────────────────────────────┐
│  Features Editor, larger paper; Chief │
│  Features Editor; or Managing Editor  │
└─────────────────────────────────────┘

┌─────────────────────────────────────┐
│           Features Editor            │
└─────────────────────────────────────┘

┌─────────────────────────────────────┐
│  Features Writer or Reporter,        │
│  General Assignment Reporter, or      │
│  Beat Reporter                        │
└─────────────────────────────────────┘
```

Position Description

Browse through the pages of a daily newspaper and you will notice a difference in the headlines. Some are clearly news-breaking pieces about events that have happened since the last issue came out. However, there are also stories that focus on more in-depth coverage. For example, there may be a piece profiling the spouse of a candidate for election or a report about a recent health trend. These in-depth stories and human-interest coverage are known as features.

In addition to pieces throughout the paper, features departments also include the special sections that many newspapers tend to incorporate regularly. The *New York Times,* for one, has a Science section on Tuesday, a Dining section on Wednesday, and a House and Home Section on Thursday, as well as a daily Arts section, among others. Usually, the Sunday issue is another time for additional features and sections.

These sections, with stories that focus on lifestyle, entertainment, and informative tidbits, often fall under the realm of the Features Editor. Features Editors may be responsible for all of these sections; larger papers may employ a different Features Editor for each one.

Features topics may include:

- Food
- Wine
- Home
- Gardening
- Families
- Travel
- Fashion
- Entertainment: movies, television, theater
- Art and culture
- Money and business
- Careers and job market

Features Editors edit and oversee the process of reporting on these features stories. Beginning by projecting a vision for what the features section should cover, they supervise reporters. They assign pieces, run meetings, and work with them to conceptualize ideas. Features Editors work with features writers and reporters who are responsible only for in-depth stories, as well as general assignment reporters and beat reporters working on features.

The features section is an important component of a newspaper because some believe it gives it character. Many people get their news from television and the Internet, and after picking up the newspaper and scanning the headlines, they want to settle down to read something more interesting. Features Editors shape this content and need to have an understanding of cultural issues as well as current events. Enjoying and being able to relate to pop culture is also a plus.

In addition to projecting the vision to conceptualize the features section, Features Editors perform hands-on editing. When stories are complete, Features Editors get to work, often line editing the copy and making changes and corrections. They also may perform some page design, determining what goes where and why.

Since there are many areas that constitute features, some Features Editors develop specific niches for themselves, in such realms as entertainment, food and wine, or jobs and careers.

Their duties may include:

- Developing new features components or sections
- Creating features series
- Overseeing columns and columnists
- Writing feature stories as well as editing
- Managing a sizable staff
- Interacting with senior management
- Assuring that content is reader-friendly
- Keeping up on news and trends
- Coordinating with other departments (especially news) to avoid overlap

Features Editors enjoy greater freedom, perhaps, than other newspaper editors. Because their work is not as time sensitive as breaking news, they are often able to have more creative control over content. Also, Features Editors simply have more time to both write and edit their stories. While they need to stick to deadlines, they do not face the same daily pressure that occurs constantly on the news side. Features Editors also have more time to focus on their writing and hone their style.

Furthermore, Features Editors have more time to work on page design and creation, using their vision to lay out their pages to the optimum effect. This also allows for more specific photo selection and design, as well as headline creation.

Among newspaper staffers, Features Editors may also enjoy more regular hours. Without the breaking news component, they often work day shifts. However, workweeks can still be long, averaging 50 hours or more.

Salaries

Each year, the Inland Press Association conducts the Newspaper Industry Compensation Survey, which is the authoritative "industry standard" for newspaper industry compensation planning. In 2004 lifestyle editors (comparable to Features Editors) earned an average of $50,634 per year as their base salary. Their total direct compensation, including bonuses and other commissions, was $51,776.

Salaries for Features Editors may have a large range depending on the size and circulation of the paper. The survey participants reported a range spanning a low in total direct compensation at $17,680 and a high at $225,000.

Employment Prospects

Employment prospects are fair for Features Editors. For every one Features Editor, there are numerous features writers and reporters. The best opportunities are for those with extensive experience writing features and who have proven their leadership skills.

Advancement Prospects

Advancement prospects are also fair. Since advancement in journalism often moves from smaller papers to larger ones, Features Editors may go on to run the features department at a larger newspaper. They may take on responsibility for several features areas instead of just one. Also, Features Editors may advance to roles where they manage larger staffs and have ownership over writing columns or specific departments.

Furthermore, some Features Editors seek to advance within the ranks of the newspaper hierarchy. They may look to become managing editors. However, this may be more difficult since the job might be more likely to go to someone with a strong news background.

Education and Training

Most Features Editors have bachelor's degrees in journalism or a related field. A combination of a journalism and liberal arts education is generally considered the ideal balance in order to become the most well rounded journalist possible. An undergraduate major or minor in journalism is common, as is a liberal arts major and a master's degree in journalism.

In addition, Features Editors may have specific training in specialty areas. For example, a Features Editor of a food and wine section probably had experience as a restaurant critic and perhaps some culinary school or a wine course.

Most training for Features Editors comes on the job and through internships. Many have written features extensively before taking on an editorial role. They need training in writing, reporting, and editing, as well as some past leadership and management to supervise staff.

Experience, Skills, and Personality Traits

Features Editors should be interested in people and their daily lives. They want to know the story behind the scenes and they have the desire to bring these stories and lives into other people's living rooms. Features Editors are curious and creative; they use these skills to craft human interest content that appeals to readers.

Additionally, Features Editors must be good leaders and managers. They motivate and supervise reporters to develop creative ideas and to help bring their own visions into fruition. Also, they need to ensure that writers stick to deadlines and work on stories appropriate to their expertise.

Excellent writing, reporting, and editorial skills are also critical for Features Editors. In addition to grammar, punctuation, and spelling, they need a good sense of style to craft and edit stories with the right tone for their paper.

As with other editorial positions, it is extremely helpful for Features Editors to know page design programs such as QuarkXPress and Adobe Photoshop.

Unions and Associations

The main professional association specifically for Features Editors is the American Association of Sunday and Features Editors. Features Editors may also belong to the American Society of Newspaper Editors, the American Journalism Review, and the Newspaper Guild.

Tips for Entry

1. Take a look at the Web site for the American Association of Sunday and Features Editors at http://www.aasfe.org/. It offers news about features as well as job listings.
2. Skim through several local and national newspapers. See if you can identify the difference between news and feature stories on the front page.
3. Also, consider the specific features sections of different newspapers. How many different sections can you find? Which of them appeals to you the most? Explore how you can get training in that particular area.
4. Get started writing features for your local or campus paper. Be aware of people, places, and things that can be interesting to the students around you.
5. To work in features, one should have a good understanding of popular culture. Take courses that help build your knowledge base and hone your writing and editing skills.

CITY EDITOR

CAREER PROFILE

Duties: Oversees local coverage for a newspaper; may manage a city desk, assign stories, and edit copy

Alternate Title(s): Metro Editor, Regional Editor

Salary Range: $30,000 to $75,000 and up

Employment Prospects: Fair

Advancement Prospects: Fair

Best Geographical Location(s): All, with the greatest opportunities in larger cities and metropolitan areas

Prerequisites:

Education or Training—Bachelor's degree in journalism or related field; graduate degree can be helpful

Experience—Three to seven years of prior newspaper work is typical

Special Skills and Personality Traits—Excellent writing, editing, and reporting skills; knowledge of local news, business, and politics; leadership and management ability; strong organizational skills and ability to meet tight deadlines

CAREER LADDER

```
┌─────────────────────────────────────┐
│    News Editor or Managing Editor    │
└─────────────────────────────────────┘

┌─────────────────────────────────────┐
│             City Editor              │
└─────────────────────────────────────┘

┌─────────────────────────────────────┐
│      Assistant City Editor,          │
│      Copy Editor, or Reporter        │
│    (General Assignment or Beat)      │
└─────────────────────────────────────┘
```

Position Description

Every day, each city has news of vital importance to its readers. Whether it is a three-alarm fire in a small town or corruption in the mayor's office of a major city, readers still depend on newspapers to keep them informed about their hometown, regardless of its population. City Editors are responsible for managing the local coverage at their papers.

The job of a City Editor varies in a small town as opposed to a large metropolis. Big cities can mean big stories, including major issues such as crime and heated political battles. However, regardless of the scope, the City Editor must decide what will be covered and how. Whether he or she works with just a few others or manages a large city desk staffed by assistant city editors, copy editors, and reporters, local news coverage must be anticipated, planned out, organized, and handled daily.

City Editors must always be on the pulse of breaking local news. As they check in with news wires, the Internet, and sources constantly, they assign stories to reporters with local beats. They must be plugged in with the city or community in which they work, including police, mayor's office, schools, and other public officials.

Leading reporters and providing their direction is a major part of the work of a City Editor. City Editors can help reporters plan their coverage and ensure that no important stories are overlooked. Also, City Editors help reporters to set priorities; they may mentor and advise reporters with regard to general reporting, chasing leads, and generating stories.

Although breaking news is a major component, the city desk also covers local feature and enterprise stories. City Editors develop ideas for these stories and make sure they are staffed. They are aware of local and regional personalities and events that will make for good reporting. At many papers, they write some of these pieces themselves.

Depending on the size of the newspaper, City Editors often have additional responsibilities along with managing staff. They frequently write and report on local news. Furthermore, they often edit copy from reporters as it comes in, paying attention to spelling, grammar, punctuation, usage, and style. Other City Editors may work on page design to structure, assemble, and organize the local sections.

Their duties may include:

- Developing relationships with local community leaders and city officials
- Working closely with other departments such as news, graphics, and photography to coordinate coverage
- Writing and editing online content
- Hiring, supervising, and evaluating reporters
- Developing budgets for their section
- Searching wire services for stories
- Training new reporters
- Responding to readers and interacting with the public

Like other editors, City Editors have a vision for their section that they carry out along with staff members. They have ideas about the type of local coverage that will best meet the needs of their readers. Furthermore, they can conceptualize the best ways to write and present it visually to the public.

Hours for City Editors can be especially long and grueling. Tight deadlines are a daily reality and as news comes in around the clock, City Editors must work irregular hours to be there as it happens. At some point in their careers, they must work the night shift, which can range from 5:30 P.M. to 2:30 A.M., or the earliest morning shift, which can begin at 3:00 A.M.

Salaries
According to the Inland Press Association's annual Newspaper Compensation Survey, in 2004 City Editors earned an average of $56,188 as their base salary. Like all other journalism positions, this figure can vary greatly based on the size and circulation of the paper. The same survey reported a range in total direct compensation (base salary and any other applicable bonuses) for City Editors to be from a low of $20,983 to a high of $176,000.

Employment Prospects
Employment prospects for City Editors are fair. At most papers, there are more reporters needed to handle local coverage than there are editors to supervise them. The greatest opportunities will be for those City Editors who have paid their dues as reporters and copy editors.

Advancement Prospects
Advancement prospects are also fair for City Editors. They may advance by moving from smaller newspapers to larger ones, where the scope of their coverage is greater. Other City Editors may seek to move up the editorial ladder to managing editor or news editor positions. These jobs are

competitive; City Editors who have proved themselves with strong managerial and editorial skills will be in the best position to move up.

Education and Training
City Editors should hold a bachelor's degree in journalism or a related field. Those who do not major in journalism take related courses and/or get a graduate degree. A master's degree in journalism can supplement a different undergraduate major, as well as enhance a journalism background and offer essential skills and training. Liberal arts courses are also helpful in providing a well-rounded education.

For a City Editor, training comes on the job and through prior newsroom positions, such as reporting and copy editing. Furthermore, internships and campus newspaper experience are invaluable.

Experience, Skills, and Personality Traits
Excellent writing, editing, and reporting skills are required in order to be a City Editor. A strong command of language and style helps City Editors to line edit copy, write their own pieces, and guide reporters on the best ways to present their coverage.

Sound news judgment and overall journalistic curiosity are important as well. City Editors must be aware of and interested in crucial issues not only in local news but also in the nation and world. They should be flexible and able to jump on spot news as it happens. They need high energy and passion for their job to work long, late hours and juggle multiple tasks and deadlines.

Furthermore, City Editors must have very good leadership and management skills. As managers of city desks and supervisors of reporters, they must be able to motivate and retain staff. City Editors challenge themselves and their reporters to provide exciting coverage and content.

As with other editorial positions, it is helpful for City Editors to know page design programs such as QuarkXPress and Adobe Photoshop.

Unions and Associations
City Editors may belong to a variety of professional associations including the American Society of Newspaper Editors, the Newspaper Guild, the Newspaper Association of America, and the World Editors Forum.

Tips for Entry
1. Gain experience reporting on local coverage for a campus or local publication. What are the hot-button issues affecting your community?
2. Pay attention to local coverage in your hometown paper. Which issues are highlighted each day, revealing what is most important to readers? Contrast this

information by reading online versions of other local papers in different cities.

3. Explore Web sites such as http://www.journalismjobs.com and others to read job descriptions for City Editors. See how these jobs differ from those of other editors.

4. Take journalism courses to hone reporting and editing skills. Learn how to write a catchy lead.

5. Copyediting experience is good preparation for the work of a City Editor. Seek these positions, which are sometimes entry-level, as a way to break into the field.

NEWS RESEARCHER

CAREER PROFILE

Duties: Handles news research requests from reporters and editors at a newspaper

Alternate Title(s): Librarian, News Research Manager

Salary Range: $20,000 to $50,000 and up

Employment Prospects: Fair

Advancement Prospects: Fair

Best Geographical Location(s): Major cities

Prerequisites:

Education or Training—Most positions prefer or require a master's degree in library science (MLS); journalism training/education also helpful

Experience—Three to five years

Special Skills and Personality Traits—Superior research skills; proficiency in using research databases; excellent communication ability; good customer service

Special Requirements—Some positions require an MLS degree and related certification

CAREER LADDER

```
┌─────────────────────────────────────┐
│  Research Chief, Research Department  │
│   Director, or Library Director       │
└─────────────────────────────────────┘

┌─────────────────────────────────────┐
│            News Researcher            │
└─────────────────────────────────────┘

┌─────────────────────────────────────┐
│      Assistant Researcher or          │
│  News Researcher, smaller paper       │
└─────────────────────────────────────┘
```

Position Description

Think about the last time you read an in-depth news story. Statistics are often quoted and studies cited. Experts are interviewed from around the world. As reporters work to craft their features, these in-depth pieces are often a team effort. News Researchers are behind the scenes, gathering critical information to make each story successful.

A typical day in the life of a News Researcher usually begins at the computer. News Researchers check their e-mail for research requests, paying special attention to any requests that are for immediate time-sensitive stories. Most News Researchers respond to both in-house and external requests.

Internal requests come from reporters and editors that need information for their stories. For example, they may need the names of employees at certain companies, a list of people who contributed to a political campaign, the license plate numbers of specific cars, or verification of property ownership. Furthermore, they may also need access to past articles from their paper, as well as other sources about a particular person or subject. News Researchers find this information through research databases, books, archival material, and phone calls, using their skills to find the most efficient method for each request.

External requests can come from a variety of clients. Some newspapers provide public research as a free service, but many charge clients a fee for access to detailed information. Many News Researchers have access to databases such as IQ Data and others that only information professionals can obtain. Businesses and individuals may also request archived issues or articles from the paper.

As News Researchers provide reporters and editors with reports for their research requests, they frequently spend time explaining how to read the reports. They help decipher any technical language and help them to understand how the information can be relevant to their story. News Researchers may go through these reports, highlighting or isolating important material.

News Researchers often maintain research requests in a database that helps them keep track of activity. They record information such as which department or desk made the request, what it was for, how much time it took to complete, and what resources were used.

Since archived materials are crucial to any newsroom library, News Researchers also work to create and maintain archives. They enhance text and index before archiving, comparing it from different editions to ensure consistency. Also, they add header information and scan for correctness, making sure all coding is done properly. Photo archives are a major part of this process as well, and many research requests are specifically for photos.

Furthermore, News Researchers are an active part of the newsroom operations. They attend regular news and editorial meetings and comment on stories, as well as express ideas. They may have thoughts about new stories, as well as suggestions about ways that research can help reporters with existing stories.

Additional duties may include:

- Searching through prior newspaper records
- Providing support for weekend editions
- Scanning editions for errors
- Maintaining calendars of events
- Working on special projects
- Acquiring, ordering, and maintaining materials such as periodicals, books, and electronic subscriptions for the news library
- Developing procedures to store and classify information
- Managing newsroom Intranet databases
- Providing technical training and support to database users
- Working as a liaison with library vendors
- Preparing library budgets
- Maintaining and developing digital archives for photos

News Researchers are part of a research department that may include assistants, database managers, archivists, managers, and directors. Working both independently and as team players, they interact with reporters, editors, bureau staff, and the general public.

Work schedules and hours for News Researchers tend to be more regular than others in journalism. However, there may also be night shifts through which News Researchers need to rotate, or where they may begin their careers.

Salaries

According to the Inland Press Association's annual Newspaper Industry Compensation Survey, the authoritative "industry standard" for newspaper industry compensation planning, in 2004 librarians (comparable to News Researchers) earned an average of $32,011 in base salary. Their base salary as well as total direct compensation ranged from a low of $11,243 to a high of $73,010. News Researchers who direct research departments at large papers can earn somewhat higher salaries.

Employment Prospects

Job opportunities for News Researchers are fair. Many small papers cannot afford to have News Researchers on staff, so the greatest employment prospects are at larger papers in major cities. News Researchers may start out as database researchers, archivists, or assistants. Furthermore, they may need to find part-time positions to start out, or positions working the night shift. A good resource for job listings is the one maintained by the News Division of the Special Libraries Association, at http://www.ibiblio.org/slanews/.

Advancement Prospects

Advancement prospects for News Researchers are also fair. They may move from smaller to larger papers, or take on more responsibility in a management position. News Researchers can become research chiefs, news research department directors, research directors, or head librarians. In these types of positions, they supervise staff and all research operations.

Education and Training

News Researchers may have a background in library science, a background in journalism, or both, depending on their position. A degree in library science, particularly with a specialization in news, provides a solid foundation in research. However, some News Researchers do have degrees and experience in journalism.

The master's degree in library science (MLS) may be required, or at the minimum, preferred for many positions. The degree usually takes between one and two years to complete and offers a variety of specializations. The American Library Association (ALA) provides a list of accredited programs and educational information on their Web site at http://www.ala.org/ala/accreditation/lisdirb/lisdirectory.htm.

Special Requirements

Some newsrooms may require News Researchers to be librarians with MLS degrees from ALA-accredited institutions. A list of accredited programs is available at http://www.ala.org/ala/accreditation/lisdirb/lisdirectory.htm.

Experience, Skills, and Personality Traits

It is important for News Researchers to be excellent communicators. In addition to the research they conduct, they frequently must explain reports and other pieces of information to reporters, editors, or clients. They help others to make sense of information in a way that is usable. Also, News Researchers may train staff on the use of particular database systems.

Of obvious importance is the ability to conduct thorough, effective, and efficient research. News Researchers must be familiar with public records, campaign finance data, census data, and government documents in order to handle many common requests. They must be proficient at using electronic research and public records databases such as Lexis/Nexis, Factiva, Autotrack, Accurint, and Dialog. Expertise at conducting Internet research is expected as well.

News Researchers should also have a strong customer service orientation. They deal with difficult people placing complicated requests; they must take them in stride and work well under pressure. Journalistic curiosity is also an asset.

Unions and Associations

News Researchers may belong to a variety of professional associations. News Researchers who are professional librarians may belong to the Special Libraries Association, News Division. Others may belong to associations for librarians or journalists, such as the American Library Association or the Newspaper Association of America.

Tips for Entry

1. Learn more about News Researchers, including job profiles, at the Special Libraries Association, News Division's Web site, at http://www.ibiblio.org/slanews/.
2. Become familiar with electronic research databases. Check out sites such as http://www.iqdata.com, http://www.factiva.com/, and http://www.accurint.com/.
3. Gain experience through a newspaper internship. Find a position in the research department or speak to professionals working in that area.
4. Consider graduate programs in library science. Review the Web site of the American Library Association to explore information, at http://www.ala.org/ala/education/educationcareers.htm.
5. Also consider graduate programs in journalism that have a strong research bent. Look at the Web site for the Journalism Education Association at http://www.jea.org/.

COPY CHIEF

CAREER PROFILE

Duties: Leads a team of copy editors through each editing and production process for a newspaper; reviews all content before it goes to print, checking for correct grammar, punctuation, spelling, usage, and style

Alternate Title(s): Copy Desk Chief, Slot Chief

Salary Range: $40,000 to $65,000 and up

Employment Prospects: Fair

Advancement Prospects: Fair

Best Geographical Location(s): All

Prerequisites:

Education or Training—Bachelor's degree in journalism or related field

Experience—Three to 10 years, depending on the size of the paper

Special Skills and Personality Traits—Superior organization and managerial skills; excellent command of language including spelling, grammar, and usage; close attention to detail; knowledge of AP (Associated Press) style

CAREER LADDER

```
┌─────────────────────────────────┐
│      Copy Chief, larger paper    │
│         or News Editor           │
└─────────────────────────────────┘

┌─────────────────────────────────┐
│           Copy Chief             │
└─────────────────────────────────┘

┌─────────────────────────────────┐
│  Copy Editor, Assistant Copy Chief, │
│      or Deputy Copy Chief        │
└─────────────────────────────────┘
```

Position Description

Accuracy is crucial to the integrity and validity of journalism. Newspapers strive to make sure misprints are avoided, facts are checked, and there are no glaring errors to tarnish the pages. Copy Chiefs are ultimately responsible for ensuring that all newspaper content is correct in each issue.

There is a specific flow to copyediting work. After a reporter completes a story, it usually goes next to the editor of their desk (i.e., news, sports, features). After the editor has reviewed the piece and made any necessary changes, the next line is the Copy Chief. At this point, Copy Chiefs do not edit the story themselves but decide which editors will handle it. Management of stories as they come in from editors is important, and Copy Editors must decide on assignments and priorities. Assignments may be given by timing, or based on the specialty and skills of specific editors.

Newspapers often have several copy editors, but usually only one Copy Chief whose job it is to supervise them all. Some large papers do have Copy Chiefs that manage each desk, such as one for news, one for sports, and so on. At

these papers, different desks are responsible for editing their own copy and managing their own copy editors, while other papers use a universal copy desk model.

While Copy Chiefs delegate much of the hands-on editing to their copy editors, they are always the last word. Depending on the paper, they may reread all stories personally for grammar, spelling, usage, and style, or they may only read the headline and lead. Editors look to them for guidance about any controversial material, as well as problems that may keep occurring with certain writers. Additionally, Copy Chiefs are the go-to people for any questions about incorrect facts or libelous materials.

Copy Chiefs are experts on the style and tone of their paper. They advise editors as to the technical idiosyncrasies followed by their paper with regard to numbers, abbreviations, jargon, slang, and more. As most newspapers adhere firmly to AP (Associated Press) style, Copy Chiefs are AP masters, but they add their own personal stylistic touch as well.

For each newspaper issue to go out flawlessly, cooperation is key. Copy Chiefs work closely with other newspaper professionals. Collaboration with assigning and news editors is important to keep the flow of work going smoothly. Together, they may make decisions that affect content and deadlines. Furthermore, Copy Chiefs work with the production and design staff to determine story placement and layout.

Furthermore, Copy Chiefs oversee some page design and layout. Since space is an issue, the size of each story and its ability to fit in its assigned slot is crucial. Along with copy editors, Copy Chiefs may cut or add content to stories in order to make them fit. Tough decisions about placement and editing fall to them, as they are careful to exercise their excellent journalistic judgment along with their pragmatism. Copy Chiefs are well versed in computer programs for layout and pagination. Their eye for not only crisp words but also catchy design helps create pages that work on several levels.

Additional duties may include:

- Scheduling and running daily/weekly meetings with copy editors
- Answering questions and handling problems with writers
- Assigning work to copy editors
- Maintaining schedules and checking deadlines
- Providing training and professional development opportunities for copy editors
- Watching for late breaking news through the wire services
- Writing and editing headlines
- Editing Web content
- Overseeing a variety of desks, including news, features, sports, local, or business
- Attending meetings with editorial management

In the past, before the advent of computers and modern technology, copy editors sat in a horseshoe configuration with the Copy Chief in the center. The editors were known as the "rim" while the Copy Chief was known as the "slot." These were the days when editing was done with pencil and typesetting prepared pages for publication.

However, some papers still use this horseshoe configuration but with computers instead. Copy Chiefs sit nearby to distribute assignments when they come through the wire, remaining close in order to receive completed work and hand pages back to editors for revisions, if necessary. The flow of work and back-and-forth style, even though it now takes place by pressing a key on the computer, is at the heart of copyediting.

As supervisors, Copy Chiefs also serve as teachers and mentors to the copy editors. They may manage staffs ranging from one or two members to more than 20. Part of their role is to train the copy editors; the better skilled they are, the easier the work of the Copy Chief is. They may train them with regard to AP style, educate them about the tone

of their newspaper, and help them to write effective captions and headlines. Copy Chiefs are responsible for hiring copy editors, as well as fact-checkers and proofreaders.

Hours for Copy Chiefs are usually long and intensive. While editors will have different shifts, Copy Chiefs must be there until the last story comes in, usually working late into the night. However, at some papers, Copy Chiefs have deputies that alternate shifts.

Salaries

The Inland Press Association's annual Newspaper Industry Compensation Survey is considered the authoritative "industry standard" for newspaper industry compensation planning. According to their most recent survey, Copy Chiefs earned an average of $50,966 per year as their base salary in 2004. Total direct compensation including bonuses was $51,860.

However, the range can be great depending on the size of the newspaper and level of experience of the Copy Chief. The same survey reports a range in total direct compensation for Copy Chiefs from a low of $19,500 to a high of $129,900.

Employment Prospects

Employment prospects are fair for Copy Chiefs. Since there is only one Copy Chief and several copy editors at each paper, jobs are not as plentiful and are more competitive at the chief level.

Most Copy Chiefs have between three and 10 years of experience as a copy editor. Some go through the ranks as assistant and/or deputy copy chief before reaching a full Copy Chief position. Many also have reporting experience. Past experience and geographic flexibility are key factors for finding employment.

Advancement Prospects

The main way for Copy Chiefs to advance is through moving from smaller papers to larger ones where they can supervise a larger staff and have greater responsibility. Other Copy Chiefs that only manage single desks may aspire to a position managing a universal copy desk, while others may seek the reverse, deciding to specialize with specific copy. With considerable reporting experience and time on the news desk, Copy Chiefs may also advance to news editor positions.

Education and Training

Most Copy Chiefs have bachelor's degrees in journalism or related fields. In order to achieve this level and manage other editors, they need a clear understanding of the structure of a news story; this background is best gained through journalism coursework. Also, expertise in grammar, spelling, and usage is honed by the reading and writing required at the college level. Some Copy Chiefs may have bachelor's degrees in liberal arts fields and master's degrees in journalism.

Training comes from prior experience as a copy editor. Work on the copy desk is the ultimate way to understand the responsibilities of a Copy Chief and his or her relationships with copy editors. Work as a copy editor also fine tunes necessary skills such as writing headlines and captions; proofreading for style, spelling, and grammar; organizing stories; and page design and layout.

Experience, Skills, and Personality Traits

As supervisors, Copy Chiefs should have strong leadership skills. They need the ability to manage, mentor, and inspire staff members with authority as well as understanding. Copy Chiefs work well under pressure and can adhere to strict deadlines. Not only are they well organized but they are also able to organize and prioritize the work of their staffs.

Copy Chiefs must have an excellent command of the English language. Since they are managers, they are held to the highest standard, and they should have impeccable punctuation, grammar, spelling, and usage. Additionally, their eye for detail and ability to find errors has been honed to a science.

However, their job is not only about detail. Copy Chiefs should be creative with a vision of how their pages should look. Good visual skills help content to fit and keep layout fresh and interesting. Excellent news judgment is also essential to know how to appropriately trim, pad, and place stories.

Familiarity with computer programs such as QuarkXPress, InDesign, Photoshop, and/or NewsEdit is needed for layout work. Copy Chiefs also need a firm grasp of AP (Associated Press) style, the format in which most newspapers are written.

Unions and Associations

Copy Chiefs may belong to professional associations including the American Copy Editors Society, the American Society of Newspaper Editors, and others.

Tips for Entry

1. Consider internships that will give you insight into copyediting. The New York Times Company offers the Dow Jones Newspaper Fund Editing Internship for a copyediting intern. See http://www.nytco.com/intern.html#dowjones for more information.

2. Gain experience on a copy desk. Begin as a reporter or copy editor and try to work your way up to a Copy Chief position at your campus paper.

3. Copy Chiefs need to know how to be good copy editors first. See *Copy Editor* (http://www.copyeditor.com/copy/copy.asp), a leading newsletter for copy editors working in a variety of settings.

4. Search http://www.journalismjobs.com to read job descriptions for Copy Chiefs.

5. Take a look at this site compiled by Moorhead State University for journalism students looking for copyediting help. It brings together many useful copyediting links: http://www.mnstate.edu/gunarat/ijr/writing.html.

6. The Web site for the Journalism Education Association (http://www.jea.org/resources/curriculum/copyediting/copyediting.html) offers excellent copyediting resources, including quizzes, copyediting symbols, and information about AP style.

GENERAL ASSIGNMENT REPORTER

CAREER PROFILE

Duties: Writes and reports on a variety of topics for a newspaper

Alternate Title(s): Reporter, Correspondent

Salary Range: $20,000 to $100,000 and up

Employment Prospects: Fair to Good

Advancement Prospects: Good

Best Geographical Location(s): All

Prerequisites:

Education or Training—Bachelor's degree with a major or minor in journalism or a bachelor's degree in a liberal arts discipline with a graduate degree in journalism

Experience—One to five years

Special Skills and Personality Traits—Excellent writing and reporting skills; persistence; strong interviewing, listening, and communication skills; ability to work well under pressure and meet deadlines

CAREER LADDER

```
┌─────────────────────────────────────────┐
│      General Assignment Reporter or       │
│  Beat/Specialized Reporter, larger paper  │
└─────────────────────────────────────────┘

┌─────────────────────────────────────────┐
│        General Assignment Reporter        │
└─────────────────────────────────────────┘

┌─────────────────────────────────────────┐
│      General Assignment Reporter or       │
│      Beat Reporter, smaller paper         │
└─────────────────────────────────────────┘
```

Position Description

General Assignment Reporters cover a wide variety of topics for a newspaper. Unlike beat reporters, who have specific specialty areas, General Assignment Reporters go where the news is. Their versatility and reporting skills enable them to handle whatever assignment comes their way.

Typically, General Assignment Reporters begin their day by checking in with their editors. Depending on the size and scope of their paper, they can be sent anywhere from covering a small local fire to a distant location where a natural disaster has occurred. Their work depends on the news each day—they go where it is. Since they are not tied to only one topic, they chase late-breaking news stories to get to the heart of the matter.

After figuring out their current assignment, General Assignment Reporters begin the job of writing their daily piece. This usually involves a combination of live interviews, telephone conversations, meetings with primary and secondary sources, visits to scenes, and other forms of background research. After this research is complete, they get to the task at hand: writing their article.

Some General Assignment Reporters are responsible for writing about certain related topics. Although they do not cover one specific beat, they may cover groupings such as courts, police, and safety all together. General Assignment Reporters take direction and assignments from their editors, but they also may generate their own stories as news arises. They can conduct research, consult news and wire releases, and speak to sources to find ideas.

General Assignment Reporters must be creative and versatile. As generalists, they need to be skilled at writing about different subjects. With each day being different, General Assignment Reporters often work without a routine and they must get to know a variety of sources. They need initiative to cultivate these sources and generate ideas. These relationships, as well as relationships with other reporters, who can share information related to their specific beats, can be very important to making their stories both valid and appealing.

There is great responsibility in the hands of General Assignment Reporters to affect their readers. With each story, they make decisions about the angle they choose to take and the facts they want to highlight. In a typical day, they may interview several people in person and speak to dozens on the phone in order to uncover facts about a particular story. Their words can influence public opinion, so they need to be ethical and meticulous, as well as have a gift for telling a story.

Depending on the paper, General Assignment Reporters may wear any number of hats. Their assignments are often a combination of feature stories and more in-depth explorations of issues. They may also take on some more long-term investigative pieces where they will scour public records to uncover wrongdoings. At some publications, they may also take photographs, work on layout, edit copy, or participate in design. This also will depend on their journalism training.

Additional duties may include:

- Attending editorial news meetings
- Working closely with editors
- Covering local events
- Meeting with sources at their places of businesses
- Conducting online research
- Performing digital editing
- Filing audio clips for newscasts
- Filing news updates for the Internet
- Selecting stories

General Assignment Reporters may need to travel to follow the news. During election campaigns, they can be assigned to travel with candidates and follow the political whirlwind on a local, state, or national level. While entry-level General Assignment Reporters might not have much control of their assignments, with experience they gain niche areas for themselves. Even without being tied to a beat, they become recognized for specific types of writing and they work with their editors to find those assignments that are the best fit for their style and skills.

The hours for General Assignment Reporters reflect the never-ending hours of news. They usually work eight- or nine-hour shifts that can be from anywhere from 6 A.M. to 2 P.M. or 3 P.M. to midnight. Those General Assignment Reporters who work the evening shift are responsible for updates to stories and late-breaking news.

Also, some General Assignment Reporters specifically work weekend shifts. In addition to those shifts, extra hours may be necessary to meet with sources, fine-tune stories, or work on special assignments. However, most General Assignment Reporters will tell you they thrive on the adrenaline rush of their work.

Salaries

According to the Inland Press Association's annual Newspaper Industry Compensation Survey, the authoritative "industry standard" for newspaper industry compensation planning, in 2004 entry level reporters earned an average of $28,162 per year in total direct compensation. With considerable experience, that average went up to $43,292.

However, the salary range is quite diverse depending on newspaper size and experience. In 2004 the same survey reported figures ranging from a low salary of $10,042 at the entry-level to a high salary of $163,926 at the experienced level.

Additional information about reporters' salaries comes from the media union, the Newspaper Guild. Each year, they produce a collective bargaining manual that lists the top minimum weekly salaries for reporters throughout the country. The 2004 figures for reporters/photographers show a high weekly minimum of $1,445.17 per week with two years of experience at the *New York Times* ($75,148.84 annually) and a low weekly minimum of $387.50 at the Utica, N.Y., *Observer-Dispatch* ($20,150 annually). This further underscores the salary range based on circulation and experience.

Employment Prospects

Employment prospects are fair to good for General Assignment Reporters. With mergers and related layoffs, newspaper positions are dwindling in the 21st century. However, positions for General Assignment Reporters remain available but competitive, particularly in geographically desirable areas.

New professionals are expected to pay their dues, beginning at local weeklies before moving up to daily papers. Students fresh from journalism school have to check glamour and their egos at the door, taking positions in small towns where they can gain reporting experience. Journalism school can provide valuable contacts and job leads.

Advancement Prospects

In the newspaper hierarchy, advancement often means moving from paper to paper. Typically, General Assignment Reporters begin at local weeklies, covering small-town events for little pay. They can move up to small-town dailies, and then advance further to larger city papers, where they will cover issues of increasing depth.

Some General Assignment Reporters advance to editorial positions once they have achieved their reporting goals. They can become news editors, feature editors, or assignment editors, among others.

Education and Training

The vast majority of General Assignment Reporters have some formal journalism education. Through this course of study, they learn the art and science of reporting and the tangible skill of crafting a news story, as well as some layout, design, and important software programs.

However, journalists are split about the best educational course of study for future journalists. Some will argue that a bachelor's degree in journalism is the best training, while others maintain that a well-rounded liberal arts curriculum is the ideal preparation. Through courses in fields such as literature, economics, and political science, students learn to write and research, as well as become knowledgeable and educated over a variety of genres.

If students choose to go the liberal arts route, most seasoned journalists do agree that some formal journalism training is necessary in addition. Future reporters who major in the liberal arts often minor in journalism or continue on for a master's degree. This is extremely helpful and may be even required for employment.

Training for General Assignment Reporters also comes from hands-on work. Virtually all have had student journalism experience through campus newspapers and internships.

Experience, Skills, and Personality Traits

In addition to superb writing and reporting skills, General Assignment Reporters must have excellent communication skills. They need to know how to speak to and interview people in a way that gains their trust and respect. Their writing must accomplish that same goal as well. General Assignment Reporters are skilled storytellers and know the dynamics of journalistic writing inside and out.

General Assignment Reporters must understand news and the public's relationship to current events. With a natural curiosity, they are not afraid to delve into issues and persist in their quest for information. They use their good judgment to make tough decisions and choose the most relevant facts and issues. It is also important for General Assignment Reporters to be honest, ethical, and cognizant of legal concerns in their writing such as slander or libel.

Furthermore, General Assignment Reporters must be flexible. Since they are generalists, they need to be comfortable reporting on a variety of issues. Additionally, they must be able to take direction from their editors and respond to the stories to which they are assigned, even if they are not the best ones.

The intense schedule of the newsroom requires General Assignment Reporters to work under constant deadline pressure. They need to work hard on their stories, but then let them go to the expert team of editors that will prepare

them for publication. As they may be working on several stories simultaneously, including more in-depth pieces for the weekend edition, they need to balance many responsibilities without getting frazzled.

At some papers, General Assignment Reporters also work on page design and other layout tasks. It is helpful to know programs such as QuarkXPress, CopyDesk, InDesign, and others.

Unions and Associations

General Assignment Reporters may belong to a variety of professional associations including the American Society of Newspaper Editors, the Newspaper Association of America, and Investigative Reporters & Editors.

Tips for Entry

1. Reporters are avid readers and observers. Read newspapers, magazines, novels, and literature to immerse yourself in the written word. Be aware of the world around you and how people interact.
2. In addition to reading, hone your skill at writing. Take courses in journalism, English, creative writing, and other fields where you can express yourself. Try out different writing genres for size.
3. Never underestimate the power of an internship. Take a look at the internships listed on the Web site of the American Society of Newspaper Editors. Many of these are paid opportunities at newspapers nationwide: http://www.asne.org/index.cfm?id=3749.
4. Speak to General Assignment Reporters working for your local paper. What do they like best and least about their jobs? See if you can visit them at the newsroom to understand the way it works.
5. Do you know Associated Press (AP) style, the format in which most newspapers are written? Learn more about it at http://www.utexas.edu/coc/journalism/SOURCE/journal_links/AP_style.html and consider ordering your own copy of the stylebook at http://www.apstylebook.com/.

BEAT REPORTER

CAREER PROFILE

Duties: Covers a specific beat or topic for a newspaper such as police, education, or government

Alternate Title(s): Reporter, Correspondent

Salary Range: $18,000 to $110,000 and up

Employment Prospects: Good

Advancement Prospects: Good

Best Geographical Location(s): All

Prerequisites:

Education or Training—Bachelor's degree in journalism or undergraduate degree in liberal arts field and master's degree in journalism

Experience—Entry-level to five years and up

Special Skills and Personality Traits—Excellent writing and reporting skills; persistence and patience; strong communication, listening, and interviewing skills; good judgment and analytical skills

CAREER LADDER

```
┌─────────────────────────────────────┐
│  Beat Reporter, larger beat/paper    │
└─────────────────────────────────────┘

┌─────────────────────────────────────┐
│            Beat Reporter             │
└─────────────────────────────────────┘

┌─────────────────────────────────────┐
│     Beat Reporter, smaller paper     │
└─────────────────────────────────────┘
```

Position Description

Beat Reporters are responsible for a specific beat or area of the newspaper. They become experts on their topic and get to know the related players on a personal basis. Those with daily beats also become skilled at creating a story out of the most mundane or minute changes in daily status.

Generating stories takes initiative and creativity; Beat Reporters must have both. They develop an in-depth knowledge of their beat and what constitutes breaking news. While some Beat Reporters receive assignments from editors, most know their beats best and work independently, checking in with editors for approval when necessary.

Local, city, and national newspapers may vary slightly in terms of which beats they have, but following is a general breakdown of potential beats for Beat Reporters:

- Education
- Town Hall
- City Hall (mayor's office)
- State government (governor's office)
- National government
- Courts
- Police
- Business
- Planning/zoning
- Science/medicine
- Sports

Most Beat Reporters begin their day with a series of phone calls. For example, a Beat Reporter in charge of city hall will likely check in with the mayor's office first thing each morning. Administrative assistants and secretaries can be a Beat Reporter's best friend, and earning their respect and cooperation is a key to success. They are the ones who know what is really going on, and they can make the process of getting a story or access to information easy or difficult for Beat Reporters, depending on their relationship.

A challenge for Beat Reporters is to find the news on a daily basis. In news, as in life, sometimes there are slow days. However, Beat Reporters need to find something to tell about their beat each and every day. It may be minor, such as the mayor of a town cutting the ribbon on a new store or a baby elephant being born at the local zoo, but it is still news.

As Beat Reporters begin on their beats, it is important for them to spend time getting to know their sources and the important issues at stake. Even if they have covered a similar topic at their last job or while in school, each beat is brand new in a different town and context. By creating a plan, talking to people extensively, and doing their homework, Beat Reporters earn the trust of their editors, sources, and the general public. On the other hand, they need to be careful about becoming too close to any of their sources. They must remain objective in order to report accurately and ethically.

Beat Reporters spend a lot of time attending meetings related to their beat. For example, Beat Reporters responsible for education attend all school board meetings, and those handling local politics go to all city council meetings. Beat Reporters write about what takes place at these meetings. The follow-up from these meetings also can make for stories for several days to come.

The job of a Beat Reporter varies depending on their beat, as well as the size and scope of their paper. At a small-town paper, Beat Reporters cover everything that goes on, from checking the police blotter daily to fires and other local events. More prominent beats come with more experience, as do jobs at larger city newspapers. Beat Reporters in these settings report on state politics and larger issues that can have national implications.

With each story, Beat Reporters use their skills as journalists to make decisions. They decide not only which stories make the most interesting news but also whom to interview and what angle to take. By considering what they want to convey with their words, they can influence the way people feel and respond to different issues.

While positions such as general assignment reporter allow journalists to cover a variety of topics, Beat Reporters are specialists. For this reason, the best Beat Reporters are those who feel passionate about their beats, whether they are education, health, or sports. Their commitment to their topic helps to earn the confidence and trust of their readers.

Additional duties may include:

- Meeting with sources at their places of businesses
- Setting up lunch dates with potential sources
- Conducting online research
- Generating story ideas and identifying trends
- Writing sidebars and blurbs in addition to articles
- Performing some copyediting
- Taking photographs
- Working with other Beat Reporters to minimize overlap and discuss issues
- Meeting with editors for guidance

Beat Reporters often must work irregular hours. At most daily papers, they come in during the morning and have until midnight to finish their stories. While clearly they are not working during all those hours, it may be that they come in to the office and make several phone calls in the morning, take off during the afternoon, attend a meeting in the evening, and then write until 11:00 P.M. at night.

In addition to their daily contributions, many Beat Reporters also work each week on the Sunday issue of their paper. In this larger package, they often have the space to explore an issue in depth. Beat Reporters and their editors determine which issues warrant in-depth coverage and how to get their message across.

Salaries

Salaries for Beat Reporters vary tremendously, depending on their level of experience, their beat, and the size and circulation of their paper. Entry-level Beat Reporters at small-town publications typically earn in the $18,000 to $25,000 range. Beat Reporters at a midsize paper may earn from $40,000 to $50,000 and then those with more than 10 years of experience at very prominent national newspapers can earn $100,000 or more.

Information compiled by the media union, the Newspaper Guild, each year lists the top minimum weekly salaries for reporters throughout the country in their collective bargaining manual. The 2004 figures for reporters/photographers show a high weekly minimum of $1,445.17 per week with two years of experience at the *New York Times* ($75,148.84 annually) and a low weekly minimum of $387.50 at the Utica, N.Y., *Observer-Dispatch* ($20,150 annually).

Also, according to the Inland Press Association's annual 2004 Newspaper Industry Compensation Survey, the authoritative "industry standard" for newspaper industry compensation planning, total direct compensation for entry-level reporters was $28,162 on average and $43,292 on average for those with considerable experience.

Employment Prospects

As newspapers consolidate and jobs diminish, Beat Reporters benefit from the fact that each newspaper has a number of beats it must cover. However, to be a Beat Reporter, one must be willing to go wherever the jobs are.

Particularly right out of journalism school, fledgling journalists may have idealistic dreams about uncovering scandal in Washington, D.C., or traveling with the New York Yankees. The reality is that jobs at the entry-level are going to be most likely covering school board meetings or reading the police blotter at small-town weeklies across the nation. Jobs in geographically desirable locations or at well-regarded papers are highly competitive. So are desirable beats.

Beat Reporters who understand that they need to start off small can use the opportunity to develop a niche area for themselves, as well as a portfolio of clips. By realizing that no paper is too small to begin with, they can put themselves in a position for later success. With experience, jobs at dailies are most often found through networking and professional associations.

Advancement Prospects

The advancement process at newspapers, particularly in reporting, tends to go from small to large papers, rather than a change in the actual position or job title. Beat Reporters who begin at small-town weeklies find advancement by moving to small-town dailies and then to larger daily papers in bigger cities. Others may prefer to change their beats early on in order to advance, such as moving from local crime to city hall.

Education and Training

Because positions as Beat Reporters can be highly competitive, education and training is important. Within journalism, there runs a debate about the best educational course of study for future journalists. Some will argue that a bachelor's degree in journalism is the best training. This background provides hands-on, nuts and bolts skills in writing, reporting, and research.

Yet other seasoned journalists will maintain that a well-rounded liberal arts curriculum is the best career preparation. Through courses in fields such as literature, economics, history, and political science, students learn to write and research, as well as becoming knowledgeable and educated over a variety of genres. However, with the liberal arts curriculum, most do agree that some formal journalism training is also necessary. Future reporters who major in the liberal arts often minor in journalism, or continue on for a master's degree. This is extremely helpful and may even be required for employment.

Furthermore, Beat Reporters that plan to develop their specialty area early on may also study that subject academically. For example, a Beat Reporter who specializes in business might have an economics, finance, or business background.

In addition to education, training also comes from hands-on work. Virtually all Beat Reporters have had student journalism experience through campus newspapers and internships.

Experience, Skills, and Personality Traits

Successful Beat Reporters are curious and persistent. They have good judgment and intuition in order to delve into issues and decide what will appeal to readers. Furthermore, they do not give up until they have the necessary information to make their story work. Good Beat Reporters help readers to see the relevance of their stories to their own lives.

Also, Beat Reporters must be excellent writers. A knack for words is needed to make their stories interesting. In addition to writing skills, verbal communication is also very important. As Beat Reporters work with sources, their ability to put people at ease, persuade, and extract information is crucial. They need to be thick-skinned and be able to take criticism, whether it comes from their editors, their sources, or the public. Beat Reporters also must be ethical in order to gain respect.

The nature of reporting requires Beat Reporters to be able to work under intense deadline pressure. Although many feel they are perfectionists, they need to be able to submit stories within a 24-hour turnaround time and leave the fine-tuning to the editorial staff. Sometimes they may be working on stories simultaneously for the Sunday edition or the following day, so Beat Reporters need to be able to juggle many responsibilities at once.

Unions and Associations

There are a number of professional associations for Beat Reporters. While many are specific to certain beats such as the American Society of Business Writers and Editors and the Education Writers Association, there are also a number of general organizations such as the American Society of Newspaper Editors, the Newspaper Association of America, and Investigative Reporters & Editors.

Tips for Entry

1. Take a look at the following Web site, which offers training advice for journalists: http://www.notrain-nogain. org.
2. The Dow Jones Newspaper Fund provides internships and scholarships for high school and college students interested in careers in newspaper journalism. Visit their Web site at http://djnewspaperfund.dowjones. com/fund/default.asp.
3. If you are a high school student, explore http://www. highschooljournalism.org/, a site that offers information and advice about how high school students can prepare for careers in journalism.
4. The American Society of Newspaper Editors offers helpful career information on their Web site. Explore it at http://www.asne.org/index.cfm?id=2.
5. If you want to be a Beat Reporter, begin now. Work for your high school paper, your college paper, or local paper in any capacity where they need you. Remember that no beat or paper is too small to get started.
6. Reporters are avid readers and observers. Read newspapers, magazines, novels, and literature to immerse yourself in the written world. Be aware of the world around you and how people interact.

FOREIGN CORRESPONDENT

CAREER PROFILE

Duties: Covers world issues for a newspaper, reporting from foreign locations

Alternate Title(s): International Correspondent, International Reporter, Foreign Affairs Reporter

Salary Range: $20,000 to 100,000 and up

Employment Prospects: Poor

Advancement Prospects: Fair

Best Geographical Location(s): Major world cities and regions in the news

Prerequisites:

Education or Training—Bachelor's degree in journalism or related field; background in international affairs, politics, or foreign language helpful

Experience—Several years of news reporting experience

Special Skills and Personality Traits—Excellent writing and reporting skills; international exposure; knowledge of at least one foreign language; willingness to travel; flexibility, independence, and initiative; understanding of international culture, news, and politics

CAREER LADDER

```
┌─────────────────────────────────────┐
│  Foreign Correspondent, larger paper;│
│      Editor; or Bureau Chief         │
└─────────────────────────────────────┘

┌─────────────────────────────────────┐
│      Foreign Correspondent           │
└─────────────────────────────────────┘

┌─────────────────────────────────────┐
│      Beat Reporter or                │
│   General Assignment Reporter        │
└─────────────────────────────────────┘
```

Position Description

The media helps to make the world smaller. Newspaper, television, radio, and the Internet keep us informed around the clock about breaking news across the globe. Foreign Correspondents are the journalists who cover these international stories, bringing world news into the homes of their readers. They are there, on location, telling the stories of what is really happening abroad.

Foreign Correspondents are few and far between. There are approximately 1,000 Foreign Correspondents employed by U.S. newspapers today. World news is only the domain of the 50 or so largest daily newspapers. Foreign Correspondents may report from one overseas post for a set period of time, or they may travel frequently to various international locations.

As reporters, Foreign Correspondents write a combination of stories. They handle breaking news, but most also write longer investigative/enterprise pieces. They conduct interviews, visit scenes of events, check in with sources, and scan local media just as domestic reporters do. However, this all must be done with international savvy and sensibility. Not only are languages different, but so also are the methods to access information in foreign lands.

Some foreign language skills, as well as knowledge of the politics, history, and culture of their region, are necessary for Foreign Correspondents. Equally important is the ability to work in a country very different from home. Foreign Correspondents often work with local translators that do more than merely help them with words. These locals, who are often journalists themselves, serve as guides to help Foreign Correspondents get information, connect with sources, conduct interviews, and cut through red tape. They also may help them with practical needs such as securing transportation and places to stay on assignment. These relationships are crucial to good reporting.

Unlike domestic reporters, Foreign Correspondents may not have an editor to check in with daily and hand out assignments. They may not have an office with a computer where they can collaborate with colleagues. Foreign Correspondents must be independent and resourceful. They have the initiative to generate stories and the curiosity to follow through with leads. Furthermore, they have the ambition to handle difficult topics with professionalism.

Foreign Correspondents are often sent to areas of conflict. Unfortunately, with the budget cuts prevalent at newspapers today, many U.S. newspapers can only report on major world events involving war, political unrest, disaster, or business. Foreign Correspondents who cover these conflicts, particularly those relating to war or political unrest, potentially put themselves at risk for their work. However, for these journalists, the desire to uncover the truth as danger beckons is part of the excitement.

Not all Foreign Correspondents handle dangerous assignments. Another major area for specialty is business. While business reporting does not have the glamour and intrigue of other types of international journalism, it provides a way to work overseas in a more controlled environment. As long as issues of international business affect the world economy, Foreign Correspondents will be needed to cover this news. Other issues might include trade, immigration, and global finance.

Some Foreign Correspondents find themselves enmeshed in politics—both of their region and of their newspaper. The world takes sides on international issues, particularly those that relate to politics. The political leanings of the newspaper for which a Foreign Correspondent works may affect coverage. While Foreign Correspondents strive to portray a situation objectively, the angle they take and the stories on which they choose to focus can help create public sympathy for a specific group, uncover humanitarian abuses, highlight the economic climate, and more. In this sense, Foreign Correspondents shoulder a great responsibility in offering information that can influence public opinion and affect world support.

Their duties may include:

- Writing features about people's lives
- Conducting interviews
- Working with state departments and U.S. embassies
- Meeting with other foreign correspondents in their region
- Keeping abreast of new developments in their region
- Learning one or more foreign languages
- Taking photographs or video footage
- Staying informed about local culture
- Reading, watching, and listening to all news media from their region
- Checking in with local sources

For most Foreign Correspondents, the travel required is the most exciting aspect of the job. It can be an opportunity to see the world and live in different environments. However, Foreign Correspondents do not necessarily get to choose their assignments. They may need to uproot themselves (and their families, if applicable) to move to undesirable regions for extended periods of time. Many positions require a specific time period overseas, as well as working domestically on international issues. Some Foreign Correspondents report that for their first few years, they were never home for more than six weeks at a time.

Yet few positions in journalism can match the sheer excitement of a Foreign Correspondent in the face of danger. At the heart of major developments, both tragic and joyous, their reporting can bring the world together and offer insight into other cultures.

Salaries

Salaries for Foreign Correspondents vary depending on experience. According to the Inland Press Association's annual Newspaper Industry Compensation Survey, the total direct compensation for entry-level reporters in 2004 was $28,162 on average and $43,292 on average for those with considerable experience. The overall range was very diverse and reported figures spanning a low salary of $10,042 at the entry-level to a high salary of $163,926 at the experienced level. Although this survey is not specific to Foreign Correspondents, it can be used as a guide.

Furthermore, each year the Newspaper Guild, a media union, lists the top minimum weekly salaries for reporters throughout the country in their collective bargaining manual. The 2004 figures for reporters/photographers show a high weekly minimum of $1,445.17 per week with two years of experience at the *New York Times* ($75,148.84 annually). Since Foreign Correspondents primarily work at large dailies, this figure can also be comparable.

Employment Prospects

Jobs for Foreign Correspondents are highly competitive. Only major daily newspapers in large cities employ Foreign Correspondents, so employment prospects are limited to papers large enough to have reporters overseas. Job seekers need to determine both their target papers as well as their target regions, finding out which newspapers have correspondents in which cities. These will yield the most likely job prospects.

Prospective Foreign Correspondents should consider their areas of expertise. Which countries would you want to target and why? Have you spent time living in these regions? Can you speak the language? These are important questions to ask in order to get started.

Most Foreign Correspondents pay their dues as beat or general assignment reporters before receiving a foreign post. An ideal beat through which to transition to international news might be business. Business reporting often features international issues such as trade and global finance that offer potential for overseas experience.

Furthermore, some Foreign Correspondents find opportunities through freelance work. Web sites, trade journals, and public relations firms in foreign countries are just some of the ways to work abroad as a writer while gaining enough experience to market to newspapers.

Advancement Prospects

Foreign Correspondents may advance through moving to larger papers with more high-profile posts. However, extensive travel causes some Foreign Correspondents to face burnout after several years in the field. As transitions, they may try to take on semipermanent positions at international bureaus of their paper. Others might work for journalism schools as professors training future foreign correspondents. Still other Foreign Correspondents might advance to become news editors or bureau chiefs.

Education and Training

Most Foreign Correspondents starting in the field today have bachelor's degrees in journalism or related fields. Many hold master's degrees in journalism as well. These degrees and courses provide a foundation in writing and reporting, as well as an entry into reporting jobs.

A liberal arts curriculum that emphasizes history, political science, and culture is also important. International affairs, international relations, and foreign language and culture courses are very helpful.

The best training for Foreign Correspondents comes from a combination of reporting and international experience. Time spent living, working, and/or studying abroad develops a cultural understanding, as well as a network of contacts that are invaluable.

Experience, Skills, and Personality Traits

In addition to having excellent writing and reporting skills, it is essential for Foreign Correspondents to be interested in travel and living abroad. Knowledge of at least one foreign language may be required, as is the ability to be adaptable and function in different environments. Foreign Correspondents must be comfortable with risk and potentially dangerous situations. They should be confident, with a nose for news and good judgment.

Furthermore, Foreign Correspondents must be able to work independently. They need to be flexible and resourceful as they receive less input and direction from editors than their domestic counterparts. Their insatiable curiosity drives them to uncover breaking stories and issues that can hold the world's attention. At the same time, they are sensitive to people and their differences. Foreign Correspondents should be nonjudgmental and committed to telling the accurate story.

Working under tight deadline pressure is a daily reality for Foreign Correspondents. They can juggle many tasks at once, taking photos or video as necessary. Persistence and thick skin enable them to persevere, even in tough conditions.

Unions and Associations

The Overseas Press Club of America is a professional association that has been serving the interests of Foreign Correspondents since 1939. Foreign Correspondents may also belong to associations based on their specialty region including the Foreign Correspondents' Association for journalists working in Australia and the South Pacific and the Foreign Press Association in London.

Tips for Entry

1. The Overseas Press Club of American sponsors two internships for each academic semester. Read more about their program at http://www.opcofamerica.org/internships/internships.php.
2. Read *The World on a String: How to Become a Freelance Foreign Correspondent* by Alan Goodman and John Pollack to learn more about freelancing as a Foreign Correspondent.
3. Practice being a Foreign Correspondent by selecting a country or region of interest. Research this country from its language and history to its culture and politics. As a Foreign Correspondent, think about what are the most pressing issues you would cover today? What is important to convey to readers worldwide?
4. Learn a foreign language. Language skills will broaden your options as a journalist. Consider studying abroad as a way to perfect the language you choose, as well as to gain cultural perspective.
5. Be willing to start at the bottom. It is very unlikely that you would become a Foreign Correspondent straight out of journalism school. Take a position that enables you to gain writing and reporting experience while honing and improving your skills.
6. Be a constant reader of world news. Stay abreast of current events and take note of different types of coverage.

PAGE DESIGNER

CAREER PROFILE

Duties: Designs and assembles pages for a newspaper, including placement of articles, photos, graphics, and art

Alternate Title(s): Designer, News Designer

Salary Range: $25,000 to $50,000 and up

Employment Prospects: Fair to good

Advancement Prospects: Fair to good

Best Geographical Location(s): All

Prerequisites:

Education or Training—Bachelor's degree in journalism or art

Experience—One to three years of page design experience through internships or prior jobs

Special Skills and Personality Traits—Creativity and artistic sense; excellent computer skills; strong command of language; editing, grammar, and spelling skills; good spatial vision

CAREER LADDER

```
┌─────────────────────────────────┐
│    Design Editor or Director     │
└─────────────────────────────────┘

┌─────────────────────────────────┐
│         Page Designer            │
└─────────────────────────────────┘

┌─────────────────────────────────┐
│   Page Designer, smaller paper   │
└─────────────────────────────────┘
```

Position Description

When you read a newspaper, chances are that you take for granted the way the pages are constructed and information is presented. As you read the stories and sections that interest you, you might glance at headlines, notice photos, and skim through graphs. However, putting these pages together to create a dynamic newspaper takes a lot of careful planning and hard work. Page Designers are responsible for assembling and designing newspaper pages. They conceptualize a vision for their paper and determine the way to make it work.

The process of assembling pages for a newspaper can be complex. Stories, headlines, photos, graphics, and art must all fit into a particular space. Page Designers put all these puzzle pieces together in a way that not only makes sense logically but also looks neat and organized for the readers. Page design is an art that requires close attention to detail. As visual journalists, Page Designers use design techniques to find the best way to inform readers.

Design can transform and define a newspaper's image. The look of the front page, the placement of headlines, the use of color, and the attention to photographs project the goals of each paper, defining what they deem important. A dull front page does not inspire sales at the newsstand. Page Designers have an important task in making their paper stand out. They need good journalism knowledge and news judgment to highlight the most compelling information.

Sometimes, stories must be trimmed in order to fit in a particular space. The column format of text must be integrated with graphics, art, and photos. Page Designers work with editors to determine what content can be trimmed. They often work with copy editors to fine-tune and cut articles. At some papers, Page Designers also perform copyediting themselves. This makes sense, since both professionals are responsible for ensuring that the finished page looks good and reads correctly.

In the old days, Page Designers assembled pages by hand, using a "dummy sheet," pencil, and ruler, but now most papers use computer-generated design. The process of laying out and formatting pages on a computer screen is called pagination. While Page Designers used to spend their time caught up in the logistics and mechanics of assembly, now they can focus on the actual design and creativity. Different newspapers may have their own in-house pagination programs, but some common ones are CCI Layout Champ, InDesign, Harris, and QuarkXPress. Most use both PC and Mac platforms.

There are many ways that Page Designers can use creativity to make their pages aesthetically pleasing. Some use shaded boxes, contrast, and color tints. Others tend toward vertical or horizontal column formats. Page Designers can also alter the width of columns and size of type to make stories more readable. Good design usually avoids large columns of gray and breaks them up with variety. However, consistency is a key in making a particular format work.

Their duties may include:

- Brainstorming with editors
- Reading other publications for design ideas
- Creating charts, tables, or graphics
- Copyediting text
- Cropping photographs and deciding on photo size
- Designing section fronts
- Writing headlines and/or captions
- Enhancing visual elements
- Creating Web content

A combination of independent work and working with people is typical for Page Designers. While hours are needed to be spent at their computers, they also need to consult with editors, photographers, reporters, and graphic artists. Furthermore, they may work on design teams with other designers.

Most Page Designers report to design/art editors or directors, news editors, or copy editors. Many work on all sections, while others specialize in particular areas such as news, sports, or front-page design. Hours can be long and nontraditional, especially for entry-level positions. Since final page design occurs once all other content is in, night shift and weekend work is common.

Salaries

Salaries for Page Designers will vary depending on the size and location of their paper. The Inland Press Association conducts an annual Newspaper Industry Compensation Survey, which is considered to be the "industry standard" for newspaper industry compensation planning. In 2004 news designers/artists earned an average of $40,307 per year as their base salary. Their total direct compensation, including bonuses and other commissions, was $40,594. The survey participants reported a range spanning a low in total direct compensation at $17,680 and a high at $94,278.

Employment Prospects

Traditional newspaper employment for Page Designers is fair to good. As newspapers consolidate, positions diminish and grow more competitive. Like other journalism professionals, Page Designers should expect to begin at small papers and to be geographically flexible. A willingness to work the night shift is also helpful.

However, the Internet is a growing market for Page Designers. Rather than face the limits of a conventional page, the online paper is boundless, opening up design possibilities. It is essential for new and aspiring Page Designers to get computer training to be competitive in the job market.

Advancement Prospects

Page Designers can advance by moving from smaller papers to larger ones. They may move from small weeklies to small dailies, and then up to bigger dailies where they have more responsibility, handling different types of sections and graphics.

Additionally, Page Designers can advance into editorial positions, both on the art/design side and the copyediting side, depending on their skills and background. In these positions, they have managerial responsibility. Also, Page Designers can move from print journalism to Internet-based publications, branching into Web design.

Education and Training

In this competitive market, virtually all Page Designers hold bachelor's degrees. Among Page Designers, bachelor's degrees are typically in either journalism or art. Since the job is really a marriage of the two, Page Designers with degrees in one area usually get training on the other area on the job. Journalism tends to be the more common degree since many programs offer degrees in design journalism.

Computer and graphics courses are essential in addition to any course of study. Also, courses in history and political science are always helpful for a strong news background.

Experience, Skills, and Personality Traits

Page Designers must know AP (Associated Press) style for the editing portion that is involved in many jobs. Since many Page Designers also perform copyediting, their language skills—including grammar, spelling, punctuation, and usage—must be top-notch. For some positions, a copyediting test may be required. A good eye for detail and strong organizational skills help Page Designers catch errors and discrepancies related to both text and other aspects of each page.

Furthermore, Page Designers must be skilled at using computers, particularly graphics and pagination programs such as QuarkXPress, InDesign, CCI, and Harris. A background in Web design is extremely valuable as well. Many Page Designers gain experience using these programs through internships and work on their school papers. Good Page Designers are creative, with a passion for art and design and an excellent visual sense.

Since page design is not only about page assembly, Page Designers should have excellent news judgment. As journalists, they make decisions about placement of stories, graphics, and photographs. They must understand which pieces are significant and why. Flexibility and the ability to adhere to tight deadlines are also needed.

Unions and Associations

The Society for News Design is the main professional association for Page Designers. They may also belong to the American Copy Editors Society, the American Institute of Graphic Arts, and the Society of Publication Designers.

Tips for Entry

1. Spend time on the Web site of the Society for News Design at http://www.snd.org. View their job listings and speak to experts in visual journalism.

2. Learn more about graphic design pagination programs such as Adobe Photoshop, QuarkXpress, and CCI. Gain experience with layout through coursework, internships, and work on your school paper.

3. Become an expert copy editor. The Journalism Education Association offers good copyediting resources, including quizzes, copyediting symbols, and information about AP style at http://www.jea.org/resources/curriculum/copyediting/copyediting.html.

4. Speak to a Page Designer to find out more about his or her job. See if you can shadow a Page Designer on a typical day (or night).

5. Be aware of design on a daily basis. Read a variety of newspapers, as well as news Web sites. See how they integrate text with graphics and photos. Notice which formats you like best and why.

PHOTOGRAPHER

CAREER PROFILE

Duties: Takes photographs for a newspaper; may also write some captions and copy and/or shoot video footage

Alternate Title(s): Photojournalist

Salary Range: $10,000 to $75,000 and up

Employment Prospects: Fair

Advancement Prospects: Fair

Best Geographical Location(s): All

Prerequisites:

Education or Training—Degree in journalism very helpful; some photography training necessary

Experience—Prior experience taking photographs; some previous newspaper experience (can be through internships or part-time work)

Special Skills and Personality Traits—Excellent technical photography skills; creativity and artistic vision; understanding of journalism

CAREER LADDER

```
┌─────────────────────────────────┐
│   Photographer, larger paper or  │
│           Photo Editor           │
└─────────────────────────────────┘

┌─────────────────────────────────┐
│           Photographer           │
└─────────────────────────────────┘

┌─────────────────────────────────┐
│    Photographer, smaller paper   │
└─────────────────────────────────┘
```

Position Description

Photographers play a role in newspaper journalism as critical as that of reporters. Both professionals tell a story and make the public aware of current events. However, each uses a different medium to tell their story. While reporters use words, Photographers present their vision through visual images that touch the minds and hearts of readers. The emotions they capture stay burned on our brains for years to come.

There are many components to being a newspaper Photographer. First, Photographers take photographs daily on assignment. Depending on the size of the paper, they make take between two and six photos on average. Assignments may come from the news, features, or sports departments and are usually filtered down through the photo editor. The editor then assigns various Photographers their assignments, based on timing as well as their individual strengths.

Most Photographers will have a mix of coverage in their work. Shifts will also determine assignments, as those Photographers working afternoon/evening shifts are more likely to handle late breaking news and sports. Some assignments will be known in advance (such as scheduled games or meetings), while others will come from breaking news.

Upon receiving their assignments, Photographers go to the scene of the event. With breaking news, they must tread lightly and with caution, especially at any kind of accident scene. Since it is important that they do not interfere with police or medical assistance, Photographers usually set up a perimeter where they can work without getting in the way. As outside observers, they can often get the best type of footage this way.

For more general news and features coverage, Photographers often arrive early to spend some time talking to the people they will be shooting. Sometimes a brief phone call the day before will help put people at ease and translate into better pictures. With features photography, Photographers can really be creative and experiment with different ways to tell their stories. As journalists, Photographers are able to note important quotes or themes and pass them along to reporters.

Technology facilitates the work of Photographers, enabling them to send photos directly from their location back to their office via an FTP (file transfer protocol) using a laptop, cell phone, and/or landline. Once they are finished shooting an event or subject, images are sent to the office computers and are reviewed by the Photographer and photo editor. While the photo editor has final say in determining which footage will be used, good Photographers edit themselves by knowing what to focus on in their coverage. Adobe Photoshop is generally the industry standard computer program for editing photographs digitally.

However, in the digital age, Photographers are aware that there is only so much a picture can be altered on a computer. Photographers are bound by their journalistic ethics to be responsible and keep to the truth. Anyone who has ever experimented by putting their own photographs online knows how undesirable images can easily be deleted, light and dark adjusted, and focuses shifted. Photographers strive to present the image as is and go with the code of ethics that anything they do by computer should also be something they could do in a darkroom.

Their duties also may include:

- Photographing sports events
- Photographing breaking news
- Taking posed pictures of people and things for feature stories
- Performing digital photo editing
- Developing film in a darkroom
- Working with reporters and editors
- Attending meetings
- Generating story ideas
- Shooting photo essays
- Writing captions
- Some reporting and writing (usually at smaller papers)

Photographers can work during a variety of shifts and hours that often include evenings and weekends. Travel may be a big part of the job, or none at all, depending on the size and scope of the paper. While clearly not all Photographers are sent off to cover a war, there are some that are. Furthermore, Photographers must capture a wide range of domestic and international events. This can be an exciting and high stress aspect of the work.

Salaries

There is quite a bit of a range for Photographers' salaries. According to the Inland Press Association's annual Newspaper Industry Compensation Survey, the authoritative "industry standard" for newspaper industry compensation planning, in 2004 entry-level photographers earned an average of $14,560 per year in total direct compensation. With considerable experience, a position they deem as "Photographer Level III," that average went up to $43,418. The high end of the entry-level salaries capped out at $92,321, while more experienced Photographers can earn $125,000 per year and more.

Additional information about Photographers' salaries comes from the media union, the Newspaper Guild. Each year, they produce a collective bargaining manual that lists the top minimum weekly salaries for reporters and photographers throughout the country. The 2004 figures for reporters/photographers show a high weekly minimum of $1,445.17 per week with two years of experience at the *New York Times* ($75,148.84 annually) and a low weekly minimum of $387.50 at the Utica, N.Y., *Observer-Dispatch* ($20,150 annually). This also demonstrates the salary range based on circulation and experience.

Employment Prospects

Employment prospects are fair for newspaper Photographers. Jobs are competitive, and like other newspaper positions, recent graduates must be prepared to start at small papers in tiny towns.

Prior photography experience is crucial to finding a job and a portfolio of photography is a prerequisite. Aspiring photographers gain experience through working for campus or local papers, as well as through photojournalism courses. These provide opportunities to take the types of photographs that would be appropriate for a professional portfolio.

Freelancing can be another good way to break into the job market. Working for hire at several different papers helps Photographers get to know the management staff and gives them a chance to prove their skill. Some Photographers may then move into full-time staff positions, while others enjoy the freedom they get from freelancing and find they can earn enough to sustain their careers.

Advancement Prospects

Photographers can advance in several ways. They can work their way up to becoming photo editors at their papers, where they would make decisions and manage a staff of photographers. Others advance by moving from smaller papers to larger ones with a greater variety and scope of assignments, as well as higher salaries. Still other Photographers start their own businesses where they do freelance work.

The future of photojournalism involves technology. Photographers say that video work is becoming more common at newspapers, as many include interactive components on their Web sites. Photographers who also know how to shoot video and have a multimedia/Internet background make themselves more marketable.

Education and Training

In the past, it was not necessary for Photographers to hold bachelor's degrees. However, in today's competitive job market, the vast majority do, studying photojournalism, photography, or other liberal arts fields supplemented with photography course work.

Above all, Photographers at newspapers need training in photography. Insiders agree that regardless of the move from the traditional darkroom to the "digital darkroom," as they call their computers in a well-lit room where editing and development now takes place, Photographers still must know the darkroom process. Photography curricula includes the history of photography, as well as learning the operation of different types of cameras. While Photographers must know how to operate digital cameras, they must also train in developing pictures by hand to learn the craft. By seeing their mistakes and successes and spending time getting the exposures right, they can transfer that knowledge to their digital work.

Photojournalism education is a big plus and is required for many positions. Courses include photography education, as well as journalism classes. Subjects such as news writing help Photographers to see the reporter's perspective to telling a story and also are useful when Photographers are the only ones on a scene and must jot down notes.

Experience, Skills, and Personality Traits

Photography has changed with the times. Roughly 75 percent of newspaper photography is shot digitally now, although some small papers still use film or a combination. However, starting in the mid 1990s, insiders say that both color and black and white darkrooms are being phased out.

Yet it is still crucial for Photographers to know their craft both past and present. Photographers must be able to use both digital and regular cameras, know how to expose film, edit, and use a darkroom. They need to know how to expose film and balance color, along with other technical processes involved with film development and editing. Photographers must understand the role of light and its challenges, adapting to different conditions. In addition to understanding how to "soup" their film with darkroom chemicals, they must also know how to process a raw digital image into a JPEG file.

On the nontechnical side, flexibility is another skill essential for Photographers. They must be able to cover a wide variety of assignments with ease, switching gears as needed. Also, they must be able to meet tight deadlines. They know what to look for as they are shooting an image, to maximize time and minimize editing. Photographers are quick thinkers, able to make spot decisions and changes in order to get the best coverage.

Photographers must be creative. Through their cameras, they capture emotion and see things that many of us cannot. Along with the mechanical expertise, an artistic vision is still crucial and always will be. Computer programs such as Adobe Photoshop and others that are customized are vehicles through which they can portray their creativity.

Furthermore, Photographers must be thick-skinned and resilient. As witnesses to difficult events, they must be able to remain objective and deal with their emotions. Additionally, people may resent their presence, and they must be able to handle animosity with professionalism.

Like all journalists, Photographers should be curious. They must be interested in people and wonder what lies beneath the surface. It is important for them to be aware of their surroundings. Photographers work with all kinds of people from billionaire CEOs to impoverished victims of torture; they must be able to treat all with respect.

Unions and Associations

Photographers may belong to the National Press Photographers Association, a professional association dedicated to the advancement of photojournalism. They may also belong to the American Society of Media Photographers, the Society of Professional Journalists, the Newspaper Guild, or the American Institute of Graphic Arts.

Tips for Entry

1. Begin by picking up a camera. Take pictures for pleasure to get a feel for photography. Practice editing them on the computer and learning how to manipulate the images.
2. Move photography from your hobby to career goal by trying your hand at photojournalism. Volunteer for the staff of your high school, college, or local paper. Learn what constitutes news photography and let your vision come through.
3. Take care putting together your portfolio. Experts suggest getting several experienced journalists to review it and offer their suggestions. It is also important to pay attention to the order of photographs and begin with your strongest work.
4. Even if you did not major in journalism, take journalism courses. Learning how to write and report will be a tremendous asset on the job.
5. Explore the video aspect of photojournalism. Surf the Web sites of different newspapers to see how they use video and live feed to add to their content.
6. Visit the Web site of the National Press Photographer's Association for excellent career information about photojournalism, at http://www.nppa.org/.
7. Go online and read the current issue of the *Digital Journalist* (http://digitaljournalist.org/), a multimedia magazine for photojournalism in the digital age.

EDITORIAL WRITER

CAREER PROFILE

Duties: Writes opinion pieces for a newspaper that reflect the viewpoint of the paper's top management; shapes and impacts public opinion through these editorial pieces

Alternate Title(s): None

Salary Range: $20,000 to $100,000 and up

Employment Prospects: Fair

Advancement Prospects: Fair

Best Geographical Location(s): All

Prerequisites:

Education or Training—Bachelor's degree in journalism or related field

Experience—Five years or more of newsroom experience

Special Skills and Personality Traits—Excellent writing, reporting, and editing skills; ability to write a persuasive argument; good understanding of community, national, and world issues and politics

CAREER LADDER

```
┌─────────────────────────────────────┐
│      Editorial Page Editor or        │
│  other high-level editorial position │
└─────────────────────────────────────┘

┌─────────────────────────────────────┐
│           Editorial Writer           │
└─────────────────────────────────────┘

┌─────────────────────────────────────┐
│  General Assignment Reporter, Beat   │
│  Reporter, Copy Editor, or News Editor │
└─────────────────────────────────────┘
```

Position Description

Have you ever opened a newspaper to the editorial page? Unlike the rest of the contents, which strive to be objective, this part of the paper offers an opinion about politics, government, community, education, and other current public issues. Editorial Writers are responsible for writing these pieces.

Editorials, as these opinion pieces are called, are considered to voice the collective opinion of the newspaper. The viewpoint is coming from the highest management, such as the publisher and executive editor. It works best when Editorial Writers work for newspapers that share their basic political beliefs, although they should be able to write convincing opinion pieces even when they do not agree. Usually, these editorials do not have a byline with someone's name since they are considered to be the collective viewpoint of the paper.

Some Editorial Writers also write individual opinion pieces with their names attached to them, usually called commentary. These articles or columns do reflect their own opinions. Once again, this is usually when Editorial Writ-ers and the management are in agreement with their basic views. However, there might be one or more Editorial Writers with different beliefs. This can offer insight into several sides of an issue.

In order to gather support for the opinion, Editorial Writers conduct research and compile facts. They gather the background information needed to make a convincing argument. The goal of editorial pieces can be to sway public opinion—in an election, to support reform, and to impact change. They write about issues that are important to the community, the state, the country, and the world, as seen by their readers.

According to the National Conference of Editorial Writers (NCEW), a nonprofit professional association that exists to improve the quality of editorial pages and broadcast editorials, there are several goals of editorial pieces:

- To serve as the conscience of the community in mobilizing public actions
- To alert readers to important public issues and problems
- To challenge readers to think and form their own opinions

- To relate one problem to another, such as through historical perspective
- To spotlight wrongdoing.
- To advocate for improvements in community, state, national or world situations.

NCEW states in their "Basic Statement of Principles" that "editorial writing . . . is a profession devoted to the public welfare and to public service. The chief duty of its practitioner is to provide the information and guidance toward sound judgments that are essential to the healthy functioning of a democracy."

For this reason, it is critical for Editorial Writers to write well-developed arguments that are well researched and thoroughly backed up by evidence. While pieces express an opinion, they always take care not to reveal prejudice, inaccuracies, or fact distortion that will weaken and discredit their point. This is how readers can come to fair conclusions about important issues.

To write a strong editorial, Editorial Writers first state their point. They put the issue on the table, as well as why it is important. Next, they formulate their argument, defending each statement they make with facts and evidence. These facts are carefully researched and studied. Finally, they reach a conclusion that may propose a course of action to move forward.

Additional duties may include:

- Researching complex issues through the Internet, databases, and by speaking with people
- Developing community contacts and sources
- Checking facts
- Investigating claims made by the government and public figures
- Responding to readers' questions and concerns about pieces
- Meeting with policy makers and community members to learn more about their issues
- Attending editorial board or committee meetings to discuss potential topics and positions on issues

People often do not know what to believe about controversial issues. They do not know whom to support in a presidential election, if they should be in favor of a new mass transit system in their state, or which side to take about a new housing development in their community. Editorial Writers help people to understand these issues and offer sound and persuasive arguments supporting their points of view. While readers do not have to agree, the goal is that the writing will stimulate their thoughts and invite them to gather more facts and form their own opinions.

Editorial Writers tend to experience high job satisfaction among journalists. While many face the deadline pressure of completing editorials on a daily basis, they enjoy their work and the way it serves the public good. It also enables them to express themselves through their writing. Furthermore, because they are not reporting on breaking news, Editorial Writers may have more regular hours than other newspaper staff, although hours can still be quite long.

Depending on the size of the paper, there may be a team of Editorial Writers or only one at a very small local. They may write editorials daily, several times a week, or for a Sunday issue. Additionally, Editorial Writers may specialize in their areas of expertise such as international affairs, U.S. government, or education.

Salaries
Editorial Writers can have a large salary range depending on the size and scope of their paper. Each year, the Inland Press Association conducts the Newspaper Industry Compensation Survey, which is the authoritative "industry standard" for newspaper industry compensation planning. In 2004 Editorial Writers earned an average of $57,062 per year as their base salary. Their total direct compensation, including bonuses and other commissions, was $57,518. The survey participants reported a range spanning a low in total direct compensation at $10,648 to a high at $170,000.

Employment Prospects
Overall, employment prospects are fair for Editorial Writers. Positions are quite competitive, and small papers do not usually employ a large editorial staff.

Editorial Writers begin in the newsroom often as beat or general assignment reporters. Some are copy editors and others even advance to news editor before looking for a position as an Editorial Writer. Contacts with newspaper publishers and executive editors are valuable.

Advancement Prospects
Editorial Writers can have different goals for their professional future. They may go on to be editorial page editors, handling all the editorial writers and various columns, commentaries, and opinion pieces. Others aspire to become part of the top management as executive editors, although this can be very competitive.

At smaller papers, Editorial Writers may advance to work at larger ones where they comment on issues greater in scope. Still others find advancement through developing a following for their work, expanding into columns, freelance pieces for other publications, and books.

Education and Training
A bachelor's degree in journalism is helpful for an Editorial Writer. Formal journalism training teaches methods of news researching, writing, and analyzing that will benefit anyone in the profession.

In addition, liberal arts and social science subjects, including English, history, political science, international relations, and economics, can also be valuable for providing a sound knowledge base. Composition courses that teach how to write a persuasive argument are the building blocks to learning the craft.

Experience, Skills, and Personality Traits

In addition to the strong writing skills that are clearly necessary to becoming an Editorial Writer, a measure of self-knowledge is also important. Editorial Writers need to be insightful about themselves and their sources, realizing prejudice that detracts from an effective argument. Furthermore, they must be skilled researchers, able to draw out complicated information and use it in a way that supports their point.

Several years of newsroom experience are expected for Editorial Writers where they can hone their writing, editing, and layout skills as needed. They must be able to produce copy under deadline pressure, taking the initiative to come up with thought-provoking and insightful topics. Language, including grammar, spelling, punctuation, usage, and style is second nature to Editorial Writers.

Furthermore, Editorial Writers should be intellectually curious. Their role is not to vent their frustrations for the world to read. Rather, they understand what topics are important to the public and they use their format to guide people into making choices. Editorial Writers know how to make intelligent arguments so that even if readers disagree, they will still learn something.

Unions and Associations

Many Editorial Writers belong to the National Conference of Editorial Writers (NCEW). Other professional associations include the American Society of Newspaper Editors, the National Writers Union, and the National Society of Newspaper Columnists.

Tips for Entry

1. Look at how newspapers of different size and scope handle their editorials. Notice how they are developed, as well as the differences between the editorials, commentary, and columns. Many papers also have an "Op-Ed" page, which can include two pieces on the same topic, representing opposite viewpoints. Also see the "Letter to the Editor" section where readers can voice their response to the editorials.

2. Being able to write well is the key to being an Editorial Writer. Take a variety of writing courses that teach you different kinds of structure. Learn how to write research papers and analytical papers, as well as persuasive position papers.

3. Staying informed about the world is also crucial for an Editorial Writer. If you are considering this career, become a news junkie, staying aware of what is happening in the world around you. Be a voracious reader.

4. Take courses in a wide range of subjects. One cannot form opinions in a vacuum. The more educated you are, the better you will be able to express an effective opinion.

5. Spend time on the NCEW Web site at http://www.ncew.org. See their job listings to understand more about what the job of an Editorial Writer entails.

6. Hone your persuasive skills by taking part in a debate team, attending community forums about issues, and/or writing opinion pieces for your campus publications.

INVESTIGATIVE REPORTER

CAREER PROFILE

Duties: Writes longer, in-depth stories for a newspaper, usually ones that uncover new information

Alternate Title(s): Enterprise Reporter

Salary Range: $30,000 to $100,000 and up

Employment Prospects: Fair

Advancement Prospects: Fair

Best Geographical Location(s): All, but best opportunities are at bigger city papers

Prerequisites:

Education or Training—Bachelor's degree in journalism or related field

Experience—Several years of reporting experience

Special Skills and Personality Traits—Innate curiosity; excellent writing and reporting skills; strong research skills; persistence and patience

CAREER LADDER

```
┌─────────────────────────────────────┐
│      Investigative Reporter,         │
│  larger paper or an editorial position│
└─────────────────────────────────────┘

┌─────────────────────────────────────┐
│       Investigative Reporter          │
└─────────────────────────────────────┘

┌─────────────────────────────────────┐
│  General Assignment Reporter or       │
│           Beat Reporter               │
└─────────────────────────────────────┘
```

Position Description

If a reporter's job is to expose the truth, then the work of an Investigative Reporter defines the profession. Investigative Reporters work on long-term stories, spanning several weeks to a year or more. In each story, their goal is to uncover new and significant information. This information can be quite dramatic, ranging from the revelation of corruption or crime to the lesser-known effects of a newly FDA-approved drug. Their assignments are usually kept quiet to the rest of the newspaper staff, with only a few top editors knowing their plan of action. In addition to information, Investigative Reporters can expose problems, issues, and wrongdoings, holding public officials and private corporations accountable for their actions.

Generally, Investigative Reporters begin each story using the same formula. After generating an idea (or receiving an assignment), they determine which people they will need to speak with to find information. Furthermore, they consider the public records that will also help to uncover details and support the idea or supposition. This can be challenging, requiring intense persistence and determination on the Investigative Reporter's part, since the information is often being kept hidden by those who stand to suffer if it is revealed.

In order to flesh out an idea, time is crucial to show patterns. For example, if an Investigative Reporter supposes that a local school board member has been appropriating school funds for personal use, he or she will need to demonstrate how this pattern has occurred over a period of time. The time may be several weeks, months, or even longer. It is necessary to take the time to show the history in order to give the stories more credibility.

Examining patterns is also a way that Investigative Reporters might generate stories. Good Investigative Reporters can see something in the news that appears like a coincidence, such as two cases of breast cancer among next-door neighbors. If this seems questionable, the reporter will dig deeper, looking for reasons why. Have other neighbors been sick in a five-year period? They will scan health records, as well as records from power companies, water and sewage, and more to find any evidence that this was not random.

It is important for Investigative Reporters to be great writers and storytellers. Not only do they dig for information but they also must be able to present it in a way that is interesting and exciting to the public. Big investigative, or enterprise, stories, as they are also called, appear on page

A1 and are often the among the first pieces to capture the readers' attention.

Investigative Reporters must be able to organize complicated material and make sense of detailed records. They have a sense of what makes a good story, yet they realize they may spend weeks pursuing dead ends in order to find the piece that will make a difference.

Investigative Reporters can work a number of different beats, having specializations in areas such as hard news, politics, government, business, sports, health, and more. While many have specialties, others work on a wide variety of topics.

Their duties may include:

- Scouring public records and court documents
- Interviewing people in person and by telephone
- Conducting extensive research using the Internet, databases, and public records
- Meeting with editors
- Discovering tips and trends
- Complying with the U.S. Freedom of Information Act to access records
- Coordinating with graphics, design, and photography departments for stories
- Writing both individual and series of articles

Most Investigative Reporters will tell you that they find their jobs to be extremely exciting and rewarding. Investigative Reporters are among those whose ultimate goal might be a Pulitzer Prize for the category of investigative reporting, as they fight injustice. However, while discovering the key details is a rush, they need the patience to spend weeks and months going over mundane data until they find the proof they need. Travel may be required during the course of a story to speak to people and peruse records.

Compared to other reporters, Investigative Reporters enjoy the freedom of not adhering to tight deadlines and focusing on one story at a time. They may work alone or as part of an investigative team, lead by an investigative or enterprise editor.

Salaries

Depending on their years of experience as well as the scope of their reporting, Investigative Reporters can have a wide salary range.

The Inland Press Association conducts an annual Newspaper Industry Compensation Survey, which is the authoritative "industry standard" for newspaper industry compensation planning. According to the survey, reporters with considerable experience (which can be descriptive of most Investigative Reporters) earned an average of $43,292 per year in 2004 in total direct compensation. The range for reporters was from a low of $17,680 to a high salary of $163,926 at the experienced level.

Additional information about reporters' salaries comes from the media union, the Newspaper Guild. Each year, they produce a collective bargaining manual that lists the top minimum weekly salaries for reporters throughout the country. The 2004 figures for reporters/photographers show a high weekly minimum of $1,445.17 per week with two years of experience at the *New York Times* ($75,148.84 annually) and a low weekly minimum of $387.50 at the Utica, N.Y., *Observer-Dispatch* ($20,150 annually). This further demonstrates the salary range based on circulation and experience.

Employment Prospects

Employment prospects are fair for Investigative Reporters. The positions are competitive, usually going to seasoned reporters who have proved themselves through years of work as general assignment or beat reporters.

Like other reporters, Investigative Reporters should expect to start out in small towns at even smaller papers. By proving themselves with good writing, they can try to incorporate hard-hitting news into their stories when possible. This can help them build up enough clips to move into an investigative role after three to seven years.

Advancement Prospects

Investigative Reporters have several options for advancement. Those who work at smaller papers and want to tackle bigger, national investigative pieces can move to larger publications. Others may find that they are interested in an editorial role and can work their way up to managing a team of reporters.

Still other Investigative Reporters who have received national recognition for their work may move on to turn their stories into larger pieces, such as books.

Education and Training

Most Investigative Reporters have some formal journalism education. Journalism school offers concrete training in writing and reporting, including how to craft a news story, as well as some layout, design, and important software programs. While some Investigative Reporters have bachelor's degrees in journalism, others may hold degrees in English, history, or other liberal arts fields. Many seasoned journalists believe that the combination of a journalism and liberal arts education provides for the most well-rounded reporters. These reporters with liberal arts majors may have minored in journalism, or they may have gone on to receive master's degrees in journalism.

Investigative Reporters with specialties may also have education or training in a specific area. For example, an Investigative Reporter specializing in business may have significant business coursework, while another with a health niche may hold a master's degree in public health.

Training for Investigative Reporters also comes from hands-on work. Virtually all have had student journalism experience through campus newspapers and internships.

Experience, Skills, and Personality Traits

A novice reporter does not finish journalism school and find himself or herself in an investigative role right away. These jobs usually require between four and seven years of newspaper experience, depending on the position.

Investigative Reporters should be, by nature, curious and skeptical. Rather than accepting things at face value, they are intuitive and want to dig deeper to find what lies beneath. Their natural curiosity is supplemented by superb writing skills and the ability to tell a story. With clear organization and a catchy style, they draw readers in and make them understand the significance of what they are reading. Research skills are also paramount in searching records and databases.

Furthermore, Investigative Reporters are thick-skinned and able to face adversity. They are often "snooping around" where others do not want them to go, but they can remain professional and not get discouraged. Good Investigative Reporters are skilled at communication and are able to put people at ease and get them talking. With patience and determination, they can spend extensive time conducting research with little results.

Ethics are a key factor for Investigative Reporters. The information they uncover has consequences, and they must remain impartial and objective. Their goal is to serve the greater good, as well as to uphold the First Amendment of freedom of speech, and they remember this in all their pieces.

Unions and Associations

Investigative Reporters may belong to professional associations such as Investigative Reporters and Editors, located at the Missouri School of Journalism. They may also be members of the Society of Professional Journalists, the Newspaper Association of America, and the National Writers Union.

Tips for Entry

1. Learn more about the U.S. Department of Justice's Freedom of Information Act, which enables people to gain access to public records through written requests at http://www.usdoj.gov/04foia/.
2. Spend some time on the Web site of Investigative Reporters and Editors at http://www.ire.org/. Among other features, it offers a resource center with an investigative story database, tipsheets from conferences, and reporter contacts. It also contains job listings.
3. Look on the front page of a national newspaper. Can you identify an investigative story? Also look on the front pages for other sections such as sports and business and take note of investigative stories you find there.
4. Find opportunities for investigative reporting at your campus paper or through internships.
5. Speak to an Investigative Reporter about his or her job. Find out about the career path as well as the daily experience. You can find names of people to interview through professional associations (such as Investigative Reporters and Editors) and personal contacts, as well as your campus career center.

NEWS OMBUDSMAN

CAREER PROFILE

Duties: Investigates and responds to the public's issues, complaints, and concerns for a newspaper; maintains ethical standards

Alternate Title(s): Public Editor, Readers' Representative, Readers' Advocate

Salary Range: $75,000 to $100,000 and up

Employment Prospects: Poor

Advancement Prospects: Poor to fair

Best Geographical Location(s): Major cities

Prerequisites:

Education or Training—Minimum of a bachelor's degree in journalism

Experience—Usually 10 or more years of newspaper experience, most recently in a senior editorial role

Special Skills and Personality Traits—Extreme journalistic integrity and ethics; superb judgment; ability to be objective; excellent writing and reporting skills; extensive knowledge of journalism and public issues

CAREER LADDER

```
┌─────────────────────────────────────┐
│  Return to previous editorial position; │
│    Executive Editor; or News          │
│  Ombudsman, larger publication        │
└─────────────────────────────────────┘

┌─────────────────────────────────────┐
│          News Ombudsman              │
└─────────────────────────────────────┘

┌─────────────────────────────────────┐
│  Senior Editorial Position such as    │
│  Managing Editor or News Editor       │
└─────────────────────────────────────┘
```

Position Description

As newspapers continue to struggle with maintaining ethical standards and raising their esteem in the eyes of the public, the role of a News Ombudsman becomes increasingly important. News Ombudsmen uphold journalistic integrity and fairness at their publications. They serve as advocates for the readers, hearing their complaints and concerns, as well as crafting responses and suggesting courses of action to newspaper management. In current times of tight budgets and deadlines, News Ombudsmen ensure accuracy and accountability on the part of newspapers as they have a responsibility to their readers.

Regularly, newspapers print content that angers or causes strong reactions in their readers. Sometimes, readers feel that stories were too biased. Other times, they may be concerned that facts were not valid or issues were misrepresented. Most papers invite readers to submit "letters to the editor," where they can voice their concerns. At newspapers large enough to employ a News Ombudsman, he or she is often the editor who manages the process of responding to these complaints.

A News Ombudsman listens to readers, reports back on their concerns to the newspapers' management, and uses this discussion to help improve and change their newspaper.

The role of a News Ombudsman is a relatively new idea in American journalism. According to the Organization of News Ombudsmen, "the first newspaper ombudsman in the U.S. was appointed in June 1967 in Louisville, Kentucky, to serve readers of the *Courier-Journal* and the *Louisville Times*." In part, the field was started to help bridge the gap between journalists and readers, helping to make newspapers more credible and accessible.

News Ombudsmen may monitor a variety of newspaper sections, including news, features, columns, opinion pages, and more. They can serve as the voice of balance both internally and externally. Internally, as they see problematic material, they bring it to the attention of the appropriate staff members, as well as the management if necessary. News Ombudsmen may handle some internal complaints from staff, help develop ethical policies and procedures, and ensure a balance in coverage.

On the external side, which is the main function of their job, News Ombudsmen represent their readers. A typical day may involve perusing reader letters and/or e-mails to determine issues of concern. As the electronic age continues to impact the newsroom, there is greater opportunity for reader/editor dialogue via e-mail. News Ombudsmen may be responsible for selecting letters to print based on a thoughtful range of opinions expressed. Furthermore, they may respond directly to some readers' concerns, or work with reporters to acknowledge inaccuracies noted by readers.

Most News Ombudsmen write regular columns (weekly or bimonthly) or opinion pieces themselves that directly address issues of importance to readers. These pieces may help the public to better understand the journalistic process, making it more accessible. As public advocates, they may also lead public forums or run advisory boards to help build the connection between readers and their paper's management.

Additional duties may include:

- Supervising and/or writing corrections to text
- Writing/editing newsletters representing readers' viewpoints
- Talking to groups about media practices
- Following up on news stories for accuracy purposes
- Conducting interviews and running roundtable discussions with reporters and editors
- Working closely with newspaper leadership such as executive editors and publishers
- Answering angry reader e-mails, letters, and telephone calls
- Investigating validity of reader complaints and inaccuracies
- Writing weekly reports
- Building trust and relationships with readers
- Lobbying for specific stories to meet readers' needs

Although most small newspapers do not have the budget to hire a News Ombudsman, they can be very beneficial for a paper to have on staff. Firstly, News Ombudsmen demonstrate to the public that the newspaper is attuned to their concerns. The existence of this position shows that the paper is regulating itself and keeping itself in check, enhancing its credibility to readers. Furthermore, the presence of a News Ombudsman can save the newspaper both time and money. Centralizing complaints to one person who can then get others involved as needed frees up time for editors, and dealing with issues head-on helps to avoid lawsuits that can be costly to both finances and reputation.

News Ombudsmen are advisers more than anything else. By ensuring that the public has an outlet to be heard, they validate their concerns for balanced coverage. This is a critical part of the journalistic process, as reporters, editors, and readers participate together to ensure fairness and accuracy.

Salaries
Salaries for News Ombudsmen are typically in the $75,000 to $100,000 range, according to a past survey of public editors. Since this is a mid- to late-career position, salaries reflect those of the top editorial positions from which News Ombudsmen come. Since many News Ombudsmen do earn more than $100,000 per year, this makes it challenging for newspapers to add this costly position to their staff.

Employment Prospects
Employment prospects are limited for News Ombudsmen, with less than 50 working in the United States today. Only large daily newspapers will employ them, and they are selected from among the newspapers' senior management. At some papers, the position is rotated among the senior editors (such as managing or news editors), with each editor working in an ombuds capacity for one to two years. Occasionally, senior editors from one newspaper may move to become a News Ombudsman at another newspaper similar in scope and size.

News Ombudsman is a senior position for a journalist with at least 10 years of experience; more typically they have 20 to 30 years. Sometimes, retired journalists may seek positions as News Ombudsmen, where they can leverage their years of knowledge to assist a paper for several more years.

Insiders believe that many more newspapers would like to hire News Ombudsmen but do not have the budgets to do so. Sometimes, it is public criticism or a crisis of the paper that forces them to take action and hire News Ombudsmen to show their readers that they are accountable for their mistakes. Furthermore, as public distrust of the media grows, the need for more News Ombudsmen, even in the face of budget cuts, may become necessary.

Advancement Prospects
Since News Ombudsman is a senior-level position, there is not tremendous opportunity for advancement. After completing their tenure as ombudsmen, many journalists return to prior positions as managing or other top editors. Yet others may advance to become executive editors, or News Ombudsmen at larger publications.

Education and Training
Like other senior journalists, News Ombudsmen have extensive journalism education and training. With bachelor's degrees in journalism or related fields, many also have advanced degrees in journalism.

Training comes through the years on the job necessary to take on such a position. Experience with writing, reporting, and editing, as well as managing people and dealing with difficult personalities enables News Ombudsmen to do their jobs.

Experience, Skills, and Personality Traits
It is crucial for News Ombudsmen to be scrupulously fair and ethical. They face a continuous conflict of inter-

est as they are challenged to criticize the newspaper that employs them. However, good News Ombudsmen are able to toe this line with good judgment. By maintaining good relationships with the newspapers' management as well as their readers, they can do their jobs with fairness and accuracy.

Furthermore, News Ombudsmen need to be levelheaded and calm. Faced frequently with angry readers, who project their fury onto them through phone calls and e-mails, they must be good listeners who are able to diffuse difficult situations. They cannot project arrogance or indifference that can create public perception that the newspaper is inaccessible. Also, they must be intelligent, well-read, and well-informed about public issues.

News Ombudsmen must be seasoned journalists, often with 20 years or more of work behind them. They have extensive experience working in different newsroom roles as both reporters and editors. This experience gives them the credibility needed to advise senior management of the paper about changes.

Unions and Associations

The main professional association for News Ombudsmen is the Organization of News Ombudsmen, founded in 1980. Many News Ombudsmen may also belong to the American Society of Newspaper Editors.

Tips for Entry

1. Begin by exploring the Web site for the Organization of News Ombudsmen (ONO) at http://www.newsombudsmen.org/what.htm. This site provides a detailed understanding of the field and why it was created.
2. Also on the ONO's Web site (http://www.newsombudsmen.org/what.htm), see the links for Ombudsmen columns. See what different News Ombudsmen are writing about around the country, highlighting which issues are important to readers in various places.
3. Gain experience in customer service to handle complaints. Try to remain objective even when faced with irrational anger. Seek out positions to review reader mail at a local newspaper.
4. Conduct an informational interview with a News Ombudsman. Learn about his or her career path and current role.
5. Hone your editorial skills. Apply for leadership positions at campus publications to understand the responsibilities and challenges faced by senior editors.

SPORTS EDITOR

CAREER PROFILE

Duties: Edits the sports section for a newspaper; supervises sports writers, reporters, and columnists

Alternate Title(s): Sports Page Editor

Salary Range: $25,000 to $70,000 and up

Employment Prospects: Fair

Advancement Prospects: Fair to good

Best Geographical Location(s): All, with greater opportunities in bigger cities

Prerequisites:

Education or Training—Bachelor's degree or higher in journalism or related field

Experience—At least three to five years of sports writing and reporting experience

Special Skills and Personality Traits—Strong editing skills, including good grasp of language, grammar, spelling, and usage; good writing and reporting skills; astute visual sense; knowledge of and interest in sports

CAREER LADDER

```
┌─────────────────────────────────┐
│  Sports Editor, larger paper or  │
│      Syndicated Columnist        │
└─────────────────────────────────┘

┌─────────────────────────────────┐
│         Sports Editor            │
└─────────────────────────────────┘

┌─────────────────────────────────┐
│    Sports Writer or Reporter     │
└─────────────────────────────────┘
```

Position Description

We all know people who immediately flip to the sports pages before reading any other part of a newspaper. The sports section of a typical daily newspaper features updates on all professional sports being played during the current time, as well as high school and college scores. Additionally, it may include feature stories about different sports issues, topics, and personalities, as well as columns with commentary. The Sports Editor is at the helm of this section.

Sports Editors plan out the sports section, including decisions about story and photograph placement. It is their vision as to how the section should look and what should be included. Sports Editors make quick decisions based on breaking stories and decide which pieces should be highlighted. Also, they give assignments to sports writers and reporters and set deadlines.

As the leaders of the sports desk, Sports Editors work closely with sports writers and reporters. They help them to plan their coverage and discuss any pending issues or problems. Furthermore, they are aware of daily sports schedules, ensuring that each game is covered and all reporters have

assignments. Their feedback helps sports writers to challenge themselves and tackle in-depth coverage. Sports Editors may supervise staffs ranging in size from one or two reporters to eight or more.

Editorial responsibility is an important component of being a Sports Editor. Sports Editors often line edit copy after reporters hand it in, checking for content, style, and structure. As writers themselves, they know what makes an effective story. Their strong attention to detail enables them to catch errors of facts or grammar. Some Sports Editors have a dual role as copy editors, while others work closely with copy editors to make sure final copy is perfect.

While each game has a tangible outcome, reporting style can make a big difference. Sports Editors work hard to distinguish their section from the local competition. They need a good visual and editorial eye to create pages that capture attention. Additionally, they need to bring in top-notch writers and columnists who can provide critical analysis and make their pieces engaging and enjoyable to read. Sports Editors set the tone of what their sports section should be about.

Sports Editors may wear a number of hats, particularly at smaller papers. They often do some writing and reporting. At some papers, they may even take photographs, while more typically they work closely with photographers on getting the best shots. Also, they are involved in pagination and copyediting.

Page design is another key component of being a Sports Editor. Sports Editors have a visual and creative sense of how stories, photos, and graphics should fit together on the page. An appropriate balance and good judgment about placement can make or break their success. The way the front page looks, for example, can determine readers' responses to the whole section.

Additional duties may include:

- Hiring and training new sports reporters and writers
- Developing sports budgets
- Running daily sports meetings
- Coordinating with the graphics department on matching visual images with stories
- Working with other editors on overlapping stories
- Developing relationships with sports professionals including athletes and coaches
- Conducting in-depth interviews for sports features
- Working with the local community
- Responding to readers' questions and concerns

Sports Editors collaborate with editors of the other major desks, such as news, features, metro/city, and others. They usually report to the managing editor and may be part of the senior staff. As the sports authorities, they may advise managing editors and other senior staff members about reporting assignments and editorial decisions affecting the sports desk.

Long and late hours are an inevitable part of being a Sports Editor. They must stay until after all games are played and all reporters get their pieces in. Evening and weekend work is required, although at some papers deputy sports editors may alternate shifts.

While most travel is for writers and reporters who cover games, many Sports Editors are still a vital part of the writing team. They may travel also, especially for big games or significant events. Many report on big events or write interesting features as well. Sports Editors have taken the passion for sports that drove them to become sports writers in the first place to the next level as the managers who run the show.

Salaries

Salaries for Sports Editors can vary greatly depending on their roles and responsibilities, as well as where they work. Each year, the Inland Press Association conducts the Newspaper Industry Compensation Survey, which is the authoritative "industry standard" for newspaper industry compensation planning. In 2004 Sports Editors earned an average of $50,058 per year as their base salary. Their total direct compensation, including bonuses and other commissions, was $51,381. The survey participants reported a range spanning a low in total direct compensation at $21,000 and a high at $217,000.

Employment Prospects

Employment prospects are fair for Sports Editors. Since virtually all newspapers cover sports in some capacity, editors are needed to manage the section. Furthermore, larger papers often hire more than one Sports Editor, designating them as assistant sports editors, deputy sports editors, or associate sports editors.

Sports Editors typically begin as sports reporters in small towns. They pay their dues covering high school beats and gaining experience in editing and page design as well as reporting. Aspiring Sports Editors should be geographically flexible and willing to start at the bottom. There are some entry-level Sports Editor positions that require a combination of writing, editing, reporting, and design. Also, some entry-level positions may combine the Sports Editor and copy editor position.

Advancement Prospects

Sports Editors may advance by moving from smaller papers to larger ones. Since some newspapers break down editorial roles with an executive sports editor, a deputy sports editor, an assistant sports editor, and so on, other Sports Editors advance by taking on increasing responsibility at their current paper.

Another advancement option for Sports Editors could come from pursuing other writing opportunities such as articles, books, and/or becoming a syndicated columnist whose work appears in several papers. Also, they may specialize in writing about specific types of sports or sports issues, such as the history of baseball or women tennis players.

Education and Training

Sports Editors have bachelor's degrees in journalism or related fields. Those who have liberal arts degrees also need journalism coursework that teaches not only about writing and reporting but also about design, layout, and editing. Some Sports Editors have master's degrees in journalism as well.

While no formal education in sports is necessary, it is expected that Sports Editors are very knowledgeable about a wide range of sports. Some Sports Editors are former high school or college athletes; all are sports enthusiasts.

Experience, Skills, and Personality Traits

The overriding personality trait needed for a Sports Editor is a passion for sports. Sports Editors never get tired of discussing a game, analyzing a play, or commenting on the personalities that make it fun to watch. While they cannot possibly know everything about all sports, Sports Editors generally have several favorite sports but some knowledge of others. Possibly former athletes, but definitely lifelong fans, Sports Editors translate their enthusiasm into a career choice.

Prior experience as a sports writer or reporter is a necessary step to becoming a Sports Editor. Positions with supervisory responsibility may require at least three to five years of experience. Leadership and management skills are needed to supervise and mentor staff members. Writing and reporting skills should be excellent, along with editing ability. Sports Editors should have a strong command of language, spelling, grammar, and usage, as well as a good sense of tone and style. Attention to detail keeps copy error-free.

Part of sports editing involves making sure the sports pages look the right way. Sports Editors should know about design and layout with programs such as QuarkXPress and Adobe Photoshop. The ability to work under pressure, meet tight deadlines, and stay energetic through long hours is also important.

Unions and Associations

Sports Editors may belong to professional associations including the Associated Press Sports Editors, the American Society of Newspaper Editors, and the American Copy Editors Society. Additionally, they may belong to associations for sports writers by state or region.

Tips for Entry

1. Learn more about becoming a Sports Editor by visiting the Web site of the Associated Press Sports Editors at http://apse.dallasnews.com/job_board/apse_job_board.html.

2. Gain experience writing about sports. Work for your campus or local paper handling a variety of sports coverage including games, features, and enterprise stories. See if you can take on an editorial role as well.

3. Copyediting experience is also valuable preparation for a career in sports journalism. See the resources section of the American Copy Editors Society (http://www.copydesk.org/) for tips on honing your skills.

4. Some journalism schools offer programs or courses in sports journalism. Explore the offerings at the University of Tennessee at Knoxville (http://web.utk.edu/~foley/SportsJour/courses.htm), the University of Texas at Austin (http://journalism.utexas.edu/undergraduate/sportsjournalism.html), and the University of Wisconsin–Whitewater (http://www.uww.edu/Catalog/02-04/Degree/courses/164.html), among others.

5. Read the sports section of your local newspaper, as well as other publications. Note how coverage varies from paper to paper. Which type of coverage do you admire and why? Can you identify their coverage goals? See if you can set up an informational interview with the Sports Editor to discuss his or her job.

EDITORIAL CARTOONIST

CAREER PROFILE

Duties: Creates cartoons for a newspaper that combine humor with political statements

Alternate Title(s): Political Cartoonist

Salary Range: $5 to $10 per cartoon to salaries of $40,000 to $60,000 per year and up

Employment Prospects: Poor

Advancement Prospects: Poor to Fair

Best Geographical Location(s): Large cities for newspaper work; all for freelance work

Prerequisites:

Education or Training—No specific requirements, but bachelor's degrees in art or journalism can be helpful

Experience—Portfolio of cartoons from college newspaper or freelance work

Special Skills and Personality Traits—Artistic and creative talent and vision; good sense of humor; excellent knowledge of politics and current events; strong writing skills

CAREER LADDER

```
┌─────────────────────────────────────┐
│  Syndicated Editorial Cartoonist     │
└─────────────────────────────────────┘

┌─────────────────────────────────────┐
│ Editorial Cartoonist (newspaper staff)│
└─────────────────────────────────────┘

┌─────────────────────────────────────┐
│  Freelance Editorial Cartoonist or   │
│    college Editorial Cartoonist      │
└─────────────────────────────────────┘
```

Position Description

Editorial Cartoonists express their views about politics and current events through an artistic medium. Using the tools of caricature, composition, light and shade, they create cartoons that inform and enlighten people about what is going on in the world. Their cartoons criticize, defend, and comment on public figures and issues, offering an opinion for readers to consider.

The idea is central to the work of an Editorial Cartoonist. A good editorial cartoon is centered on a powerful concept. While artistic skill and talent are needed to back it up, Editorial Cartoonists begin by finding an issue to which they have a strong reaction. As part of the brainstorming process, they read several newspapers each day, as well as checking other news mediums such as the Internet, radio, and television. They note issues of interest and importance and jot down words, pictures, and images that come to mind. Later, they will go back and flesh out some of these concepts.

Ideas may be national or local in scope, depending on the size of the newspaper for which the Editorial Cartoonist is writing. Cartoons may center on world politics, state government, or local environmental concerns. As commentators and critics, Editorial Cartoonists focus on issues that will have relevance to their readers. Each day brings a potential wealth of new material.

As they find issues that cause a personal rise, Editorial Cartoonists decide the best way to present their feelings through their cartoons. They use artistic techniques such as caricatures, size, and shading to produce recognizable images in a new way. Furthermore, they try to find the humor in the situation. They capture the heart of an issue through drawing and captions that will express their opinion and hit the right note with their readers. By using visual images as metaphors, they are able to convey a commentary and explanation of a complicated political or social situation.

Like editorial writers, Editorial Cartoonists express their politics through their work. They may be Democrats or Republicans, liberals, conservatives, or moderates. Usually, newspapers hire Editorial Cartoonists and publish editorial cartoons that keep in line with the opinion expressed by the editors and publishers of the newspaper.

In this way, editorial cartoons are an important part of the U.S. political process. Editorial Cartoonists bring controversial issues to the forefront and encourage people to have an opinion. They express their criticism for politicians, world leaders, and other public issues through humor, usually a non-offensive way to bring these concerns to public attention. Editorial Cartoons represent the social commentary of an era. They are a serious part of the journalism mission, as evidenced by the fact that there is a Pulitzer Prize category for editorial cartooning.

Editorial Cartoonists may be employed full-time by newspapers, although these jobs are extremely competitive and limited. Many Editorial Cartoonists work as freelancers, selling their work to local newspapers. The ultimate goal for many Editorial Cartoonists is syndication. Syndicated cartoonists have agreements for their work to be published in more than one paper. Their work is sold through a syndicate, which is an agency that represents cartoonists and sells their work for simultaneous publication in a number of markets.

Additional duties may include:

- Drawing several cartoons per week
- Conducting research on political issues
- Dealing with complaints and questions from readers and editors
- Keeping abreast of news and local, state, national, and/or world events
- Taking art or technique classes
- Working with editors and designers

Editorial Cartoonists primarily work at newspapers, with limited cartoons appearing in newsmagazines. However, the Internet is a whole new market in which to get published. There is a growing number of Editorial Cartoonists who get paid for their Internet cartoons, which can also include animation in addition to digital drawing. Editorial Cartoonists with strong computer graphic skills will have an edge in today's market.

Most Editorial Cartoonists employed by newspapers work for editorial page editors. They discuss controversial content with them and can work together to handle readers' concerns.

Salaries

Editorial Cartoonists beginning in the field should expect very low salaries. Cartoons may sell for as low as $5 per drawing, with rates going up as experience does. Larger papers may buy cartoons for $100 or more from experienced cartoonists.

For the lucky few Editorial Cartoonists to be employed full time by newspapers, salaries can be in the $40,000 to $60,000 range with experience. The even luckier Editorial Cartoonists who achieve syndication can earn up to six figures and more.

Employment Prospects

According to the Association of American Editorial Cartoonists, there are only about 100 full-time job openings at newspapers for cartoonists in the United States. Needless to say, this makes employment prospects quite competitive and difficult.

There are a limited number of major syndicates for cartoonists, and they get thousands of submissions each year. Syndication opportunities are available only for Editorial Cartoonists with current or previous newspaper experience. Addresses for syndicates are available in *Editor and Publisher* magazine's annual Syndicate Directory (published each July).

Since the job market is so difficult, insiders liken earning a living as an Editorial Cartoonist to making it as an actor or sports figure. However, they do say that persistence is the key. Editorial Cartoonists must expect to start small. Most begin by creating cartoons for their college newspaper. A portfolio of work is essential.

Furthermore, Editorial Cartoonists should think locally to begin building up their freelance work. Local papers often need cartoonists that can comment on local matters, since syndicated cartoonists are bound to larger issues.

Advancement Prospects

Advancement for Editorial Cartoonists comes through more recognition for their work. Those who are freelancing are usually looking to secure full-time positions at newspapers. This takes extreme perseverance. Developing relationships with editors is important, as is knowing the market and content they want.

Editorial Cartoonists who already are on staff at newspapers can advance by moving to larger papers with larger markets. Syndication can be an ultimate goal, as it assures more longevity of work and income.

Education and Training

Some Editorial Cartoonists have a traditional journalism background, with bachelor's or master's degrees in the field and writing and reporting experience. Others have art training, including degrees in fine arts, studio art, or drawing. While some Editorial Cartoonists can be successful without a bachelor's degree, in this competitive market it has become almost a necessity.

Since editorial cartoons are often political, coursework in history and political science is helpful. Editorial Cartoonists must be able to combine this knowledge with artistic skill and talent, writing, and humor.

Experience, Skills, and Personality Traits

Artistic skill and talent are a must for Editorial Cartoonists. They need these tangible skills to bring their ideas and opinions to life. Whether or not they have formal art training, they should be comfortable with different artistic mediums including ink, pencil, drafting pens, and others. Furthermore, they should be able to create computer images using a digital tablet and programs such as Adobe Photoshop.

In addition to their artistic sense and creativity, Editorial Cartoonists should be sharp and intelligent. They must be well-read and well-informed about politics and world history. Also, they should be astute observers and critics who have something to say about our society. They form strong opinions based on evidence. Editorial Cartoonists need good writing skills to create captions that capture the essence of their point.

Most of all, Editorial Cartoonists must be passionate about what they do. It is very difficult to succeed in this field, and only those who truly love it will have a chance for any success.

Prior experience working on cartoons as early as possible is helpful. Most Editorial Cartoonists worked for their college papers where they developed their style.

Unions and Associations

The main professional association for Editorial Cartoonists is the Association of American Editorial Cartoonists (AAEC).

Tips for Entry

1. Mike Keefe, an Editorial Cartoonist for the *Denver Post* and a member of the AAEC, offers his tips for getting started in the cartooning business on the AAEC's Web site: http://aaeconline.org/cartoonist/howto/Keefe/. One tip recommends that "if you have a portfolio of cartoons on regional subjects, you may be able to convince the local newspaper that they need a hometown point-of-view on their editorial page. Most small papers don't have full-time cartoonists and subscribe, instead, to syndicated work covering mostly national and international topics. That's your selling point. You can provide the local material. You will probably be paid some insultingly small amount per cartoon but now you've got your foot in the door. Then you can begin to broaden your range of issues, building up the portfolio. Next step: take your cartoons to a larger paper."

2. Nurture your artistic talent. Doodle, sketch, and paint at every opportunity that you have. Take courses to help fine-tune your technique. Develop a portfolio of images, especially those that are difficult to draw. You can use this to consult each time you create a cartoon.

3. Get to know the cartoonist on your local paper. Mike Keefe suggests that he or she is usually glad to look over your work and offer constructive criticism.

4. Read newspapers avidly—especially the editorial page. How do different writers express their opinions? Also, read editorial and political cartoons. How do they differ from the editorial writing? Which cartoonists do you admire and why? Borrow elements from their various styles of drawing and commentary until you fully develop your own.

5. There is a wealth of information on the Internet for aspiring Editorial Cartoonists. Perform a Google search for "becoming an Editorial Cartoonist" and see what comes up.

SUNDAY EDITOR

CAREER PROFILE

Duties: Edits the Sunday issue of a newspaper

Alternate Title(s): Weekend Editor

Salary Range: $40,000 to 80,000 and up

Employment Prospects: Fair

Advancement Prospects: Fair

Best Geographical Location(s): All

Prerequisites

    Education or Training—Bachelor's degree in journalism or related field; master's degree also may be helpful

    Experience—Five to seven years of newspaper experience as a reporter and/or editor

    Special Skills and Personality Traits—Excellent writing and editing skills; strong organizational skills; management and supervisory ability; ability to work well under pressure and meet tight deadlines; interest in and knowledge of popular culture, arts, and entertainment

CAREER LADDER

```
┌─────────────────────────────────────────┐
│      Sunday Editor, larger paper;         │
│    News Editor; or Managing Editor        │
└─────────────────────────────────────────┘

┌─────────────────────────────────────────┐
│              Sunday Editor                │
└─────────────────────────────────────────┘

┌─────────────────────────────────────────┐
│    Arts and Entertainment Editor,         │
│  Features Editor, or Features Reporter     │
└─────────────────────────────────────────┘
```

Position Description

Many people look forward to spending a leisurely morning with the Sunday paper. This issue is usually double or triple the size of the weekday copy, containing special features sections such as arts, entertainment, styles, book reviews, travel, food, money and business, job listings, television, and more. Hard work goes into producing that Sunday issue each week. At the helm of the process is the Sunday Editor.

Sunday Editors determine the editorial content for the Sunday issue. Adding new special sections to appeal to the changing needs of readers or rotating out existing ones is their responsibility. Brainstorming ideas with their staff in order to keep content fresh is essential. Staffing the right reporters and photographers for each story is important as well.

Because of its size and complexity, the Sunday issue takes all week to put together. Sunday Editors must have excellent time management skills to stay on top of the deadlines and manage staffing. Sunday content tends to consist more of longer feature and human-interest stories in addition to breaking news. Sunday Editors must make sure the story ideas will capture the interests of readers and that they are long and in-depth enough to fill the pages of the issue.

As visionaries and managers, Sunday Editors supervise reporters. Since the Sunday issue is so diverse, they supervise specialists in a number of different areas from travel writers to food critics. They assign pieces, run meetings, and work with them to conceptualize ideas. Sometimes stories are assigned several weeks in advance. It is necessary for Sunday Editors to have an understanding of popular culture, as well as issues of importance to their audience. Giving readers what they want helps to justify the advertising necessary to support this large and detailed section.

Furthermore, Sunday Editors also perform hands-on editing along with overall vision. When stories are compete, they get to work line editing the copy and making changes and corrections. They also may perform some page design, determining what goes where and why. The Sunday section often has more color, graphics, and photographs, which can help add to its appeal.

Their duties may include:

- Managing the Sunday story budget
- Selecting editorial cartoons for the issue
- Developing new features components or sections

- Creating ongoing series
- Overseeing columns and columnists
- Writing articles
- Managing a sizable staff
- Interacting with senior management
- Keeping up on news and trends

Although it takes all week to compile the issue, Sunday Editors must expect to work on weekends. Breaking news still appears on the front page and Sunday Editors must ensure that all last-minute news and concerns are addressed. However, even with the long hours, Sunday Editors often enjoy creative control over content. Sunday issues tend to be like weekly magazines, with the opportunity to cover more in-depth issues and investigative pieces. Creativity comes into play in writing style, as well as page design.

Moreover, Sunday Editors must be in touch with the communities that their newspaper represents. In order to sell and perform well in their market, they must know the types of articles and sections that interest their readers. This includes everything from featuring appealing travel destinations, financial advice, and movie reviews. A Sunday Editor who is in touch with his or her readership can greatly impact the success of the paper, since many subscribers receive Sunday issues alone.

Salaries
Salaries for Sunday Editors vary depending on the position. According to the Inland Press Association's annual Newspaper Industry Compensation Survey, in 2004 Sunday Editors earned an average of $58,776 per year as their base salary. Total direct compensation was $61,290. The survey reported salary ranges in total direct compensation spanning a low of $23,317 to a high of $182,000. Earnings tend to be higher than other editorial positions due to the level of experience needed for the job.

Employment Prospects
Employment prospects are fair for Sunday Editors. While very large papers may have several Sunday Editors for their different specialty sections, smaller newspapers have just one or none at all, delegating the work to news editors and features editors. Opportunities are best for those editors with extensive experience reporting and editing. Previous work in features, arts and entertainment, or in areas of the specialty sections is helpful.

Advancement Prospects
Advancement prospects are also fair. Sunday Editors may aspire to become news editors or managing editors, where they face strong competition. They also may look to move from smaller papers to larger ones, where the Sunday issue is more complex. Those who have made strong contributions at their current papers may be recruited to revamp or revitalize an unsuccessful Sunday issue. Keeping up with news trends and the breaking news component of their work may help for advancement to news editor.

Education and Training
Most Sunday Editors have bachelor's degrees in journalism or a related field. A combination of a journalism and liberal arts education is generally considered the ideal balance in order to become the most well-rounded journalist possible. An undergraduate major or minor in journalism is common, as are a liberal arts major and a master's degree in journalism.

In addition, Sunday Editors might have specific training in specialty areas, such as business or travel. Most training for Sunday Editors comes on the job and through internships. Many have written features extensively and/or have worked as copy editors before taking on an editorial role. They need training in writing, reporting, and editing, as well as some leadership and management to supervise staff.

Experience, Skills, and Personality Traits
Sunday Editors usually need at least five to seven years of prior editorial and reporting experience. For this reason, they should be good leaders, communicators, and managers. They motivate and supervise reporters, photographers, and editors, helping them to develop ideas and bring their stories to the page. Furthermore, they need to ensure that writers stick to deadlines and work on stories appropriate to their expertise. Sunday Editors also need creativity and the ability to generate fresh and compelling story ideas. Good organizational skills help them stay on track of deadlines.

Excellent writing, reporting, and editorial skills are also essential for Sunday Editors. In addition to grammar, punctuation, and spelling, they need a good sense of style to craft and edit stories with the right tone for their paper. Knowledge of and interest in culture, including arts, travel, entertainment, and food helps them to do their jobs well. As with other editorial positions, it is helpful for Sunday Editors to know page design programs such as QuarkXPress and Adobe Photoshop.

Unions and Associations
The main professional association for Sunday Editors is the American Association of Sunday and Features Editors. Here, they can network with others who have the same unique set of responsibilities. Founded in 1948 with 17 members, membership has now risen to more than 200. Sunday Editors may also belong to the American Society of Newspaper Editors, the American Journalism Review, and the Newspaper Guild.

Tips for Entry

1. Take a look at the Web site for the American Association of Sunday and Features Editors at http://www.aasfe.org/. Editors just starting out can be mentored with more experienced Sunday Editors, and the site also has a job board.

2. What do you like about the Sunday issue of your local paper? Which are your favorite sections and which do you think are least effective? Have you noticed any new components or changes since you've been reading?

3. Read Sunday issues of different sized papers throughout the country to gain insight into the important issues for those readers. Sunday Editors must be in touch with their communities. Before going on a job interview, make sure you have conducted research on the demographic audience for the newspaper.

4. Read the classifieds on *Editor & Publisher* at http://www.editorandpublisher.com/eandp/classifieds/index.jsp. The magazine is America's oldest journal covering the newspaper industry.

5. Write features for your local or campus paper. What topics will appeal to students on your campus or to people in your community? Develop a portfolio of clips that will help you secure your first job.

6. Copyediting experience is also very valuable. The following link provides tips about frequent errors caught by copy editors: http://www.well.com/~mmcadams/words.html.

GRAPHIC ARTIST

CAREER PROFILE

Duties: Creates and assembles graphics and images for a newspaper, including bars, charts, maps, and drawings

Alternate Title(s): Graphic Designer, Infographics Specialist

Salary Range: $25,000 to $60,000 and up

Employment Prospects: Fair

Advancement Prospects: Fair

Best Geographical Location(s): All

Prerequisites:

Education or Training—Bachelor's degree in art or graphic design required for most positions

Experience—One to three years of prior graphic art experience and a portfolio of work

Special Skills and Personality Traits—Creativity and excellent visual arts skills; good communication skills; strong attention to detail; ability to multitask and work well under pressure; knowledge of computer design programs

CAREER LADDER

```
┌─────────────────────────────────┐
│     Art or Graphics Director     │
└─────────────────────────────────┘

┌─────────────────────────────────┐
│         Graphic Artist           │
└─────────────────────────────────┘

┌─────────────────────────────────┐
│    Intern or Graphic Artist,     │
│         smaller paper            │
└─────────────────────────────────┘
```

Position Description

In addition to the text, there are many visual elements to be found in a newspaper. Photographs, drawings, charts, graphs, boxes, and empty space are just some of the other components that make up each page. Graphic Artists create, organize, and arrange these elements that make pages aesthetically pleasing and easy to read.

Graphics serve different purposes on a news page, depending on what they are. Illustrations bring stories to life, perhaps portraying a sketch of an individual described. Charts and graphs are information graphics, which organize facts and data for easy reference. Boxes help readers locate relevant information; shaded areas may point out useful links. Graphic Artists develop these graphics, playing a crucial role in visual communication and transforming information into eye-catching images.

As Graphic Artists work, the images become the elements that pages are built around. They are used to help guide the reader through the stories and supplement the text. However, text size and type can be an element of graphic design as well. Arranging graphics can include headlines, photographs, line or clip art, text, white space, and boxes. Graphic artists must understand typography, color, space, contrast, and other design elements and how they come into play on a page.

While page designers focus on the overall page layout, Graphic Artists work closely with them, concentrating on the graphics themselves. Some Graphic Artists draw images freehand; most also use computer-aided design programs. For each story, page, or assignment, they assess the goal, determining the appropriate graphic accompaniment. Then, they create a sketch or layout as a preliminary plan for the graphic. Graphics developed by Graphic Artists can include realistic illustrations, clip art or pop images, charts, graphs, tables, maps, diagrams, and more.

Graphic Artists work with their art or graphics directors to select the final images to use. For each assignment, there may be different types of visual elements needed. Since headlines are part of the graphics package, some Graphic Artists with good copywriting skills may also write and choose headlines. A good visual eye is essential for creating and selecting images that attract the reader, complement the story, and make the page stand out.

Some Graphic Artists also have responsibility for news Web sites. Here, they have the opportunity to utilize video and animation to convey their message. This is a growing area for the field, and Graphic Artists with these skills will make themselves more marketable as newspapers and magazines move toward multimedia.

Additional duties may include:

- Toning color photos
- Writing headlines
- Collaborating with reporters, editors, and page designers
- Reading other publications for design ideas
- Cropping and resizing images
- Selecting fonts and typography
- Building advertisement graphics
- Converting electronic files
- Scanning images

Graphic Artists work typically long newsroom hours. They must be able to handle the busy flow of work handed down from the graphics director, which can include many assignments per day. Some Graphic Artists, especially those just starting out, will be needed to work late night or weekend shifts, particularly because Sunday issues often include more color and graphics than weekday papers. However, it is an ideal position for a creative person who enjoys the visual aspect of journalism. In addition to newspapers, Graphic Artists can work in other areas of journalism, including magazines, Web sites, new media companies, advertising agencies, and others.

Salaries

According to the Bureau of Labor Statistics (BLS), median annual earnings for graphic designers were $38,030 in May 2004. Graphic Artists working for newspaper, periodical, book, and directory publishers earned a median of $32,390. The BLS also offers information from the American Institute of Graphic Arts, which reported the 2005 median annual total cash compensation for graphic designers according to level of responsibility. Entry-level designers earned a median salary of $32,000 in 2005, while staff-level graphic designers earned $42,500. Senior designers with supervisory responsibility earned $56,000.

Additional salary information comes from the Inland Press Association's annual Newspaper Industry Compensation Survey. In 2004 news designers/artists earned an average of $40,307 per year as their base salary. The survey reported salary ranges spanning a low of $17,680 and a high of $94,278.

Employment Prospects

The BLS states that employment for Graphic Artists is expected to grow as fast as average for all occupations through 2014. Demand will grow in the areas of computer graphics and multimedia, especially as many newspapers and magazines consolidate and move toward expanding their Web sites. Since competition will be tight, Graphic Artists who are skilled in computer design will have an advantage. Graphic Artists looking to work at newspapers must be geographically flexible and willing to work in small towns to get started. Freelancing is another option for those looking to build a portfolio and gain experience.

Advancement Prospects

Graphic Artists have several paths for advancement. At newspapers, they may advance to become art or graphics directors, running the entire visuals department. Also, they may move from smaller papers to larger ones with greater graphic variety. Furthermore, Graphic Artists may move around between newspapers, magazines, Web sites, and other publications. Some choose to work in areas outside of traditional journalism, such as advertising or specific graphic design firms that are contracted by clients. Other Graphic Artists may begin their own firms or build their own freelance careers.

Education and Training

Virtually all Graphic Artist positions currently advertised require a bachelor's degree. A Bachelor of Fine Arts degree (BFA) in art, graphic design, or visual communication may be required. Some Graphic Artists at newspapers do have journalism degrees or coursework, supplemented by design classes. It is essential for aspiring Graphic Artists to learn computer graphics and design software programs. Associate's degrees or certificates in graphic design may be good beginnings for the field, but a bachelor's degree will ultimately be required for advancement.

The National Association of Schools of Art and Design currently accredits more than 245 programs in art and design. See their Web site at http://nasad.arts-accredit.org for more information.

A portfolio is essential for finding employment. Education provides the opportunity to learn the necessary graphic design computer skills and develop samples of one's work. Internships are also a valuable part of the training process.

Experience, Skills, and Personality Traits

Graphic Artists must be creative with excellent visual skills. As artists, they can both typically draw by hand and use computers to create images with ease. They have a good eye and aesthetic sensibility, coupled with knowledge of visual communication and journalism.

Additionally, Graphic Artists should be good verbal and written communicators. They work closely with supervisors, colleagues, and/or clients and must be able to understand and meet their goals. Also important is the ability to be a team player, as well as work independently with little supervision or direction. Graphic Artists must be well organized and detail oriented. They should be able to stay calm under pressure, meet close deadlines, and juggle multiple tasks at once.

Knowledge of specific computer design programs is also needed. Some of the useful and/or required programs may include the Mac-based Macromedia FreeHand, Adobe Photoshop, Lightwave, Flash, Illustrator, QuarkXpress, InDesign, ArcView, and other 3-D programs.

Unions and Associations

Graphic Artists may belong to professional associations including the Society for News Design, American Institute for Graphic Arts (AIGA), the Art Directors Club, and the Society of Publication Designers.

Tips for Entry

1. Take a look at http://www.newsdesigner.com/blog/, a Weblog about newspaper design.

2. About.com offers useful information about graphic design on its site for desktop publishing. Read about trainings, tutorials, and careers in graphic design at http://desktoppub.about.com/od/graphicdesign/.

3. The Poynter Institute, a school for journalists and an online resource, has design and graphics information on their site as well. Read articles and gain tips at http://www.poynter.org/subject.asp?id=11.

4. Create a Web site to showcase your work. This will enable you to try out some of the multimedia aspects of graphic design such as streaming video and animation. Sites such as http://www.killersites.com/ and http://www.jessett.com/ can help.

5. Conduct an interview with a Graphic Artist to learn more about the field. Joining a professional association such as AIGA (http://www.aiga.org/) can help put you in touch with professionals. Having a Graphic Artist review your portfolio and offer suggestions can be extremely valuable as well.

MAGAZINES

EDITOR IN CHIEF

CAREER PROFILE

Duties: Leads the editorial content and overall editorial direction of a magazine

Alternate Title(s): Editor

Salary Range: $40,000 to $180,000 and up

Employment Prospects: Fair

Advancement Prospects: Fair

Best Geographical Location(s): New York and other major cities

Prerequisites:

Education or Training—Bachelor's degree in English, journalism, or related field; master's degree may be helpful

Experience—Ten to 15 years or more of prior magazine experience

Special Skills and Personality Traits—Excellent managerial and leadership skills; very strong writing, editing, and communication skills; good organization; editorial insight and vision; business savvy

CAREER LADDER

```
┌─────────────────────────────────────┐
│  Editor in Chief, larger publication │
└─────────────────────────────────────┘

┌─────────────────────────────────────┐
│           Editor in Chief            │
└─────────────────────────────────────┘

┌─────────────────────────────────────┐
│ Managing Editor, Executive Editor,   │
│  Deputy Editor, or other high-level  │
│         editorial position           │
└─────────────────────────────────────┘
```

Position Description

Editors in Chief are the top editorial positions at magazines. They are responsible for setting goals, developing a vision, and assembling the staff that will carry it out. The ultimate success of failure of the publication rests on their shoulders. The pressure is felt by many to be a challenge. Editors in Chief thrive on making their magazines the best they can be.

Everything from the look of the magazine to the quality of its articles to the placement of advertisements is approved by the Editor in Chief. He or she has final say as to what is included in each issue and why. The cover artwork or photo, as well as the lead articles, can have tremendous impact on sales. Editors in Chief are savvy about the business of publishing as well as the actual writing, and they use this expertise to advance their magazines.

Furthermore, the Editor in Chief is expected to maintain the ethical standards for the magazine. By setting editorial policy, they develop an atmosphere of journalistic integrity. The stories and topics they choose and how they will be handled represent the magazine's ideals. Editors in Chief

ensure that the magazine's contents are always consistent with its vision.

More than anyone else at the publication, it is important for Editors in Chief to have creative ideas, strategy, and vision. They must understand their readers and sense the type of stories that will bring them in. As they run editorial meetings, they can generate successful story ideas and assemble the appropriate editorial and writing teams to make each article work.

When a magazine is struggling, a new Editor in Chief is frequently brought in to "save" the publication. They need to shake things up and make changes that will result in more advertisers and broader circulation. Editors in Chief draw on their experience to determine what changes should be made that will help achieve its new vision. Sometimes it involves reinventing the magazine to go with the changing times, while other times it may involve getting back to the roots of the magazine. Either way, Editors in Chief develop a new formula for success when they are brought into their jobs.

By the time they reach this position level, most Editors in Chief have created a niche area for themselves. Frequently, they are specialists in an area such as trade publications, health, or travel. Yet they also remain generalists in the sense that they can oversee content in a variety of topics. Editors in Chief understand what makes effective writing across different genres.

Depending on the size of their magazine, responsibilities vary for Editors in Chief in terms of hands-on writing and editing. At smaller publications, they may be responsible for writing regular columns or features, while at larger magazines, they may submit a "letter from the editor" or editorial opinion piece each issue. Some Editors in Chief perform editing on copy themselves, while others delegate it to other senior-level editorial staff.

While the editorial staff can handle most editorial responsibilities, special circumstances usually fall to the Editor in Chief. Dealing with high-profile clientele of any kind, from writers to models to advertisers, is often up to the Editor in Chief. Skilled communicators and negotiators, Editors in Chief can work with difficult personalities and soothe conflicts when necessary.

Additional duties may include:

- Overseeing design and layout
- Running regular meetings
- Managing editorial budget
- Supervising editorial work flow and approving schedules
- Working with writers, photographers, and artists
- Creating ad maps
- Negotiating contracts with vendors
- Cultivating freelancers
- Generating new ideas
- Maintaining relationships with Editors in Chief at similar publications
- Deciding on story placement

Editors in Chief often serve as the face of their magazine. It is important for them to share the values and project the image of their publication. For example, the Editor in Chief of a magazine focusing on pets would be expected to own some animals and so on. In trade magazines and others focusing on specific fields, the Editor in Chief has relationships with those in the industry, and these continue to build in order to add to the magazine's success. He or she must be well-informed about all industry news and trends and be able not only to comment on it to readers and the public when necessary but also to analyze it thoughtfully.

Also, Editors in Chief serve as representatives for their magazines in the public eye. They may appear on television or radio to promote specific issues or contribute their expertise to other publications.

Working as an Editor in Chief is not a 9-to-5 job. The hours can be intense and insiders say that it is not uncommon to become very wrapped up in the work, leaving less time for outside interests. Travel may be required to attend trade shows, events, conferences, and more. However, most Editors in Chief thrive on their work and find satisfaction in seeing the direct application of their efforts on the newsstand.

Salaries

Salaries for Editors in Chief are as diverse as the magazines found on a newsstand. The range can be tremendous, with figures in the low $40,000s and the high $180,000s. Editors in Chief at business and trade magazines, or small local publications are at the low end, and those at large, national consumer publications are at the high end.

According to *Folio Magazine*'s 2004 Editorial Salary Survey, salaries for Editors in Chief averaged $93,561. Broken down by age, the survey showed Editors in Chief age 39 and younger earning an average of $67,543 annually and those 40 and older earning $101,799 annually. The average age for Editors in Chief in that survey was 45.9.

The survey also breaks salaries down by circulation. Salaries vary here too but not as dramatically as they do by age, accounting for years of experience. Editors in Chief at publications with circulation under 50,000 earn an average of $81,057, and those at magazines with circulation of 100,000 to 499,999 earn $105,923 on average.

Folio also states the average bonus for Editors in Chief in 2004 to be $12,285; a bonus was expected by 63.7 percent of Editors in Chief.

Employment Prospects

Because of the high level of the position, employment prospects for Editors in Chief are fair. Typically, one finds a job as an Editor in Chief by working his or her way up at a publication and/or by moving to a similar or competing magazine. Jobs are often not advertised and are found through networking, word of mouth, or through recruiting firms and headhunting agencies.

Some Editors in Chief are recruited based on the success they had at another magazine. Those who have made names for themselves in the publishing industry for increasing circulation at certain magazines or using a new and innovative format are often sought after by other publications.

Advancement Prospects

Advancement prospects are also fair. Many Editors in Chief are the top of their field and are content to stay where they are. Others move from smaller magazines to larger ones, or transition to publications that fulfill personal goals or interests. Still others may advance by being recruited to competitors for higher salaries and opportunities to affect change.

Some Editors in Chief pursue other related media options including professional speaking, consulting, or freelance writing (books and/or articles).

Education and Training

Most Editors in Chief hold bachelor's degrees in English, journalism, or related fields. Additionally, they may have advanced degrees in these subjects, as well as in subjects related to their publishing specialty area. Business courses may also be helpful to understand budgeting and management.

Most training for Editors in Chief comes on the job, both past and present. They have had extensive magazine experience where they have learned the ropes about working for a periodical.

Experience, Skills, and Personality Traits

It is common for Editors in Chief to have 10 to 15 years of magazine experience before reaching their position. They have usually advanced through the editorial hierarchy, holding positions such as senior editor, managing editor, and executive editor. Through this experience, they gather the necessary skills to be successful as an Editor in Chief.

Editors in Chief must have superior written and verbal communication skills. On the written side, they must have an excellent command of language and an eye for the fluid writing of others. Verbally, they need to express themselves clearly and engage, persuade, and manage others as necessary.

The job of Editor in Chief requires a combination of business and editorial skills. Editors in Chief must understand the bottom line of publishing and be aware of how to sell successfully. However, they must also be journalists who are committed to their editorial mission and will not compromise their integrity.

Also, Editors in Chief must be well-organized and comfortable with close deadlines. They need to manage and motivate staff, delegate tasks, and keep everyone on schedule. It is important for Editors in Chief to be decisive. As strategic visionaries, they need the foresight to solve problems and move forward, bringing their staff along for the ride.

As leaders, Editors in Chief should be knowledgeable about all the computer programs and environments that may be used in publishing. These include Word, Excel, QuarkXPress, Adobe Photoshop, Illustrator, InDesign, and others.

Unions and Associations

There are a number of professional associations to which Editors in Chief may belong. These include the Society of Magazine Editors, the Society for Professional Journalists, or the City and Regional Magazine Association.

Tips for Entry

1. Take a look at the book *The Editor in Chief: A Practical Management Guide for Magazine Editors* by Benton Rain Patterson and Coleman E. P. Patterson. This handbook for Editors in Chief provides a guide for those in or interested in the field.
2. Conduct an informational interview with the Editor in Chief of a local magazine. Find out about his or her career path as well as any advice for people trying to get into the field.
3. Browse through three magazines that you regularly read or ones that you admire. As you skim through the first several pages, see if they have a letter or introduction from the Editor in Chief. What is this person commenting on and how does it function in the magazine?
4. Visit your college career center to see if they have any alumni contacts in the magazine industry or internship leads.
5. Work your way up to a high-level position at your school newspaper, literary magazine, or other publication. This will give you a taste of the combination of managerial and writing responsibilities needed to be a successful Editor in Chief.
6. Explore courses in magazine editing, such as "Basic Training: An Introduction to Magazine Editing" offered through Mediabistro.com at http://www.mediabistro.com/courses/cache/crs486.asp.

EXECUTIVE EDITOR

CAREER PROFILE

Duties: Leads the editorial team of a magazine; manages editorial and operational objectives

Alternate Title(s): None

Salary Range: $50,000 to $90,000 and up

Employment Prospects: Fair to good

Advancement Prospects: Good

Best Geographical Location(s): New York and other major cities

Prerequisites:

Education or Training—Bachelor's degree, English or journalism preferred; master's degree may be required and/or helpful at some magazines

Experience—Four to 10 years of prior magazine experience

Special Skills and Personality Traits—Editorial vision and creativity; good leadership and managerial skills; strong time management skills; ability to juggle many projects at once and work under time pressure

CAREER LADDER

```
┌─────────────────────────────────────┐
│           Editor in Chief            │
└─────────────────────────────────────┘

┌─────────────────────────────────────┐
│          Executive Editor            │
└─────────────────────────────────────┘

┌─────────────────────────────────────┐
│  Managing Editor or Senior Editor    │
└─────────────────────────────────────┘
```

Position Description

Executive Editors lead editorial teams at magazines. Using their editorial experience and vision, they determine the overall goals and direction for the magazine. Through overseeing day-to-day editorial work, Executive Editors develop the content and lineup for each issue. They assign features and departments to freelancers and staff, coordinating format, visual direction, and editorial flow.

Furthermore, Executive Editors are responsible for the overall execution of each magazine issue. Along with the editorial staff, they edit articles and write headings, sidebars, and other supplementary materials. They may write particular sections of each issue as well. Working closely with the art department, they also select the cover and article layout. Before each issue is ready to go, Executive Editors ensure that everything is as it should be. This means they may need to pitch in to tackle tasks large and small themselves, including fact-checking, photo retouching, and copyediting.

The calendar is important at magazines. Finding the right placement for articles based on time of year can be critical for success. Executive Editors are responsible for planning the editorial calendar. They determine what will be published and when. By staying abreast of all current news affecting the industry of their magazine, as well as what their competition has been covering, Executive Editors make sure their stories will sell.

While assistant, associate, and senior editors may be responsible for specific areas, Executive Editors must be generalists to some extent in order to manage the editorial team. They must have excellent judgment about what makes a good story and a clear idea about what their magazine is striving to accomplish. Often, they have final decision-making power about which stories make it into each issue. They also may guide staff and writers about the angle with which to tackle a topic.

Part of being a good Executive Editor involves balancing the magazine's editorial vision and organizational objectives with the needs of readers. This may be achieved by running reader focus groups to learn more about what readers are looking for. Since the success of a magazine is ultimately determined by its sales, Executive Editors strive to give the people what they want while maintaining editorial integrity. Marketing and branding opportunities are part of their realm, and they are constantly thinking about how to reach new markets and keep their ideas fresh, current, and in demand.

In addition to leading the editorial team, Executive Editors are also involved with the business of running a magazine. They set policy and procedure and make sure that the editorial goals are met with the financial resources they have. Also, they may be responsible for recruiting, hiring, evaluating, and terminating full-time editorial staff, as well as freelance writers and photographers.

Their duties may include:

- Overseeing the editorial budget
- Making presentations to internal and external audiences
- Brainstorming on advertising strategies
- Developing editorial contracts
- Working with printers
- Approving final copy and files
- Overseeing subscriber satisfaction initiative
- Managing online editorial content and/or creating an online presence
- Conducting outreach with related vendors
- Working with the benefits administrator
- Setting advertising strategy
- Developing communications priorities
- Writing monthly columns or features
- Informing the sales team about the editorial objectives
- Serving as a magazine spokesperson

With their experience and leadership, good Executive Editors also help to develop and mentor their editorial staff. They provide guidance and offer feedback on their work that will help them to become stronger editors and writers.

Executive Editors often work long hours before publication deadlines. Meetings with editors, writers, photographers, and others are required and may sometimes take place after traditional business hours.

Salaries

According to the results of the *Folio*: 2004 Editorial Salary Survey conducted annually by *Folio Magazine*, average salaries for Executive Editors were $80,322. The figure was broken down by age, showing an average of $61,015 for Executive Editors age 39 and younger and $86,119 for those 40 and older. This discrepancy by age also reflects the higher earnings of those with more experience in the field.

Furthermore, the survey goes on to show salary differences by magazine circulation. Executive Editors working for publications with circulation of less than 50,000 earned

an average of $62,470, while those at magazines with circulation over 100,000 earned $90,626 on average.

In addition to base salary, the same survey states that 48.1 percent of Executive Editors expect to receive a bonus each year, averaging $8,500.

Employment Prospects

According to the Bureau of Labor Statistics (BLS), employment for magazine editors overall is expected to increase through 2012 as demand for varied publications will increase. Executive Editors will be needed to manage editorial staff members and lead magazines into new directions. However, keep in mind that some smaller publications do not employ Executive Editors. The most opportunities will be at large publications with sizable editorial departments.

Advancement Prospects

Since they are already at a high level, Executive Editors can find advancement by moving from smaller publications to larger ones, or by seeking editor in chief positions. There are numerous local, regional, or trade magazines with circulation of less than 50,000 where Executive Editors can gain experience and then move to national or consumer mass-market publications. Furthermore, their experience managing an editorial staff and creating a vision and plan for a magazine also prepares them for work as an editor in chief.

Magazines tend to have high turnover rates and it is common for the top editors to move around frequently within their same genre, often securing a new position with a competitor. It is in this way that they try to stay fresh and bring in new ideas.

Education and Training

Executive Editors have bachelor's degrees in a variety of fields, commonly English, journalism, or communications. They are often veterans of their campus publications and frequently have held editorial leadership positions since early on. Some Executive Editors have master's degrees in journalism or related fields, depending on their journalistic niche area and publication genre. Others may hold degrees or have completed coursework in business or management.

To become an Executive Editor, one must have four to 10 years of prior editorial experience on average. This training is crucial, as it provides the necessary experience and exposure to the inner workings of the editorial operations of a magazine. By taking on progressively more responsibility, Executive Editors learn how to lead an editorial staff and develop their own style and vision.

Experience, Skills, and Personality Traits

Executive Editors should be experienced leaders. It is important for them to have a vision and to work with their staff to get them on board. In addition to their editorial skill, Executive Editors are hands-on operations people who can implement as well as strategize.

Also, Executive Editors must have excellent organizational skills. They are creative, yet meticulous, and must be able to juggle multiple tasks at once and meet deadlines. As strong communicators, Executive Editors can express themselves well in their speech and writing, and they are often asked to present to crowds. At their level, Executive Editors must be knowledgeable and passionate about the genre of their publication, be it politics, pets, fashion, or food.

Computer skills are also a must. Necessary programs may include Microsoft Word, Excel, and QuarkXPress, as well as databases such as LexisNexis.

Unions and Associations

Executive Editors may belong to professional associations including the American Society of Magazine Editors, the American Society of Business Publication Editors, or the Society for Professional Journalists.

Tips for Entry

1. Take a look at job listings for Executive Editors at http://www.journalismjobs.com.
2. Gain experience while a student for campus publications. Work up to leadership positions such as managing editor or editor in chief of a school newspaper, magazine, or journal.
3. Apply for an internship with a magazine. Spend time speaking to the editorial staff and sitting in on meetings.
4. Conduct an informational interview with an Executive Editor. Find out what he or she likes best and least about the position.
5. Explore courses in business and management. These classes can provide a useful background for managing operations and understanding budgets.

CREATIVE DIRECTOR

CAREER PROFILE

Duties: Manages all layout for a magazine; oversees art and design departments

Alternate Title(s): Art Director, Design Director

Salary Range: $50,000 to $100,000 and up

Employment Prospects: Fair

Advancement Prospects: Fair

Best Geographical Location(s): Major cities

Prerequisites:

Education or Training—Some jobs may require a bachelor's degree in art, graphic design, or related field; portfolio more important than formal education

Experience—At least five to seven years of experience in art or design for a magazine

Special Skills and Personality Traits—Creativity; good artistic sense; strong management and organizational skills; knowledge of graphic design and related computer programs; understanding of magazine journalism

CAREER LADDER

```
┌─────────────────────────────────────┐
│  Creative Director, larger magazine  │
└─────────────────────────────────────┘

┌─────────────────────────────────────┐
│         Creative Director            │
└─────────────────────────────────────┘

┌─────────────────────────────────────┐
│         Art, Design, or              │
│      Photo Director or Editor        │
└─────────────────────────────────────┘
```

Position Description

Magazine journalism offers a wide range of positions. In addition to writers and editors, there are other creative professionals that contribute their talents to produce a quality publication. One of these professionals is the Creative Director.

The look of a magazine has much to do with the image it projects to readers. Before they even have the opportunity to open it up and scan the contents, consumers see a magazine cover and make a quick judgment as to what it is all about. Together with the editorial staff, the Creative Director leads the artistic team to create a product that will meet its goals and be a success. They strive to create a format that is eye-catching, appealing, and targeted to the magazine's market.

For each issue of a magazine, the writing is only part of the picture. In order for readers to connect with the contents and articles, the design, illustrations, and photographs play a crucial role. Creative Directors are responsible for the overall look of each issue. They oversee every page to make sure the layout is flawless. It is their artistic sense and creative vision that determines the structure of the pages.

As managing editors and executive editors determine the editorial direction, Creative Directors guide the artistic direction for their magazine. Their realm includes the art, photography, and design departments where they supervise all staff. This staff can be comprised of full-time art editors and directors, photo editors and directors, designers, and freelancers.

For each story that comes in, the creative team gets to work. Creative Directors assign illustrations and photography to appropriate staff members and freelancers, determining who would be the right artist for each piece. Working together with these professionals, they decide how the art should be approached and what the final copy should look like. Along the way, Creative Directors may approve sketches, check in, and oversee the work process.

Once the artwork and photographs are complete, Creative Directors and their teams begin the layout process. In order to create a story, they must interpose art with words in a way that makes the copy clear and readable. The art serves to enhance the words and draw the reader in. Most of this work is done via computer, and Creative Directors and their teams are experts on these systems.

Additional duties may include:

- Managing online layout and Web design
- Designing specific magazine departments
- Overseeing the art and design budget
- Running regular meetings
- Hiring freelance and full-time staff
- Collaborating with the editorial department to combine stories and art
- Planning photo shoots
- Following through with the production process
- Designing other media contents such as brochures, press kits, and inserts

Creative Directors often serve as leaders and mentors. They run their departments using a combination of artistic sensibility and savvy management. Good Creative Directors help to develop the talent of their artists, designers, and photographers by helping them to express their vision. They have both the big ideas and the ability to engage in the process of getting them realized.

While they may not have journalism training, those Creative Directors who choose to work at magazines are interested in journalism. They enjoy the flow of words and ideas and the idea of collaborating to publish something tangible.

Long hours may be required for Creative Directors, especially close to deadlines. Some travel may also be necessary for photo shoots or other on-site features.

Salaries

Salaries for Creative Directors vary by both geographical location and circulation size. A range can be anywhere between $50,000 and $100,000, with Creative Directors at large magazines earning considerably more, at $200,000 and up.

According to *HOW* magazine's 2004 Design Salary Survey, featuring salary information about graphic design careers, Creative Directors earned an average of annual salary of $60,781. However, insiders say the average at large magazines tends to be higher—closer to $80,000.

Employment Prospects

Employment prospects are fair for Creative Directors. Small magazines often do not have the budget to centralize their art departments and may not employ a Creative Director. Instead, they will have an art director or design director that functions in a similar role.

Larger magazines hire Creative Directors who can oversee many art and design functions. The best opportunities are for those who have proven themselves in the magazine industry through solid experience and an impressive portfolio.

Entry-level creative positions may include art assistant, photo assistant, design assistant, or assistant to the cre-

ative director. Internship experience can be very helpful for breaking into the field.

Advancement Prospects

For artistic professionals working at magazines, a Creative Director position is often their ultimate goal. It usually takes at least five years to advance to this position and can take as much as 10 or more. For Creative Directors who are looking for more advancement, they may move from smaller magazines to larger ones. They also might choose to work as freelancers, consultants, or even start their own creative design businesses.

Education and Training

While many people working for magazines have bachelor's degrees in English or journalism, those subjects are not necessary for Creative Directors. Some may study journalism, but most have degrees in art or graphic design fields instead. Even if the degree itself is not in art, Creative Directors have at the minimum taken some art courses. Design skills are more important than degrees, and an excellent portfolio can compensate for lack of formal education or academic training.

Experience, Skills, and Personality Traits

Creating a portfolio is essential for aspiring Creative Directors or any other art professionals who are interested in working at a magazine. A portfolio is a collection of samples that showcases one's artistic work, whether it be illustration, photography, design, or layout.

There are several ways in which people who want to break into the field can create their first portfolio. Firstly, it is necessary to take computer courses to learn graphic design programs. The required programs may include QuarkXPress, InDesign, Adobe Photoshop and Illustrator, and other layout programs.

After acquiring the layout knowledge, a prospective job applicant can put together his or her own portfolio. According to industry insiders, one good way to get started is simply to target magazines and construct sample layouts by taking several pages that include both copy and art, scanning them to your own computer, and then reorganizing them into your own layout that showcases your artistic sensibility. There are also specific portfolio courses where the class project is to produce a portfolio for those who might prefer more structure and assistance. Either way, the key to becoming a good Creative Director is showing that you have both the creative vision and the technical skills to do the job.

It goes without saying that Creative Directors need an innate artistic sense as well as the necessary technical skills to do the job. In addition, at least five years of work in design at a magazine is required to advance to this level. One must understand the inner workings of magazines and be familiar with photography and typography. Furthermore, Creative Directors must be able to multitask and juggle many projects at once. They must be good leaders who can manage a department and motivate others to work hard. Also helpful is the ability to pay close attention to detail and to communicate effectively.

Unions and Associations

There are a number of professional associations to which Creative Directors at magazines may belong. These include the Society of Publication Designers, the Art Directors Club, the Type Directors Club, the American Institute of Graphic Arts (AIGA), and the Society of Illustrators.

Tips for Entry

1. Begin exploring resources that will enable you to put together a portfolio. Check out information at sites such as http://www.rhodesstate.edu/applications/e-portfolio/portcourses.asp, http://graphicdesign.about.com/cs/designerportfolios/a/portfolio.htm, and http://www.allgraphicdesign.com/onlinecourses.html.

2. Become an avid magazine reader. Study the format of different magazine genres and note the differences in photography, illustrations, design, and type.

3. Create a résumé that highlights your artistic experience. Make sure it is well organized and has an effective layout

4. Learn more about the computer programs necessary for a career as a Creative Director. Take a look at Adobe programs (InDesign, Photoshop, and Illustrator) at http://www.adobe.com and QuarkXPress at http://www.quark.com.

5. Visit the Web site of *HOW* magazine (http://www.howdesign.com/) for information related to the graphic design community.

MANAGING EDITOR

Duties: Oversees all editorial content for a magazine; develops ideas, manages scheduling, reviews edits, and assigns stories

Alternate Title(s): None

Salary Range: $45,000 to $70,000 and up

Employment Prospects: Fair to Good

Advancement Prospects: Good

Best Geographical Location(s): New York and other major cities

Prerequisites:

Education or Training—Bachelor's degree, preferably in English or journalism; master's degree may be helpful

Experience—Five to 10 years of editorial experience

Special Skills and Personality Traits—Excellent organizational skills; good management ability; superior writing skills and command of language; careful attention to detail; good computer skills

```
┌─────────────────────────────────┐
│  Editor in Chief, Executive      │
│  Editor, or Editorial Director   │
└─────────────────────────────────┘

┌─────────────────────────────────┐
│       Managing Editor            │
└─────────────────────────────────┘

┌─────────────────────────────────┐
│  Senior Editor or Copy Editor    │
└─────────────────────────────────┘
```

Position Description

At some point, all editorial copy at a magazine must flow through the Managing Editor. Features, columns, and departments are all filtered through the Managing Editor who has both editorial input and management responsibilities. Managing Editors often make assignments and follow up on their progress. For each issue, they see that editing is being covered by staff and facts are being confirmed. Additionally, they work closely with senior editors to make sure that their responsibilities for each issue are going according to plan.

Furthermore, Managing Editors are decision makers. They are instrumental in determining the editorial direction of their magazine. Developing both content and overall focus for each issue, they often decide which queries will be approved for publication, which stories will be covered, and who the writers will be. Managing Editors also help advise writers and editors about their goals and tone for each piece.

Scheduling is a major part of the Managing Editor role. Regardless of whether their magazine is published weekly, monthly, or only several times a year, each issue has a date on which it must be ready and available to its readers. Managing Editors keep schedules to ensure that each issue will get out on time. From working with editors and freelancers on each issue to planning ahead with schedules for future issues, they are dedicated to making the process run seamlessly.

At many magazines, there are several sets of deadlines to which staff must adhere. The early deadline is usually for columns and feature stories that are not especially time sensitive. However, there is a later deadline for timely information, especially at magazines that review restaurants or movie openings, or discuss local events. An article might critique a concert that takes place only several days before the issue is to go to print. Managing Editors help to set and enforce these deadlines.

Furthermore, Managing Editors do not just consider each monthly schedule, but they look ahead to the annual schedule and beyond. When the editorial staff has brainstorming meetings for story ideas, Managing Editors determine which upcoming issue would be the best fit for each feature. They oversee the nitty-gritty, including the date stories need to be assigned to writers, the date they need to be completed by writers, and when each issue must be planned. Without their careful eye, the contents of each installment would not flow.

In order to coordinate all editorial copy, Managing Editors work not only with the editorial staff of their magazine but with many other departments as well. They work with the production department to ensure that deadlines will be met and the art department to discuss illustration, photo layout, and overall design. As leaders within their magazine, they may serve as liaisons and mentors to much of the staff.

Additional duties may include:

- Leading brainstorming meetings
- Managing concepts and designs for magazine covers
- Working as a liaison with advertisers
- Training and supervising editorial staff
- Tracking cost and quality of editorial production
- Inspecting printing quality
- Writing magazine copy
- Tracking editorial spending
- Managing the editorial budget and specific story budgets
- Handling writer contracts and payment requests
- Running special issues

It is important for Managing Editors to be generalists, even if they have served as specialized editors in the past. Writers approach articles from different styles and points of view. There is an overall tone for travel pieces, entertainment, and editorials that may differ greatly. Managing Editors strive to keep the individuality of each piece, yet to sustain consistency, uphold standards, and portray the tone of the magazine as a whole. They should be appreciative of and knowledgeable about many different styles of writing to do this well.

In their role, Managing Editors must always have the overall goals of the magazine in mind. Sometimes seasonal events and current trends cause writers to focus on similar themes, and Managing Editors make sure that each issue does not contain duplicate material or overused phrases. They also check headlines to make sure they fit the stories to which they are attached.

Like many others in the journalism field, Managing Editors often work long hours before their issues go to print. They must be able to work well under pressure and tight deadlines. Some travel may be required, depending on the topic of the magazine.

Salaries

The results of the *Folio*: 2004 Editorial Salary Survey conducted annually by *Folio Magazine* showed average salaries for Managing Editors to be $59,216. Statistics varied by age, showing an average of $54,446 for Executive Editors age 39 and younger and $62,094 for those 40 and older.

Higher earnings are typical for those who have paid their dues and have more experience in the field.

Salaries for Managing Editors also vary by the size of their magazine. The same survey shows that Managing Editors working for the smallest types of publications, those with circulation of less than 50,000, earned an average of $46,196.

Other factors can add to the overall salary for Managing Editors. The *Folio* survey states that 42 percent of Managing Editors expect to receive a bonus each year, averaging $2,971.

Employment Prospects

Most magazines, large and small, do employ Managing Editors, making job prospects fair to good. However, there is usually only one Managing Editor per magazine, creating competition for positions. Jobs vary depending on the size of their publication, and Managing Editors may do more writing, editing, or supervising, depending on the situation.

Most opportunities are found through job boards and industry networking. Good Managing Editors may become known in their circles, and insiders say that they are often contacted by headhunters or recruiters to come work for larger magazines. Managing Editors may be required to submit writing and/or editorial samples when they apply for jobs to show their editorial history.

Advancement Prospects

Managing Editors may advance in several ways. Firstly, they may move from smaller magazines to larger ones. At smaller publications, each editor is often required to take on a number of roles, so these Managing Editors get a wide range of experience. Also, they may get promoted from within, taking on the role of editor in chief, executive editor, or deputy editor, depending on the hierarchy of their publication. Other Managing Editors may decide to become more specialized and create a niche for themselves working for specific types of genre magazines.

Education and Training

Like many others in the journalism field, most Managing Editors have bachelor's degrees in English or journalism. If they do not hold degrees in these particular fields, they have taken courses that have developed their writing, editing, and research skills. Their editorial experience frequently starts at the undergraduate level or even earlier, where they have worked for campus publications and/or completed internships.

Some Managing Editors have master's degrees in journalism, or in other fields related to the genre of their magazine. Interest and experience in that genre is valuable as well. For example, the Managing Editor for a ski magazine is often an avid skier, or at least somewhat knowledgeable about the sport.

Experience, Skills, and Personality Traits

In order to get a job as a Managing Editor, it is typical for one to have five to 10 years of related experience. Many professionals have previously worked as senior editors or copy editors, where they have honed their editorial and management skills.

Organizational skills are key for Managing Editors, as is the ability to balance time, deadlines, and workload. They should be confident leaders with superior editorial skills who can offer an editorial voice and vision to their department. Creativity and big ideas combined with practicality and logistics are the hallmarks of a good Managing Editor. Their attention to detail ensures that each issue will be launched as close to flawless as possible.

Managing Editors complete much of their editing and scheduling by computer, and it is essential for them to have strong skills. The Macintosh-based QuarkXPress program is critical for overseeing proofreading changes at most magazines. Also, Managing Editors should know how to use PC-based programs such as Microsoft Word and Excel databases.

Unions and Associations

Managing Editors may belong to a variety of professional associations, including the American Society of Magazine Editors, the City and Regional Magazine Association, and the Society of Professional Journalists.

Tips for Entry

1. One advantage of attending an undergraduate or graduate journalism program is access to alumni networks and job boards. Explore the programs listed in Appendix I.
2. Consider city and regional magazines as a good way to break into the industry. These publications are focused, yet encompass many different types of writing. Local candidates certainly have an edge, so research magazines in your hometown and apply for internships to improve your chances. Take a look at the Web site of the City and Regional Magazine Association at http://www.citymag.org/.
3. Hone your computer and graphic design skills through courses at universities, community colleges, local community centers, and online sites such as http://www.computertrainingschools.com/ and http://desktoppub.about.com/.
4. Contact the Managing Editor at a magazine you read for an informational interview. Find out about his or her career path and the advice he or she has for new professionals trying to break into the field.
5. Improve your editorial skills through writing classes that require you to read and evaluate the work of your classmates. Peer editing is a valuable skill that translates directly to the journalism field.

SENIOR EDITOR

CAREER PROFILE

Duties: Writes and edits a variety of copy for a magazine; leads editorial projects; generates story ideas

Alternate Title(s): None

Salary Range: $45,000 to $80,000 and up

Employment Prospects: Fair to Good

Advancement Prospects: Good

Best Geographical Location(s): New York and other major cities

Prerequisites:

Education or Training—Bachelor's degree in English, journalism, or related fields; master's degree may be helpful

Experience—Three to six years of prior magazine experience

Special Skills and Personality Traits—Excellent writing skills; superb editing ability; creativity and ability to generate story ideas; good communication skills; time management and ability to juggle multiple tasks

CAREER LADDER

```
┌─────────────────────────────────────┐
│  Managing Editor or Executive Editor │
└─────────────────────────────────────┘

┌─────────────────────────────────────┐
│           Senior Editor              │
└─────────────────────────────────────┘

┌─────────────────────────────────────┐
│   Assistant or Associate Editor      │
└─────────────────────────────────────┘
```

Position Description

As an editor moves up the corporate ladder of a magazine, he or she gains more experience and responsibility with editing, writing, and reporting. Senior Editors are at the top of the chain for pure editorial positions. Whereas executive editors and managing editors are high-level positions, they also entail management and supervisory responsibility that often take time away from writing and editing. Senior Editors are the professionals who have hands-on involvement with planning, writing, and editing of each issue.

What separates Senior Editors from the editors working below them is in the quality and quantity of the articles they both write and edit. Often they are responsible for more copy in terms of sheer number of stories. Also, they oversee the more substantial pieces of the magazine. A major article covering an important issue may only be trusted in the hands of a Senior Editor.

Senior Editors handle all aspects of story development, from generating ideas and formulating concepts to final edit-ing and proofreading. They may assign stories to in-house staff writers or assistant editors, or recommend appropriate freelancers. Also, Senior Editors may take on many writing responsibilities themselves. They usually have ownership over specific facets of the magazine and handle all editorial work in their assigned area.

Most consumer magazines are comprised of several feature articles, as well as "departments" or specific contents that are included in every issue. Departments can be very diverse, including horoscopes, advice, humor, editorials, entertainment guides, and more. Frequently, another aspect of the job of Senior Editor is to handle specific departments for each issue.

Because they oversee this department continuously, they are able to shape its contents and give it their voice or flair. Some Senior Editors write the content for these departments, while others delegate the writing and perform the editing themselves; most do a combination of the two. Their experience provides a solid foundation that makes them assured of their writing style and editorial goals.

While assistant and associate editors often work on assignment, Senior Editors take initiative and come up with ideas regularly. They can shift between different types of writing and are comfortable both writing and editing components such as features, news, headlines, captions, and more.

Additional duties may include:

- Writing headlines and captions
- Working with designers on layout concepts
- Writing Web copy
- Reporting on current trends
- Reading competing publications to learn about their angles on issues
- Conducting research on news and trends
- Leading editorial meetings
- Overseeing special projects
- Hiring freelancers
- Performing some copyediting and proofreading
- Editing final copy
- Heading editorial features departments
- Mentoring and managing more junior editors

Depending on the magazine, editorial jobs may blend together and the distinctions between various titles can blur. While sometimes viewed as middle managers at large publications, at small magazines Senior Editors may have more leadership and managerial responsibility. They may supervise editorial assistants or assistant or associate editors, as well as interns and/or freelancers. Furthermore, in some cases they may also be responsible for editorial assignments, scheduling, and management of deadlines.

Senior Editors may need to work long hours before each issue goes to print. Some travel may be required depending on the type of stories and genre of the magazine.

Salaries

According to the results of the *Folio*: 2004 Editorial Salary Survey conducted annually by *Folio Magazine*, average salaries for Senior Editors were $61,519.

Furthermore, the survey goes on to show salary differences by magazine circulation. Executive Editors working for publications with circulation of less than 100,000 earned an average of $51,160, while those at magazines with circulation over 100,000 earned $71,877 on average.

In addition to base salary, the same survey states that 51 percent of Senior Editors expected to receive a yearly bonus, averaging $4,953.

It is interesting to note that although managing editors are generally higher up the corporate structure, their overall earnings may be similar or less, according to some sources. This discrepancy reflects the variation in titles by a magazine. A Senior Editor looking to advance to managing editor would seek out a situation where that title change commanded a higher salary.

Employment Prospects

Employment prospects are relatively good for Senior Editors. Unlike some other editorial professionals, most magazines employ Senior Editors, sometimes more than one. Because they are still competitive, job opportunities are likely to be found through networking and contacts made through prior magazine experience. Headhunters may seek out editors who have proved themselves at their respective magazines. They may be recruited for Senior Editor positions at competing or larger publications.

Advancement Prospects

Advancement prospects are also good for Senior Editors. With more than five years of magazine experience, they are in a good position to advance to different jobs within the magazine world. Frequently, they have carved out an editorial and writing niche for themselves and may be known for their work. Also, they may do some freelance work on the side.

Some Senior Editors may move from trade magazines to consumer magazines or from small publications to larger ones. Others may seek positions as managing editors or executive editors for higher pay and more responsibility. Yet other Senior Editors may even be qualified for some editor in chief jobs.

Education and Training

Most Senior Editors have bachelor's degrees in English, journalism, or related fields. A strong grasp of language is necessary to do the job well. Course work that emphasizes writing, editing, and research is essential. The training that comes from work on campus publications or through internships is also invaluable.

At some magazines, Senior Editors may have master's degrees in journalism or other related fields. Additionally, other Senior Editors may hold undergraduate or graduate degrees related to the genre of their specific magazine. For example, a Senior Editor at a magazine focused on international issues may hold a degree in international affairs or relations.

Experience, Skills, and Personality Traits

Senior Editors must have superior writing and editing skills. As they are often among the final editors of copy, they need a strong grasp of grammar, usage, and style. Creativity is necessary to generate story ideas, as well as write articles that are interesting and engaging to readers.

Also, Senior Editors must be excellent at time management. They need to be able to multitask and handle their many projects all at once. Deadline pressure is always present, so they must thrive in these situations and not get flustered. Senior Editors must also have leadership qualities and the ability to exert authority as they manage other editors and freelance writers. Good communication skills are necessary to work with article subjects and magazine staff alike.

Like other editorial professionals, Senior Editors may be required to know specific computer programs used for magazine layout and editing. These may include QuarkXPress for the Macintosh and Microsoft Office for the PC.

Unions and Associations

Senior Editors may belong to a variety of professional associations, including the American Society of Magazine Editors, the City and Regional Magazine Association, the Society of Professional Journalists, and the National Conference of Editorial Writers.

Tips for Entry

1. Set up an informational interview with a Senior Editor at a magazine that interests you. This is an excellent way to learn more about the job, career path, and ways to break in.

2. Read position descriptions for Senior Editors on sites such as http://www.journalismjobs.com and http://www.mediabistro.com. See how the job of Senior Editor is distinguished from other editorial positions.

3. Gain experience through an internship at a magazine. Instead of focusing only on the summer, consider an internship during the academic year at a local or regional publication. At least one magazine can usually be found in even the smallest of cities.

4. Even if you are not a journalism major, take a course related to journalism or writing to hone your skills.

5. Volunteer at your campus career center. You might be able to find a position proofreading résumés and cover letters, which will give you great editorial practice.

STAFF WRITER

CAREER PROFILE

Duties: Writes a variety of articles for each issue of a magazine; writes on assignment as well as by pitching ideas

Alternate Title(s): Staff Correspondent, Staff Reporter, Correspondent, Correspondent at Large

Salary Range: $40,000 to $100,000 and up

Employment Prospects: Fair

Advancement Prospects: Good

Best Geographical Location(s): New York and other major cities

Prerequisites:

Education or Training—Bachelor's degree in English or journalism preferred; master's degree may be helpful

Experience—Three to five years or more of magazine and writing experience

Special Skills and Personality Traits—Excellent writing and reporting skills; strong communication skills; creativity; initiative; ability to work with deadline pressure; ability to generate story ideas

CAREER LADDER

```
┌─────────────────────────────────┐
│  Senior Editor, Senior Writer, or │
│  other senior editorial position  │
└─────────────────────────────────┘

┌─────────────────────────────────┐
│          Staff Writer            │
└─────────────────────────────────┘

┌─────────────────────────────────┐
│ Editorial Assistant, Associate Editor, │
│    or other entry to mid-level   │
│        editorial position        │
└─────────────────────────────────┘
```

Position Description

For many people who choose to pursue a magazine journalism career, their ultimate goal is to write. They may be skilled editors, but their true passion is to see their byline under a story that they developed and brought to fruition in their own style. For this reason, Staff Writer is often a coveted magazine job.

Staff Writers contribute specific content for each issue of their magazine. They may be responsible for writing certain sections found in every issue, as well as covering new stories and features each month. Sometimes they are assigned articles developed by senior, managing, or executive editors. However, they are also expected to contribute their own story ideas and pitch them regularly.

For Staff Writers, the creative process is exciting. It is one thing to have a good idea, but another thing altogether to conceptualize how to bring this idea to life. For each story they initiate, they have a vision about what it will achieve in print. They plan out how it will meet the goals of the magazine and serve its readers. As Staff Writers get ready to pitch their ideas, they conduct background research and develop outlines that will guide their brainstorms into finished projects. This is how they sell their ideas to the editorial staff.

Furthermore, Staff Writers must be creative not only when they generate their own story ideas but also when they work on assignment. If an editor assigns a story, Staff Writers need to determine how to make the most of it and make it their own. However, they also need to work with that editor to make sure his or her vision and goals for the story will be met as well.

In order to get story ideas, Staff Writers constantly must have their fingers on the pulse of the genre or industry covered by their magazine. Whether their area is fashion, travel, or politics, Staff Writers scour the media to find out about new developments. They read competing publications to see what topics are covered and with what angle, log onto numerous Web sites daily, read newspapers, and watch related television programs. Furthermore, they extend themselves, speaking to people who are knowledgeable about new trends and happenings that will be of interest to their readers. This helps Staff Writers build up a crucial network of contacts for stories.

For each of their pieces, whether they are feature articles, cover stories, or brief reviews, Staff Writers work diligently to write and rewrite. They must decide how to handle each story, always considering who the target audience is, what it will cover, and how it will meet the needs of their readers. Staff Writers must know the art of reporting and how tell a story in a way that is interesting.

It is important for Staff Writers to understand various genres of writing and develop their own styles. Style is partially dictated by the publication, but it is also up to the writer to put his or her own stamp on it. Some writers are known to write in a narrative form, while others develop informative lists, essays, investigative pieces, columns, or profiles. Staff Writers strive to develop ideas and text that will engage and appeal to their readers. Additionally, the layout plays a role in determining the style of each story. Staff Writers may also work with designers to organize artwork and text into a format that fits the tone.

Additional duties may include:

- Interviewing subjects for stories
- Writing Web copy and articles in addition to print material
- Writing special interest columns
- Developing a network of sources
- Attending and covering events related to stories
- Line editing and copyediting
- Working on story layout

Staff Writers must remain organized as they work on their stories. They must be skilled at sifting through large amounts of complicated information and selecting the most interesting and relevant parts to focus on. As they put together interview transcripts and research notes, Staff Writers must keep track of all their paperwork so that facts can be checked by researchers or fact-checkers later on.

Travel may be required for work on some stories, and long hours as deadlines approach are common. Staff Writers may have some flexibility in terms of actual work hours, and some may complete assignments from home.

Salaries

The salary range for Staff Writers is diverse and depends on their level of experience and the type of publication for which they work. Insiders say that a typical magazine Staff Writer's salary is in the $50,000 to $70,000 range with senior writers earning six figures.

Additional information comes from the Council for the Advancement of Science Writing, where according to their information, Staff Writers specializing in science may start at salaries of around $30,000 per year and go up to $100,000 per year for experienced senior correspondents.

Employment Prospects

For Staff Writers, employment prospects are fair overall. These desirable positions are not easy to obtain, except for those with exceptional writing experience. Jobs are often found through networking and contacts that have been developed through entry-level positions.

Often, a prospective Staff Writer will gain experience writing while working as an editorial assistant or editor for a smaller magazine. Since magazines may be flexible and titles may vary, those in editorial positions can sometimes contribute a significant amount of writing if they are persistent. Then they may apply for Staff Writer positions at larger publications once they have some clips to show.

Advancement Prospects

Because of their strong writing skills, advancement prospects are good for Staff Writers. They can move in a variety of different directions, depending on their interests.

Many Staff Writers work on freelance projects, but their ability to do so depends on their employer. Staff Writers generally need to get approval from their magazine for freelancing. Some magazines restrict their Staff Writers from taking freelance assignments, while others allow it as long as the pieces are do not create conflicts of interest or contain competitive material. Some will use a pen name to ease concerns. Additionally, some Staff Writers may pursue book projects in addition to freelance articles.

Those Staff Writers who want to stay full-time at magazines may advance to become senior writers for bigger articles and higher pay. Others may move over to the editorial track, in mid- to senior-level positions.

Education and Training

For a position as a Staff Writer, a bachelor's degree in English or journalism is helpful. Magazine veterans will say that while there is a debate about the most appropriate degree, no one has a definitive answer. A liberal arts curriculum offers a broad education that teaches its students to read and write critically, whereas journalism courses cover the nuts and bolts of reporting. A combination of classes with different major and minors may be useful.

The same debate rages about whether or not the master's degree in journalism is a necessary credential. Although those in the field agree that most training comes on the job, journalism school at the graduate level often provides invaluable contacts and practical exposure. Internships are crucial, whether at the undergraduate or graduate level.

Experience, Skills, and Personality Traits

Staff Writers should have experience with investigative journalism. For those who report on different topics, they need to be skilled at speaking to people, interviewing, and putting them at ease to open up. Their communication skills must be sharp and their energy level high, as they tackle the task of reporting with tact and enthusiasm. Positions usually require three to five years of experience or more and a portfolio of writing clips.

Furthermore, an innate talent for putting words together is required to be a Staff Writer. Staff Writers may have styles that are funny, confrontational, or informative, but they all are able to convey their thoughts in a way that enables people to read and respond. Regardless of their assignments, they understand basic rules of grammar and sentence structure.

Additionally, Staff Writers should be able to work under pressure and meet deadlines. Focused yet flexible, they may need to juggle several writing assignments at once. Flexibility also comes into play in that Staff Writers need to be thick-skinned and able to respond well to criticism. They must make the most of boring assignments and respect the changes editors may make to their work.

Unions and Associations

Staff Writers may belong to a variety of professional associations including the National Writers Union, the National Conference of Editorial Writers, Investigative Reporters and Editors, and the Society of American Business Editors and Writers, among others based on their specialty areas.

Tips for Entry

1. Create a writing niche for yourself. Whether your passion is for the stock market, beauty products, or foreign films, focus your writing around your interests whenever possible. This helps you to develop an area of expertise that will make you more marketable.

2. Gain as much writing experience as possible. No matter how menial the assignment, cover events for campus publications, review books for literary journals, and report on news for local tabloids.

3. Be a reader. Read everything ranging from newspapers and magazines to Webzines and novels. The best writers in the world will tell you that they credit their voracious appetites for reading as much as their natural talent. The more you read other people's writing, the better you will be at your own.

4. Visit the Web site of the National Writers Union at http://www.nwu.org, the only labor union representing freelance writers in all genres.

5. Make valuable contacts in the magazine industry through the internship program offered to college juniors by the American Society of Magazine Editors. To learn more, see http://www.magazine.org/Editorial/Internships/.

ASSISTANT EDITOR

CAREER PROFILE

Duties: Edits copy for a magazine; may write a variety of articles and other content

Alternate Title(s): Associate Editor

Salary Range: $28,000 to $50,000 and up

Employment Prospects: Fair to Good

Advancement Prospects: Good

Best Geographical Location: New York City and other major cities

Prerequisites:

Education or Training—Bachelor's degree in English, journalism, or related field; master's degree can be helpful and/or necessary at some publications

Experience—One to three years of work as an editorial assistant

Special Skills and Personality Traits—Excellent writing and editing skills; strong organization and attention to detail; effective communication ability; good judgment and stylistic sense; ability to meet deadlines and work under pressure

CAREER LADDER

```
┌─────────────────────────────┐
│  Associate or Senior Editor  │
└─────────────────────────────┘

┌─────────────────────────────┐
│      Assistant Editor        │
└─────────────────────────────┘

┌─────────────────────────────┐
│     Editorial Assistant      │
└─────────────────────────────┘
```

Position Description

After paying their dues as editorial assistants, the next step on the magazine ladder for editorial professionals is as Assistant Editors (or at some magazines, the title is associate editor). Assistant Editors have increased responsibility for both writing and editing. Particularly at smaller magazines, they have a major role in shaping magazine content.

Overall, Assistant Editors have advanced editorial duties. Since magazines vary so much from each other, the title of Assistant Editor can bring with it different levels of responsibility. At small publications, they may review editorial copy for the entire magazine, while at larger periodicals, they may only handle specific sections. Their tasks typically include checking copy for grammatical, factual, and punctuation errors. Additionally, Assistant Editors evaluate and alter each of their assigned pieces to make sure it is consistent with their magazine's tone and style.

As one moves up the editorial ladder, job responsibilities grow in both the quality and quantity of their editing and writing. In terms of writing, Assistant Editors may write short articles or features for each magazine issue. Rather than covering only what is assigned to them by more senior editors, Assistant Editors may decide what they want to write and find a place for it that makes sense stylistically. They pitch ideas that both fit with the current issues and represent topics they want to write about. Using their creativity, they think of catchy headlines and titles that will draw in readers. Their writing assignments also vary depending on the size of the magazine staff.

Assistant Editors frequently have ownership over specific magazine contents. Depending on the type of publication, these "departments" vary greatly and can include quizzes, reviews, beauty, sports, travel, or gossip. Assistant Editors can oversee these departments, including writing, editing, design, and layout. For each issue, they ensure that these departments are well covered. Assistant Editors may work alongside senior editors who have final say for some departments, or they may have autonomy over smaller departments.

Furthermore, Assistant Editors contribute to the overall direction of their magazine. They participate in weekly or monthly meetings and brainstorming sessions where their ideas help to shape the content. No longer at the entry-level at most magazines (note that the occasional small publication may use the terms editorial assistant and Assistant Editor interchangeably), Assistant Editors use their experience to understand the inner workings of magazines.

While editorial assistants communicate with freelancers and photographers, it often falls to Assistant Editors to manage and supervise them. This can include selecting the right freelance writer and photographer for each story, as well as setting deadlines and ensuring they are adhered to. Assistant Editors might also help current writers work on their stories as well as cultivate new writers. Being able to negotiate this role is a challenge for Assistant Editors. They must be able to stress the importance of deadlines and deal with grievances over salary and other issues in a friendly, yet professional manner.

Also, Assistant Editors can be responsible for cleaning up the work of writers. When each piece comes in, they make sure the writer has met the goals of the article. If changes need to be made, Assistant Editors may contact the writers with suggestions or, more often, make changes themselves. Often this will involve adding catchy language, writing strong introductions and conclusions, and devising other reader-friendly components.

Additional duties may include:

- Writing, editing, and rewriting press releases
- Selecting photographs and artwork for various pieces
- Creating layout for stories
- Conducting research
- Developing story ideas
- Proofreading final copy
- Tracking progress of pages from proof to final copy
- Developing and writing Web content
- Performing fact-checking on some stories

Some travel may be required for Assistant Editors at certain magazines to attend events, trade shows, or other happenings related to magazine content. At large magazines with international editions, Assistant Editors may even serve as liaisons with editors from all over the world in order to work together and create brand consistency.

At not quite the entry level or senior level, Assistant Editors can make the most of their jobs by being go-getters. They have a great opportunity to take initiative and commit to bigger projects as long as they can manage their current workloads. Assistant Editors can be in an exciting position to shape their jobs and their careers to fit their strengths and interests. To do so, they can expect to put in some long hours to complete assignments.

Salaries

Assistant Editors earn salaries that are a step up from those of editorial assistants. However, the numbers vary depending on the size, genre, and circulation of the magazine. Assistant Editors may earn $28,000 to start at small magazines where they come in with little or no experience. At a larger magazine where they have put in several years as editorial assistants, they can earn salaries of $40,000 to $50,000.

Employment Prospects

Employment prospects are fair to good for Assistant Editors. Magazines depend on the work of their mid-level staff to get each issue out on time. For those with one to three years of prior magazine experience, there are a number of openings for Assistant Editors at all types of publications. However, positions at major magazines remain competitive.

Networking within the industry often provides the best job leads. When turnover occurs, it is often a good time to explore new opportunities. For example, if an editor in chief or other high-level editor leaves to go to a competing publication, he or she will often take along additional staff members.

Advancement Prospects

Since they have enough experience to become more senior members of an editorial team, employment prospects are good for Assistant Editors. At this point, they must evaluate the direction in which they want their career to go. It is important for Assistant Editors to be knowledgeable and/or interested in the type of publication for which they work. As they look to advance, many seek to carve out a niche for themselves, whether it is beauty, food, fiction, entertainment, sports, travel, or features. Their next move may help to determine the path of their career.

In addition to defining themselves by a specific genre, Assistant Editors also decide if they want to advance to senior editor, or pursue more writing-related positions, such as staff writer. They also may advance by moving to larger publications for better salary and overall growth.

Education and Training

Assistant Editors hold bachelor's degrees in a variety of fields, with English, journalism, and communications being the most popular. Course work involving significant writing, editing, and research is very valuable. Most also have significant training in writing and editing through work on campus publications.

Increasingly, some Assistant Editors have graduate degrees as well. A master's in journalism can offer a significant advantage and may even enable a new professional with considerable internship experience to come in at the Assistant Editor level and bypass editorial assistant work. Furthermore, Assistant Editors may also be required to hold graduate degrees that are related to the content of their publication. For example, an Assistant Editor at a political magazine may hold an advanced degree in political science, public policy, or law.

Most Assistant Editors learn the ropes as editorial assistants, where they receive extensive training for their next step. Additionally, they often have internship experience in different areas of journalism, and they may also have freelance writing credits.

Experience, Skills, and Personality Traits

To perform their jobs well, Assistant Editors must be able to work well under deadlines and to handle many tasks at once. They need excellent writing and editing skills, with a good grasp of grammar, punctuation, and usage. It is important for them to be familiar with different types of writing styles and the standard style used by their magazine such as Associated Press (AP) style.

Strong communication skills help Assistant Editors to work as part of the editorial team. They also come in handy for working with writers as well as story subjects. Detail orientation helps Assistant Editors to catch mistakes and stay focused.

Also, Assistant Editors must be computer literate. They may be required to know certain computer word processing, database, and design/layout programs. Such programs include both PC-based Microsoft Office (Work, Excel, and others) and Mac-based QuarkXPress. Furthermore, they may need to know Adobe programs such as InCopy and InDesign.

Unions and Associations

Assistant Editors at magazines may belong to a variety of professional associations including the American Society of Magazine Editors, the City and Regional Magazine Association, and the Society of Professional Journalists.

Tips for Entry

1. Most editorial positions expect candidates to be familiar with AP (Associated Press) style. Learn more about it by checking links such as http://www.utexas.edu/coc/journalism/SOURCE/journal_links/AP_style.html and http://www.ku.edu/~edit/ap15.htm.

2. Learn more about the variety of magazines published today. Browse newsstands, bookstores, and Web sites such as http://www.findatoz.com/cgi-bin/cgi/x.fcgi?category=magazines to explore the different genres.

3. Visit your campus career center and set up an appointment with a counselor or adviser. He or she can offer help and support with the career process, including assistance with preparing your résumé and finding a magazine internship.

4. Consider freelance writing opportunities as a way to put together a portfolio of clips. Check out listings for freelancers on Web sites such as http://www.freelancewriting.com/forumdir/fjb/ and http://freelancewrite.about.com/.

5. Become a skilled editor. Seek a position as a teaching assistant where you review the writing of your peers, volunteer at the writing help center on campus, or work for any local publication that may need your help.

EDITORIAL ASSISTANT

CAREER PROFILE

Duties: Supports the editorial staff of a magazine with editorial, writing, and administrative responsibilities

Alternate Title(s): None

Salary Range: $25,000 to $35,000

Employment Prospects: Good

Advancement Prospects: Good to excellent

Best Geographical Location(s): New York and other major cities

Prerequisites:

Education or Training—Bachelor's degree in English, journalism, or related field; master's degree may be helpful for some positions

Experience—Internship experience at a magazine or other publication

Special Skills and Personality Traits—Excellent writing and editing skills; good communication ability; strong organizational skills and attention to detail

CAREER LADDER

```
┌─────────────────────────────────┐
│   Assistant or Associate Editor  │
└─────────────────────────────────┘

┌─────────────────────────────────┐
│       Editorial Assistant        │
└─────────────────────────────────┘

┌─────────────────────────────────┐
│             Intern               │
└─────────────────────────────────┘
```

Position Description

Editorial Assistants pitch in where they are needed to support the editorial operations of a magazine. Whether pitching ideas, editing features, writing captions, or answering phones, Editorial Assistants serve a crucial function at magazines. Not only do they provide the administrative support necessary for more senior editors to perform their jobs but they also ease their burden by writing and editing pieces. This entry-level position provides a way for those interested in careers in magazine journalism to learn the ropes.

One area in which Editorial Assistants spend much time is conducting background research. For example, a senior editor might ask an Editorial Assistant to find five articles written on a given topic relating to a story she is writing. Editorial Assistants use the Internet, databases such as LexisNexis, and other media contacts to find relevant information. For different articles in their magazine they may find interview subjects, obtain necessary pictures or supplementary notes, and follow up with leads.

Another component of research involves being well-read and well-informed. Editorial Assistants read all magazines in similar genres to their own as soon as the new issues are released. They look to see what these magazines are doing, make sure there is not too much overlap, and find out how their own publication compares with the competition. Additionally, Editorial Assistants scan newspapers, Web portals, and other media sources for stories of interest. They pull anything they might be able to use that relates to the content of their magazine, and then share it with their editors.

Skills in communication are necessary as Editorial Assistants maintain contact with people from a variety of fields. In order to find subjects to interview for articles they must be resourceful. For example, if an editor asks an Editorial Assistant to find breast cancer survivors between the ages of 25 and 35 for a piece, he may reach out to cancer support groups and nonprofit organizations, as well as posting on e-mail Listservs.

Also, Editorial Assistants are good networkers and use their personal contacts to gather information. They can interact with different types of people and convince them why participation in a particular article might be a good idea.

As their title suggests, Editorial Assistants also perform editing. They may be asked to edit various features and components of the magazine. Many Editorial Assistants have particular responsibilities such as selecting reader mail to be published each month (or week) and editing those letters. They proofread work to look for errors of grammar, spelling, and usage. Furthermore, they can also help craft language and tone to make it more interesting, clear, engaging, or logical.

Most Editorial Assistants begin their positions with the hope that they will have some opportunity to write. For many, this wish is granted within several months of hard work. Depending on the magazine, they may report on short pieces, write captions or small articles, and contribute to other pieces for which they will receive writing credits. They may pitch ideas directly to their boss, suggest them at regular editorial meetings, or receive assignments from editors.

In addition to some of the more interesting job tasks, all Editorial Assistants also perform many administrative duties. They may answer the telephone, respond to reader e-mails, file paperwork, photocopy documents, or enter data in the computer. Additionally, they frequently schedule appointments, file expense reports, work with vendors, and offer any other general support needed by the editorial department.

Additional duties may include:

- Screening article queries from new writers and making recommendations to editors
- Handling permissions for articles
- Fact-checking
- Writing and posting online content for magazine companion Web sites
- Selecting photos and graphics for stories
- Conducting interviews by telephone and in person
- Writing and editing press releases

Editorial Assistants may work for one specific editor, or they may report to a group of several editors in a particular department such as features or entertainment. To some extent, the daily tasks of their job as well as their writing opportunities will depend upon their supervisors. Some top editors, particularly at high-profile magazines, expect their assistants to perform personal tasks for them. It is not unheard of for Editorial Assistants to fetch coffee, pick up lunch, or even babysit for the children of their editors.

However, for most Editorial Assistants, the payoff for these tasks is worthwhile as they get to see their names in print. Editorial Assistants usually do not stay in their positions for more than three years, and most feel that the less-than-glamorous aspects that come along with their job are part of paying their dues.

Editorial Assistants typically work from 10:00 A.M. to 6:00 P.M., with some overtime (which may be paid or unpaid) common around deadlines. Depending on their publication, they may be required to attend social and cultural events in the evening or travel for stories.

Salaries

Editorial Assistant jobs are notorious for offering low pay. According to insiders, salaries generally range from $25,000 to $35,000 per year. Some magazines pay their Editorial Assistants overtime, which can increase their earnings toward the higher end of the spectrum. Some Editorial Assistants supplement their income with freelance writing work, while others find that the demands of their job do not allow time to pursue independent writing projects.

There may be other job perks for Editorial Assistants in addition to salary. For example, at fashion magazines, Editorial Assistants may receive free designer clothing and shoe samples; at food magazines, they may enjoy many complementary meals at fine restaurants.

Employment Prospects

Employment prospects for Editorial Assistants are fair to good. Positions at highly regarded consumer magazines are quite competitive. However, since the turnover is high and many magazines employ several Editorial Assistants, there are opportunities to be found. Networking is the best way to break in, as many positions are not advertised. Internships are a key way to gain valuable experience, as well as make important contacts.

Advancement Prospects

Because Editorial Assistant positions are considered entry level, opportunities for advancement are good to excellent. Typically, an Editorial Assistant works at his or her job for one to three years before being promoted to assistant or associate editor. They may advance within the same magazine or move on to another magazine in a similar genre.

Additionally, after gaining experience at one magazine, Editorial Assistants may decide to move on to another area of print journalism such as newspapers or new media, as well as magazines of a different genre. Depending on their experience, they may be eligible for the next level of assistant editor, or they may need to make a lateral move and take another position as an Editorial Assistant to compensate for the change in responsibilities. Either way, by working as Editorial Assistants, they have gained skills in writing, researching, and editing that will be valuable in their future journalism careers.

Working for a high-powered editor, such as the editor in chief, may have pros and cons for an Editorial Assistant looking to advance. These editors are well connected and often introduce their former assistants to other journalism players that can help them take the next step in their career. However, good help is hard to find, and some editors are reluctant to let go of a strong assistant. Editorial Assistants may or may not be forthcoming with their editors about their job search, depending on the situation.

Education and Training

Editorial Assistants hold bachelor's degrees, usually in fields such as English or journalism. They have taken courses that hone their writing, research, and editing skills.

Furthermore, some Editorial Assistants have graduate degrees in fields like English or journalism as well. The advanced education, internship opportunities, and networking contacts obtained from graduate school may be helpful for employment at prestigious publications. Editorial Assistants at special interest magazines such as science or business may hold undergraduate or graduate degrees in those fields as well.

The best training for work as an Editorial Assistant comes from internships. It is unusual to be hired without this crucial experience on a résumé. Internships provide exposure to the inner workings of a magazine and an understanding of what the job of an Editorial Assistant is all about. Internships in other aspects of print journalism, such as newspapers, new media, or even book publishing, can be helpful as well.

Furthermore, many Editorial Assistants prove themselves as writers while in college. They may write for their school newspapers or literary magazines, as well as newsletters, Web sites, and other publications.

Experience, Skills, and Personality Traits

It is essential for Editorial Assistants to be excellent communicators. Not only must they be superb writers with an eye for detail, but they also need strong verbal communication skills and the ability to deal well with people. They should have a good command of the English language and editing skills that include an understanding of grammar, syntax, spelling, usage, and proofreading.

Also, Editorial Assistants should be well organized. They can schedule appointments and handle other office tasks with the same efficiency they use to tackle their writing assignments. Furthermore, they understand the genre of the magazine for which they work. It is easy for them to adapt their own writing style and the style of others to fit the tone of their publication.

The ability to be flexible, multitask, and accept criticism is also important for Editorial Assistants. Although at times they may feel "I went to college for this?" when asked to perform a task that seems beneath them, they must be able to look at the big picture and remain positive.

Unions and Associations

Editorial Assistants working for magazines may belong to the American Society of Magazine Editors, among others.

Tips for Entry

1. A good Web site for magazine positions is http://www.mediabistro.com. Search for Editorial Assistant listings.
2. Internships are of key importance for securing that first job as an Editorial Assistant. Explore the program offered through the American Society of Magazine Editors at http://www.magazine.org/Editorial/Internships/.
3. Another proactive way to find an internship is through contacting magazines directly. Send a résumé and cover letter directly to a senior editor of the magazines that you read. Names and address information can be found on the masthead page, found at the beginning of most magazines.
4. Cover letters are particularly important for editorial and writing jobs. In your letter, make sure to articulate why you want to work for each particular magazine. It is important to have read the magazine and demonstrate that you understand its audience and contents. Have a friend or career counselor proofread your letter carefully.
5. Check out the site http://www.ed2010.com, a community of young magazine editors and editor-hopefuls. It offers fun and irreverent but useful information (such as salary reports from different publishers and job listings) as well as networking resources for those who want to make it in the magazine business.
6. Most people immediately think of consumer magazines when they consider the magazine industry, but business, professional, and trade magazines offer a wealth of opportunities. Explore entry-level positions at these publications as a way to break into magazine journalism and gain valuable experience.

RESEARCHER

CAREER PROFILE

Duties: Researches and gathers information for magazine stories; verifies facts prior to publication

Alternate Title(s): Fact-checker, Editorial Researcher

Salary Range: $30,000 to $45,000

Employment Prospects: Fair

Advancement Prospects: Good

Best Geographical Location(s): New York and other major cities

Prerequisites:

Education or Training—Bachelor's degree in English, journalism, or related field

Experience—One to five years of magazine experience

Special Skills and Personality Traits—Excellent research skills; careful attention to detail; good investigative and communication skills; knowledge of research systems and databases

CAREER LADDER

```
┌─────────────────────────────────────┐
│ Research Director or Research Chief  │
└─────────────────────────────────────┘

┌─────────────────────────────────────┐
│             Researcher               │
└─────────────────────────────────────┘

┌─────────────────────────────────────┐
│      Editorial Assistant or          │
│      Research Assistant              │
└─────────────────────────────────────┘
```

Position Description

Journalism is as good as the truth and integrity of the information it offers. If journalists did not confirm facts, reputations could be destroyed, lawsuits would follow, and the general public would not be able to believe what they read, see, and hear from the media. When a magazine publishes an article, information must be gathered and facts need to be verified before it goes to print. Researchers are responsible for this very important job, among other things.

Researchers working for magazines confirm facts and details about a wide range of topics. From statistics and numbers to celebrity gossip, they use research skills to ensure that the writers have used correct information in their articles. The genre of the magazine drives the type of content and research that must be done.

In addition to checking facts, Researchers are often called upon to develop or flesh out story ideas. They also perform background research for writers and editors. This can involve finding interview subjects for articles, identifying resources, and locating related news.

It is crucial for Researchers to have the investigative skills of a journalist to do their jobs well. Research has many components, and a typical day can involve hours on the telephone, time spent on the Internet, and periods perusing electronic databases such as LexisNexis.

While almost anyone can conduct a Google search, Researchers are experts about the different methods of conducting research. Knowing which source to use and where to begin helps them do their jobs effectively. Researchers need to be persistent and proactive to find out what they need. Talking to people is essential and adds an interactive component to their often-independent work.

At some magazines, Researchers also have writing and editing components to their jobs. They may create lists, charts, and graphs, as well as write blurbs or short pieces. Researchers might hunt down correct contact information, investigate organizations that provide specific services, or compile resource sidebars to articles. Furthermore, some magazines run annual surveys or questionnaires. Researchers may be responsible for designing, analyzing, or compiling this information.

Yet another role for a Researcher may be to support other aspects of the magazine in addition to the editorial side. Researchers may also conduct market research to help increase circulation and grow the business. With the appropriate skill set, they may identify new markets, conduct focus groups, and make presentations on their findings.

Additional duties may include:

- Performing administrative tasks such as office organization
- Working with freelance writers
- Assisting the photography, design, or art departments
- Managing time schedules
- Learning about industry trends
- Proofreading and analyzing material
- Reading newspapers and competing publications
- Leading research projects

While the task of verifying information or conducting primary research may seem daunting to some, Researchers know where to look and what to do. Many see their job as a stepping-stone to other, potentially more glamorous, magazine work, but others get great satisfaction from their work. For those who find a challenge in hunting down information, the thrill of that chase makes their jobs exciting.

Additionally, the role of a Researcher will differ depending on the type of magazine. At some publications, Researchers assist writers and editors, while others have a major research component that requires more responsibility. For example, scientific magazines might require Researchers to have scientific backgrounds as they identify important issues and uncover relevant details. Researchers may be involved with writing reports, performing statistical analysis, or assessing data.

Salaries

Salaries for Researchers can vary depending upon their position level. At magazines where Researchers mainly check facts and assist the editorial staff, their salary is comparable to those of editorial assistants or assistant editors in the $30,000 to $35,000 range. However, at publications where Researchers manage research assistants and perform independent studies, their salaries can be in the $40,000 to $45,000 range and above.

Employment Prospects

Employment prospects are fair, since not all magazines employ Researchers. Those who do tend to be larger or have greater research needs, such as regular statistical information. Most Researchers find their jobs through publishing job-listing sources and industry networking.

Advancement Prospects

Researchers can advance on several different magazine paths, depending on their areas of interest and expertise. At some magazines, Researcher is close to an entry-level position, and a Researcher can move up the editorial ladder to an assistant editor, copy editor, or other editorial position. Yet others may enjoy research greatly and seek out a position that enables them to manage other Researchers and lead a department, such as research chief. Other Researchers might want to get more involved with writing.

Education and Training

Most Researchers have bachelor's degrees in English, journalism, or related fields. A strong liberal arts curriculum is also helpful. As students, Researchers become skilled in the art of conducting research for various class assignments. A journalism background can be an advantage as well since it offers tangible investigative skills.

Some Researchers may hold undergraduate or advanced degrees in research methodology or specific fields related to the subject of their publication. For example, it would be an asset for a Researcher for a health-related trade or consumer publication to have a degree in a health, medical, or scientific field. Social science or statistics backgrounds may be useful for those Researchers who design research studies.

Experience, Skills, and Personality Traits

As their title implies, above all Researchers should have excellent research skills. They must be meticulous and persistent, utilizing different types of research methods until they find the information they need. Their attention to detail must be strong, as they may be the last stop for verifying the accuracy of information.

Furthermore, Researchers must be excellent communicators. Not only do they need to ensure that their research findings are clear and easy to understand but they also must speak to people regularly as sources of information. It is important for Researchers to be articulate, well-informed about their subject matter, and able to break through bureaucracy at times to speak to the necessary people.

Good Researchers are curious, with a desire to find facts and pertinent information. They must be able to work independently and spend many hours in front of a computer when necessary.

Knowledge of specific electronic research databases such as LexisNexis is also required. Computer literacy is a must. Some magazines may expect Researchers to be familiar with computer programs such as QuarkXpress, CopyDesk, and others.

Unions and Associations

Researchers at magazines may belong to a number of professional associations including the Society of Professional Journalists, the National Press Club, and the American Society of Magazine Editors.

Tips for Entry

1. Take a look at the book, *The Fact Checker's Bible: A Guide to Getting it Right,* by Sarah Harrison Smith.

2. Virtual libraries can be an invaluable resource for Researchers. They are organized by all types of subjects. The following link is a good start to see a virtual library that comprises all academic subject areas: http://vlib.org/.

3. Learn more about LexisNexis, one of the largest subscription-based research databases, at http://www.lexisnexis.com/.

4. Look on the masthead of several magazines that interest you. Do all employ Researchers? See which type of publications list Researchers and which do not to get a better idea of the work that Researchers do.

5. Explore magazine internships that enable you to conduct research.

COPY EDITOR

CAREER PROFILE

Duties: Line edits magazine copy for grammar, punctuation, and style

Alternate Title(s): None

Salary Range: $25,000 to $45,000

Employment Prospects: Good

Advancement Prospects: Good

Best Geographical Location(s): New York and other major cities

Prerequisites:

Education or Training—Bachelor's degree in English, journalism, or related fields

Experience—One to three years editing experience

Special Skills and Personality Traits—Excellent command of the English language including punctuation, grammar, spelling, and usage; keen attention to detail; well-organized; ability to work under deadline pressure

Special Requirements—May need to pass a copy editing test

CAREER LADDER

```
┌─────────────────────────────────────┐
│  Copy Chief, Associate Editor, or    │
│            Senior Editor             │
└─────────────────────────────────────┘

┌─────────────────────────────────────┐
│            Copy Editor               │
└─────────────────────────────────────┘

┌─────────────────────────────────────┐
│      Editorial Assistant or          │
│      Assistant Copy Editor           │
└─────────────────────────────────────┘
```

Position Description

Do you instinctively correct people's grammar when you hear or read words misused? Are you a stickler for spelling? Do friends seek you out to proofread their papers? If you are someone who has an innate sense of the way words should flow together on a page, then a career as a Copy Editor may be for you.

Quite literally, Copy Editors are responsible for "editing the copy" at their magazines. "Copy" refers to all written material—articles, headlines, sidebars, blurbs, and more. The Copy Editor ensures that each issue goes out with text that is error-free.

More than any other editors, Copy Editors need to have meticulous attention to detail. Their grammar, punctuation, spelling, and usage must be impeccable as they scan material for final errors. However, Copy Editors are not just proofreaders. In addition to merely correcting mistakes on the pages, Copy Editors also look at style, consistency, and overall fit with the tone of their publication. They must

understand what makes good writing as well as what style best serves readers of their magazine.

Copy Editors spend much of their time reading text written by other writers and editors. They scan it carefully and often rewrite and edit portions or entire articles. Some fact checking of any information that sounds questionable might also be needed, especially if there is not a separate fact-checker on staff.

Furthermore, some Copy Editors also do have writing responsibilities. They may write blurbs, headlines, or other material. However, this depends on the needs of the magazine and size of the staff, as well as the interests and talents of the particular Copy Editor.

Each magazine has its own editorial idiosyncrasies. For example, one publication may always write out "New York City" or specify "Manhattan," while another will choose the style of writing "NYC." Based on their audience, they each have quirks in terms of how they begin their sentences, the way they identify subjects in the stories, and more.

The preferred way to handle capitalization, abbreviations, numbers, and hyphenation all may vary. Copy Editors are the gatekeepers of these stylistic points. Since punctuation can change the meaning of a sentence, Copy Editors are not only thorough to a fault but also exercise good judgment and know their magazine genre well.

Sometimes Copy Editors may need to work with specific editors or writers to fix their pieces. For example, if a story needs more work than a Copy Editor can do in a short time, or requires major rewrites, the Copy Editor will meet with the writer to discuss changes. They will often begin by sending queries, or questions, to the writer about specific stylistic choices. All of these changes need to be negotiated carefully so as not to step on anyone's toes. Copy Editors have their own vocabulary for grammatical and stylistic writing problems that help them to defend their decisions.

Magazines go through a number of stages before they get to publication. At different publications, the phases may go by different names, but they always include several draft stages and a final stage. Part of the role of a Copy Editor is also to make sure deadlines are being met at each stage of the process. They work with other editors and production staff alike to help everything run smoothly.

Additional duties may include:

- Log work coming through the copy department
- Proofreading pages immediately before they go to print
- Editing both on computer and on paper
- Understanding different typography, type fonts, and type styles
- Working with designers on layout
- Entering copy into specific software
- Writing and editing Web site text and content

In general, Copy Editors find that their jobs play more to their organizational skills than their creativity. For many, this is what they like about their work. They are detail-oriented people who enjoy working in a creative environment without the pressure of having to generate ideas themselves. As they put in long hours when each issue goes to production, they can see the tangible results of their skills in each issue.

Salaries

Salaries for Copy Editors will vary depending on their work situation and extent of experience. Full-time, in-house Copy Editors may earn in a range from $25,000 to $42,000 depending on the level of their position, which can be entry-level or several steps above entry-level. For example, a salary survey at http://www.payscale.com calculated the salary for a magazine Copy Editor (with three years of experience and working in New York City) to be $39,900. However, this figure can be considerably lower for those with less experience and working in different parts of the country.

Freelancers are usually paid on an hourly basis and earnings can range from $15 to $35 per hour.

Employment Prospects

Employment prospects are good for Copy Editors, as most magazines employ Copy Editors in some capacity. While there are many full-time positions for Copy Editors posted on journalism job boards throughout the country, there are a growing number of part-time and freelance positions available as well.

Since the job of Copy Editor is very specific, some magazines find it cost effective to bring in several freelancers to do the work. This can be another option for Copy Editors who also want to work on their freelance writing or balance a number of assignments.

Advancement Prospects

There are a number of different directions in which Copy Editors can go for advancement. Many choose to stay with copy editing and seek positions of more responsibility and management such as copy chief. Yet others find that they prefer general editorial positions that enable them to be more creative and do more writing. These Copy Editors may advance to become associate or senior editors, depending on their level. The skills they developed as Copy Editors will serve them well in any editorial role.

Education and Training

Most Copy Editors hold bachelor's degrees in English, journalism, or related fields. The skills required for the job—spelling, punctuation, grammar, and usage—are best developed through a liberal arts curriculum with much reading, writing, and editing built in.

Copy Editors must be well versed in the writing style of their magazine. There are several different style manuals and formats that magazines may employ including the most commonly used Associated Press (AP) Style, the Chicago Manual of Style, and even the Modern Language Association (MLA) Style for academic journals. Copy Editors should be familiar with all, but expert in the one favored by their magazine.

Experience, Skills, and Personality Traits

Outstanding spelling, grammar, punctuation, and usage skills are required for work as a Copy Editor. Copy Editors must pay close attention to detail and be meticulous in their approach. They need the ability to stare at printed material for long periods of time. Furthermore, Copy Editors are able to adhere to close deadlines and work well under pressure. They can communicate well with other editors and authoritatively convince them about their improvements to sentence structure and more.

There are specific computer programs used by Copy Editors at various magazines. A working knowledge of QuarkXPress, Quark CopyDesk, Words into Type or similar publishing systems is often required.

Special Requirements

Some Copy Editors may be required to take a copyediting test before being hired. This test is not standardized and it varies by magazine. However, each test covers the same basic material and deals with identifying and correcting errors in grammar, spelling, punctuation, and usage.

Unions and Associations

Copy Editors may belong to various professional associations including the American Copy Editors Society, the Editorial Freelancers Association, and the American Society of Magazine Editors.

Tips for Entry

1. Become familiar with standard proofreaders' marks, which help Copy Editors to mark up their pages. You can find a list at http://www.m-w.com/mw/table/proofrea.htm.
2. Take a look at this site, http://www.well.com/user/mmcadams/copy.editing.html, which features a syllabus for a course taught by Mindy McAdams in magazine copy editing. It provides useful insight into the most common mistakes fixed by Copy Editors, as well as insight into the profession.
3. Purchase a copy of William Strunk, Jr., and E. B. White's *The Elements of Style,* a bible of grammar and usage since its first publication in 1957. Also check out a newer title, *Eats, Shoots & Leaves: The Zero Tolerance Approach to Punctuation* by Lynne Truss.
4. Review the 100 most often misspelled words in English at http://yourdictionary.com/library/misspelled.html, as well as the 100 most common usage errors at http://www.medill.northwestern.edu/faculty/roth/rr100/contents.html.
5. Try your hand at the number of copyediting tests found on the Internet. Take a look at, "The John Bremner editing test," http://www.ku.edu/~jschool/school/bremnertest.shtml, to get started.
6. Review the highlights of correct AP style through a quick reference at http://www.utexas.edu/coc/journalism/SOURCE/journal_links/AP_style.html.

PUBLISHER

CAREER PROFILE

Duties: Runs the business operations of a magazine, including advertising, marketing, sales, circulation, finance, and editorial; may also be the founder and/or owner of a magazine

Alternate Title(s): None

Salary Range: $50,000 to $200,000 and up

Employment Prospects: Fair

Advancement Prospects: Fair

Best Geographical Location(s): New York and other major cities

Prerequisites:

Education or Training—Bachelor's degree in journalism, business, or marketing; may have advanced degree

Experience—Ten or more years of experience to be hired at an established publication; varies for entrepreneurs

Special Skills and Personality Traits—Excellent understanding of the magazine publishing industry; strong sales and marketing skills; very good leadership and management skills

CAREER LADDER

```
┌─────────────────────────────────┐
│  Publisher, larger magazine or  │
│  magazine group or Magazine     │
│  Founder and Owner              │
└─────────────────────────────────┘

┌─────────────────────────────────┐
│           Publisher             │
└─────────────────────────────────┘

┌─────────────────────────────────┐
│  Associate Publisher, Director of│
│  Business Development, or        │
│  other high-level position       │
└─────────────────────────────────┘
```

Position Description

More often than not, everyone working for a magazine becomes invested in its success. If the magazine is doing well, so are its employees. The financial and critical success can be seen as a reflection of their jobs well done. However, when it comes to the bottom line, it is the Publisher who is accountable for it all.

Publishers determine the vision for a magazine and then the budget with which to carry it out. While editors in chief lead the magazine's contents, Publishers are responsible for all departments, including editorial, circulation, sales and marketing, advertising, promotions, and so on. The Publisher works closely with the heads of each of these departments to follow the progress for each issue, as well as the overall big picture—success. Publishers are always watching the numbers and making sure all is on track.

In terms of business functions, Publishers participate in and oversee sales, marketing, and advertising. They may direct national advertising sales, launch new campaigns, and direct marketing programs. Working with the financial department, they also allocate budgets for each area. Publishers direct their input to internal staff as well as external advertising agencies or other consultants.

Magazine Publishers come in all shapes and sizes. Some are employed by one magazine, while others are responsible for a magazine group. Other Publishers are journalists who combine their editorial background with business acumen. Still others are entrepreneurs, working in other business fields until they come up with an idea for a magazine they want to launch. These Publishers have a difficult job early on as they need to find financial capital as well as the appropriate staff to bring their dream to reality. Becoming a Publisher requires knowledge of entrepreneurship, how to write a business plan, and starting your own business.

Regardless of their realm, all Publishers are strategists. They can identify new business opportunities and implement goals. Their job requires them to combine corporate and financial targets with editorial vision to produce a magazine that works in both areas. A united vision is necessary for the magazine to succeed. Publishers work with editors in chief to formulate game plans and content that are consistent with the mission they both have in mind.

Advertising is another big part of a Publisher's job, as the revenue generated by ads drives much of the magazine's budget. Publishers often manage and maintain existing accounts, as well as generate new business. Experienced Publishers bring with them industry contacts that can be very valuable when expanding accounts. They work to build and grow a core base of advertisers that can be relied on for each issue.

Publishers also oversee circulation. They monitor such issues as newsstand distribution, direct mail, and subscription sourcing. Always thinking about how to reach new markets, Publishers work with the marketing and circulation departments to develop creative marketing plans and circulation strategy.

Their duties may include:

- Performing financial analysis
- Developing Web site expansion
- Working with vendors
- Negotiating contracts
- Working with production and design staff
- Evaluating plans for subscriber acquisition
- Reviewing materials for audits
- Meeting with clients
- Initiating new business opportunities
- Raising initial capital and funding
- Implementing creative launch ideas
- Interacting with the press and media
- Some writing and editing, depending on the publication
- Managing a sizable staff
- Speaking to community groups

At trade publications, Publishers may serve as ambassadors within the industry. Along with the editor in chief, they can serve as the face of the publication and build relationships with professional associations and industry leaders.

Furthermore, Publishers may have additional corporate responsibilities when they work for large companies. They frequently meet with the senior management of the magazine group or parent company. Publishers might prepare presentations for the senior management to inform them about the status of the magazine and how it is meeting its goals and targets.

Publishers hold high-level positions and they work long hours. When problems arise with the magazine, they are the troubleshooters, day and night. Travel can be frequent, taking place for conferences, stories, client meetings, and press opportunities.

Salaries

The salary level for magazine Publishers can vary considerably depending on their affiliation with the magazine. Some Publishers may also own the magazine, which can create virtually limitless salary opportunities, depending on its success. Publishers who own lucrative magazines can earn in the high six figures and more. However, those Publishers who own their magazines also face tremendous risk if the magazine fails or suddenly goes under.

Publishers who are employed by corporations can earn anywhere from $50,000 to $200,000 and up. Salary will depend upon years of experience, size and circulation of the magazine, and level of responsibility.

Employment Prospects

Technically, anyone with an idea for a magazine can become a magazine Publisher, given the capital or the ability to raise capital. However, employment prospects at established magazines are fair, since this high-level position does not frequently open up. Often, professionals are recruited from other magazines where they have demonstrated success or other business areas.

Advancement Prospects

Advancement prospects for Publishers are also fair. Publishers who have brought financial success at smaller magazines may move to larger magazines or to magazine groups for more responsibility. Others who have had extensive experience working for corporate-owned publications may find advancement through entrepreneurship and beginning their own magazine.

Education and Training

Magazine Publishers have a variety of educational backgrounds. While Publishers who are entrepreneurs do not have to conform to any educational requirements, those who are employed by magazines and the vast majority of all others hold bachelor's degrees. Many have majored in fields such as business, advertising, or marketing; however, some have studied journalism or English.

Graduate school in business or journalism may also be helpful for ultimate success. A combination of business training in marketing, advertising, finance, and sales along with knowledge of journalism and the publishing industry is ideal for running the helm of magazine.

Experience, Skills, and Personality Traits

Publishers usually have 10 to 15 years of experience in the publishing industry or related fields. Through this experience, they gather sales, marketing, circulation, and advertising expertise, as well as an understanding of what makes a successful magazine. They need a firm grasp of business concepts and models and how this relates to magazines in particular. Insiders say that it is very beneficial to have worked in several magazine areas, such as editorial, art, and business.

In addition to business skills and experience, Publishers need to be excellent communicators. As they work with staff, clients, and vendors, they need to be articulate, persuasive, and professional. They must be able to work independently, yet value teamwork greatly. Also, Publishers should have strong leadership and management skills, as they often supervise high-level staff members.

To remain competitive in the publishing industry, Publishers must stay one step ahead of the curve. They must know their market and anticipate changes before they occur as much as possible. By becoming experts in their area, Publishers can grow both professionally and personally.

Unions and Associations

Publishers may belong to professional associations including the Magazine Publishers of America, as well as others by type of publication such as the City and Regional Magazine Association.

Tips for Entry

1. Learn more about the magazine publishing industry and how to start a magazine through the following articles at: http://www.publishingbiz.com/html/articles.html and http://www.laughingbear.com/lbn.asp?mode=article&subMode=110_magazine.
2. Take courses in business, advertising, and entrepreneurship. Learn about business models, how to write a business plan, and how to be a successful manager.
3. Gain experience on the business side of publishing and journalism through internships and part-time jobs.
4. Read job descriptions for Publishers at sites such as http://www.mediabistro.com and http://www.journalismjobs.com.
5. Follow your passion to develop a niche area for yourself. Intern at magazines in that niche area and speak to professionals on staff.

PHOTOGRAPHER

CAREER PROFILE

Duties: Takes photographs for a magazine; may shoot video footage and/or write some captions and copy

Alternate Title(s): Photojournalist

Salary Range: $10,000 to $75,000 and up

Employment Prospects: Fair

Advancement Prospects: Fair

Best Geographical Location(s): Major cities, especially magazine publishing hubs like New York City

Prerequisites:

Education or Training—Bachelor's degree not required, but may be helpful in subjects such as photography or arts fields; some photography training necessary

Experience—Prior experience taking photographs and a viable portfolio; previous work on a magazine

Special Skills and Personality Traits—Creativity and artistic vision; excellent technical photography skills; good visual eye; ability to put people at ease; ability to work well under pressure

CAREER LADDER

```
┌─────────────────────────────────┐
│  Photographer, larger magazine or │
│         Photo Editor             │
└─────────────────────────────────┘

┌─────────────────────────────────┐
│         Photographer             │
└─────────────────────────────────┘

┌─────────────────────────────────┐
│ Photographer, smaller magazine or │
│         Photo Assistant          │
└─────────────────────────────────┘
```

Position Description

Magazine Photographers capture the visual effects that accompany the articles in their publications. Whether shooting high fashion models, victims of torture, war-ravaged landscapes, natural wonders, or simply ordinary people, they are responsible for the photo shoots that bring these stories to life. They use their artistic vision to tell the story behind the words and give readers more information to interpret the articles' meanings.

Unlike newspaper photographers, who often complete several assignments in one day, magazine Photographers often work on broader deadlines. Since magazines often are published weekly or monthly, Photographers usually complete one or two assignments per issue. Sometimes Photographers will go on location for magazine photo shoots. This may be to an exotic tropical locale or to a small town where the interview subject for the article lives. Other times, photos are taken in a studio near the magazine's offices.

Photographers run the photo shoots from start to finish. This can include scouting locations, deciding what equip-

ment to use, and hiring models. Furthermore, subjects for photographs must sign releases that they agree to have their pictures used in a magazine. Photographers may obtain these signed releases, sometimes working with the subjects to feel comfortable with the process.

Once the photos are taken, Photographers process the film. This process is often performed digitally, using computer disks. Photographers may send the images digitally back to the studio or magazine headquarters from on location if necessary. They work with photo editors to edit and make decisions about which shots will work best with the stories.

Without the pressure of breaking news, magazine Photographers can often focus more on the art of their photography. Setting the scene for a shoot is very important. When photographing people, it is important for Photographers develop good rapport with their subjects. The ability to put people at ease comes into play as Photographers build relationships and enable people to open up. Photographers also make use of lighting, exposure, shadows, and other features to convey the right mood for the shoot.

Their duties also may include:

- Taking posed pictures of people and things for feature stories
- Performing digital photo editing
- Developing film in a darkroom
- Working with reporters and editors
- Attending meetings with magazine management
- Taking direction from photo editors and other senior staff
- Shooting photo essays
- Writing captions

Photographers at magazines may have specialties (such as fashion or nature photography) or work as generalists. They usually complete assignments as handed down by the photo editor, art director, or creative director, but they may also play a role in brainstorming ideas and deciding which assignment to take. Many Photographers work on a freelance basis. They may work a variety of shifts and hours that often include evenings and weekends. Travel may be a big part of the job, or none at all, depending on the size and scope of the magazine.

Salaries

Salaries for magazine Photographers can vary greatly. In-house Photographers typically earn anywhere from $20,000 to $70,000 and up, depending on their magazine. At large national magazines, they can earn more. Since many Photographers work on a freelance basis, they are paid per assignment. Their salaries reflect the amount of hours they work, the reputation they have developed, and their entrepreneurial skills at marketing themselves and their work.

Employment Prospects

Employment prospects are fair for magazine Photographers. Staff Photographer positions are quite competitive and generally go to those who have considerable freelance experience and impressive portfolios.

To get prior photography experience and build a portfolio, working on a small scale is key. Aspiring Photographers can build their body of work through internships and photography and photojournalism courses. Furthermore, working as an assistant to a professional photographer can provide valuable exposure and contacts to break into the magazine industry.

Freelancing can be another good way to break into the job market. Working for hire at several different magazines helps Photographers get to know the staff and gives them a chance to prove their skill. Some Photographers may then move into full-time staff positions, while others enjoy the freedom they get from freelancing and find they can earn enough to sustain their career.

Advancement Prospects

Photographers can advance in several ways. Some work their way up to becoming photo editors at magazines, where they make decisions about artistic direction and manage a staff of photographers. Others advance by moving to staff positions at larger magazines with a greater variety and scope of assignments, as well as higher salaries. Still other Photographers start their own businesses where they do freelance work. Photographers who also know how to shoot video and have a multimedia/Internet background make themselves more marketable.

Some Photographers at magazines consider themselves journalists, while others consider themselves artists; many are a bit of both. Photographers with more of a photojournalism bent, working on news stories, may work for both magazines and newspapers.

Education and Training

While it is not necessary for Photographers to hold bachelor's degrees, it can help them get started in today's competitive job market. Photographers may take courses in a variety of fields, including art, photography, and photojournalism. Journalism course work helps Photographers to see their role as visual storytellers and may help them learn to write captions and other copy.

It is essential for magazine Photographers to have training in photography. Although there has been a move from the traditional darkroom to the "digital darkroom," consisting of computers in a well-lit room where editing and development now takes place, Photographers still must understand and know how to perform the darkroom process. Good Photographers must know how to both operate digital cameras and also develop pictures by hand in order to learn the craft.

Experience, Skills, and Personality Traits

Photographers at magazines should be creative and flexible, with a good eye and a strong artistic vision. As visual storytellers, they must be able to read an article and develop a sense for the right accompanying image. They must be able to shoot a variety of coverage while managing tight deadlines. Strong communication skills enable Photographers to work with writers, editors, and subjects effectively. This natural rapport, particularly with article subjects, is reflected in the emotion captured by their work.

Furthermore, they need the technical skills to back up this artistic vision. Photographers must be able to use both digital and regular cameras, know how to expose film, edit, and use a darkroom. They need to know how to expose film and balance color, along with other technical processes involved with film development and editing. Photographers must understand the role of light and its challenges, adapting to different conditions. In addition to understanding how to "soup" their film with darkroom chemicals, they must also know how to process a raw digital image into a JPEG file. Computer programs for editing such as Adobe Photo-Shop are also needed.

Unions and Associations

Magazine Photographers may belong to the National Press Photographers Association, a professional association dedicated to the advancement of photojournalism. They may also belong to the American Society of Media Photographers, the American Society of Picture Professionals, and the Professional Photographers of America.

Tips for Entry

1. Take a look at the Web site for the American Society of Media Photographers at http://www.asmp.org. The site offers information about membership, as well as educational programs and seminars.
2. Become an avid Photographer. Shoot pictures using both digital and regular cameras, learning how to develop images with both.
3. Intern at a magazine to gain a better understanding of magazine photography. Speak to photo editors about what they look for when they hire photographers for freelance or in-house positions.
4. Read a variety of magazines and note the differences in photography. Learn about style and technique, as well as how the pictures supplement the written text.
5. Gain experience shooting video as well, which can make you more marketable as more magazines go digital and feature streaming video on their Web sites.

SPECIALIZED WRITING AND REPORTING

POLITICAL CORRESPONDENT

CAREER PROFILE

Duties: Covers politics for a newspaper, magazine, Web site, publication, or television/radio station; reports on all issues relating to politics

Alternate Title(s): Political Writer, Political Reporter, White House Correspondent, Washington Correspondent

Salary Range: $25,000 to $60,000 and up

Employment Prospects: Fair

Advancement Prospects: Fair

Best Geographical Location(s): All, especially Washington, D.C.

Prerequisites:
   Education or Training—Bachelor's degree required; journalism or related field helpful; may also have educational background in political science, government, or law
   Experience—Most positions require at least five years of experience as a reporter; political and/or Capitol Hill experience can also be a plus.
   Special Skills and Personality Traits—Excellent writing, reporting, and editing skills; strong communication, interpersonal and interviewing skills; understanding of issues in government and politics and the legislative process

CAREER LADDER

```
┌─────────────────────────────┐
│  Political Correspondent,    │
│  larger market or Editor     │
└─────────────────────────────┘

┌─────────────────────────────┐
│  Political Correspondent     │
└─────────────────────────────┘

┌─────────────────────────────┐
│ Beat Reporter; General Assignment │
│ Reporter; or Political Correspondent, │
│ smaller market               │
└─────────────────────────────┘
```

Position Description

Reporting on politics is an important aspect of free speech and the democratic process of our country. It makes the public aware of what is happening in government at the local, state, and national level. Because politics has a different meaning at each of these levels, political beats can include:

- White House
- Congress
- National politics
- National security
- Foreign policy
- Economics
- Consumer economics
- Legal affairs
- Health policy and science
- Local congressional delegations
- State capitol
- Mayor's office

During election times, Political Correspondents may work seven days a week for intensely long hours. They accompany candidates on the campaign trail, informing readers or their audience about significant moments, new developments, and other issues that will affect voting. Political Correspondents cover what the candidates do and say, investigating their backgrounds and their views. Furthermore, they analyze the race as it progresses, as well as the tough questions that will help the public make decisions. Talking to voters and presenting their views and decision-making process also illuminates the public climate.

While Political Correspondents often focus on breaking news, they also handle longer, feature or investigative pieces. They delve into controversial issues and spend time interviewing politicians and voters alike, conducting background research. These stories often serve to drive support for candidates or issues. Some Political Correspondents cover one party or another with a subjective slant, while many remain neutral and objective. Columnists and editorial writers tend to be more partisan and offer their opinions.

Some Political Correspondents specifically cover the White House. They cover all issues related to the President—bills that are currently in progress, State of the Union, speeches, decisions, and more. They offer and interpret the facts to give their audience an understanding of what is happening. Knowledge of complex government issues helps them explain in terms that the public can follow.

Other Political Correspondents have a general Washington focus, including Congress, the Senate, the Supreme Court, and other Capitol Hill concerns. International politics is another area of specialization. On the state and local level, Political Correspondents cover the mayor or governor's office and state legislature.

Cultivating sources can be especially important and tricky for Political Correspondents. Developing relationships with major players is essential for getting the stories. However, becoming too much of an insider inhibits a reporter's ability to remain objective. Once again, ethics remain crucial for presenting the facts. Political Correspondents need excellent relationship-building skills, as well as reputations for being fair.

Their duties may include:

- Covering debates
- Reading and reporting on budgets
- Reporting on general news assignments as needed
- Covering spot and breaking news as well as longer in-depth pieces
- Attending press conferences and sessions of Congress
- Working with other departments such as news or features to prevent overlap
- Conducting interviews
- Bringing in exclusive stories
- Writing columns
- Identifying political trends
- Following politics at all levels

The press has a unique role in politics, with Political Correspondents inadvertently driving the political process at times. By covering major events and uncovering information, aspects are revealed that affect voting and public opinion. Political Correspondents have a responsibility to be fair and ethical, but to make sure voters have the facts as well.

Political Correspondents generate story ideas as well as receive assignments from their editors. Their hours are typically long and nontraditional. Travel is frequently required during elections, unless they cover a specific beat like a state capitol or Washington, where many are based.

Salaries

Political Correspondents face a wide range in salary depending on their employment setting as well as their level of experience. The Inland Press Association conducts an annual Newspaper Industry Compensation Survey, which is the authoritative "industry standard" for newspaper industry compensation planning. According to the survey, reporters with considerable experience (which is the level of most Political Correspondents) earned an average of $43,292 in total direct compensation in 2004. The range for reporters was from a low of $10,042 to a high salary of $163,926 at the experienced level. While these figures are for general reporters and are not particular to politics, they can be used as a guide.

Furthermore, Political Correspondents working for magazines and Web sites earn comparable ranges. In broadcasting, Political Correspondents may earn $80,000 or considerably more, especially if they are on-air in the national realm.

Employment Prospects

Employment prospects are fair for Political Correspondents. Because their topic is specialized, there are not as many opportunities as exist for generalists. Competition is tight, and jobs will go to those with extensive knowledge of politics and government.

As is the case with all reporting jobs, aspiring Political Correspondents should expect to start at the bottom at small papers covering any available beat. After proving themselves as reporters, they can look to focus some articles on politics and develop a specialty. During this time, developing a better understanding of the political process and cultivating relationships with key players can be very helpful.

Advancement Prospects

Political Correspondents often advance by moving from smaller publications to larger ones. At national newspapers, covering politics becomes more influential with greater responsibility. Political Correspondents may also specialize as Washington or White House reporters. They can move from local and state to national politics. Within broadcasting, the lucky few may even have their own programs where they moderate political debates.

Education and Training

Political Correspondents have bachelor's degrees in journalism or related fields. They may have degrees in other subjects including liberal arts as well as political science, government, and economics, which can be very helpful, especially when combined with some journalism course work or training. Other Political Correspondents may hold master's degrees in journalism or other fields.

While Political Correspondents must be journalists first with mastery over writing and reporting, they also need to have a good knowledge of politics and government. Whether it comes from academic study, internships and work experience, or personal interest, a knowledge of U.S. government on different levels, the legislative process, and the structure of political campaigns is essential. Internships not only in journalism but also on Capitol Hill can be very beneficial.

Experience, Skills, and Personality Traits

Political Correspondents need excellent writing and reporting skills. Creativity and curiosity help generate interesting and informative stories. Persistence, tenacity, and a desire to dig deeper enable them to get the facts of a story without backing down. Also, strong communication and interpersonal skills help them to conduct interviews and deal with politicians, constituents, lobbyists, and voters on a variety of levels. Confidence and the ability to gain people's trust and put them at ease add to good reporting. Most Political Correspondents have at least five years of prior reporting experience.

Furthermore, Political Correspondents must be passionate about politics and government—some are self-described "policy wonks"—in order to write about it with intelligence and insight. They need to know about government and how it works. Ambitious and savvy, they can go after difficult stories and adhere to tight deadlines. They are not afraid to uncover scandal, but they need strong ethics to guide their decisions.

Unions and Associations

While there is not a professional association specifically for journalists covering politics, Political Correspondents can belong to a variety of professional associations including the National Writers Union and the American Society of Journalists and Authors.

Tips for Entry

1. Consider an internship on Capitol Hill to learn more about the workings of the government. Get some advice from ehow.com at http://www.ehow.com/how_ 11151_internship-capitol-hill.html.
2. Volunteer on a political campaign for a candidate you support. You will gain valuable insight about both the political process and the role of the press.
3. Read about politics in several different newspapers, including columns and editorials. Take note of which articles are objective and which offer opinions. What slant do they take, and how does it reflect the demographics of its readership? Which reporters do you admire and why?
4. Take courses in both journalism and politics to hone your writing and reporting skills, as well as your government knowledge.
5. There are many Web logs on the Internet that relate to political journalism. Sites to explore include http:// journalism.nyu.edu/pubzone/weblogs/pressthink/ 2003/08/18/introduction_ghost.html and http://www. usatoday.com/news/politicselections/nation/2003-12- 30-blogging-usat_x.htm.

SCIENCE WRITER

CAREER PROFILE

Duties: Writes and reports about science, health, or medical topics and breakthroughs for a newspaper, magazine, Web site, or other publication

Alternate Title(s): Health Writer, Medical Writer, Science Reporter, Science Journalist

Salary Range: $20,000 to $60,000 and up

Employment Prospects: Good

Advancement Prospects: Good

Best Geographical Location(s): All

Prerequisites:

    Education or Training—Bachelor's degree in science or journalism

    Experience—Several years of writing and reporting experience

    Special Skills and Personality Traits—Excellent writing and reporting skills; strong research ability; knowledge of science, health, or medicine, and scientific issues

CAREER LADDER

```
+---------------------------------------+
|   Science Editor or Science Writer,   |
|            larger publication          |
+---------------------------------------+

+---------------------------------------+
|            Science Writer              |
+---------------------------------------+

+---------------------------------------+
|    General Assignment Reporter,        |
|    Staff Writer, or Scientist          |
+---------------------------------------+
```

Position Description

Each day, there are new breakthroughs in science and health that change our society. News large and small, ranging from space exploration and fossil discoveries to new drugs that fight disease and nutrition tips that promote weight loss, is critical for the public to hear. Science Writers are responsible for bringing these scientific discoveries into our homes, keeping people informed about the advances that affect their lives.

Many topics comprise science writing. Astronomy, geology, biotechnology, and engineering are accompanied by medicine and health. A Science Writer may cover global warming, a new comet in the solar system, and continental shift, as well as new pharmaceuticals and FDA approval, treatments for cancer, health insurance, animal behavior, and a low-fat diet. Some Science Writers have specialties in different areas such as medical, health, or psychology writing, while others cover a variety of topics.

Science Writers may be employed by newspapers, magazines, Web sites, or as freelancers, among other settings. They often cover a combination of breaking news, feature, and investigative stories. It is important for Science Writers to be up-to-date with all science news. They are avid researchers, scanning the Internet and wire services for scientific information. Furthermore, they read scientific and medical journals as well as other publications to get ideas and information. They may attend scientific meetings and conferences as well. Through interviews and interactions with scientists, Science Writers get much of their most valuable information.

An essential part of the job of a Science Writer is to make technical language accessible to the public. While scientists have their epiphanies in their labs, their findings may be difficult to explain to people without scientific knowledge. Science Writers know how to make information relevant to their readers. Depending on their publication, they set the tone and level of complexity to fit their audience. In this way, Science Writers serve as a link between scientists and the public, helping to make people aware of issues that can impact them. By translating news that can have legal, ethical, and political implications, they help people become educated.

Furthermore, Science Writers that specialize in health and medicine perform a service for their communities. As Americans age and develop habits that interfere with a healthy lifestyle, Science Writers can focus on issues that may help them make changes. Science Writers working for local publications can emphasize issues of concern to their specific audience.

Science writing can be quite technical, or more newsy and informative. Different publications vary greatly. For example, writing for a serious science magazine involves a different style than working for a health and fitness magazine or covering science for a national newspaper. Science Writers may use quantitative detail statistics, graphs, and charts to demonstrate information. Furthermore, they may use qualitative methods as well such as personal interviews and anecdotes.

Their duties may include:

• Interviewing scientists, doctors, and other health professionals
• Writing profiles and human interest stories about scientists, doctors, and other health professionals, as well as patients and people affected by health issues
• Attending scientific conferences and meetings
• Working with editors to brainstorm ideas
• Collaborating with photographers and artists to find the right graphics for a story
• Developing relationships with people in the scientific community
• Reporting on public health concerns stemming from disasters such as earthquakes or oil spills
• Researching issues of importance to their readers
• Keeping abreast of cutting-edge developments and research trends
• Reading science-related publications
• Visiting hospitals and research institutes

Some Science Writers write for the general public, while others write for professional audiences of doctors, engineers, and scientists. This underscores the point that Science Writers must know their readers and write and report accordingly. When working for scientific publications, Science Writers use the language and terminology of those professions.

Travel may be required for Science Writers. Occasionally, they will accompany scientists on discovery missions such as paleontology digs and report on the process and findings. Other travel may occur for interviews and for attending conferences.

Science Writers can use a wide variety of journalistic skills. A good news sense and hard-nosed reporting is required for acting quickly on breaking developments, while creativity and humor may come into play during feature stories. Curiosity and persistence drive investigative

pieces, and technical expertise helps Science Writers handle more scholarly work. Whether they develop niche areas for themselves or stay as generalists, this diversity is the reason many Science Writers greatly enjoy their work.

Salaries

The Council for the Advancement of Science Writing (CASW) offers salary information for Science Writers working in a variety of settings, including newspapers, magazines, new media, and freelance. According to the CASW, starting salaries are in the $20,000 to $30,000 range for journalism school graduates in entry-level general assignment reporters' jobs, depending on the size of the newspaper. Higher starting salaries are more likely for journalists with specialized master's degrees in science writing, who begin as Science Writers at larger newspapers. Experienced science writers and editors at major newspapers may make more than $60,000 a year.

The CASW also reports that magazine staff Science Writers may start at slightly better salaries of around $30,000 per year, ranging to $100,000 per year for experienced senior correspondents and editors at national magazines. Salaries in new media for content producers at Web sites tend to be somewhat higher than those for print journalists, with beginning salaries around $35,000.

Freelance Science Writers often earn less than other science journalists who work full-time as staff writers. They usually earn about $1.00 per word for magazine articles and even less for newspaper articles. A 3,000-word magazine article may take a month to produce, and one such article per month translates into a $36,000 annual salary for an experienced freelancer.

Some Science Writers become authors of science books, though they usually hold down other staff writing jobs. The CASW states that despite occasional six-figure advances for major books, authors earn average advances on royalties of between $5,000 and $25,000. However, science writers who are committed to writing many books and establishing a reputation can earn a living at it.

Employment Prospects

Overall, employment prospects are good for Science Writers. Because of the diversity of science, medical, and health topics, they can work for more types of publications than some other reporters and writers. In addition to a traditional journalism setting such as newspapers and magazines, Science Writers may also work for health organizations, where they write material to explain the organization's programs and overall mission.

Many Science Writers begin as general assignment reporters at small newspapers before they are able to specialize. Others work through the magazine industry as staff writers. Still others develop a science niche as freelance writers before landing a staff job. Scientists, doctors, and health professionals with an interest in and ability for journalism may also make the transition to become Science Writers.

Advancement Prospects

Science Writers can advance by moving to larger publications for higher salaries, responsibilities, and prestige. Those who have developed a niche area or a following for their work may be offered more promising assignments or their own columns. Other Science Writers may choose to become science editors, managing a staff of writers.

Another writing opportunity comes through authoring books, since there is a large market for popular science and health books. Science Writers may write books on a wide range of topics, and the more journalism experience they have, the easier it can be for them to break into this market.

Education and Training

Science Writers typically have bachelor's degrees in either journalism or science. Knowledge in both of these areas combines the best of both worlds. Courses in science writing are offered through many journalism programs and can be very helpful. Graduate degrees in science and journalism are also common. Some schools offer specializations in science journalism, such as the program offered by the University of Maryland at http://www.physics.umd.edu/academics/ugrad/psci/scijour.html.

Whether or not Science Writers have formal education in science, it is essential that they understand scientific fields, particularly those about which they write. Science fields may include the biological sciences, the physical sciences, health fields, and medicine. Some Science Writers may hold joint graduate degrees in science and journalism. This combination of training is crucial for success in science writing since it demonstrates both the writing and reporting ability needed to be a strong journalist and the science understanding to make sense of news and gain credibility in the scientific community.

Experience, Skills, and Personality Traits

A passion for science and the desire to continue learning is needed in order to be a Science Writer. The field is not for a reporter interested in maintaining the status quo. Science Writers continuously need to learn new jargon, as well as new developments that affect science overall. They must have intellectual curiosity to succeed and stay on top of breaking news.

Science Writers also must have excellent writing, reporting, and editing skills. Often, they need the ability to translate complex information into terms that the average person can understand. They must be able to read their audience and write in a style that is both engaging and informative.

Additionally, Science Writers need knowledge of science. While work experience in a scientific, medical, or health field is an asset, it is not required. However, a desire to learn more about science, as well as a logical, analytical mind and excellent research skills is crucial.

It is also important for Science Writers to be able to adhere to tight deadlines and juggle many responsibilities at once. They need initiative and creativity to generate stories and the ability to work independently. Strong communication skills enable them to work with scientists, editors, and other professionals.

Unions and Associations

There are a number of professional associations geared toward science writers of different specialties. They include the American Medical Writers Association and the National Association of Science Writers.

Tips for Entry

1. Explore and read science magazines such as *Scientific American* (http://www.sciam.com/), *Discover* (http://www.discover.com/), and *Popular Science* (http://www.popsci.com/popsci/), as well as health publications such as *Men's Health* (http://www.menshealth.com) and *Prevention* (http://www.prevention.com). Consider internship opportunities in these settings.

2. There are many books that help people learn how to become Science Writers. Take a look at *The Health Writer's Handbook* by Barbara Gaster, M.D. and *A Field Guide for Science Writers* by Deborah Blum.

3. Visit the Web site of the National Association of Science Writers at http://www.nasw.org. Also see the Web site for the Council for the Advancement of Science Writing at http://www.casw.org/. These sites offer good information about the field of science writing.

4. Which area of science or health interests you? Find a specialty area and study the field. At the same time, hone your writing skills through courses in English and journalism.

5. Try an internship at a science-related magazine, public relations firm, or museum.

BUSINESS REPORTER

CAREER PROFILE

Duties: Covers business and finance topics for a newspaper, magazine, Web site, or other publication; reports on all issues relating to business

Alternate Title(s): Business Writer, Financial Reporter, Financial Writer

Salary Range: $25,000 to $80,000 and up

Employment Prospects: Fair

Advancement Prospects: Fair

Best Geographical Location(s): All

Prerequisites:

Education or Training—Bachelor's degree in journalism or related field helpful; educational background in business or finance also valuable

Experience—Several years as a reporter; business experience also a plus

Special Skills and Personality Traits—Excellent writing, reporting, and editing skills; good communication and interviewing skills; understanding of business and financial issues

CAREER LADDER

```
┌─────────────────────────────────┐
│  Business Reporter, larger paper or │
│         Business Editor          │
└─────────────────────────────────┘

┌─────────────────────────────────┐
│        Business Reporter          │
└─────────────────────────────────┘

┌─────────────────────────────────┐
│  Beat Reporter or Business Reporter, │
│           smaller paper           │
└─────────────────────────────────┘
```

Position Description

Money drives the news in many different ways. The economy affects the job market, real estate, politics, funding for the arts and education, and just about everything else in our daily lives. Business Reporters bring this information to readers and explain its relevance. The stereotype might maintain that Business Reporters just follow the stock market, but in actuality, they cover many different aspects of business news that have implications for all of us.

Business Reporters can work for newspapers, magazines, Web sites, or other publications; they can also do freelance work. While there are a number of publications that entirely focus on business, most daily newspapers and news magazines have business sections. Some Business Reporters have specific specialty areas, while many others cover a variety of topics.

Possible business beats include:

- Banking and finance, including the stock market
- Labor and unions
- Real estate
- Hospitality and tourism
- Retail
- Health care
- Technology
- Job market
- Manufacturing
- Personal finance
- U.S. economy

Assignments can vary tremendously, ranging from covering corporate mergers and CEO scandals to the grand opening of a local retail shop. Business Reporters should be versatile, with the ability to talk to billionaire tycoons and unemployed union workers alike.

Like other writers and reporters, Business Reporters receive some assignments from their supervisor (usually a business editor), as well as through generating ideas on their own. Often they cover a combination of breaking news stories with short deadlines and longer feature and investigative pieces that delve deeper into people, problems, solutions, and results.

Depending on their employment setting, Business Reporters may need to find a daily story, complete several per week, write on a monthly basis, or take even longer on enterprise stories. In any situation, they need to be able to find the news and understand what will make an interesting story. They use a combination of interviews with contacts as well as thorough research to accomplish their goals. Good relationships with reliable sources spanning different business areas are essential.

In the world of business journalism, numbers matter. Business Reporters must ask the question of "how much" and not hesitate to bring up issues of money in their interviews. This focus on cost and the bottom line is what distinguishes business stories from others. A skilled Business Reporter can take most topics in the news—such as education, politics, and entertainment—and find a business angle on which to report.

Additional duties may include:

- Reading and understanding documents such as annual reports and earnings reports
- Analyzing SEC (the U.S. Securities and Exchange Commission) findings
- Filling in for the business editor on occasion
- Reporting on general news assignments
- Working with other departments such as news or features to prevent overlap
- Conducting interviews with a variety of sources
- Working with the graphics department to present graphs and charts
- Reviewing public records
- Attending meetings with editors to brainstorm story ideas
- Conducting research
- Identifying trends

Business Reporters must have an understanding of business and finance and be comfortable working with numbers. They often read and analyze complex information so they can make sense of it to their readers. Therefore it is important not only that they can follow business and finance but also that they can translate its technical jargon into simple language.

Hours for Business Reporters can vary depending on their specific focus and their type of employment. For example, those covering foreign markets for a newspaper may begin their day at 4 A.M. in order to coordinate with time differences. Generally, Business Reporters at magazines or at publications that do not feature breaking news have more regular daytime hours. Those Business Reporters who freelance will also have flexibility. However, in all cases, some interviews may also be conducted at unlikely times. Travel may be required for certain stories.

Salaries
There can be much salary difference for Business Reporters depending on their employment setting, educational background, and level of experience.

Within the newspaper industry, the Inland Press Association conducts an annual Newspaper Industry Compensation Survey, which is the authoritative "industry standard" for newspaper industry compensation planning. According to the survey, entry-level reporters earned an average of $28,162 per year in 2004 in total direct compensation. With considerable experience, that average went up to $43,292. The range for reporters was from a low of $10,042 to a high salary of $163,926 at the experienced level.

While these figures are for general reporters and are not particular to business, they can be used as a guide. Insiders say that Business Reporters tend to earn slightly more than the average, particularly at financial publications.

Furthermore, Business Reporters working for magazines and Web sites earn comparable ranges. They may work as freelancers for several types of publications.

Employment Prospects
Business Reporters have fair employment prospects. With a specialized topic, they might not find as many opportunities as a generalist can. However, since business is a common beat, their expertise can make them marketable for the jobs that do come up.

While some Business Reporters work exclusively for newspapers, magazines, and Web sites, others write for a combination of the three. They may be contributing writers to several publications based on their niche area and contacts. Some make their career out of freelancing, which can offer a variety of writing assignments but no guaranteed stability.

As is typical in journalism, aspiring Business Reporters should expect to start at the bottom at small papers covering any available beat. Business may be overlooked by some journalists as dry or boring, so those with an interest may be able to get some stories early on. Entry-level jobs at business-specific publications can also be a good way to get started.

Advancement Prospects
Business Reporters can advance by moving into an editorial role, such as a business editor, where they supervise other reporters and writers. Also, they can move from smaller publications to larger ones, where they cover more prominent topics for more money and recognition.

As Business Reporters move to handle issues of national attention, this can open other doors. By developing a following through their insight and writing style, they may write columns, freelance articles, or even books.

Education and Training
Many Business Reporters hold bachelor's degrees in journalism or a related field. Others may study liberal arts

with some journalism course work or training as well. It is also common for Business Reporters to hold master's degrees in journalism to complement their undergraduate background.

While it is not required for Business Reporters to have formal degrees in the business field, it is crucial that they have some understanding of business, economics, and finance. This can be accomplished through coursework or even undergraduate majors in these fields, or through the Master of Business Administration (MBA) graduate degree. Some Business Reporters may hold joint graduate degrees in business and journalism.

The combination of journalism and business knowledge is essential for success in the field. It demonstrates the mastery of skills like writing and reporting to be a good journalist, as well as the financial understanding to conduct hard-hitting interviews and gain credibility.

Experience, Skills, and Personality Traits

Business Reporters need superior writing and reporting skills. Inquisitive and skeptical, they can't be afraid to ask tough questions about money and earnings, topics most of us have been taught to avoid. Their strong communication skills enable them to interview people from all types of backgrounds and present their stories in a fair and objective way.

Also, Business Reporters must be able to adhere to tight deadlines. They often juggle numerous tasks at once, including working on more than one story at a time. In addition to their knowledge, Business Reporters should be passionate about business. Whatever their beat, they need to not only know it but also to care about it in order to make their readers care too.

Knowledge of computer programs such as QuarkXPress can be helpful for Business Reporters who also work on copyediting, layout, or design.

Unions and Associations

Many Business Reporters belong to the Society for Business Editors and Writers, the largest association for business editors and writers in North America. They may also belong to the American Society of Business Publication Editors (http://www.asbpe.org/), the National Writers Union, and the American Society of Journalists and Authors.

Tips for Entry

1. There are many publications specific to business. Explore the different types of writing in newspapers such as the *Wall Street Journal* (http://online.wsj.com/public/us) and magazines such as *BusinessWeek* (http://www.businessweek.com), as well as their online features.

2. Network through the Society for Business Editors and Writers (http://www.sabew.org/) to learn more about the field.

3. Take courses in economics, business, and finance to better understand these topics. What are the specific elements that interest you?

4. Become an avid reader of the business section of your local daily paper. Study the different topics that fall under the business realm, as well as the different types of articles (news, features, investigative).

5. Gain valuable experience through internships. Try working in a variety of settings such as newspapers, magazines, and new media to see which format is best for you.

SPORTSWRITER

CAREER PROFILE

Duties: Covers sports for newspapers, magazines, and Internet publications; may write, report, and edit; attends games and other sporting events

Alternate Title(s): Sports Journalist, Sports Reporter

Salary Range: $20,000 to $200,000 and up

Employment Prospects: Fair

Advancement Prospects: Good

Best Geographical Location(s): All

Prerequisites:

Education or Training—Bachelor's degree in journalism or related field

Experience—One to 10 years of journalism experience and sports coverage; varies by position

Special Skills and Personality Traits—Interest in and knowledge of sports; excellent writing, reporting, and editing skills; tact and diplomacy; good interviewing and communication skills

CAREER LADDER

```
┌─────────────────────────────────┐
│   Sportswriter, larger market or │
│           Sports Editor          │
└─────────────────────────────────┘

┌─────────────────────────────────┐
│           Sportswriter           │
└─────────────────────────────────┘

┌─────────────────────────────────┐
│   Sportswriter, smaller paper or │
│           Beat Reporter          │
└─────────────────────────────────┘
```

Position Description

Combining a passion for sports with a passion for writing is the ideal goal of a Sportswriter. One of these passions alone is not enough. Many people are sports fans but cannot sit down and write an article giving the play-by-play of a game. Others are reporters who know their craft but are not enthusiastic enough for the lively and insightful coverage needed for success. Sportswriters are able to bring their knowledge of both sports and journalism to their jobs.

Sportswriters may report, write, edit, and design pages at various points in their careers. At small papers, they may even take pictures. This is why the knowledge of journalism is so critical. The line between sports and news is often blurred. For example, a Sportswriter may be covering a game where a fire breaks out. He or she will need to jump into news reporting mode to get the whole story, not merely the score of the game.

Typically for the field, Sportswriters usually begin at small-town weekly or daily papers. Here, the scope of what they cover can be very broad. They might cover high school games in all sports, as well as local colleges and regional events. Coverage is also determined by the region, and can include a diverse range like minor league baseball, Little League, skiing, boating, auto racing, horse racing, and golf, among others.

As Sportswriters work their way up to larger papers, they will often begin with the high school or college beat. With experience, they may work up to the professionals and specialize in one or several sports. For example, a Sportswriter covering basketball may cover the local professional team as well as the area men's and women's college teams. He or she may also write features and cover a second sport such as tennis.

Additionally, Sportswriters often handle a combination of breaking news, features, and longer enterprise pieces. Early in their careers, they report on games. With more experience, they provide more analysis and commentary. They may give their opinions on the personalities of the athletes, the coaches, the referees, and the fans. Some Sportswriters have weekly or even daily columns where they comment on current sports topics.

Telling the story behind the scores is what sports journalism is really about. Anyone can watch a game or find out the winner; it is the Sportswriter that goes beyond the numbers to engage readers. By getting to know the teams and their successes and failures, they develop material that gives readers more than just what they can see on the screen. In addition to game coverage, there are many other stories within sports. Changes and developments, ceremonies, and hot issues such as steroid use are just a few of the other areas about which Sportswriters may write.

Relationships with coaches and players are crucial to a Sportswriter. He or she needs to walk the fine line between putting people at ease but not getting too close. Mutual respect is the key here. Coaches and players will not talk to journalists they do not like. Once they have that respect, Sportswriters need to value these relationships, yet remain objective in order to tell the true story. With a good rapport in place, the teams can take criticism without insult, and Sportswriters can give them advance warning about any controversial content so they can be prepared.

Occasionally, tensions may arise between Sportswriters and their fellow newspaper staffers. For example, during an event such as the World Series, decisions must be made about how news will be handled on the front page. Reporters, photographers, and editors in both sports and news all will have a say about their opinions.

Additional duties may include:

- Performing page design, layout, and pagination
- Writing columns or opinion pieces
- Writing longer features and human interest pieces about sports personalities
- Meeting with the news department to determine coverage
- Meeting with players, coaches, and other sports professionals
- Conducting interviews
- Taking photographs
- Attending games and other sports industry events
- Working with editors and other reporters
- Keeping up on sports news

Some travel is required for Sportswriters, with more extensive travel common at larger papers. They may travel locally to games and go long distances for playoffs or tournaments.

Hours will vary by shift, but they are also determined by the various beats and game times. Since most sports are played in the late afternoon and evenings, Sportswriters should expect some late night work to be a regular part of their routine.

Sportswriters often know more about their schedule in advance than other types of reporters. Since games are planned ahead, certain coverage will be known each week rather than waiting for breaking news to happen. Along with that regular coverage, however, there often is breaking news as coaches resign, players are traded, and scandals come out.

Salaries

Sportswriters can have a large salary range, depending on the size of their paper. According to the Inland Press Association's Newspaper Industry Compensation Survey, entry-level reporters earned an average of $28,162 per year in 2004 in total direct compensation. With considerable experience, that average went up to $43,292. The range for reporters was from a low of $10,042 to a high salary of $163,926 at the experienced level. While these figures are for general reporters and are not particular to sports, they can be used as a guide.

Furthermore, some Sportswriters work as columnists. The Inland Press Association's survey shows that the average total direct compensation for a columnist was $61,323 in 2004. The range spanned from a low of $16,640 to high of $385,000 for those who achieve national syndication.

Sportswriters working for magazines or Web sites generally earn comparable salaries to the newspaper industry.

Employment Prospects

Becoming a Sportswriter is one of the more competitive areas within journalism. Prospective Sportswriters must be willing to start out at small papers in tiny towns, beginning with whatever beats they are given. For those who find early jobs on other beats, insiders recommend developing a relationship with the sports editor in order to be considered for any openings as they arise.

Internships are essential for aspiring Sportswriters. Covering sports for high school or college papers develops the interest and skills early on and helps Sportswriters get hired after graduation. Also, knowledge of design, layout, and photography can help Sportswriters land their first job.

Advancement Prospects

The hierarchy in sports journalism is similar to that in news. One may begin as a sports reporter for a small weekly and advance to a similar position at a larger paper. Some reporters will want to go on to the editorial track after several years, becoming assistant sports editors and then sports editors. Others will continue to make a name for themselves by reporting and writing, developing a following through their opinion and insight.

Sportswriters also write for sports-related magazines, Web sites, and different publications other than newspapers. They may write books, articles, and columns about sports topics.

Education and Training

Most Sportswriters have bachelor's degrees in journalism or related fields. Through journalism education, they learn not only about writing and reporting but also about design, layout, and editing. Some Sportswriters have master's degrees in journalism as well.

Some Sportswriters may work their way up into the field with an athletic background, rather than a journalism background, but this is very unlikely in print journalism. Broadcasting is a much more common fit for former athletes interested in sports journalism.

Experience, Skills, and Personality Traits

To put it simply, Sportswriters must know sports. They cannot possibly know everything about every sport, but beginning with good knowledge of several is a good starting point. Some Sportswriters were high school or college athletes themselves, but that is not required. However, being a sports fan is.

In addition to sports, Sportswriters must also know journalism. They need the tangible writing, reporting, and editing skills; layout and design helps for many newspaper reporting positions. A firm grasp of AP (Associated Press) Style is a must.

Furthermore, Sportswriters must be deadline-oriented and able to work under pressure. They need high energy to work nights and stay until the last overtime is played. The ability to think and reason quickly and logically is important as stories may come up suddenly and Sportswriters need to react quickly. Good communication skills and tact are valuable in developing relationships with coaches and players.

Unions and Associations

Sportswriters can belong to a variety of professional associations including the Associated Press Sports Editors, the Association for Women in Sports Media, and the Society of Professional Journalists.

Also, different cities and states have associations for sports writers. Some include the Philadelphia Sports Writers Association (http://pswa.org/) and the Florida Sports Writers Association (http://www.fswaonline.org/). More associations can be found by searching the Internet with key words.

Furthermore, the site sportswriters.net (http://www.sportswriters.net/) has links to the Football Writers Association of America, the Arena Football League Writers Association, the United States Basketball Writers Association, and the National Collegiate Baseball Writers.

Tips for Entry

1. Make yourself marketable by developing a range of valuable skills. Learn how to report, edit, and design through journalism courses.
2. About which sports are you passionate? As you watch and attend games, consider the behind-the-scenes stories. Read newspaper sports sections avidly, as well as publications such as *Sports Illustrated*. Think about which sports writers you admire and why.
3. Gain experience covering sports for your high school, college, or local paper. Be willing to work for free just to get your foot in the door. Remember that even covering Little League games is a good way to start.
4. Take a look at the Web site for the Associated Press Sports Editors at http://apse.dallasnews.com/. It contains information about membership, conferences, job listings, and more.
5. Although sports journalism has been historically male-dominated, there are a number of prominent women sports journalists and the field is becoming wide open. If you are a woman, developing a niche area and finding mentors can be very helpful. Check out the Web site of the Association for Women in Sports Media at http://www.awsmonline.org/ and the Women's Sports Foundation at http://www.womenssportsfoundation.org/.

FOOD WRITER

CAREER PROFILE

Duties: Writes about food and/or wine for a newspaper, magazine, or other publication; offers critiques and ratings

Alternate Title(s): Food Critic, Restaurant Reviewer, Food and Wine Writer

Salary Range: $20,000 to $70,000 and up

Employment Prospects: Poor to Fair

Advancement Prospects: Fair

Best Geographical Location(s): All, with the best opportunities in larger cities

Prerequisites:

Education or Training—Degree in journalism or culinary training

Experience—Several years of writing and reporting experience and/or culinary work

Special Skills and Personality Traits—Excellent writing and reporting skills; knowledge of food and wine; adventurous palate; strong communication skills

CAREER LADDER

```
┌─────────────────────────────────────┐
│  Food Writer, larger publication or  │
│            Food Editor               │
└─────────────────────────────────────┘

┌─────────────────────────────────────┐
│             Food Writer              │
└─────────────────────────────────────┘

┌─────────────────────────────────────┐
│   General Assignment Reporter,       │
│      Staff Writer, or Chef           │
└─────────────────────────────────────┘
```

Position Description

Imagine getting paid to eat for a living. In essence, that is what Food Writers do. However, the job entails much more than simple wining and dining. Food Writers offer critiques on new restaurants, wines, eating trends, and more.

Food Writers can work in a variety of settings. At newspapers, they often write for a dining, food and wine, arts, entertainment, or features section. They might review restaurants in a number of different price or food categories, cover openings of new food stores and events, rate wines, interview chefs or restaurant owners, write feature stories related to food, and write pieces that include recipes. They may cover similar topics for general magazines and Web sites; in addition, they can work for specialty publications dedicated to food and wine. Furthermore, some Food Writers work as freelancers and authors.

While not all Food Writers are also critics, many do write restaurant reviews. Like other critics, they devise a rating system to account for all factors that contribute to a restaurant's success—food, service, atmosphere, price/value, cleanliness, noise level, presentation, and overall dining experience. They must be willing to try many things on the menu and to analyze them with an expert's palate, not just based on taste alone. Food Writers consider how the chef prepared the meal, looking for creativity in terms of ingredients and presentation. They examine the menu, looking to see new and innovative ideas and approaches. Some offer a star system as a rating with five stars being outstanding.

Food Writers may be faced with the challenge of chefs and restaurant owners who expect good publicity in exchange for free meals. Since a review by a prominent critic can have an impact on a restaurant's success, chefs can become very angry, questioning the writer's expertise and wanting to strike a deal. Food Writers who develop personal relationships with chefs or proprietors may find it difficult to remain objective. However, it is important for Food Writers to remain professional and detached, offering their ratings as a guide to readers. Some Food Writers may visit a restaurant several times before writing about it, in order not to base their review on only one experience.

Chefs and restaurant staff are often nervous when a critic arrives. If a prominent critic is dining, the staff may feel the need to give special treatment in exchange for a positive review. Some Food Writers report going to restaurants incognito and providing false names on their reservation. While some see this as dishonest, others say it is the only way to judge the restaurant experience for the average person. Their reviews serve to help people decide where to spend their money for dining.

Food Writers offer a combination of facts and opinions to serve as credible sources. In their reviews and articles, they provide tangible facts about prices, menu items, and decor. Furthermore, they share their educated opinion about less tangible factors such as taste and service. Food Writers must have excellent background knowledge of food and culinary history to make their judgments. They use evidence to justify their conclusions and analyze their experience.

In addition to reviewing restaurants, Food Writers cover other issues of importance in dining. They may have specialties in areas such as wine, Italian cooking, budget dining, vegetarian lifestyle, family establishments, or desserts and pastries. Some may focus on food preparation and cooking, rather than dining. Furthermore, different communities have various food trends and important issues such as organic produce or free-range farms.

Often, Food Writers conduct interviews and write human-interest pieces that relate in some way to food. They may offer tips about barbecuing in the summer and suggestions about pairing food and drink. Their writing contributes to their readers' lifestyles. Some Food Writers have columns as well.

Their duties may include:

* Covering food events
* Visiting wineries, farms, or factories where food or wine is produced
* Researching and reporting on food trends
* Contributing to cookbooks
* Trying exotic dishes
* Speaking to restaurant patrons and wait staff
* Collaborating with travel or entertainment writers
* Working with editors to generate story ideas and complete assignments
* Creating a diverse list of restaurant genres and locations to review
* Writing books in conjunction with chefs
* Answering reader mail
* Working with copy editors and page designers on formatting
* Working with photographers and food stylists

Food Writers may eat in restaurants several times a week. While for many this is one of the best parts about their job, some Food Writers do say that it gets tiring to go out all time. Others note that they need to exercise in order to balance out the sometime excess of rich and fattening foods.

Although they enjoy their meals, Food Writers cannot merely sit back and relax while they dine. They must take notes and pay attention to every detail of their experience. Staff Food Writers have expenses covered by their publication and may get to bring a guest. Freelance Food Writers and those at small publications typically have much smaller budgets.

An interesting aspect of food writing is that it can combine several types of journalism. Food Writers often include components of travel, entertainment, and health for different stories. With our culture of celebrity chefs and trendy restaurants, the lucky few Food Writers become something of celebrities themselves. The rest, however, are satisfied informing their local communities and doing something they enjoy.

Salaries

Salaries for full-time staff Food Writers vary depending on the level and responsibility of their position. In the newspaper industry, experienced reporters can earn in the $40,000 to $50,000 range. The Newspaper Industry Compensation Survey, conducted annually by the Inland Press Association, shows that experienced reporters earned an average of $43,292 per year in 2004 in total direct compensation.

At magazines, Web sites, and publishing companies, Food Writers can earn comparable salaries and sometimes even higher ones. Typical ranges are from $25,000 for entry-level positions to $60,000 and above with experience. Freelance Food Writers can earn anywhere from several hundred dollars per year up to $50,000 and more, depending on their previous writing experience, connections, and contracts. However, it is difficult to earn enough money to make a living as a freelancer without extensive prior journalism experience.

In addition to base salary, Food Writers enjoy perks such as expense accounts for dining and related travel. Their work may give them the opportunity to eat in fine restaurants that they could never afford on their journalist's salary alone.

Employment Prospects

As a whole, Food Writers love their work. For this reason, staff positions are extremely competitive. Anyone who is persistent may find a way to review new local eateries for their small-town paper, but staff positions that enable Food Writers to make a living this way are not plentiful.

If you love to eat as well as write, be prepared to start small and gather the right combination of skills. Food Writers may start as journalists at local papers, while gathering expertise in the food industry through training and courses. Food Writers may also find positions at magazines, Web sites, and publishing companies that produce cookbooks and restaurant/travel guides, as well as through freelancing.

Advancement Prospects

Although staff positions for Food Writers are very competitive, new restaurants are always opening, creating a buzz and need for reviews. Specialty niches can be important as a way for Food Writers to market themselves. Food Writers can advance by finding bigger markets—larger city newspapers, specialty magazines, and others. They may also supplement staff work with freelance articles, columns, and books.

Education and Training

Food Writers can become professionals in several different ways. Many have degrees in journalism. These Food Writers usually start out as general assignment reporters and slowly build up experience with entertainment and features in order to switch over to food. Others begin as editorial assistants or staff writers at food-themed magazines.

While some come from journalism and build up food expertise, yet others come from the food industry and build up their writing skills. Food Writers may be former chefs or restaurant owners, as well as amateur cooks. Some may have degrees in culinary arts or certificates from cooking schools. Wine courses and training are also very valuable. A combination of writing and culinary training is ideal.

Experience, Skills, and Personality Traits

Successful Food Writers have a passion for food. They are adventurous eaters who enjoy varied and exotic food and drink. While of course they have particular likes and dislikes, they are generally willing to try most things.

This passion for food must be combined with excellent writing skills. Food Writers need to know how to write a critical analysis, as well as report on news and events. A good command of language and an engaging style make their pieces enjoyable to read. As journalists, they are able to adhere to tight deadlines and generate creative ideas.

Furthermore, Food Writers need excellent observation skills and a good eye for detail, as they use their senses at all times. Strong communication skills enable them to conduct interviews and interact with "foodies" of all kinds.

Unions and Associations

Food Writers may belong to professional associations including the Association of Food Journalists, the International Food, Wine, and Travel Writers Association, and the International Association of Culinary Professionals.

Tips for Entry

1. Explore and read food and wine magazines such as *Gourmet* and *Bon Appetit* (http://www.epicurious. com/), *Food and Wine* (http://www.foodandwine.com), and *Wine Spectator* (http://www.winespectator.com). Consider internship opportunities in these settings.

2. Visit the Web site of the Association of Food Journalists at http://www.afjonline.com. They offer such features as critics' guidelines, recipes and news, and spelling tips for exotic food terms.

3. Browse through the dining section of your local bookstore. Read the bios of cookbook authors and other types of food-related publications to learn more about their professional backgrounds. You can also learn about food writing from books such as *Dining Out: Secrets from America's Leading Chefs, Critics and Restaurateurs* by Andrew Dornenburg and Karen Page.

4. See if you can write restaurant reviews for a campus or local publication. Offer to work for free as a way to build a portfolio.

5. Have you ever seen the Zagat Survey guides to restaurants in various cities? See the Web site at http://www. zagat.com.

6. Read the dining section of different newspapers. Take note not only of the restaurant reviews, but also the food news and other components of the section.

7. Take a wine tasting course. Local courses are often available through college and universities, as well as culinary institutes. See the offering at New York University at http://www.scps.nyu.edu/departments/ course.jsp?courseId=58887.

FILM CRITIC

CAREER PROFILE

Duties: Writes reviews of current cinema for newspapers, magazines, and online publications

Alternate Title(s): Movie Reviewer, Movie Critic, Film Reviewer

Salary Range: $20,000 to $70,000 and up

Employment Prospects: Poor

Advancement Prospects: Fair

Best Geographical Location(s): All, especially large cities

Prerequisites:

Education or Training—Bachelor's degree in journalism or related field; film background also helpful

Experience—Previous writing and reporting experience

Special Skills and Personality Traits—Excellent writing, reporting, and editing skills; knowledge of and passion for film; critical and analytical skills; strong observation and attention to detail

CAREER LADDER

```
┌─────────────────────────────────┐
│   Film Critic, larger paper or   │
│  Features/Entertainment Editor   │
└─────────────────────────────────┘

┌─────────────────────────────────┐
│           Film Critic            │
└─────────────────────────────────┘

┌─────────────────────────────────┐
│        Reporter, including       │
│  General Assignment or Features  │
└─────────────────────────────────┘
```

Position Description

As the price of movies continues to rise, people think twice before paying close to 10 dollars and more to see a film. One way to learn more about a movie is by consulting the experts. Magazines, newspapers, and online publications feature movie reviews that offer critical analysis of the current cinema. Film Critics are the professionals who write these reviews.

While every moviegoer feels like a reviewer at times, there is more to film criticism than merely offering an opinion about a movie. Film Critics are trained journalists who have mastered the craft of writing reviews. Furthermore, they are knowledgeable about film and different movie genres. Rather than just professing their opinion, they share an analysis of movies—the good, the bad, and the questionable—that is based on a background in both what makes a successful film and how to write effective criticism.

Film Critics must understand movies for more than their entertainment value. They analyze them based on their goals and their meanings. Do they have historical or political context? What was behind this movie being made? Film Critics watch hundreds of films each year. In doing so, they become familiar with directors and actors, getting to know their styles, strengths, and weaknesses.

In newspapers, movie reviews usually appear in print on the day the film has been released. Online publications offer similar immediacy, whereas magazines that are published weekly or monthly may include reviews of selected movies that have opened during that time period. Film Critics may write several reviews per week or per month, depending on where they work. They may also review older movies that have recently been released on DVD or video.

Movie reviews usually contain a summary of the movie; however, Film Critics are careful not to reveal too much of the plot. They can rate the skill of the director (perhaps in comparison to his or her previous works), the quality of the screenplay, and the finesse of the actors. Film Critics discuss what worked and what did not in all these components, giving thought-provoking reasons as to why. Effective reviews should be both entertaining and analytical.

In reviewing a movie, Film Critics also analyze it in several categories. They consider its era and genre (such as action, romantic comedy, science fiction, etc.), comparing it with similar films of its time and type. Also, they look at the type of budget the film had—was it a large, mainstream movie or a small independent film? Furthermore, they look at other aspects such as cinematography and score and how these add or detract to the film's quality.

In addition to reviewing movies, Film Critics comment about other issues in current cinema. They attend film festivals and speculate about favorites to win the Academy Award or Golden Globe. Also, they may interview actors and directors. Film Critics notice patterns and trends in film and share interesting developments with their readers.

Their duties may include:

- Discussing their views in broadcast media forums
- Screening five or more movies per week
- Meeting with editors
- Attending movie premieres, film festivals, and special screenings
- Developing relationships with people in the entertainment industry
- Writing about other entertainment news
- Meeting close deadlines
- Working on special issues and features, such as Top Ten Lists, Oscar picks, and others
- Analyzing box office trends

Film Critics usually work for arts or entertainment editors. There may be a team of Film Critics, but most newspapers and magazines usually have just one or two. The Film Critics may work as part of a team with other entertainment and arts reporters and critics. Some Film Critics also write occasional television or book reviews.

Tension can exist between Film Critics and the entertainment industry. Respected Film Critics can exert major influence over a movie's success at the box office. They can affect actors and directors getting their next films made, depending on their performances.

Good Film Critics know how to work with this tension without letting it affect their work. They are able to remain objective and balance their reviews with examples for all their opinions and claims. In this way, they help to shape the way our society thinks about film and entertainment and give us a guide by which to make our choices. Whether we agree or disagree, Film Critics' analyses are sure to spark interesting debates.

Salaries

Salaries for Film Critics will vary depending on the size and scope of their market. Critics employed at small papers can earn less than $20,000 per year, while those six-figure salary critics like Roger Ebert do exist as well.

For Film Critics at newspapers, the Newspaper Industry Compensation Survey, conducted annually by the Inland Press Association, offers information about reporters' salaries. According to the survey, reporters with experience earned an average of $43,292 per year in 2004 in total direct compensation. At magazines and Web sites, Film Critics can earn comparable salaries, or possibly higher ones with a range typically between $30,000 and $60,000 for staff writers.

Employment Prospects

Employment prospects are quite competitive for Film Critics. For many new graduates, it seems like an ideal job, yet few will find their way into a position without paying their dues as a writer and reporter for a number of years. While newspapers have many general assignment reporters, most have only a few Film Critics.

Aspiring Film Critics should expect to begin like other reporters—at small papers in small towns. As it becomes available, taking on features and entertainment pieces is helpful, as is developing a good relationship with the features editor. After one proves himself or herself as a good writer, in addition to having a background understanding of film, then opportunities may come up to write reviews.

Most Film Critics begin their careers in newspapers, and move between newspapers and magazines later on if they wish. Yet some do go the magazine journalism route from the beginning, working their way up through the editorial ranks and becoming staff writers. Other Film Critics work in television or radio, but they usually have a print background as well. Film Critics can also freelance but usually cannot earn a living this way without the backing of an established publication.

Advancement Prospects

Once one is established as a Film Critic, advancement is not easy. Film Critics are generally quite satisfied in their jobs and turnover is low. However, Film Critics who make a name for themselves and develop a following may be able to move into bigger markets. They may move between newspapers, magazines, and broadcast media.

The rare successful Film Critics can achieve a measure of fame for their work. The glamour of the Oscars and Sundance does not happen to everyone, but some Film Critics do get to this level. Television appearances and programs, articles, and books can also be possible for the lucky few.

Education and Training

While anyone can set up a Web site, review movies, and call himself or herself a Film Critic, this is not a likely way to earn a living. Reputable, employed Film Critics frequently hold bachelor's degrees in journalism or related fields. They have extensive knowledge of writing and reporting, particularly writing a critical analysis.

Furthermore, Film Critics should have some formal education or training in film. Whether it is course work in the history of cinema or a master of fine arts degree in film, a background in film is crucial to their job and complements their writing skills to establish credibility.

Internships are one of the most useful ways to get training in the field. Writing movie reviews for campus papers, entertainment Web sites, or other publications is a great way to gain experience and get a feel for the work. These positions usually do not pay a salary; however, the training they offer builds a portfolio of clips that can help one break in later on.

Experience, Skills, and Personality Traits

Experience in journalism is crucial for Film Critics who are looking to work at newspapers and magazines. Several years as a general assignment or features reporter are typical, before getting the chance to tackle some reviews. Many Film Critics write freelance reviews during this time as well, to gain additional experience.

In addition to being excellent writers and reporters, Film Critics need to be thoughtful, analytical, insightful, and critical. They are skilled at looking beyond the surface and are able to recognize patterns, possibilities, and implications. Their observation skills are astute, and they have good memories for people and visual details.

It almost goes without saying that Film Critics must be passionate about movies. They need to have the patience to watch thousands of films throughout their career, spanning all types of genres. A genuine love and respect for the process of filmmaking is key.

Also, Film Critics should be knowledgeable not only about film but also about pop culture and the arts. Understanding theater, music, television, and art provides an intellectual and cultural framework that will make their reviews more effective. At the beginning of their careers, Film Critics may write different types of arts reviews before specializing.

As critics themselves, Film Critics must be thick-skinned and able to take criticism from others. People will not always agree with their reviews and will not hesitate to tell them so. They must also be open-minded and tolerant of different films. Even if a Film Critic does not like a film personally, he or she needs to be able to separate personal opinion from filmmaking technique, holding movies to a standard higher than merely his or her own.

Unions and Associations

Film Critics may belong to professional associations including the regional New York Film Critics Circle, the Los Angeles Film Critics Association, and the Chicago Film Critics Association. They may also join the Online Film Critics Society, as well as the International Federation of Film Critics or the Society of Professional Journalists and Authors. Film Critics working for television or radio may belong to the Broadcast Film Critics Association.

Tips for Entry

1. Consider creating your own Web site to review movies. While this will not earn you money, it can be a great way to demonstrate your commitment to the field and practice your writing. Alone it will not get you hired, but combined with the right education and work experience, it can help an editor take notice of your skills.

2. Take courses about film including its history as well as film criticism. Some continuing education programs even offer courses on how to become a Film Critic. Check out this course at New York University: http://www.scps.nyu.edu/departments/course.jsp?courseId=56826.

3. Go to the movies! Every chance you get, hit the big screen as part of your education. In addition to viewing current movies, rent all the classics. Start with the American Film Institute's list of the top 100 movies of all times at http://www.afi.com/tvevents/100years/movies.aspx.

4. Read movie reviews regularly. Are there reviewers you agree with most often? Why? Notice the way the reviews are written and the components on which they comment.

5. After you see a film, write up a quick analysis of it. Then, compare your review to three others: a large national newspaper, an entertainment magazine, and a smaller local paper. How did your critique compare?

BOOK CRITIC

CAREER PROFILE	CAREER LADDER

Duties: Writes reviews of current books for newspapers, magazines, and online publications

Alternate Title(s): Book Reviewer, Literary Critic

Salary Range: $20,000 to $70,000 and up

Employment Prospects: Poor

Advancement Prospects: Fair

Best Geographical Location(s): All, especially large cities

Prerequisites:

Education or Training—Minimum of a bachelor's degree in English, journalism, or related field; background in literature helpful

Experience—Previous writing and reporting experience; many Book Critics are published authors themselves

Special Skills and Personality Traits—Excellent writing, reporting, and editing skills; knowledge of and passion for books; understanding of literary analysis; ability to read much material in short amounts of time; critical and analytical skills; good attention to detail

---

```
┌─────────────────────────────────────────┐
│  Book Critic, larger or more prestigious  │
│  publication; Arts and Leisure Editor;    │
│      Book Editor; or Author               │
└─────────────────────────────────────────┘

┌─────────────────────────────────────────┐
│              Book Critic                   │
└─────────────────────────────────────────┘

┌─────────────────────────────────────────┐
│      Reporter, including General          │
│      Assignment or Features;              │
│      Freelance Writer; or Author          │
└─────────────────────────────────────────┘
```

Position Description

Book Critics help shape the national attitude about reading. They can influence which book becomes a best seller, which novels win prestigious book awards, and what nonfiction titles are being read by book clubs. As experts, they offer summaries and analyses of books to help readers make decisions about what to try.

Although everyone is in touch with their likes and dislikes, Book Critics offer a more complex analysis of books. They are journalists, writers, and editors who share more than a mere opinion. Trained in the art of literary criticism or the genre in which they review, they understand the components of a successful book. Book Critics comment on books based on their writing styles, stories, complete contents, and overall goals. They can contrast it with other similar titles on the market, determining how it compares to the competition.

Book Critics break down the elements of a book in their reviews. With a novel, they will comment on the plot, the dialogue, the depth of characterization, and the consistency of the author's style and voice throughout. When reviewing a biography, they might discuss whether it sheds new insight on the subject's life. With a how-to book, Book Critics may analyze whether or not it provides the reader with a better understanding of the topic at hand. Overall, they consider how a book entertains, enlightens, affects, or informs its readers.

Some Book Critics specialize in certain genres. Regardless of their specialty, it is essential for Book Critics to be well-read across a number of areas. Additionally, they must know the market to determine how well a book works compared to others of its type. It does not have to appeal to everyone, but it must work for its target audience. To be a good critic, one must be objective. Regardless of whether she loved the author's previous five books, if a Book Critic does not like the new one, she must analyze it fairly. Book Critics must be honest and justify their opinions with concrete data.

The work of Book Critics appears in newspapers, magazines, and Web sites. Some big city papers offer book reviews daily in an arts section; others offer a book review section or individual reviews on Sundays. Magazines may offer several reviews in each issue, whether weekly or monthly. Online publications offer immediacy, with reviews entered more frequently. Targeted publications offer targeted reviews; for example, a magazine geared toward teachers will review new books on education topics. Reviews often appear on or soon after the release date of the book.

In addition to reviewing current books, Book Critics may also write about other issues in the literary and publishing world. They may attend publishing events and conferences, as well as speculate about book awards. Furthermore, they often interview authors and take note of current patterns and trends in writing.

Additional duties may include:

- Reading several books per week
- Meeting with editors and authors
- Writing about other entertainment news
- Meeting tight deadlines
- Working on special issues and features, such as Notable Books of the Year and others
- Analyzing publishing trends

Some Book Critics work on a freelance basis, writing for several publications and getting paid per review. Others are on staff at newspapers or magazines, usually working for arts or entertainment editors. Book Critics may also work for industry publications such as *Publishers Weekly*. The Book Critics may work as part of a team with other entertainment and arts reporters and critics. Some Book Critics also write occasional television or film reviews.

Book Critics use their own skills as writers to provide reviews that will inform and advise their audience. Reviews should give a feel for the book without giving away too much about the plot. While no Book Critic can account for all readers' personal tastes, reviews should help readers make decisions about what they want to read in their leisure time.

Salaries

Salaries for Book Critics can vary greatly, depending on the size and scope of their market. For example, some freelance Book Critics may earn $20 per review, while well-respected literary analysts at papers such as the *New York Times* can make six figures. Typically, Book Critics on the staff of newspapers may earn between $30,000 and $60,000 per year, with similar figures for staff writers at magazines and Web sites.

Employment Prospects

Employment prospects are very competitive for Book Critics. While anyone can find a forum to post his opinions, positions where one can earn a living as a Book Critic are hard to find. Many new journalists must pay their dues as writers and reporters for a number of years.

Those interested in becoming Book Critics should expect to begin like other reporters—at small papers in small towns. As assignments become available, taking on features and entertainment pieces is helpful. Developing a good relationship with the features, arts, or book editor is also helpful. After one proves him or herself as a good writer, in addition to having a background understanding of literature, then opportunities may come up to write reviews. Many writers begin by selling their reviews on a freelance basis before being offered a full-time position.

Advancement Prospects

Book Critics may advance in several different ways, depending on their background and ultimate goals. Some Book Critics on the staff at newspapers and magazines look toward editorial roles. Positions such as book editor, arts/entertainment editor, or features editor might be some next steps. Others are already established or plan to pursue careers as authors themselves and look to publish their own work. Yet others may move to larger and more prestigious publications where they can have more of an impact on the industry.

Education and Training

It goes without saying that Book Critics should love to read. Studying writing and literature with the opportunity to read and analyze great authors is the best preparation for being a book critic. Reputable Book Critics hold bachelor's degrees in English, journalism, and literature, as well as other liberal arts fields. Some may have advanced degrees as well. Learning the craft of writing and establishing one's own writing success is also helpful for success.

In addition to merely loving books, Book Critics must know how to write a critical analysis. They must be able to analyze the elements in a thoughtful and insightful way. Studying literature on the college (or higher) level often provides this type of training.

Experience, Skills, and Personality Traits

Book Critics need to be thoughtful, analytical, and insightful. They are skilled at looking beyond the surface and are able to recognize patterns, themes, and subtleties of language. Additionally, they must pay close attention to detail. Furthermore, Book Critics should be avid readers and adept writers. They should be interested in books across many genres and well read in literature both past and present. They must be both quick and careful readers, able to handle many books in a short period of time with the attention they deserve.

To be well-rounded, Book Critics should have an overall knowledge of culture and the arts. Understanding theater, music, television, and art provides an intellectual and cultural framework that will make their reviews more effective. At the beginning of their careers, some Book Critics may write different types of arts reviews before specializing.

Reviews can cause controversy, so Book Critics must be able to accept criticism from others and stand by their opinions. If authors or readers do not agree with their reviews, they must have thick skins in order to hear their concerns. Also, they should be open-minded and objective. Even if they do not like a book personally, Book Critics must be able to separate that from their analysis of the work.

Unions and Associations

Book Critics may belong to a variety of professional associations, including the American Society of Journalists and Authors and the National Writers Union.

Tips for Entry

1. Become familiar with *Kirkus Reviews*, online at http:// www.kirkusreviews.com/kirkusreviews/index.jsp. According to their Web site, *Kirkus Reviews* is published 24 times annually and reviews approximately 5,000 titles per year, including fiction, mysteries, sci-fi, translations, nonfiction, and children's books. Specialists selected for their knowledge and expertise in a particular field write the reviews.

2. Read a variety of book reviews regularly. In addition to your local paper, read the *New York Times* *Sunday Book Review* (http://www.nytimes.com/pages/ books/index.html), where the famous best seller list originated. Note which reviewers you agree with most often and why. Pay attention to the way the reviews are written and the components on which they comment.

3. See *Publishers Weekly,* the international voice for book publishing and book selling. View the book reviews on their Web site at http://www.publishersweekly.com/.

4. After reading a book you like, and one you dislike, write up a quick analysis of it. Then, contrast your review to others and see how your critique compared.

5. Review books for a local publication, Web site, or student newspaper. Think about any genre where you might have some expertise; for example, if you are an avid knitter, perhaps you can review a knitting book for a knitting magazine to which you subscribe.

6. Check out reader comments on http://www.amazon. com. For most books, Amazon offers links to published reviews as well. Compare and contrast reader comments with Book Critics' analyses.

7. Gain amateur experience writing reviews for sites such as http://www.bookreporter.com. While you will not get paid, you will get free books and a published byline.

8. Never underestimate the power of the classics. Read great literature from lists such as http://www.time. com/time/2005/100books/the_complete_list.html and http://www.randomhouse.com/modernlibrary/100best. html.

TRAVEL WRITER

CAREER PROFILE

Duties: Writes and reports on travel in a variety of formats, including newspaper, magazine, and online articles, as well as guidebooks

Alternate Title(s): Travel Reporter

Salary Range: $25,000 to $60,000 and up

Employment Prospects: Fair

Advancement Prospects: Fair

Best Geographical Location(s): All

Prerequisites:

Education or Training—Bachelor's degree in English, journalism, or related field

Experience—Previous writing and publishing experience; familiarity with a particular region and/or extensive travel experience needed

Special Skills and Personality Traits—Excellent writing, reporting, and editing skills; passion for travel and visiting new locations; adventurous spirit; respect for other cultures; openness to new experiences and flexibility; good organizational skills; critical eye

CAREER LADDER

```
┌─────────────────────────────────┐
│  Travel Editor or Travel Writer, │
│         larger markets           │
└─────────────────────────────────┘

┌─────────────────────────────────┐
│          Travel Writer           │
└─────────────────────────────────┘

┌─────────────────────────────────┐
│   Editorial Assistant, General   │
│  Assignment Reporter, or Intern  │
└─────────────────────────────────┘
```

Position Description

The last time you took a vacation, how did you make your plans? While many people consult travel agents for some of the particulars, chances are that you read material that helped you to decide what to do, where to stay, and where to eat. Travel Writers transport their audience to a far-off locale. They write these pieces that acquaint readers with a specific place, giving them information and advice they need to plan and enjoy their trip.

The work of Travel Writers appears in a variety of formats. They can write for newspapers and/or magazines, including articles profiling cities, beaches, and lesser-known villages around the world. Also, Travel Writers can work for one of the many online sites dedicated to travel planning. Furthermore, some Travel Writers author guidebooks for major travel publishers. Guidebooks include complete information about a region, including tips for getting there, hotels, restaurants, activities, and day trips.

Travel topics can include (among others):

- Hotels
- Restaurants
- Nightlife
- Arts and culture
- Entertainment
- Sports and outdoor activity
- Budget/luxury travel
- Travel arrangements: air, bus, train, and car; also may include directions
- Local history
- Adventure travel
- Travel for specific groups or populations
- Travel to specific areas such as Disney World or Caribbean cruises

Travel Writers may have a variety of specialties. Some find their niche writing for a particular population. There is much special-interest travel including family vacations, traveling with pets, gay- and lesbian-friendly locales, and best spots for singles, to name just a few. Other Travel Writers focus on a specific region. To write extensively about a place for a major publication such as a guidebook, it is necessary for the Travel Writer to have lived there for several years. For a shorter article, however, Travel Writers working for newspapers or magazines might be sent to visit a place where they have never been, offering readers a fresh and critical perspective.

In order to be a Travel Writer, one must obviously love to travel. While that sounds exciting, it also requires a willingness to deal with the not-so-glamorous aspects of travel including dealing with airport security, waiting on long lines for museums, eating at dingy restaurants, and trekking around to find an obscure hotel in the rain. As they enjoy their trips, Travel Writers are always thinking critically and analytically. They try to view their experiences from the point of view of their readers, thinking "how would I rate this sight, who would most enjoy this activity, and is this hotel worth the price?" When Travel Writers are on location, they are working, rather than on vacation, and many find it hard to relax, especially on shorter trips.

Good travel writing involves careful research and planning. For each story, Travel Writers must determine their focus and what they need to cover. Outlines help them to stay organized and keep track of the sights, hotels, and restaurants they may need to visit in a short period of time. Often, they develop a rating system to help readers make decisions about how to spend their time. Travel Writers strive to offer their opinions in a factual and objective way that can enhance people's travel experience. In a sense, they do the research so the average traveler does not have to.

Articles may be written daily, weekly, and/or monthly depending on the publication. Travel Writers usually complete a combination of stories they have generated on their own, as well as those that have been assigned by their editors. Travel Writers that write guidebooks usually have a set period of time (such as six months to one year) to complete their manuscript.

Additionally, Travel Writers have the responsibility of finding fresh and exciting new things in places that have been visited before. They must keep up-to-date on the travel industry, aware of new trends and events. Furthermore, they must be up on the news of the regions they visit. Not only should they be aware of tourism-related business news but also any political, cultural, and economic news that can affect tourism.

Their duties may include:

- Traveling domestically and internationally
- Working with photographers, including shoots for different articles
- Taking photographs to accompany writing
- Conducting interviews and speaking with local residents and proprietors
- Attending meetings with editors to brainstorm story ideas
- Editing articles
- Conducting background research using the Internet and other databases
- Answering questions from readers

It is important for Travel Writers to know their market and its demographics. Understanding not only what the editors want but also what the readers need is essential. For example, certain publications target the wealthy, the adventurous, or the budget-conscious. With each of their trips, Travel Writers need to find the stories that appeal to their population.

The amount of time that a Travel Writer actually travels can vary tremendously. A Travel Writer living in and working on a guidebook about Phoenix, Arizona, can spend a year only focusing on local information, while a Travel Writer on staff at a newspaper or magazine may be on a plane more than three times in a month. In most cases, the publication for which the Travel Writer is working provides a budget that covers travel and writing-related expenses.

Salaries

To earn a living as a Travel Writer, one is usually employed by a newspaper or magazine. Salaries vary depending on the level and responsibility of the position. In the newspaper industry, experienced reporters can earn in the $40,000 to $50,000 range. The Newspaper Industry Compensation Survey, conducted annually by the Inland Press Association, shows that experienced reporters earned an average of $43,292 per year in 2004 in total direct compensation.

At magazines and Web sites, Travel Writers can earn comparable salaries and sometimes even higher ones. Typical ranges are from $25,000 for entry-level positions to $60,000 and above with experience. Freelance Travel Writers can earn anywhere from several hundred dollars per year up to $50,000 and more, depending on their previous writing experience, connections, and contracts. They may be paid per word, per piece, or per book, possibly including an advance for travel expenses and royalties. However, it is difficult to earn enough money to make a living as a freelancer without extensive prior journalism experience.

However, Travel Writers often receive other perks aside from base salary. The free travel expenses make the job worthwhile for many, especially those who earn at the lower end of the spectrum. In addition to those covered by editors, hotels and restaurants may also offer rooms or meals on the house in exchange for being included in an article or guide. Although accommodations and meals may not be luxurious, and only the lucky few are successful enough to join the jet set, travel writing offers a way for writers to experience new things. For those with a passion for seeing the world, this is well worth it.

Employment Prospects

Employment prospects are fair for Travel Writers. While anyone with a passion for travel can find a forum to post their opinions, only the fortunate and qualified will be able to earn a living this way. Competition is great for staff jobs at newspapers and magazines. The best opportunities will be in large cities such as New York with big papers and magazine headquarters.

Travel Writers should be willing to start at the bottom to develop their specialty. Positions such as editorial assistant at a travel magazine or general assignment reporter at a newspaper can be good entry points. Travel Writers should expect to get started by writing and reporting on whatever topics are needed, not just travel.

A portfolio of clips is essential for employment. Aspiring Travel Writers should also consider freelancing as a way to get started and develop some published pieces. Insiders say that writing the brief pieces at the front of travel magazines (product reviews, blurbs), rather than trying for lengthy articles, can be a good way to get published initially. Trade and regional magazines with small sections on travel may be also good places to begin.

Advancement Prospects

In order to advance, many Travel Writers look to find more lucrative and stable work. Freelancers might look for staff positions at newspapers and magazines, while Travel Writers already employed by publications may look to move to larger markets. Those who are looking for managerial responsibility may also become editors where they run a department or manage a team of staff.

However, most Travel Writers look to stay in writing as financially and personal rewarding a setting as they can. They seek opportunities to travel to more interesting places and reach larger numbers of readers. Travel Writers who develop niche areas may write columns, books, or even travel series.

Education and Training

While most people love to travel, that is not enough to make one a Travel Writer. A bachelor's degree in English, journalism, communications, or a related field is very valuable. Some Travel Writers may also have degrees in other subjects including liberal arts. Many journalists agree that a combination of a liberal arts and journalism curriculum provides an ideal background for a writing and reporting career.

Travel Writers that attend journalism school can also make valuable contacts that will help them get a first job at a newspaper or magazine. For this reason, internships are also a key way for those interested in travel writing to break in.

Experience, Skills, and Personality Traits

Like other writers and critics that offer opinions and advice, Travel Writers must be able to deal with criticism and diffi-

cult people. A hotel manager or restaurant chef may be very disappointed if their establishment does not get high marks. Travel Writers need to stick to their guns and remain ethical, doing their duty as journalists rather than advertisers.

Travel Writers must have very strong writing and reporting skills. While a love for travel is required, it does not amount to much without writing talent and ability. They must know how to structure articles or guides with the appropriate balance of information, fact, opinion, and interesting tidbits. The best travel pieces are not dry but are peppered with amusing anecdotes about people and places.

Furthermore, Travel Writers need initiative and curiosity help them to generate interesting and informative stories. It is important to be open-minded, respectful, and tolerant, especially when visiting different cultures. Travel Writers need excellent communication skills to speak to a variety of people.

Travel Writers should be passionate not only about travel but also about people. They must be avid travelers who want to truly experience each place they see rather than stay within their comfort zone. Like all journalists, Travel Writers must be able to work under tight deadline pressure. They need to be flexible in order to adapt to sudden changes of plans and schedules.

Unions and Associations

The North American Travel Journalists Association (http://www.natja.org/) is a professional association dedicated to writers, editors, and photographers in the travel industry. Travel Writers may also belong to professional associations including the regional Outdoor Writers Association of California and the Midwest Travel Writers Association, as well as the International Food, Wine and Travel Writers Association and the Society of American Travel Writers.

Tips for Entry

1. Plan a trip, either working within your realistic budget or a fantasy vacation for the future. Once you select your location, read everything you can about this place. Search the Internet for newspaper and magazine articles, use online sites, and browse through guidebooks. Take note of how the different articles help you make decisions.

2. Check out major guidebook sites such as http://www.fodors.com, http://www.frommers.com, and http://www.lonelyplanet.com. See how they are written and the types of information they include.

3. You do not need a lot of money to be a traveler. As your budget allows, backpack through Europe, study abroad, volunteer for the Peace Corps, visit a museum in your home city, take a road trip, or go camping, to name a few ideas both large and small. These experiences will help you to be a better Travel Writer.

4. Read travel magazines such as *Conde Nast Traveler, Travel and Leisure, National Geographic Traveler,* and others. What types of articles do they include? Look on the masthead to see if most seem to be written by staff members or freelancers.

5. Get started as a freelancer by writing about what you know. How would you advise a visitor to your hometown? Develop an idea for an article and send a query letter outlining the piece to a local publication. See http://www.poewar.com/archives/2004/10/24/how-to-write-a-query-letter/ and http://www.fictionwriters.com/tips-query-letters.html for some ideas about writing query letters.

6. Many good links to becoming a Travel Writer can be found at the following site: http://www.yudkin.com/travel.htm.

FASHION/BEAUTY WRITER

CAREER PROFILE

Alternate Title(s): Fashion/Beauty Reporter

Salary Range: $25,000 to $60,000 and up

Employment Prospects: Fair

Advancement Prospects: Fair

Best Geographical Location(s): Major cities

Prerequisites:

Education or Training—Bachelor's degree in English, journalism, or related field

Experience—Previous writing or reporting experience through jobs or internships

Special Skills and Personality Traits—Excellent writing, reporting, and editing skills; strong communication and interviewing skills; passion for and knowledge of fashion and beauty; good sense of style

CAREER LADDER

```
┌─────────────────────────────────┐
│      Fashion/Beauty Editor       │
└─────────────────────────────────┘

┌─────────────────────────────────┐
│      Fashion/Beauty Writer       │
└─────────────────────────────────┘

┌─────────────────────────────────┐
│   Editorial Assistant, General   │
│  Assignment Reporter, or Intern  │
└─────────────────────────────────┘
```

Position Description

From the runways of Paris to the streets of Manhattan, many people consider themselves slaves to fashion. Both women and men pour through magazines and devour articles to find out what is in style this season, what products will help them look younger, and where they can buy these items. Fashion and Beauty Writers craft these articles, reporting on trends, products, and events that help people stay on the cutting edge of style.

Fashion Writers work for magazines, newspapers, Web sites, and other publications. They may also freelance for several types of publications. Women's magazines such as *Vogue* and *Harper's Bazaar* have always been fashion standbys, and men's interest magazines such as *GQ* and *Esquire* include much about men's fashion. These days, as our society is increasingly fascinated by celebrity culture, many general magazines include fashion components.

Furthermore, fashion and style is a fixture in many large newspaper features sections. It may be included in a Sunday section or as a regular feature when products or events are launched. Fashion Writers can also work for the online equivalents of these publications, as well as specific fashion and beauty sites.

While fashion is obviously not hard news, those who follow it will always want the lowdown on new arrivals.

Fashion Writers can have a diverse range of writing responsibilities including current news as well as features. Often, they review designer shows, lending their critical analysis to new collections. Also, Fashion Writers may report on new store openings, write personal profiles of designers, or write features about how to dress for different occasions.

With our culture's ongoing obsession with youth and beauty, Beauty Writers stay busy covering the many ways we can do so. Hair products and salons, makeup and skin care, and spas and stress relievers are just some of the areas covered by Beauty Writers. They also write a combination of features and reports on beauty events and openings. Both Fashion and Beauty Writers may have particular specialties on which they focus.

Like other writers and reporters, Fashion and Beauty Writers are on the pulse of their subject. They are constantly on top of news and trends, chatting with sources daily. It is up to them to find the news, and their network of designers and fashion insiders help them to develop stories that will be interesting and exciting to their readers. Their stories are carefully researched, detailed, and outlined, yet written in a tone to which readers can relate.

Articles may be written daily, weekly, and/or monthly depending on the publication. Fashion and Beauty Writers usually complete a combination of stories they have generated on their own, as well as those that have been assigned by their editors.

Fashion and Beauty Writers often spend much time working with photographers. They are involved in shoots for different articles, which can include scheduling, finding locations, and other logistics. Furthermore, they work closely with designers and other key players in the fashion and beauty world. Like sports writers who have to navigate carefully with players, Fashion and Beauty Writers cultivate and manage these relationships. The press is important to the fashion industry and can make or break the sales for a season. Fashion Writers must maintain good terms with designers to get the coverage they want, but without compromising their objectivity.

Their duties may include:

- Identifying trends
- Conducting interviews with designers, stylists, models, and other experts
- Attending meetings with editors to brainstorm story ideas
- Editing articles
- Collaborating with photography and design departments
- Attending fashion shows, press conferences, and other events
- Conducting background research using the Internet and other databases
- Writing about the business side of the fashion and beauty industries
- Answering questions from readers

Fashion and Beauty Writers bring readers into a world of glamour and style, offering up ways to incorporate celebrity and runway gloss into their own living rooms. For this reason, most Fashion and Beauty Writers are passionate about their work. They use their writing and reporting skills to help make people feel better about themselves and make a glamorous lifestyle accessible.

Hours for Fashion and Beauty Writers will vary, but they generally keep to a more regular daytime schedule than reporters who handle breaking news. Some travel may be required to attend fashion shows or other location events.

Salaries

Fashion and Beauty Writers will vary in their compensation levels, not only in the case of their salaries but also in other job perks. For those Fashion and Beauty Writers that work at newspapers, the Newspaper Industry Compensation Survey, conducted annually by the Inland Press Association, offers information about reporters' salaries. According to the survey, entry level reporters earned an average of $28,162 per year in 2004 in total direct compensation. With considerable experience, that average went up to $43,292. The range for reporters was from a low of $10,042 to a high salary of $163,926 at the experienced level. While these figures are for general reporters and are not particular to fashion, they can be used as a guide.

At magazines and Web sites, Fashion and Beauty Writers can earn comparable salaries, and sometimes even higher ones. Typical ranges are from $25,000 for entry-level positions to $60,000 and above with experience. Fashion and Beauty Writers who freelance for different publications will have salaries dependent on the quantity and quality of their work.

In addition to base salaries, Fashion and Beauty Writers enjoy some of the most plentiful perks in journalism. It is not uncommon for them to receive free designer clothes, haircuts, makeup, beauty products and treatments, spa visits, and other style goodies.

Employment Prospects

Employment prospects are fair for Fashion and Beauty Writers. Competition is great for existing jobs, and as specialists, their opportunities can be limited. While newspapers nationwide may include fashion features, the majority of opportunities will be found in major cities such as the U.S. home of most fashion magazines and designers, New York.

Fashion and Beauty Writers should be willing to start at the bottom to develop their specialty. Fashion magazines are often a good entry into the field for those who are willing to toil as editorial assistants for several years. This will provide exposure to the industry as well as a network of editors and insiders that can be crucial for advancement later on. Furthermore, working as an assistant at a magazine may offer some writing opportunities directly related to fashion and beauty. Internships are also highly valued and can even be prerequisites for entry-level positions.

The ability to develop a portfolio of clips will be crucial for employment. Aspiring Fashion and Beauty Writers should also consider freelancing as a way to get started.

Advancement Prospects

For Fashion and Beauty Writers to advance, they can either move up the corporate ladder or move on to larger markets. If they are looking for managerial responsibility, they may become fashion or beauty editors, running a department and managing a team of staff. Other Fashion and Beauty Writers may advance by moving to larger magazines or newspapers where they have responsibility for greater coverage. Covering Fashion Week in Paris may be the ultimate goal for a writer in a small town. They can develop niche areas for themselves, writing columns, freelance articles, and even books.

Education and Training

Bachelor's degrees in English, journalism, communications, or a related field are valuable for Fashion and Beauty Writers. Some may also have degrees in other subjects including liberal arts. Many journalists agree that a combination of a liberal arts and journalism curriculum provides an ideal background for writing and reporting career.

Most Fashion and Beauty Writers do not have formal education in fashion, although some coursework can be helpful. Most find that their training comes from the job, as well as from their ongoing personal interest in fashion and beauty. Internships are also a key way for those interested in fashion writing to break in.

Experience, Skills, and Personality Traits

Fashion and Beauty Writers must have very strong writing and reporting skills. Their writing talent, along with ambition and initiative, help them to generate interesting and informative stories. They need excellent communication skills to conduct interviews and speak to a variety of people.

Additionally, Fashion and Beauty Writers must have a passion for fashion and beauty and a good sense of style. They are usually lifelong readers of fashion and beauty articles, having the background knowledge of the field necessary to offer an informed opinion. By understanding the industry, they can network with the players and keep on top of news and developments.

Like all journalists, Fashion and Beauty Writers must be able to work under tight deadline pressure. Creativity and curiosity enable them to constantly come up with fresh ideas, and organizational skills help them to get their stories in on time. Fashion and Beauty Writers thrive under stress and stay calm in dealing with difficult and volatile personalities.

Unions and Associations

Fashion and Beauty Writers may belong to associations such as the National Writers Union, the American Society of Magazine Editors, and the American Society of Journal-ists and Authors. They may also belong to fashion specific associations such as the Fashion Association.

Tips for Entry

1. Fashion is more than what you see in the window of your local department store. Take a course on the history of fashion to understand how different societies have been affected and influenced by the clothes they wore.

2. Go after an internship with a fashion magazine. These positions are very competitive but can be an ideal way to break into the field. Contact the fashion or beauty editor at different magazines directly, or check out these sites for more information: http://www.magazine.org/Editorial/Internships/ and http://www.mediabistro.com. Also, visit your campus career center to see what internship information they may have.

3. Become an avid reader of fashion copy. Discover the style and focus of different magazines and see how various Web sites cover fashion and beauty.

4. Also, see how newspapers cover fashion and beauty. If you cannot find anything in your local paper, try big nationals such as the *New York Times* which includes a Sunday Styles section, a Thursday Styles section, and daily fashion news in the Arts section.

5. Start small. Try to get your writing published wherever you can, in campus publications or small local magazines and newspapers. When opportunities arise to cover fashion or beauty related events, such as a local fashion show for charity, volunteer for the story.

6. In addition to writing and journalism internships, also consider other aspects of the fashion industry. If you are taking writing and journalism courses, internships for design houses, fashion public relations firms, and cosmetics companies may be interesting ways to gain a business background in the field.

OTHER WRITERS

FREELANCE WRITER

CAREER PROFILE

Duties: Writes articles, stories, and other copy for magazines, newspapers, Web sites, and publishers on a contractual basis

Alternate Title(s): Freelancer, Stringer

Salary Range: Varies from less than $.10 per word to $2.00 per word and more; may also pay by assignment ranging from $100 for short articles to $20,000 and up for books

Employment Prospects: Good

Advancement Prospects: Good

Best Geographical Location(s): All

Prerequisites:

Education or Training—A bachelor's degree in English, journalism, or related field is very helpful, but not required.

Experience—Prior writing experience and published clips

Special Skills and Personality Traits—Excellent writing skills; strong grasp of spelling, grammar, and usage; high level of motivation and persuasive ability; creativity and initiative; good research skills

CAREER LADDER

```
┌─────────────────────────────────────┐
│  Staff writing, reporting, or editing │
│  position at a variety of publications │
└─────────────────────────────────────┘

┌─────────────────────────────────────┐
│         Freelance Writer             │
└─────────────────────────────────────┘

┌─────────────────────────────────────┐
│  Staff writing or reporting in another │
│  career or begin freelancing          │
│  directly from school                 │
└─────────────────────────────────────┘
```

Position Description

Imagine being able to live anywhere you want and work without having to leave your house. The life of the Freelance Writer has numerous trials and tribulations, but those who make a career out of it swear that the flexibility and freedom it offers outweigh the risks and negative aspects.

Freelance Writers write stories, articles, Web content, and other copy for newspapers, magazines, Web sites, and other journalistic media. Their niche areas are completely varied, based on their interests and background prior to freelancing. For example, a doctor, nurse, or nutritionist may decide to pursue freelance writing specializing in health issues, or a former business reporter will freelance as a business writer.

There is great variety in the quantity of assignments that Freelance Writers have. Some have a schedule of regular assignments, such as a monthly column or biannual features for a specific publication. Others may be guaranteed a spe-

cific number of pieces per month without knowing exactly what they are. Yet others work on specific lengthy jobs, taking up several months at a time.

However, many Freelance Writers have no job security. Their income is dependent on their ability to go out and pitch ideas. They live from story to story, trying to line up more work as they complete their current assignment.

There are a number of ways in which Freelance Writers get assignments. Some complete stories and go out and try to sell them in the appropriate venue. This can be quite time consuming and frustrating, working without the guarantee of publication.

More frequently, Freelance Writers write query letters or proposals to get their ideas across. These letters are sent to editors at newspapers, magazines, Web sites, and publishing companies, and they outline the story idea that a writer has in mind. They are usually considered the standard first step to getting published.

Query letters begin with a catchy opening that gets the editor intrigued to read further. They outline the prospective article contents, as well as potential sources that will be used. Furthermore, queries offer insight as to why the article or idea is relevant and right for their particular publication. Freelance Writers sometimes submit résumés with their queries, and always a portfolio of previous writing clips when possible.

When an editor accepts a query or proposal, the Freelance Writer is given a contract. The contract is a legal agreement that summarizes the terms such as payment for the article, word length, due date, and "kill fee," if the publication decides not to run the article.

Freelance Writers use their creativity, writing, and other journalistic skills to plan their articles. They may interview subjects, spending time meeting with them in person or speaking to them by telephone. Also, they often conduct extensive research, using the Internet and research databases. By outlining the contents, they develop a plan for a story that will engage readers and fit the tone of the particular publication. If Freelance Writers work for several different publications in the same time frame, it can be challenging and interesting to capture all the different tones required.

Additional duties may include:

- Transcribing taped interviews
- Meeting with editors
- Reviewing notes and outlines
- Brainstorming ideas
- Editing their work
- Negotiating assignments
- Promoting their work

Freelance Writers may work several hours a week to 40 or more, depending on whether their work is full-time or part-time in any given period. The hours are flexible, depending on the writer's most productive time, as well as the availability of interview subjects. Freelance Writers may have a month or more to complete an article for a magazine, while those with regular newspaper assignments often work on tight deadlines of several days or less.

Salaries

Salaries for Freelance Writers vary tremendously. Many do not earn enough to make a living, usually writing to supplement their work as full-time writers, reporters, editors, or in completely different professions. These part-time writers may earn several hundred or thousand dollars per year, primarily writing because they enjoy it. Beginning Freelance Writers may even write a number of articles for free in order to build up a portfolio of published clips.

Yet other Freelance Writers, generally the best and the lucky, find they can earn a lucrative income. Former reporters or magazine writers with good contacts and specialty areas can make this transition most easily. With a built-in network of editors for assignments, as well as the credibility that comes with past experience and writing credits, they are often able to get consistent work. Salaries can range from $30,000 per year to $80,000 and beyond.

Freelance Writers who work on nonfiction books and other original, long-term assignments may receive cash advances and/or royalties for their work.

Employment Prospects

Employment prospects are good for Freelance Writers. As newspapers merge and magazines downsize, employees who do not command health benefits and office space become increasingly attractive. These publications utilize Freelance Writers as a way to get content written without the costly overhead.

Furthermore, new media is becoming an increasingly lucrative area of publishing and journalism. Opportunities arise for Freelance Writers to write Web content and articles. Again, Freelance Writers are attractive because of their flexibility and low cost compared to full-timers.

While freelance writing can be a career change for some, for others, it is an excellent way to begin a career in journalism. Right out of school, publications may be reluctant to hire a new graduate without considerable clips and experience. Freelancing, especially for those willing and able to do it for little money, can be a great way to build a portfolio and make valuable industry contacts.

Advancement Prospects

Advancement prospects are also good for Freelance Writers. Those who are beginning journalism careers can advance to staff positions at newspapers, magazines, new media companies, and other publications. Others, who start midcareer, can use their freelance writing accomplishments to help them advance within their own fields. For example, a therapist who writes some self-help articles can use the experience to build his or her private practice.

Furthermore, many Freelance Writers start small and expand their writing goals. Once they have gained experience, they can then query larger publications that pay considerably more. Some Freelance Writers may go after longer, more in-depth assignments such as writing books and other full-length manuscripts.

Education and Training

Freelance Writers come from a wide variety of educational backgrounds. They hold bachelor's degrees in a range of subjects from anthropology to zoology, although many do hold degrees in English or journalism. Some have education and training in different professions, including law, social work, accounting, and other fields.

While not all Freelance Writers have formal journalism education, they do need training in writing. Whether it comes from formal course work, on-the-job training, or natural aptitude, Freelance Writers need to understand what makes good and successful writing. A business background may also be helpful for negotiating contracts and being self-employed.

Experience, Skills, and Personality Traits

First and foremost, it is imperative for Freelance Writers to have excellent writing skills. They need a strong grasp of grammar, spelling, punctuation, and usage, as well as the ability to alter tone and style based on the assignment. Flexibility and comfort with ambiguity is also needed. Freelance Writers need to switch gears based on assignments and take on new projects at short notice. They need good self-discipline and the ability to stick to deadlines and stay motivated.

Additionally, Freelance Writers must be ambitious, ingenious, and creative. They need to be able to market themselves, constantly thinking up new ideas and selling their concepts to editors. Freelance Writers should have a good sense of what makes a good article or story and how to make it appeal to different publications.

Unions and Associations

Freelance Writers may belong to a variety of professional associations including the National Writers Union, the American Society of Journalists and Authors, and the Editorial Freelancers Association.

Tips for Entry

1. There are many Web sites that provide information to Freelance Writers. These include http://www.freelancewriting.com/, http://freelancewrite.about.com/, and http://www.writersweekly.com/. These sites list freelance markets and jobs that are good places to begin.

2. Hone your writing skills through courses that require different types of writing. Become comfortable writing research papers, persuasive arguments, critical analyses, and creative work.

3. Get started by writing articles for free if you have to. Contact a local paper or magazine to find out about their needs.

4. Working for a campus paper or magazine is a great way to gain clips and build a portfolio.

5. Learn how to write an expert query letter at sites such as http://www.writersweekly.com/ and http://www.geocities.com/charlottedillon2000/query.html.

6. Take a look at books that offer advice to Freelance Writers such as *How to Become a Fulltime Freelance Writer: A Practical Guide to Setting Up a Successful Writing Business at Home (Road Map to Your Writing Career)* by Michael A. Banks and *The Well-Fed Writer: Financial Self-Sufficiency As a Freelance Writer in Six Months or Less* by Peter Bowerman.

TECHNICAL WRITER

CAREER PROFILE

Duties: Writes user manuals and other material for computer, scientific, or technical companies; translates technical jargon into language that a nontechnical reader can understand

Alternate Title(s): Technical Communicator, Documentation Manager, Technical Editor

Salary Range: $40,000 to $60,000 and up

Employment Prospects: Good to Excellent

Advancement Prospects: Good

Best Geographical Location(s): All

Prerequisites:

Education or Training—Bachelor's degree, often in English or a specific technical field such as engineering, business, or science

Experience—One year or more of technical writing experience

Special Skills and Personality Traits—Excellent writing, language, and communication skills; attention to detail; ability to make sense of complex technical jargon; ability to simplify and synthesize information; patience

CAREER LADDER

```
┌─────────────────────────────────────┐
│ Director of Technical Communication  │
└─────────────────────────────────────┘

┌─────────────────────────────────────┐
│         Technical Writer             │
└─────────────────────────────────────┘

┌─────────────────────────────────────┐
│      Assistant, Intern, or           │
│      other Writer or Editor          │
└─────────────────────────────────────┘
```

Position Description

When most people need to troubleshoot their computers or install new programs, they consult with a manual designed to answer their questions. The manual is meant for the average reader to understand, enabling them to follow a procedure without needing knowledge of computer programming. While the programmers write the code to create the programs, Technical Writers help people use complex equipment by writing material that is simple and straightforward. Their writing lets people find out what they need to know and do.

Not only computers need instruction manuals. Every piece of equipment from a curling iron to a submarine has specific points for users. Employment settings for Technical Writers are vast. In addition to the computer industry, Technical Writers work in fields such as engineering, research, medicine, pharmaceuticals, banking, insurance, aviation, government, and the military. Materials they make user-friendly include employee manuals, product literature, user guides, instruction manuals, catalogs, promotional materials, parts and assembly materials, and new proposals.

Technical Writers are often involved with all stages of their material's production process. Firstly, they begin by outlining the information they need to convey. In this stage, Technical Writers conduct research by reading about the product, studying data and charts, interviewing the technical staff involved with product development, and by trying it out themselves. Consulting with engineers and product designers is critical in order to clarify their terms and get a better sense of the product and its goals.

Next, Technical Writers write their material. This can take several drafts, as they edit and refine material. In this phase, testing products is important to make sure the directions follow logically. Technical Writers try to think like their readers, wondering what they would want to know in order to operate and use the product. They strive for concise and useful language, avoiding extraneous words and unnecessary information.

Furthermore, Technical Writers spend much time editing their work, as well as the work of others. They may work as part of a team of writers. Editing can involve not only reviewing the writing but also the graphics, illustrations, and design, and how they interface with the text. Furthermore, it includes reviewing and evaluating materials.

As manuals and other documents are completed, Technical Writers may spend time testing and using the programs. They do this to ensure that the directions work and the desired results are achieved. Putting themselves in the place of the user, they follow their written documentation, troubleshooting any problems as they go along.

Scheduling is important in the production process, and Technical Writers must be able to meet their deadlines. They work with other departments such as marketing, business development, sales, graphics, and client services to make sure that the product is ready to launch.

Their duties may include:

* Working with external printing, graphics, or design companies
* Answering queries from staff and users
* Developing documentation to help users
* Drafting proposals
* Incorporating feedback and suggestions
* Meeting with technical experts
* Identifying issues and barriers to communication
* Writing documentation for software development

Technical Writers may work independently or as part of technical writing teams. They may also freelance for several different types of organizations.

Technical writing can be an interesting and lucrative option for writers and journalists who are looking for their career niche. Products will always need to be explained and documentation be necessary for their use and functioning. Writers who are skilled in teaching and training as well may be particularly well suited for technical writing.

Salaries

According to the Bureau of Labor Statistics (BLS), median annual earnings for salaried Technical Writers were $50,580 in 2002. The middle 50 percent earned between $39,100 and $64,750. The lowest 10 percent earned less than $30,270, and the highest 10 percent earned more than $80,900.

Additional information comes from the Society for Technical Communication (STC). Their 2004 survey shows that the median annual salary for entry level Technical Writers was $42,500 in 2004. For all Technical Writers and editors living in the United States, not just entry-level, the median salary was $60,240.

STC also showed salary distinctions based on whether or not Technical Writers had supervisory roles. Those mid-level technical communication professionals who supervised others earned a mean salary of $67,330 in 2004, as opposed to the non-supervisor mid-level professionals at $55,600. Senior-level supervisory professionals earned a mean salary of $80,630.

Employment Prospects

The BLS projects that opportunities should be good for Technical Writers. The 2004-05 *Occupational Outlook Handbook* states that "demand for technical writers and writers with expertise in specialty areas, such as law, medicine, or economics, is expected to increase because of the continuing expansion of scientific and technical information and the need to communicate it to others."

As technology, as well as our society's dependence on it, grows, writers will be needed to help people use technical products. Technical Writers can find job opportunities in a variety of settings, as well as working as self-employed freelancers. Another sign that the field is growing comes from the Society for Technical Communication (STC), a membership organization dedicated to technical communication professionals, which reports an 18 percent growth in membership over the last decade.

Many Technical Writers begin directly from school, or after working for several years in another writing, editorial, or journalism setting. Others may transfer from jobs as technicians, scientists, engineers, or research assistants.

Advancement Prospects

Advancement prospects are also good for Technical Writers. As demand grows, those Technical Writers with experience will be in good positions to lead departments of communications where they manage other Technical Writers. Others will move to larger organizations for more money and responsibility. Technical Writers can also work as freelancers, commanding per project salaries and giving them flexibility to choose hours and assignments.

Education and Training

The majority of Technical Writers have bachelor's degrees in English, but others hold degrees in journalism, communication, business, or technical fields such as engineering or computer science. Others have degrees in technical communications or writing; course work in these areas can be extremely helpful.

A combination of technical expertise and writing skills is an ideal background for a Technical Writer. The BLS says that "increasingly, technical writing requires a degree in, or some knowledge about, a specialized field—engineering, business, or one of the sciences, for example." Those who have course work in engineering, computer science, or technology are highly valued in the job market.

However, the writing and communication background is essential. There are many people who know about software; fewer that can describe it in a way that users will understand. Many Technical Writers begin without any technical knowledge, leveraging their writing skills and learning specifics on the job. A writer can break into the field through taking some technical writing courses and studying technical manuals. STC offers a database of schools offering academic programs in technical communication (http://www.stc.org/academicDatabase.asp).

Experience, Skills, and Personality Traits

In addition to excellent writing skills, Technical Writers need to be computer literate, with knowledge of a major word processor like Microsoft Word. Some jobs may also require experience with other publishing software such as Adobe FrameMaker and RoboHELP.

Writing skills include not only the ability to create cohesive and clear prose but also a good grasp of grammar, spelling, punctuation, and syntax. Equally important can be verbal communication skills. Technical Writers must communicate with the technical experts who have created their products or materials regularly, as well as with other staff. They must be able to extract important information and ask the right questions to get proper documentation. Always, they must be able to break down language concisely and effectively.

Technical Writers must also be able to work well under pressure. They need to work independently, but as part of a team when necessary. It is important for Technical Writers to be self-starters who can initiate projects, especially those who perform freelance work. Teaching or training experience and skills are also valuable.

Unions and Associations

The Society for Technical Communication is the largest professional association for Technical Writers and communicators, with more than 18,000 members. Technical Writers may also belong to organizations such as the National Writers Union and the Editorial Freelancers Association.

Tips for Entry

1. There are a number of books that explain the process of technical writing. Take a look at *The Complete Idiot's Guide to Technical Writing* by Krista Van Laan and Catherine Julian and *Technical Writing for Dummies* by Sheryl Lindsell-Roberts.

2. Take advantage of training opportunities for Technical Writers. In addition to the list of academic programs offered through the STC Web site, also look at free online courses such as http://www.suite101.com/lesson.cfm/17242/747.

3. Brush up on your software skills. If you are confident with your writing ability, take courses in Microsoft Office, Adobe, and other programs to become more familiar with their operations.

4. Develop a portfolio. Samples of your work will speak more for your abilities than even the best résumé. When you buy a new electronic device, check out the user manual for ideas. You can even try rewriting it in your own words to use as a writing sample.

5. Next time you are working on your computer, click on the "Help" file. This is written by Technical Writers. Consider the approach you might have taken if it was your job to explain.

NONFICTION WRITER

CAREER PROFILE

Duties: Writes nonfiction books on a variety of subjects; some authors have particular specialties

Alternate Title(s): Nonfiction author

Salary Range: $0 to $100,000 and up

Employment Prospects: Fair

Advancement Prospects: Fair

Best Geographical Location(s): All

Prerequisites:

Education or Training—Most Nonfiction Writers have bachelor's degrees or higher in a variety of subjects, depending on their specialty area

Experience—Prior published work such as articles is very helpful.

Special Skills and Personality Traits—Excellent writing skills; creativity; self-discipline and good organizational skills; entrepreneurial spirit and ability to market your work

CAREER LADDER

```
┌────────────────────────────────────┐
│   Nonfiction Writer, larger market;  │
│      Fiction Writer; Journalist;     │
│        Professor; or other           │
└────────────────────────────────────┘

┌────────────────────────────────────┐
│          Nonfiction Writer           │
└────────────────────────────────────┘

┌────────────────────────────────────┐
│   Freelance Writer, Journalist, or   │
│        professional in other field   │
└────────────────────────────────────┘
```

Position Description

In the writing world, nonfiction is a broad genre. Nonfiction books include factual information about people, events, and things that have actually existed or happened. Although they are drastically different, reference books, biographies, how-to books, cookbooks, self-help, and memoirs can all be classified as nonfiction. The similarity they share is that the author is using facts to present information or tell a story.

Like newspaper or magazine journalists, Nonfiction Writers conduct research, analyze information, and determine the facts for their books. They use their writing skills to choose the style, format, and angle that they want to portray. Some Nonfiction Writers are experts on their subject matter. They did not necessarily plan to be writers or journalists but instead have pursued careers in other fields. Because of an interest in writing, they may decide to try their hand at being a Nonfiction Writer in addition to their current profession. For example, an attorney may write a book called "How to Get Into Law School," based partly on his or her own experience. However, a good nonfiction book usually includes careful research in addition to personal experience.

Other Nonfiction Writers are professional writers or journalists. They may write for a living, on the staff of newspapers, magazines, or new media companies; they might also be full-time freelance writers. They may focus their writing on specific topics of interest, or write for hire on more general topics. Nonfiction Writers may write articles and make presentations on the same topic as their books.

Anyone with an idea can become an amateur Nonfiction Writer, but not everyone can become a published author. The first step to writing a book is coming up with the idea; next comes the proposal. A nonfiction book proposal consists of several components, including a summary of the book's proposed contents, what the book will accomplish, how it differs from other titles on the market (market analysis), who will buy the book, and an author bio (why are you the best person to write the book.) A typical proposal also includes the proposed table of contents and at least one sample chapter.

Unlike novels, where editors and agents often want to see the completed work before making a decision, Nonfiction Writers usually obtain contracts based on their proposals.

However, these proposals must be detailed and well thought out. Nonfiction Writers must have their book planned out and sell their idea. Some Nonfiction Writers submit proposals directly to editors at publishing houses, while others first go through literary agents. Frequently, a large publishing house that publishes best sellers will only accept proposals submitted through agents.

Once a proposal is accepted, a process that can take from a few weeks to a few months, Nonfiction Writers are granted contracts by the publishing house. Contracts specify that the book will be completed by a specific deadline and stick to the determined format. It also spells out the author's advance, which is a sum of money paid to the author up front (and sometimes broken down into three parts: the first part upon contract signing, the second part when half the manuscript is complete, and the third upon completion or publication). Typical nonfiction advances can range from $2,000 to $20,000 and considerably more for well-established authors. After the royalties recoup the sum of the advance, contracts specify the percentage of royalties that Nonfiction Writers will get from sales. Typical royalties might be 6 to 8 percent of the retail price on trade paperbacks and 10 to 15 percent of the retail price on hardcovers.

After the contract is signed, Nonfiction Writers can get to the task at hand: actually writing their book. This can take from six months to a year or more, as stipulated by the contract. Some Nonfiction Writers write full-time every day; many combine it with other writing or professional careers. They need to budget their time to get the manuscript completed. In addition to writing, most Nonfiction Writers spend considerable time interviewing people, conducting research, and using the Internet.

Additional duties may include:

- Working with editors
- Interviewing people via telephone and e-mail, in addition to in-person discussions
- Contacting professional associations
- Attending conferences or meetings, based on their topics
- Making public appearances
- Giving lectures
- Writing articles or Web content
- Attending book groups
- Working with publicists to promote the book
- Staying on top of the publishing industry as well as new developments in their field

Nonfiction Writers may travel to interview people or conduct specific research for their book. Once the book is published, they may travel on publicity tours, book signings, and author talks, depending on their target market. Additionally, they usually have the freedom to work from home or any location they choose, as well as to set their own hours. As long as their deadlines are met, Nonfiction Writers have the flexibility to work in their pajamas at 2 A.M.

Salaries

Salaries vary tremendously for Nonfiction Writers. Some writers barely earn several thousand dollars from a book, while best-selling nonfiction authors can earn several hundred thousand or more. Earnings come from a combination of the advance and royalties. Overall salary is determined not only by how the book sells but the expectations for sales going in. Is this a reference book that appeals to a limited audience, or a hot topic title that may interest anyone? Furthermore, some Nonfiction Writers have credibility or expert/celebrity status that will help drive book sales. A good publicist or publicity department can help increase sales and get the book noticed.

Agents can often get Nonfiction Writers higher advances or royalties, as well as placements with larger publishing houses. However, keep in mind that a percentage of the earnings must be shared with the agent, usually about 15 percent.

Employment Prospects

Employment prospects are fair for Nonfiction Writers. Editors are always looking for new and creative ideas, but getting a book published is quite competitive. Nonfiction Writers can maximize their chances of getting published by understanding what topic is best for them to write about. Categories of nonfiction include trade books for the general public, textbooks for schools, and scholarly/academic titles usually published by university presses. Developing an area of expertise through one's career can be helpful, as well as seeking out writing opportunities. For example, a nutritionist who wants to write a diet book may begin by writing a column in a local newspaper or serving as an expert for a health Web site. In addition to having a good idea, writing a strong proposal and showing that you have done your market research is key to getting published.

Advancement Prospects

Nonfiction Writers may have different ultimate goals, depending on their background. Some may use their writing as a way to advance within their own field, such as a university professor seeking tenure or a higher salary. Others may use their first published work as a way to launch a full-time writing career. It is easier to get subsequent books published after you already have one full-length manuscript, particularly if it is successful in its market. If an editor or agent enjoys working with you, he or she may seek you out for additional assignments. Experienced Nonfiction Writers may be eligible for larger advances as well.

Education and Training

Nonfiction Writers come from a variety of educational backgrounds. To gain the credibility, as well as the writing and research skills necessary to complete a full manuscript, a minimum of a college degree is expected, although not required. Celebrities and other experts or public figures may use their fame to get around formal degrees; however, they often use professional writers if they do not have the writing skills themselves.

Nevertheless, the vast majority of Nonfiction Writers hold degrees in a variety of subjects. Professional writers may have studied English or journalism, and experts may have graduate degrees in fields such as medicine, law, education, political science, psychology, and many more. Training in writing and research is very important in order to complete a full-length book.

Experience, Skills, and Personality Traits

Above all, Nonfiction Writers should have excellent writing skills. They must have a firm command of the English language, as well as spelling, grammar, usage, and style. Additionally, they must be able to engage an audience. If they are writing for a specific series or demographic group, they need to conform their style to fit the needs of the publisher or reader. Flexibility is definitely important, especially for Nonfiction Writers who may complete different types of books.

Nonfiction Writers also must be self-starters. It takes an entrepreneurial spirit to write a book proposal and research the right editors and agents to review it. They need to be able to promote themselves and their credentials with confidence.

Research skills are also critical for writing nonfiction. Since their material is based on facts, Nonfiction Writers must know the best methods for gathering and organizing information. Furthermore, they need strong communication skills to interview people when necessary, as well as work with editors, agents, and publicists.

Unions and Associations

Nonfiction Writers may belong to professional associations including the National Writers Union, the Authors Guild, the Society of Professional Journalists, and the American Society of Journalists and Authors.

Tips for Entry

1. There are virtually hundreds of books on the market that help people to become Nonfiction Writers. Take a look at some, including *Writing Nonfiction: Turning Thoughts into Books* by Dan Poynter, *Writing the Nonfiction Book* (The Successful Writer's Guides) by Eva Shaw, and *Nonfiction Writing: From the Inside Out* by Laura Robb.

2. To learn how to write a winning proposal, see books such as *Nonfiction Book Proposals Anybody Can Write: How to Get a Contract and Advance Before Writing Your Book* by Elizabeth Lyon and *The Fast Track Course on How to Write a Nonfiction Book Proposal* by Stephen Black Mettee. For additional information, see Web sites such as http://www.writing-world.com/publish/proposal.shtml, http://www.spawn.org/marketing/bookprop.htm, and http://manuscriptediting.com/proposals.htm.

3. Learn more about the world of book publishing. Reference materials can be found in any library such as *The Literary Marketplace* (http://www.literarymarketplace.com/lmp/us/index_us.asp), an alphabetical listing of publishers and agents in the United States, Canada, and international markets.

4. Additionally, there are insider guides such as *The Writer's Guide to Book Editors, Publishers, and Literary Agents* by Jeff Herman. These resources will help you determine which publishing company and editor is right for your idea, as well as if you should hire an agent.

5. Hone your writing skills. Write articles, Web content, and anything else you can on a regular basis. Do not be afraid to start small to build a portfolio of your work. There are numerous writing courses to take at colleges and institutes throughout the country, as well as online seminars. For a listing to start with, see http://manuscriptediting.com/workshops.htm.

6. Do you have an area of expertise? Whether it is through your profession or your hobby, try writing about this area. Gain recognition through talks at your local community center and membership in professional organizations. This will help you establish the necessary credibility to try writing a book in this field.

DOCUMENTARY FILMMAKER

CAREER PROFILE

Duties: Develops a film or video that offers a factual recording of events; may write, produce, and/or direct the film

Alternate Title(s): Documentary Writer, Documentary Producer

Salary Range: $0 to $75,000 and up

Employment Prospects: Poor to Fair

Advancement Prospects: Fair

Best Geographical Location(s): All

Prerequisites:

Education or Training—No specific education required, although training and/or background in film or journalism is very valuable

Experience—Varies, but typically includes some film experience

Special Skills and Personality Traits—Creativity and good visual eye; excellent observation skills; strong writing and storytelling ability

CAREER LADDER

```
┌─────────────────────────────────────┐
│  Documentary Filmmaker, higher       │
│  budget/larger scale; Producer;      │
│  or Director                         │
└─────────────────────────────────────┘

┌─────────────────────────────────────┐
│  Documentary Filmmaker               │
└─────────────────────────────────────┘

┌─────────────────────────────────────┐
│  Production Assistant or Intern      │
└─────────────────────────────────────┘
```

Position Description

According to PBS.org's Media Literacy Glossary, a documentary "refers to film or video that explores a subject in a way the public expects to be factual and accurate." As the name implies, the information used is actually coming from documents or documented sources. Since documentaries strive to present a factual account of a person, event, or situation, they can be an important part of journalism in keeping with the mission of informing the public about the truth. Documentary Filmmakers are journalists who present their stories through the video medium. Whether their telling is objective or subjective, they present facts and leave it to the public to form their own opinions.

Documentaries can be films that play in small art house theaters or mainstream multiplexes. They can also be feature-length news programs, reality programs, instructional videos, or informational broadcasts. Documentaries tell a story, often from many angles with complex layers.

Documentary Filmmakers have different motivations when they develop a project. Some will conceptualize a project for years, focusing on a personal subject that is close to their hearts. For example, one Documentary Filmmaker may choose to tell the story of her grandmother, a Holocaust survivor who came to the United States to begin a new life. Others will be inspired by something that happens in the news, where they feel they want to delve deeper into the story they have already heard. Yet others will feel passionate about pushing a certain political agenda or furthering social issues—think of Michael Moore's *Fahrenheit 911*.

The road to making a documentary is not an easy one. Having an idea is just the beginning for a Documentary Filmmaker. Assembling the crew needed to make the film and obtaining funding are the two major obstacles they face early on. Films may be funded in several ways. Some Documentary Filmmakers work for production companies who fund their projects. Others receive funding from television stations, both public and private, network and cable.

Depending on the topic, foundations may fund documentaries if they coincide with their area of interest—for example, a foundation that promotes literacy may fund a documentary about a reading program that two teachers developed in a third-world country. Furthermore, private investors may also fund documentaries.

In order to fund their projects, Documentary Filmmakers use their writing skills in another way—by writing proposals. In their proposals, they outline the description and goals of their film. This may be called a project treatment. It gives investors an idea not only of the film's objectives but also the possible audience and distribution for the film.

Above all, Documentary Filmmakers are storytellers. As journalists and writers, they create a script that captures the tone they want to take. Documentary Filmmakers may choose to tell their story in several different narrative ways. They may take an observatory stance, where they present the facts as an outside observer. Or instead, they might be participatory, where they live among subjects and describe their experience.

The team that creates a documentary includes writers, who write the script; a director, who oversees the filming of each scene; and producers, who manage the big picture. Furthermore, camerapeople actually perform the filming; documentaries are usually filmed with just one camera. A Documentary Filmmaker may have a part in all roles, but also may collaborate with others.

Like other journalists, Documentary Filmmakers spend time speaking to people and must be able to put them at ease. The process of going into people's lives and putting issues on film is invasive, and Documentary Filmmakers must be able to handle this with finesse.

Their duties may include:

- Conducting grant research and writing proposals
- Performing fundraising
- Interviewing subjects
- Conducting intense background research
- Visiting film and archival libraries for background information
- Transcribing interviews
- Logging footage
- Participating in events as part of the filming

Documentary Filmmakers work erratic hours. This is not the field for someone looking for a stable nine to five job. Extensive travel may be required depending on the documentary subject, and filming can take place around the clock.

Furthermore, the actual abundance of work is also irregular. After a movie or video wraps up, funding for another documentary might not come through for weeks, months, or even longer. Many Documentary Filmmakers have other jobs in film, journalism, or other areas to help pay the bills. However, those with a passion for making documentaries remain driven by the sheer thrill of telling a story.

Salaries
Salaries for Documentary Filmmakers vary tremendously. Initial funding covers expenses and stipends for the staff involved; overall earnings might be determined by distribution and success of the film. Documentary Filmmakers can just break even to make the film they want, or they can earn $10,000 to $50,000 or more if their film gets noticed and they continue to work on additional projects. Salary is also dependent on the budget of the film and how many projects a Documentary Filmmaker works on per year.

Employment Prospects
Employment prospects are poor to fair for Documentary Filmmakers. It is a field where one must be entrepreneurial. Occasionally, production companies may hire people to make films or videos, or producer/directors will be looking for writers or other people to join their project. However, more often than not, a Documentary Filmmaker develops his or her idea and goes after the funding to make it happen. The likelihood of these projects being completed and successful depends on the Documentary Filmmaker's ability to develop a vision into a viable film and promote and market the finished product.

Advancement Prospects
Advancement prospects are fair for Documentary Filmmakers. Once someone has made a documentary, especially if it is successful in its market, it is often easier to get funding for additional projects. The occasional Documentary Filmmaker hits it big, with movies that enjoy commercial success in theaters or on television. Some Documentary Filmmakers move into other areas of media and journalism, such as commercial filmmaking, or specialize in writing, editing, producing, or directing.

Education and Training
There is no specific educational path for a Documentary Filmmaker to follow. While anyone can make a documentary, knowledge of film certainly is critical to understand the process. Many Documentary Filmmakers formally study film at the undergraduate or graduate level. A list of film schools can be found on http://www.imdb.com/filmschools, many of them located in California. Graduates of these programs often receive a Bachelor of Fine Arts (BFA) degree or Master of Fine Arts (MFA) degree. Other Documentary Filmmakers study journalism, liberal arts, political science, or history, as well as subjects related to the topic of their film. Those who do not study film take courses or receive training to learn about technique.

The University of California at Berkeley offers the only two-year graduate documentary program in the country that is part of a school of journalism. See their Web site at http://journalism.berkeley.edu/program/documentary/. Other journalism schools, such as the University of Southern California's Annenberg School for Communication (http://www.usc.edu/dept/publications/cat2004/schools/communication/jour_graduate.html), offer cources in documentary filmmaking.

Experience, Skills, and Personality Traits

In order to make documentaries, creativity and a good visual sense are needed. Documentary Filmmakers must be able to conceptualize a project from start to finish, with the vision for what makes a compelling project and filming approach. Furthermore, they must be excellent writers and storytellers. Their approach must be able to give viewers a better understanding of a person, situation, or event and to evoke emotion, opinion, or reaction. Documentary filmmakers must be able to convey the facts, while deciding which angle they want to take and what message to send.

Furthermore, Documentary Filmmakers must be ambitious. They need to be entrepreneurial self-starters who can sell themselves and their project. Persistence and a thick skin enable them to go after funding tirelessly. Documentary Filmmakers also must be skilled at working with people. They need the ability to conduct interviews with people from a diverse range of cultures and experience. By connecting with others and displaying empathy but never condescension, they put people at ease and do their story justice.

It is also necessary for Documentary Filmmakers to be skilled in the filmmaking process. They must know the jargon and all aspects of the business, from filming to editing to directing.

Unions and Associations

Documentary Filmmakers may belong to professional associations including the Association of Independent Video and Filmmakers, the International Documentary Association, and the National Alliance for Media Arts and Culture.

Tips for Entry

1. Watch *Supersize Me,* a recent participatory documentary where filmmaker Morgan Spurlock explores the negative effects of American fast-food industry. He himself takes on an all-McDonalds diet for one month and analyzes the consequences on his own health and that of all Americans. For more information, see http://www.supersizeme.com/.

2. See the Web site for MediaRights, a community organization dedicated to maximizing the impact of social-issue documentaries and shorts, at http://www.mediarights.org/about/.

3. The Web site Documentaryfilms.net includes filmmaker resources such as film schools with documentary specialties, documentary distributors, production companies, and other resources. See http://www.documentaryfilms.net/filmmakers.htm for more information.

4. Consider joining the International Documentary Association, which promotes nonfiction film and video around the world. For more information, see http://www.documentary.org/.

5. Take courses in film to learn more about the genre. A combination of film and journalism study can be the ideal background for making documentaries, since it combines the storytelling, factual reporting, and filmmaking elements.

TELEVISION

ANCHOR

CAREER PROFILE	CAREER LADDER

Duties: Reads and presents television news from the studio or set location; serves as a regular fixture on a news program

Alternate Title(s): Correspondent, Broadcaster, Newscaster

Salary Range: $40,000 to $100,000 and up

Employment Prospects: Poor

Advancement Prospects: Fair

Best Geographical Location(s): All

Prerequisites:

Education or Training—While there are no formal requirements, a bachelor's degree is considered essential in today's market; fields such as journalism and communication are helpful.

Experience—Typically, five to 10 years of on-air work as a reporter

Special Skills and Personality Traits—Excellent communication and public speaking skills; professional appearance and on-air presence; investigative mind; good research and writing skills; ability to stay calm under pressure

---

CAREER LADDER

```
┌─────────────────────────────────┐
│  Anchor, larger/national market │
└─────────────────────────────────┘

┌─────────────────────────────────┐
│            Anchor               │
└─────────────────────────────────┘

┌─────────────────────────────────┐
│           Reporter              │
└─────────────────────────────────┘
```

Position Description

Anchors are familiar figures that we invite into our homes each morning, afternoon, and evening. In addition to journalists, they are television personalities whose success is based on the trust and rapport they build with their audience. As regular fixtures on news programs, we can depend on seeing them at 6 A.M., 6 P.M., or whenever their show is on air.

While the job of an Anchor is to read the news, most successful Anchors are much more than newsreaders. They are seasoned journalists who have worked their way up to an Anchor position through years of successful reporting. Their job is frequently a combination of presenting the news from the station, but also some live and taped reporting from different locations.

In the station, Anchors not only read the news but they also introduce live reports and different segments of the program. Here, their personalities have a chance to come through in their ability to make small talk with the other anchors, reporters, and program guests. Anchors often conduct live interviews; they must be excellent communicators who are quick thinking and flexible.

Anchors often handle a wide range of stories, including features, investigative pieces, and commentary on breaking news. Some Anchors generate ideas for their own pieces, particularly longer feature reports, as well as present the news of the day. They must know enough about each story to present it to viewers and introduce reporters who are live on the scene. Some Anchors write some of their own copy, but much is written by news writers, editors, and producers.

Successful Anchors need a combination of reporting, public speaking, and star quality to make it in the field. Depending on the scope of their program, they often become local or (the lucky few) national celebrities who are easily recognizable. Especially when the news is difficult, the public wants to hear it from people they have come to trust and respect. The likability of various Anchors can play a large role in their journalistic success, influencing both ratings and viewers' reactions.

Since many Anchors also work as reporters, much of their time is spent researching stories, following up on leads, and scanning the local and national media, including newspapers, magazines, television, and the Internet for ideas. They constantly keep up to date on breaking news. Furthermore, developing relationships with the local community is essential. Whether Anchors are introducing segments, going on the scene, or interviewing these local leaders, positive relationships will allow them easier access and/or exclusives to stories.

As Anchors are always on camera, their professional image and appearance is very important. Since Anchors are not only journalists but also television personalities, these aspects do matter. Watch any local news program and you will see that most Anchors are attractive and personable, with a commanding and pleasing on-air presence. Everything from the tone of their voice and accents to their wardrobe is under scrutiny from the public. Anchors must be comfortable being under the public eye; at times, it is a little like acting.

Additional duties may include:

- Conducting live and studio interviews
- Researching and writing stories
- Working with news directors, reporters, photographers, camera crew, and producers
- Investigating story leads
- Producing segments
- Reporting on special events
- Presenting and preparing investigative and enterprising reports
- Maintaining contacts and sources
- Developing a news series
- Reviewing background information
- Attending daily planning/story meetings
- Keeping up on local, national, and international current events
- Operating teleprompter controls
- Attending special events and making public appearances
- Introducing video clips or coverage from reporters on the scene

Whether you watch *The Today Show* or *Good Morning America, Nightline,* or *20/20,* you have seen Anchors at work during morning and evening news programs. These Anchors, such as Katie Couric and Diane Sawyer, are also program hosts with a variety of responsibilities including conducting interviews, presenting features, and traveling to various locations. While the major national network prime time news Anchors, such as the late Peter Jennings, Tom Brokaw, and Dan Rather, are celebrities in our culture, every local news program has Anchors as well who perform similar duties on a much smaller scale. News Programs have Anchors that not only handle news but also separate Anchors for weather and sports.

Anchors can be important members of their communities. You can find them atop floats at local parades or on hand when a new school opens. A crucial part of the job, Anchors are accessible to their viewers, helping to build their trust.

Being an Anchor is more of a lifestyle than a job. As the news happens around the clock, hours for Anchors can be long and difficult, including early mornings, late nights, weekends, and holidays. Program slots including the 11 P.M. news and the 6 A.M. news can require getting to the studio as much as two hours before shooting and staying late after the program is finished. Also, Anchors can be on call at all times in a sense, having to head into the newsroom when breaking news occurs for special reports. However, becoming an Anchor is often the ultimate goal of an on-air reporter. To become a regular fixture on a news program is affirmation of a reporting career well done.

Some Anchors may travel to fill their local audiences in about national and international events. Major events such as elections and political campaigns, as well as breaking tragedies such as the death of a famous figure or the flooding of New Orleans, can bring Anchors to the scene along with reporters for different types of coverage. Anchors must be flexible and able to stay calm in difficult situations. We all remember the emotion showed by major Anchors during the events of September 11th. Their ability to show their emotion, yet perform their duty as journalists, touched us and strengthened our connections.

Salaries

Anchors may be national celebrity journalists or local small-town newsreaders; salaries vary accordingly. According to the annual Radio and Television Salary Survey by RTNDA (Radio-Television News Directors Association)/Ball State University for 2005, news Anchors earned an average of $71,100. The range reported by the survey was very large— from a minimum of $9,000 to a maximum of $300,000. Those Anchors working in major markets or national news can earn considerably more.

Employment Prospects

One does not become an Anchor at the beginning of his or her journalism career. Anchor positions are highly competitive, going to reporters with a combination of journalistic savvy and on-air presence. Those who are serious about such a career must be prepared to move to small towns with tiny networks in order to get their first break. They might begin by covering frivolous local happenings in order to pave the way for more investigative news stories later on. As beginning reporters, they may produce, edit, and shoot video footage themselves as well. Reporters may begin by substituting for Anchors on occasion before being offered a permanent Anchor position.

Being able to demonstrate on-air presence and sharp journalistic skills is a must, with successful tapes of past reporting work. Anchors typically have at least five years of prior reporting experience; many also work in dual Anchor/reporter roles. Since television news is both local and national, Anchors begin in small local markets, with only the most successful advancing to national news. Anchors may work in commercial broadcasting, public television, or cable networks.

Advancement Prospects

Advancement for Anchors can occur in one of two ways. Sometimes, one works his or her way up as a reporter, moving from small to larger markets and substituting for Anchors when applicable. Other times, one secures an Anchor position in a smaller market and then looks to move to an Anchor position in a larger market. Either way, it is essential that Anchors who are looking to advance not stay in a small market for too long. They must make sure to gain experience and exposure through reporting whenever possible. Community appearances and special events can also help build their recognition.

Competition is fierce and only the lucky few will make it to national news. Network decisions can be made on a whim, and job security is scarce, with ratings determining all. However, many journalists find satisfying careers as Anchors in mid-level markets. Some may also become program hosts or other types of television personalities, with many media possibilities.

Education and Training

There is no one specific path to follow in order to become an Anchor. While experience and on-air presence is more important than education, Anchors need to be well-informed to do their jobs well. Most reporters getting hired today have bachelor's degrees in a variety of fields, and a degree is certainly essential for advancement in the current market. Journalism and communication degrees are helpful, but Anchors may also hold degrees in a range of liberal arts fields. Many journalism schools offer specialties in broadcast journalism and courses on television reporting that can help potential anchors get their first break as reporters.

In order to gain crucial experience, insiders advise that the best ways to prepare is through on-the-job training as a newsroom intern. Internships and/or working at a local or college television station offer an ideal opportunity to gain on-air reporting experience, as well as a chance to become familiar with broadcasting operations. Interns may or may not get the opportunity to be on-air, performing producing, technical, writing, and administrative tasks until they have proven themselves. Furthermore, internships and college broadcasting can be the ideal way through which prospective reporters can develop the demo or audition tapes required for employment.

Since reporting style, voice tone, and overall appearance and presentation are so important for on-air work, prospective Anchors should consider how to develop their broadcast personae. Taking voice lessons and practicing on-camera skills can be very valuable.

Experience, Skills, and Personality Traits

Above all, Anchors need excellent communication skills. Articulate and well spoken, they can read from a teleprompter as well as spontaneously ad-lib and make conversation on-air. Anchors also use their communications skills to develop relationships. They need to be able to put subjects at ease during interviews, building trust and rapport. The relationship that Anchors build with the public will determine the success and longevity of their careers.

Anchors also should be first-rate journalists. Reporting ability is essential for developing stories and reports with interesting perspectives. Writing and editing skills help Anchors write news copy and scripts that are lively and interesting. An investigative mind and strong news judgment enable them to pursue stories and interviews that get to the heart of the matter. Also important is the ability to be flexible and open-minded. Anchors work on stories covering a variety of issues and affecting different types of people. They must be able to remain objective and professional at all times, but empathetic and never judgmental. They need to work well under pressure and tight deadlines. The ability to be comfortable on-camera and to present oneself to large numbers of people is essential.

Presentation is highly important. Anchors should have high energy and the ability to project intelligence on-air. A desire to pay attention to hair, makeup, and wardrobe comes with on-camera work. A good speaking voice that is authoritative but not condescending is also needed. Anchors should also be able to create their own personal style, in both presentation and appearance. An outgoing personality and ease at making small talk is essential for success. Good Anchors draw their viewers in, making them feel like they are having a conversation.

Unions and Associations

Anchors may belong professional associations including the National Association of Broadcasters, the Society of Professional Journalists, Investigative Reporters and Editors, American Women in Radio and Television, and the American Federation of Television and Radio Artists.

Tips for Entry

1. Regularly watch the news. Become an avid watcher of all types of news programs, ranging from national morning shows to local afternoon broadcasts. Take note of different anchors and their corresponding styles. Who do you like to watch and why?

2. Before becoming an Anchor, one must make it as a reporter. Take journalism courses and seek out internships at campus or local television stations.

3. Public speaking skills are valuable in honing an on-air presence. Try programs such as Toastmasters (http://www.toastmasters.org/), as well as communications classes. Acting classes may also help you to become comfortable performing for others.

4. Be persistent. Anchors reach their positions after years of hard work. Be willing to report in very small markets to begin with, and work hard. If you develop a good relationship with the news director, he or she may think of you to fill in for the Anchors when needed.

5. Enhance your people skills through activities and volunteer work. Put yourself in situations that enable you to conduct interviews and gain people's trust.

6. Consider a training program to enhance your television skills. Programs such as Television News Center (http://www.televisionnewscenter.org/about.html) offer training services.

REPORTER

CAREER PROFILE

Duties: Develops and delivers news and feature stories on-air for a television station; may report in the studio and on location for both live and taped broadcasts

Alternate Title(s): Correspondent, Broadcaster, Newscaster, News Reporter, News Analyst

Salary Range: $20,000 to $60,000 and up

Employment Prospects: Poor to Fair

Advancement Prospects: Fair

Best Geographical Location(s): All

Prerequisites:

Education or Training—While there are no formal requirements, a bachelor's degree is considered essential in today's market; fields such as journalism, broadcasting, and communication are helpful.

Experience—Several years of on-air work through internships or full-time jobs

Special Skills and Personality Traits—Excellent communication and public speaking skills; investigative mind; good research and writing skills; professional appearance and on-air presence; ability to stay calm under pressure

CAREER LADDER

```
┌─────────────────────────────────┐
│  Senior Reporter/Correspondent;  │
│  Anchor; News Director; or       │
│  Reporter, larger market         │
└─────────────────────────────────┘

┌─────────────────────────────────┐
│           Reporter               │
└─────────────────────────────────┘

┌─────────────────────────────────┐
│  Reporter, smaller market;       │
│  Production Assistant; Intern; or │
│  expert in other field           │
└─────────────────────────────────┘
```

Position Description

Reporters who bring us television news can become familiar staples in our everyday lives. They enter our homes and keep us informed about what is going on locally, nationally, and sometimes globally. In a job that seems glamorous to many, Reporters work hard as both journalists and on-air presences to keep us up to date on news, features, and other stories that affect us in many ways.

Reporters of television news often handle a wide range of stories. General assignment Reporters cover stories on a combination of issues, while beat Reporters cover their specific topics such as education, health, entertainment, or business, like their print counterparts. Reporters often generate ideas for their own pieces, particularly related to features, as well as complete assignments given to them by their news directors. As always in journalism, much of the day-to-day work is dictated by what is going on in breaking news.

Unlike newspapers that come out once a day, television is a fluid medium. On many networks, news is on a minimum of several times a day, including a morning news program, afternoon news, evening news, and late news. Furthermore, many cable stations such as CNN handle news all day long. As breaking news happens, Reporters must be ready to go on location if needed and handle spot news. As you watch the news, picture the frequent cuts to Reporters working live in the field from the anchors in the station. In the field, they are accompanied by field producers and the technical crew to get the broadcast and handle the taping. Breaking news also may be reported on directly from the station.

To get story ideas, Reporters gather information from sources, conduct research, follow up on leads, and scan the local and national media, including newspapers, magazines, television, and the Internet for ideas. Developing relationships with the local community is essential. Reporters also monitor the news wire services to which their stations subscribe, such as the Associated Press for news and Reuters for business, which constantly update them on breaking news. Furthermore, they also receive press releases with information about different stories.

Reporters are journalists who by and large write their own stories, unlike newsreaders who are responsible for reading off of a teleprompter or script prepared by others. They prepare their copy by choosing the angle they want to take as well as the ideas they want to highlight. Television news Reporters write scripts rather than stories to capture the presentation aspect of their coverage. Spot news stories are done on a daily basis, while feature stories may take several days or even weeks to write. Reporters may perform some editing on their own work, as well as share with a news editor or news director for additional editing and direction. Frequently, they both copy edit and tape edit their pieces.

Since Reporters are almost always on camera, their professional image and appearance is very important. Television broadcasting is one of the only areas within journalism where these things matter, but to make it in the field, they are quite important. Successful Reporters are attractive and personable, with a commanding and pleasing on-air presence. Everything from the tone of their voice and regional accents to their hairstyle and wardrobe is under scrutiny from the public. Reporters must be comfortable being under the public eye; at times, it is a little like acting.

On a typical day, Reporters do much more than cover a story. They frequently have writing, editing, research, shooting, and producing responsibilities for their pieces in addition to reporting. Reporters go out with camera crews to interview people and cover current news. Often, they will produce packages that involve writing a script, presenting an on-camera bridge between segments, tracking the script, and supervising the editing process. Also, Reporters will debrief live with the anchor in the field or in the studio.

Their duties may include:

- Conducting live and studio interviews
- Researching and writing stories
- Working with news directors, photographers, camera crew, and producers
- Investigating story leads
- Producing segments
- Reporting on special events
- Presenting and preparing investigative and enterprising reports
- Maintaining contacts and sources
- Digging for information

- Reviewing background information
- Presenting accurate and clear live shots
- Attending daily planning/story meetings
- Keeping up on local, national, and international current events
- Shooting and editing their own video
- Filling in for anchors

The ability to tell a story ultimately defines one's success as a Reporter. Looking for innovative and creative ways to tell the news helps Reporters to connect with viewers. Their likability and credibility determine their rapport with their audience.

As the news happens around the clock, hours for Reporters can be long and difficult, including early mornings, late nights, weekends, and holidays. However, for most Reporters, on-air work is the fulfillment of a lifetime goal. The journalistic ambition to dig for a story, combined with the excitement of the lights and cameras, makes the long hours more than worth it.

Travel may be required for Reporters to fill their local audiences in about national and international events. Regular occurrences such as elections and political campaigns, as well as breaking tragedies such as the death of a famous figure or natural disasters, bring Reporters to the scene to report back to their network. For these reasons, it is important for Reporters to be flexible and able to stay calm in difficult situations.

Salaries

Salaries for Reporters can vary greatly depending on their level of experience and the size of their market. According to the annual Radio and Television Salary Survey by RTNDA (Radio-Television News Directors Association)/ Ball State University for 2005, News Reporters earned an average of $35,000. The range reported by the survey was very large—from a minimum of $12,000 to a maximum of $150,000. Market and staff size also plays a major role in determining salary.

Employment Prospects

The glamour of television news is not found in a first job. Positions for on-air Reporters are highly competitive. According to the Bureau of Labor Statistics, positions will grow more slowly than average through 2014. Those who are serious about such a career must be prepared to move to small towns with tiny networks in order to get their first break. They might begin by covering frivolous local happenings in order to pave the way for more investigative news stories later on. Also, Reporters may need to serve as their own producer, editor, and cameraperson, shooting video footage themselves.

Being able to demonstrate on-air presence is a must; internships and college broadcasting experience can help provide this experience. Demo or audition tapes are a key requirement for employment. These tapes display a Reporter's ability to present a newscast or program. Many prospective Reporters develop these tapes through courses, internships, or college broadcasting experience.

Since television news is both local and national, reporters begin in small local markets, with only the most successful advancing to national news. Reporters may work in commercial broadcasting, public television, or cable networks. Some Reporters begin behind the scenes as production assistants or producers while honing their on-air skills.

Advancement Prospects

It is easier to advance within television broadcasting than it is to break in from the outside. However, competition is still fierce as you get to the larger markets with high turnover and little job security. Reporters who have gained good on-air experience and have honed both their journalistic as well as presentation skills can move to larger markets. Some Reporters choose to specialize in topics of special interest such as business, health, or entertainment.

Others may look to work their way up to becoming anchors where they are regular fixtures on a news program. Yet other Reporters decide to move from the camera to behind the scenes management positions such as news directors, while others want to produce.

Education and Training

Ultimately, experience is more important than education to make it as a news Reporter. However, virtually all Reporters getting hired today have bachelor's degrees in a variety of fields. Journalism and communication degrees are helpful, but Reporters also hold degrees in a range of liberal arts fields. Many schools offer specialties in broadcast journalism and courses on television reporting. Furthermore, Reporters with specialties such as finance or politics may hold degrees in business or political science.

In order to gain crucial experience, insiders advise that the best way to prepare is through on-the-job training as a newsroom intern. Internships and/or working at a local or college television station offer an ideal opportunity to gain reporting experience, as well as a chance to become familiar with broadcasting operations. Interns may or may not get the opportunity to be on-air, performing production, technical, writing, and administrative tasks until they have proven themselves. Furthermore, internships and college broadcasting can be the ideal way through which prospective Reporters can develop the demo or audition tapes required for employment.

Since reporting style, voice tone, and overall appearance and presentation are so important for on-air work,

prospective Reporters should consider how to develop their broadcast personae. Taking voice lessons and practicing on-camera skills can be very valuable.

Experience, Skills, and Personality Traits

To be an on-air Reporter, one needs superb journalistic and communication skills. Writing, editing, and reporting ability is essential for developing stories and reports with interesting perspectives. Good journalistic sense, excellent news judgment, and an investigative mind drive Reporters to find out more and get to the heart of a matter with truth and integrity. Reporters use this curiosity to drive their investigations and break stories that their competition does not.

Communication skills are absolutely crucial. In addition to presenting articulate and professional reports, Reporters also use their communication ability to develop relationships with people. Interviews are most successful when Reporters develop rapport and put people at ease. Furthermore, the relationship between a Reporter and the public ultimately affects his or her career.

Reporters must also be flexible and persistent. General assignment Reporters must be comfortable handling a variety of issues, and all Reporters must have the ability to switch gears at a moment's notice to go where the news takes them. Reporters should thrive under pressure and tight deadlines. An ability to stay calm under pressure enables them to produce professional broadcasts even under adverse conditions. In their newscasts, Reporters must walk the fine line of checking their emotions and remaining objective, yet demonstrating sympathy and empathy for those who are suffering.

The ability to be comfortable on-camera and to present to large numbers of people is essential. Reporters must also understand how a broadcast newsroom operates, including the technical equipment needed for a broadcast, video editing, and cameras.

Unions and Associations

Reporters may belong to professional associations including the National Association of Broadcasters, the Society of Professional Journalists, Investigative Reporters and Editors, American Women in Radio and Television, and the American Federation of Television and Radio Artists.

Tips for Entry

1. Networking is essential for breaking into this competitive field. Take a look at sites such as http://www.tvspy.com, which offers information and job listings for television professionals; http://www.mediabizjobs.com, a media industry job listing site; and Broadcasting & Cable (http://www.broadcastingcable.com/), the definitive news source for the television industry.

2. Take courses in broadcast journalism. Offered at schools throughout the country, courses prepare prospective Reporters for different aspects of news broadcasting, including broadcast news writing, history, and media management.

3. Is there a Reporter whom you admire? Watch television news regularly, including local, national, and cable channels. Take note of Reporters' appearances, presentation style, and journalistic angle.

4. Call a news director from a local station for an informational interview. Ask him or her what he looks for when hiring new reporters.

5. The Radio-Television News Directors Association and Foundation lists internships on their Web site for college students. Take a look at http://www.rtnda.org/asfi/internships/internships.shtml.

6. Read about getting a job in television news at http://www.soyouwanna.com/site/syws/tvnews/tvnews.html.

BROADCAST METEOROLOGIST

CAREER PROFILE

Duties: Reports on weather as part of a news program; interprets and predicts weather patterns

Alternate Title(s): Meteorologist, Atmospheric Scientist, TV Meteorologist, Weathercaster, Weather Person

Salary Range: $30,000 to $90,000 and up

Employment Prospects: Fair

Advancement Prospects: Fair to Good

Best Geographical Location(s): All

Prerequisites:

Education or Training—At least a bachelor's degree in meteorology or atmospheric sciences; an alternative can be a degree in journalism with significant meteorology course work

Experience—On-air student experience or several years in small markets

Special Skills and Personality Traits—Excellent communication and presentation skills; knowledge of weather and meteorology; strong observation skills; good computer skills

Special Requirements—The voluntary Certified Broadcast Meteorologist (CBM) credential is offered by the American Meteorological Society.

CAREER LADDER

```
┌─────────────────────────────┐
│  Broadcast Meteorologist,   │
│       larger market         │
└─────────────────────────────┘

┌─────────────────────────────┐
│   Broadcast Meteorologist   │
└─────────────────────────────┘

┌─────────────────────────────┐
│  Broadcast Meteorologist,   │
│       smaller market        │
└─────────────────────────────┘
```

Position Description

The weather is an integral part of local television news. Interspersed between breaking stories, features, and sports, viewers tuning in want to know what to expect as they venture outside. Broadcast Meteorologists predict, interpret, and report on local weather for viewers. They provide forecasts up to one week into the future, helping their audience to be informed and prepared.

Back in the early days of journalism, those trying to break into broadcasting from the bottom were relegated to the weather. It was stereotyped as a field for attractive people without much journalism experience to simply read from a teleprompter. Today, however, you will find few stations that do not have trained Broadcast Meteorologists reporting on the weather.

Broadcast Meteorologists have a dual role in broadcasting as scientists and journalists. They understand weather patterns and can make predictions, yet they also tackle breaking news like reporters. Is a sudden storm predicted that will affect viewers? Have there been power outages or other weather-related situations of which viewers must be aware? These are the questions that Broadcast Meteorologists are constantly asking as they watch and monitor the weather.

Forecasting the weather requires technical expertise in meteorology. Broadcast Meteorologists study the Earth's atmosphere and analyze the characteristics and motions of the air, as well as the way it affects the environment. They examine components such as air pressure, temperature, humidity, and wind velocity to determine weather patterns.

Information is gleaned by using weather satellites, radars, stations, and sensors.

Additionally, Broadcast Meteorologists use computer models and other sophisticated technical equipment to study and predict the weather, as well as to measure and observe weather conditions. They follow breaking news and reports from the National Weather Service, analyzing trends and climate issues. It is necessary for Broadcast Meteorologists to know how to read meteorological data; they often use mathematical and physical principles to interpret reports and forecast the weather.

Since their job is a unique combination of science and journalism, Broadcast Meteorologists must possess a combination of technical skills and on-air presence. As they write and read their forecasts, communication skills are crucial to connect with the audience. Broadcast Meteorologists use their creativity to deliver the weather in an engaging way, since ultimately, the public decides on their credibility. On air, ratings are a constant issue and personality will be just as important as making accurate forecasts in a Broadcast Meteorologist's success.

The weather may have a 10-minute spot in some news programs or it may be ongoing in terms of storm coverage. Broadcast Meteorologists report from the station but also on location during severe weather conditions. In the station, they work with computerized weather graphics charts to show viewers weather patterns and expected temperatures. On location, their viewers see them bundled up at airports in the snow or struggling with their umbrellas overlooking major highways in the rain.

Their duties may include:

• Developing in-depth stories and/or feature segments
• Following extreme weather patterns such as tornadoes or hurricanes
• Visiting schools and educating students about weather
• Participating in network events and special programs
• Working with station's engineers and graphic designers on using a weather graphics system
• Reporting on other subjects as needed
• Attending conferences
• Keeping abreast on pertinent weather and climate issues
• Analyzing new forecasting equipment
• Studying weather trends and patterns
• Assembling material from various sources to prepare forecasts
• Making promotional announcements and/or appearances for the station
• Monitoring the weather wire for new developments
• Preparing graphics and maps

While most Broadcast Meteorologists focus on local weather, those working for national channels such as the Weather Channel may forecast weather for a number of different regions. Furthermore, Broadcast Meteorologists may work for radio stations as well as television networks.

Broadcast Meteorologists work a variety of shifts, including morning, evening, or weekend news. Hours may be quite early for morning news; with broadcasts beginning at 6 A.M. or earlier, staff may need to be in at 4 A.M. Extended hours come up in extreme weather conditions as networks provide round-the-clock coverage. As part of the news team, Broadcast Meteorologists work with anchors, reporters, and sportscasters to put together their programs.

Salaries

Careerjournal.com, the Wall Street Journal's executive career site, reports on the 2005 RTNDA/Ball State University Annual Survey, Radio-Television News Directors Association, Washington, D.C. This survey shows the median annual salary for Weathercasters as $50,000. Based on ranking, they show a salary range for Weathercasters from a high of $92,500 for stations ranked one to 25 and a low of $32,000 for stations ranked 151 and below.

According to the Bureau of Labor Statistics, median annual earnings of atmospheric scientists in 2002 were $60,200. The middle 50 percent earned between $39,970 and $76,880. The lowest 10 percent earned less than $30,220, and the highest 10 percent earned more than $92,430.

Employment Prospects

Jobs are competitive for Broadcast Meteorologists. Like others in broadcast journalism, Broadcast Meteorologists should expect to start out in very small markets. They may be presenting the earliest shift in very small towns.

Broadcast Meteorologists must submit audition tapes to news directors and networks to apply for positions. The tapes showcase their on-air presence, as well as their ability to impart the weather in an interesting way. They may also highlight their meteorologic skills. Broadcast Meteorologists may create these tapes through broadcasting courses or station internships.

Advancement Prospects

Advancement prospects are fair to good for Broadcast Meteorologists. With solid experience of three to five years, they can move into bigger markets. Those who enjoy exceptional popularity and promise as television personalities can advance to positions of both local and even national recognition on large networks.

Some Broadcast Meteorologists may branch into other areas of broadcast journalism, such as news or entertainment, but this transition usually must happen early in their careers to avoid being pigeonholed. Furthermore, other Broadcast Meteorologists may expand their meteorology focus, working for weather-related networks and producing features about weather.

Education and Training

Education in both meteorology and journalism is the best preparation for a Broadcast Meteorologist. Many have undergraduate majors in meteorology or atmospheric sciences, while others study journalism. However, Broadcast Meteorologists take courses in both areas regardless of their major. Many Broadcast Meteorologists hold joint degrees in meteorology and journalism. Those who major in journalism must have significant meteorology coursework or go on to complete a certificate program. On the other side, Broadcast Meteorologists who major in meteorology should also take journalism and communication courses. Some Meteorologists have master's degrees or Ph.D.'s.

To be called a Meteorologist, the American Meteorology Society (AMS) specifies that one must have a bachelor's degree or higher in meteorology or atmospheric science. However, the society also states that one can be a Meteorologist without a bachelor's degree in meteorology if that individual has at least three years of professional experience in meteorology, coupled with coursework. Courses required for those without degrees include atmospheric or oceanographic dynamics; atmospheric or oceanographic thermodynamics; physical meteorology or physical oceanography; synoptic meteorology (or weather systems) or synoptic oceanography; and hydrology.

Additionally, journalism students who are interested in broadcast meteorology can explore the AMS's certificate program to become a Certified Broadcast Meteorologist at http://www.ametsoc.org/amscert.

The National Weather Association maintains a listing of degree programs in meteorology or atmospheric science at http://www.nwas.org/links/universities.html. Furthermore, some schools offer specializations in meteorology and journalism. These programs include the University at Albany, State University of New York (http://www.albany.edu/main/features/2003/11-03/4meteorology/meteorology.htm) and Mississippi State University (http://www.msstate.edu/dept/geosciences/broadcast-meteorology.htm).

Special Requirements

The American Meteorological Society offers the Certified Broadcast Meteorologist (CBM) program, designed to raise the professional standards in broadcast meteorology. They may also receive the AMS Seal of Approval, which is awarded to Broadcast Meteorologists who meet established criteria for scientific competence and effective communication skills in their weather presentations. While this certification is not required to enter the field, it can be critical for employment and advancement. For more information, see http://www.ametsoc.org/amscert/. A seal of approval is also available from the National Weather Association. Consult their Web site at http://www.nwas.org/.

Experience, Skills, and Personality Traits

Broadcast Meteorologists must have excellent observation skills. A keen interest in weather is the spark to start the career, along with the scientific training to support it. Computer skills and the ability to understand weather systems and programs such as Doppler Radar and Fast Trac are also needed.

Furthermore, Broadcast Meteorologists must have superb communication skills. A congenial, engaging manner and on-air presence enables them to build a rapport with their viewers. Good grooming and a professional appearance, as well as the desire to pay attention to these aspects, is also quite important for on-air work.

To develop on-air experience, college internships are a must. Work at campus television networks, radio stations, and/or local networks are key ways to develop broadcasting skills and an audition tape.

Unions and Associations

Broadcast Meteorologists may belong to the American Meteorological Society, a professional organization for those in the atmospheric and related sciences. They may also belong to the National Weather Association and the National Association of Broadcasters.

Tips for Entry

1. USA Today.com has a weather internship for college students interested in both meteorology and journalism. See information about their program at: http://www.getthatgig.com/science_space/internships/meteorology/i_meteorology.html.

2. There are many variations on how to describe the weather. Language plays an important role in helping Broadcast Meteorologists connect with viewers. Learn about catchy weather phrasing at the following site: http://www.theweatherprediction.com/basic/terms/.

3. In a competitive field such as broadcasting, finding a mentor is invaluable. Develop a relationship with a local Broadcast Meteorologist to get tips and advice as to how to make yourself marketable.

4. Learn more about predicting weather through books such as *Air Apparent: How Meteorologists Learned to Map, Predict, and Dramatize Weather* by Mark Monmonier.

5. Take courses in math and physical sciences to prepare for studying meteorology.

SPORTSCASTER

CAREER PROFILE

Duties: Reports on sports for a television program; covers games and other sporting events

Alternate Title(s): Sports Reporter, Announcer, Sports Anchor

Salary Range: $20,000 to $250,000 and up

Employment Prospects: Poor

Advancement Prospects: Fair

Best Geographical Location(s): All

Prerequisites:

Education or Training—Bachelor's degree in journalism or related field helpful and may be required for some positions

Experience—One to 10 years of broadcasting experience and sports coverage; varies by position

Special Skills and Personality Traits—Interest in and knowledge of sports; excellent reporting and writing skills; good interviewing and communication skills; strong on-air presence; high energy and enthusiasm

CAREER LADDER

```
┌─────────────────────────────────────┐
│   Sportscaster, larger market or     │
│         Sports Director              │
└─────────────────────────────────────┘

┌─────────────────────────────────────┐
│           Sportscaster               │
└─────────────────────────────────────┘

┌─────────────────────────────────────┐
│   Sports Writer or other type of     │
│   Sports Journalist; Sportscaster,   │
│  smaller market; General Assignment  │
│      Reporter (television); or       │
│       Professional Athlete           │
└─────────────────────────────────────┘
```

Position Description

Sportscasters combine their interests in both sports and broadcasting. As television reporters and personalities, they have the on-air skills and reporters' inquisitive nature. As sports fans, they have a passion for sports news, and through this passion, they make their broadcasts exciting and lively for their viewers. Good Sportscasters bring their audience to the games along with them.

Sportscasters may serve as anchors for regular news program time slots, reading the sports news from the studio along with other anchors. Others are out in the field, attending games and interviewing coaches, players, and fans. Sportscasters may also provide the play-by-play for a live game, using his or her knowledge of sports to offer an insightful commentary that enhances the viewer's experience and understanding while watching a game.

Like other television reporters, Sportscasters may write some of their own copy as well as read copy written by news writers and other staff. Often, they decide what should go into a sportscast. They determine which parts of a game they should focus on by considering what happened that was most newsworthy. Highlights must fit into a small time portion. Good on-air presence is crucial. Sportscasters must be very knowledgeable about sports in order to report with confidence and authority.

Most Sportscasters cover a variety of sports, depending on the season. On local stations, they become experts on all the local teams. However, some Sportscasters specialize and may travel to announce at various games for particular sports teams. They may work on specialized sports programs or networks (like Sportscenter or ESPN) where they focus in on certain sports. Former athletes who become Sportscasters often focus on their own sport. For example, John McEnroe is a frequent figure on sports broadcasts during the tennis Grand Slam tournaments.

Sportscasters may have experience in other areas of journalism. They may have worked previously as sports writers, where they reported, edited, and even took photographs at games. Some Sportscasters have multiple responsibilities within broadcasting. It is not uncommon for Sportscasters, particularly early on in their careers, to report on other news, produce, and shoot video footage.

Sports coverage is more diverse than one might imagine. Sportscasters, particularly at small local stations, might cover high school games in all sports, as well as local colleges and regional events. Coverage is also determined by the region and can include a diverse range like minor league baseball, Little League, skiing, boating, auto racing, horse racing, and golf, among others.

The daily coverage of a Sportscaster is determined by the season and game schedules. While flexibility always needs to be in place for breaking news (such as players being traded and scandals involving sports figures), most Sportscasters know what they are going to cover in a given week based on schedules. Sportscasters may also handle longer investigative pieces or feature segments about sports figures.

Since anyone can watch a game and find out a score, good Sportscasters go beyond the numbers. They may give their opinions on the personalities of the athletes, the coaches, the referees, and the fans. Telling the story behind the scores is what sports journalism is really about. They help their audience to see and understand the behind-the-scenes moments and sympathize and celebrate wins and losses alongside them.

Relationships with coaches and players are important to a Sportscaster. Conducting interviews can be a big part of the job, and good communication skills are essential in getting people to talk. Mutual respect is the key here, since coaches and players will not talk to journalists they do not like.

Additional duties may include:

- Shooting and editing video footage
- Producing segments or programs
- Meeting with players, coaches, and other sports professionals
- Conducting locker room interviews
- Attending games and other sports industry events
- Keeping up on sports news
- Researching story ideas
- Writing sports news copy
- Working with other reporters at their station

Some travel is required for most Sportscasters depending on their market and/or specialty. They may travel locally to games and go long distances for playoffs or tournaments. Hours will vary by shift, but they are also determined by the various game times. Since most sports are played in the late afternoon and evenings, Sportscasters are more commonly anchors on the eleven o'clock news than on an afternoon program.

Salaries

Salaries for Sportscasters vary greatly. It can depend on the size of the market, the scope of their station, whether or not they are an anchor, and their prior experience. According to the annual Radio and Television Salary Survey by RTNDA (Radio-Television News Directors Association)/Ball State University for 2005, Sports Anchors earned an average of $53,900. The range reported by the survey was very large— from a minimum of $10,000 to a maximum of $250,000. Sports Anchors working in major markets or national news can earn considerably more.

Employment Prospects

Sportscasters face stiff competition for positions in large markets. They must be willing to start out at small stations and work their way up. Some begin as general reporters for television while others begin in print journalism as sports writers. Others transition from radio to television. A proven interest in sports, success as a reporter, and good on-air presentation skills are essential. Former athletes who are articulate and engaging also may become Sportscasters.

Internships are highly valuable for aspiring Sportscasters. The passion for watching, playing, and/or covering sports early on must be there. Covering sports for high school or college papers develops the interest and skills and helps Sportscasters get a first break after graduation.

Advancement Prospects

Advancement prospects are fair for Sportscasters. Only the lucky few will make it as anchors on national news. Sportscasters advance by moving to larger markets and bigger stations. Others may move from regular news to sports-specific programs or stations. Yet others find advancement through other media outlets such as writing sports-related books, producing sports documentaries, and more.

Education and Training

Most news directors will say that it is very difficult to get a first job in broadcasting without a bachelor's degree. Sportscasters can hold degrees in broadcasting, journalism, or communication, but those fields are not required. Others in the field recommend courses in physical education, sports management, or other areas of sports. Considerable experience as a professional athlete, coach, or other sports figure can compensate for lack of formal education.

Experience, Skills, and Personality Traits

While Sportscasters cannot possibly know everything about every sport, they are passionate and knowledgeable about their field. Whether they were athletes themselves or not, all are sports fans who love not only watching games but analyzing and dissecting them as well.

Writing skills are also valuable for Sportscasters. As they write copy for their broadcasts, they should be able to create lively and entertaining scripts. Communication skills make or break a Sportscaster's success. As entertainers as well as journalists, they need high energy and enthusiasm to draw their audience into their coverage. They must be able to stay interested and lively until the last overtime is played. Strong communication skills also enable them to conduct interviews with finesse and tact.

Good presentation skills and likability help Sportscasters to develop a following. A professional and pleasing appearance, as well as voice and overall image, help build their viewer base. They need good judgment about sports and journalism to make insightful comments that will draw an audience over their competition.

Unions and Associations

Sportscasters may belong to a variety of professional associations including the American Sportscasters Association, the Association for Women in Sports Media, and the National Broadcasters Association.

Tips for Entry

1. See the Web site for the American Sportscasters Association at http://www.americansportscasters.com/aboutus.html. They offer information and advice about becoming a Sportscaster.
2. For people interested in gaining experience in sports broadcasting, there are training camps offered through Sportscaster Camps of America. Through this experience, one can get the chance to anchor television studio sportscasts and call the play-by-play of professional sports games. According to their Web site, each camper takes home the audio and videotapes of all their camp broadcasts. See http://www.sportscastercamp.com/ for more information.
3. What makes a good Sportscaster? Watch sports coverage avidly, thinking not only as a viewer but also as a journalist. What makes good coverage? What would you do differently? Think about which Sportscasters you admire and why.
4. In addition to watching sports, read as much about sports as possible to become well informed. Your local newspaper, magazines such as *Sports Illustrated,* and Web sites are only a few of the multitude of sports information out there. Attend games whenever possible as well.
5. Gain experience covering sports for your high school, college, or local paper, or radio or television station. Be willing to work for free just to get your foot in the door. Remember that even covering Little League games is a good way to start.
6. Women Sportscasters can greatly benefit from support in this male-dominated field. Developing a niche area and finding mentors can be very helpful. Check out the Web site of the Association for Women in Sports Media at http://www.awsmonline.org/ and the Women's Sports Foundation at http://www.womenssportsfoundation.org/.
7. See http://www.onlinesports.com/sportstrust/sports41.html for more information about pursuing a sportscasting career.

PRODUCER

CAREER PROFILE

Duties: Organizes and manages the entire production process of individual television newscasts and programs from beginning to end

Alternate Title(s): News Producer, Show Producer, Line Producer

Salary Range: $20,000 to $60,000 and up

Employment Prospects: Fair to good

Advancement Prospects: Fair to good

Best Geographical Location(s): All

Prerequisites:

Education or Training—Bachelor's degree; journalism or broadcasting major helpful

Experience—One to three years of newsroom experience, often as a production assistant; advanced positions can require five years of experience or more

Special Skills and Personality Traits—Excellent writing skills; good reporting skills and knowledge of journalism; strong project management and organizational skills; ability to focus on details and visualize the big picture as well

CAREER LADDER

```
┌─────────────────────────────┐
│   Executive Producer or     │
│   Supervising Producer      │
└─────────────────────────────┘

┌─────────────────────────────┐
│         Producer            │
└─────────────────────────────┘

┌─────────────────────────────┐
│ Associate Producer, Assistant│
│ Producer, or Production Assistant│
└─────────────────────────────┘
```

Position Description

While watching a news program, people often take for granted the seamless flow of elements. As the camera moves from the anchors in the station to the reporters live in the field, programs typically also include sports, weather, and feature reports. Producers oversee a television news broadcast from conception to execution. They are involved every step of the way, from participating in brainstorming discussions about the idea, to working with reporters on their interviews and coverage, to the on-air finished product.

Writing is a large part of being a Producer in television news. Producers develop and write much of the content for each of their programs. Producers write "teasers" to be used to promote the program, and bridges between segments. They also write non-reporter copy to be used in programs, such as parts for anchors to read. Strong journalism writing skills allow Producers to develop innovative and creative news copy that fits the style of their program.

Organizational skills are essential as Producers act as the architects for each individual newscast, selecting the elements for their program. They may assign stories, or be involved with the assignment editor as to who will cover what. Furthermore, they determine the order of presentation for the different program pieces.

Producers also decide how long each component of the broadcast will be. For example, they consider how many interviews will be included and the length of each one. The process of selecting each element for a show can often fall under the title of line producer. As they select each element, Producers consider the newsworthiness of each piece. They choose the elements that they feel are the best and will most successfully meet the goals of their program.

Producers are masters of time management, and they help the other newsroom players stick to their schedules. During a broadcast, they sit in the control room and may give time cues to the anchors and directors. They make sure that a one-hour program goes exactly one hour, with each segment being the appropriate length.

Newsgathering skills are essential to come up with fresh and innovative programming ideas. Producers must be journalists who know what makes a good news story. Since they do so much writing, they also must know how to tell a story in a way that will touch their audience. Good news judgment is needed to generate compelling ideas that will expand their viewer base.

Their duties may include:

- Participating in editorial meetings
- Writing news copy and scripts to accompany pieces
- Editing audio and video content
- Generating and developing ideas for new programs
- Monitoring the live feeds
- Taking content off the wire to incorporate breaking news
- Selecting video and graphics for a particular program
- Planning coverage for special events
- Monitoring the progress of assigned features
- Coordinating the news broadcast while it is on-air
- Researching program and story ideas
- Determining the flow of newscasts

Producers work closely with different members of the newsroom team, since their job has so much overlap. On the content side, reporters, news writers, editors, and the news director work with the Producer to complete the various parts of a broadcast. Producers also work with news photographers and graphics editors to match the visuals with the audio, joining together the two parts to make a cohesive show.

Producers often work long hours; their programs are their babies. They need to make sure all elements are in place. Depending on what they are producing and the time slots of these newscasts, their hours may include early mornings, late nights, holidays, and weekends. However, Producers say that seeing the finished product and knowing they made it happen is highly rewarding.

Salaries
According to the 2005 RTNDA (Radio-Television News Directors Association)/Ball State University Annual Survey, the average salary for a television news Producer was $31,600. The figures in the survey ranged from a minimum of $15,000 to a maximum of $90,000. Like other salaries in journalism, market size and level of experience play a strong role in earnings.

Employment Prospects
Employment prospects are fair to good for Producers. Usually, one to three years of experience is required to find a position. Most Producers start out as production assistants,

assistant producers, or associate producers. Some may move directly into a Producer role from undergraduate or graduate school with significant related experience through internships and campus broadcasting. Producers must be willing to start in small markets to get their first break. The best opportunities are for those who are willing to relocate.

Advancement Prospects
Producers can advance in several ways. One way is by moving to larger markets. Here, they can have responsibility for bigger programs with more diverse and interesting coverage. Another is through becoming executive or supervising producers, where they oversee many programs for a station. Other Producers may move into other areas such as new media, commercial television, or film.

Education and Training
A bachelor's degree is standard for most positions and is preferred or required by many. While a degree is definitely necessary for advancement, experience does count more than formal education in broadcasting. However, studying journalism as an undergraduate can provide valuable exposure to news writing, as well as networking opportunities with professors and classmates.

Internships and campus media experience are ideal ways to get training in the field. Working for a campus television station or completing an internship offers hands-on exposure to broadcast journalism. Aspiring Producers can get specific experience producing a news program that will help them when they apply for jobs. Since tapes of past programs one has produced are required for many positions, this can be a good way to build a video portfolio.

Experience, Skills, and Personality Traits
Producers should have a combination of good news judgment, excellent writing skills, strong communication abilities, and sharp organizational and management skills. Each of these components is needed for them to excel at their jobs. Creativity and curiosity help Producers to develop fresh concepts for their programs and strive for different and innovative coverage. Flexibility and the ability to work well under pressure enable them to develop programs that fit their time slots and flow. Furthermore, Producers must have the vision to see the big picture and overall goals for their program, as well as the patience to focus on the minute details that will make it successful.

Knowledge of the technical aspects of television broadcasting, such as newsroom computers, Internet, satellite, and microwave newsgathering is also essential. Producers may work on programs that include coverage from helicopters, news trucks, and more—they need to be familiar with how to handle these elements.

Unions and Associations

Producers may belong to professional associations including the National Association of Broadcasters (NAB), National Federation of Community Broadcasters (NFCB), American Women in Radio and Television, and the National Press Club.

Tips for Entry

1. Take a look at job descriptions for Producers on sites such as http://www.mediabizjobs.com and http://www.tvspy.com.
2. Networking is a key way to find a Producer position. Make a list of everyone you know in journalism and media, asking family, friends, professors, and colleagues for help. Then target several professionals to meet with for informational interviews. If you are not asking for a job and your goal is to learn about the field, you will find that people are generally receptive to meeting with you.
3. The best jobs are frequently unadvertised. Contact the news director at a local station to ask about job openings for Producers.
4. TVJobs.com features a Master Station Index of 2,079 television stations in four countries. Local stations are the best way to get a first break. Take a look at http://msi.tvjobs.com/cgi-bin/index.cgi.
5. Read tips for getting a job in TV news at http://www.soyouwanna.com/site/syws/tvnews/tvnews.html.
6. See the Producer Page at http://scrippsjschool.org/producerpage.php, from the E. W. Scripps School of Journalism at Ohio University, filled with resources and a newsletter.

EXECUTIVE PRODUCER

CAREER PROFILE

Duties: Coordinates the content and presentation of broadcasts for a television station or department; oversees producing and directing

Alternate Title(s): None

Salary Range: $40,000 to $65,000 and up

Employment Prospects: Fair

Advancement Prospects: Fair

Best Geographical Location(s): All

Prerequisites:

Education or Training—Bachelor's degree required or preferred for most positions; journalism or broadcasting major helpful

Experience—Three to five years or more of experience as a producer

Special Skills and Personality Traits—Excellent leadership and management skills; good writing and editing skills; strong organizational ability; project management and attention to detail; ability to multitask

CAREER LADDER

```
┌─────────────────────────────────────┐
│ Executive Producer, larger market;   │
│ Managing Editor; or News Director    │
└─────────────────────────────────────┘

┌─────────────────────────────────────┐
│         Executive Producer           │
└─────────────────────────────────────┘

┌─────────────────────────────────────┐
│              Producer                │
└─────────────────────────────────────┘
```

Position Description

Executive Producers coordinate and manage the content of television broadcasts. While individual producers handle specific broadcasts, the Executive Producer oversees them all. He or she directs the entire presentation, making sure all aspects are complete. Additionally, Executive Producers manage multiple broadcasts, sometimes even all programming, for a station.

On the production team, there may be news producers, field producers, segment producers, and line producers. News producers develop and oversee the content for individual newscasts, including the reporters, the writing, and the filming. Field producers coordinate this process from out in the field, alongside reporters on location. Segment producers work on specific components of a broadcast, such as a guest interview or special report. Line producers select different elements to be used in a broadcast, write copy, and make sure everything is on schedule.

The Executive Producer manages this team of producers and supervises their work on a program. Along with the news director and the managing editor, he or she develops and implements programming ideas and goals. Leadership skills are necessary to run day-to-day operations of the production staff. Executive Producers play an important role in determining the editorial direction and content of newscasts.

Experience as a producer and familiarity with a newsroom is also essential. Executive Producers must utilize all their resources, from satellite and live trucks to helicopters and different bureaus. They must be able to get the best from reporters in order to create compelling broadcasts. Furthermore, they need to know their way around the technology to get this to happen.

For each broadcast, Executive Producers often have the final say about which components to include. They pore over videos, graphics, and scripts to determine which will work best with the story. Their knowledge of newsroom resources enables them to use all necessary sources. Furthermore, they also determine which stories are most interesting to their viewers and will yield the highest ratings in their market. Executive Producers use their news formatting expertise to create programs that work both intellectually and visually.

Their duties may include:

- Writing news scripts
- Editing video
- Managing editing schedules
- Approving scripts
- Working on special reports
- Overseeing the shooting process
- Coordinating the on-air broadcast
- Working with sound engineers in the control room
- Monitoring breaking news
- Handling special events coverage
- Supervising and training production staff
- Selecting graphics for broadcasts
- Conducting background research
- Interviewing guests for programs
- Critically watching and analyzing newscasts
- Preparing Web content
- Carrying out newsroom policies

Like others in broadcasting, Executive Producers work long hours that can include evenings, weekends, and holidays. They must be ready to go in for a story as breaking news happens. Furthermore, they work closely with other newsroom leaders such as news directors and managing editors to make decisions about broadcasts. Executive Producers also work with reporters and news photographers on each story.

Salaries

Each year, the Radio-Television News Directors Association (RTNDA) and Ball State University conduct a survey for television salaries. According to this annual survey in 2005, Executive Producers earned an average of $52,000 per year. Their salary range was from a reported low of $20,000 to a high of $125,000. Earnings can range greatly depending on the size of the station and market.

Employment Prospects

Employment prospects are fair for Executive Producers. While a broadcast may have several types of producers, there is usually just one Executive Producer, making the position more competitive than producer positions at different levels. Since the job usually requires at least five years of experience, most opportunities are for seasoned producers who have proven themselves through their previous work. Being open to relocation and the willingness to begin in small markets enhances employment options. Videotapes of previous broadcasts are often required with job applications.

Advancement Prospects

Advancement prospects for Executive Producers are also fair. Since it is a management position, most will need to move to larger stations and markets to find advancement. In these settings, Executive Producers may supervise more staff members and have responsibility for more in-depth and challenging stories. Yet other Executive Producers may move onto other areas of media such as commercial television or film.

Education and Training

Most Executive Producer positions require a bachelor's degree. Although experience is more important than education, a degree is usually essential for achieving this level of success. Helpful fields include journalism, broadcasting, and mass communications. However, a liberal arts or business curriculum supplemented with journalism courses and internship experience can also lead to a first job in the field.

Executive Producers often start out as production assistants, working their way up to other types of producer positions (such as general news producers, field producers, or line producers) before reaching this level. The best training comes through internships while in school and then the valuable early experience on the job.

Experience, Skills, and Personality Traits

Executive Producers need to be well-organized managers who can lead a team and visualize various broadcasts from start to finish. Their creativity and good storytelling ability enables them to assemble broadcasts that engage viewers, while their attention to detail ensures programs that make logistical sense.

Good communication skills allow Executive Producers to work with a variety of newsroom staff, as well as interview subjects and other people involved with news stories. Their strong writing skills come into play as they write news scripts to use. Staying calm under pressure is essential, as is the ability to juggle multiple tasks at once. Furthermore, Executive Producers must be skilled in the technical aspects of broadcasting. Familiarity with newsroom computers, satellite, and microwave newsgathering is crucial.

Unions and Associations

Executive Producers may belong to professional associations including the National Association of Broadcasters, the National Federation of Community Broadcasters, and American Women in Radio and Television.

Tips for Entry

1. Take a look at jobs on Variety Careers, the media and entertainment job site, at http://www.variety.com/index.asp?layout=variety_careers.

2. The Web site JournalismJobs.com features interviews with television news executives. See the 2004 interview with Steve Scully, who was the senior executive producer and political editor for C-SPAN at the time: http://www.journalismjobs.com/steve_scully.cfm.

3. Another Web site, ProductionHub.com serves as an online resource and industry directory for film, television, video, and digital media production. It includes much useful information, including job listings at http://productionhub.com/.

4. Take journalism courses with a production component. For example, the Phillip Merrill College of Journalism at the University of Maryland in College Park offers broadcasting courses that teach the production process: http://www.journalism.umd.edu/.

5. Learn more about the Robert C. Maynard Institute for Journalism Education (MIJE), the leading organization dedicated to training journalists of color and to helping the nation's news media reflect diversity in staffing, content, and business operations. See their programs at http://www.maynardije.org/programs/.

6. Begin at the bottom in order to learn more about becoming a producer. A position as a production assistant is an excellent way to start.

PRODUCTION ASSISTANT

CAREER PROFILE	CAREER LADDER

Duties: Supports the producer on a television news program

Alternate Title(s): News Assistant, News Production Assistant, Desk Assistant

Salary Range: $20,000 to $30,000

Employment Prospects: Good

Advancement Prospects: Good

Best Geographical Location(s): All

Prerequisites:

Education or Training—Bachelor's degree, especially in journalism, broadcasting, or communications, is preferred/required for most positions

Experience—Entry-level; prior experience includes internships and campus broadcasting experience

Special Skills and Personality Traits—Excellent writing and research skills; ability to be flexible and handle multiple assignments at once; good organizational skills and attention to detail; ability to follow directions and operate broadcasting equipment

```
┌─────────────────────────────────┐
│  Assistant or Associate Producer;│
│            Reporter              │
└─────────────────────────────────┘

┌─────────────────────────────────┐
│      Production Assistant        │
└─────────────────────────────────┘

┌─────────────────────────────────┐
│             Intern               │
└─────────────────────────────────┘
```

Position Description

Behind the scenes, Production Assistants help producers and other staff to develop their news programs. They are crucial to newsroom operations as they assist with diverse tasks ranging from writing copy to operating a teleprompter. As producers are responsible for the overall coordination and quality of the broadcast, Production Assistants are at the ground level making this happen. They ensure that programs go off without a hitch and that problems are minimized.

The job of a Production Assistant can vary depending on the news program on which they work. With live news, the pressure is intense and the pace is fast. Taped news offers a somewhat less frenetic environment; however, the deadline pressure is always there. Furthermore, Production Assistants also can have different responsibilities depending on the producers they assist. For example, Production Assistants for field producers often accompany reporters and producers on location, as well as coordinate live coverage from the studio.

Some Production Assistants have the opportunity to do some writing. They may be responsible for the "teasers" that

appear to advertise a news program—for example, "Coming up next on . . . " These snippets can have a major impact on drawing in viewers, so Production Assistants must use their creativity to summarize upcoming news and highlight the stories of most interest to their target audience.

Research is another component of being a Production Assistant. In order to ensure that producers have all they need for a shoot, Production Assistants often conduct background research into issues for segments. These may be feature news stories where people are interviewed. Production Assistants may help producers with booking interviews, providing biographical information, and offering detailed background on the issue at hand. Tasks can include running Internet and database searches, pulling relevant news articles and other broadcast interviews, and scanning print media.

Many Production Assistants also perform administrative duties such as answering phones, updating files, photocopying, and fact checking. While these tasks are far from glamorous, Production Assistants realize this is another part of paying their dues. To prove themselves as new professionals in the world of television journalism, Production Assistants perform a wide variety of tasks that at times can cause them to ask, "I went to school for this?" Their responsibilities can be as interesting as writing copy for newscasts and as mundane as making coffee. However, insiders agree, the job is never boring.

Production Assistants may have some technical responsibilities as well. They may coordinate graphics, check equipment, and operate cameras. Also, they might oversee studio lighting and be involved with setup, ensuring that the studio maintains the image for a professional broadcast. Production Assistants can also work with video—organizing, archiving, and maintaining past coverage.

Additional duties may include:

- Writing and editing copy
- Conducting research
- Collecting numbers or statistics
- Coordinating schedules
- Monitoring the wire services for breaking news
- Dubbing tapes
- Running a teleprompter
- Logging tapes for news stories
- Distributing scripts to reporters and producers
- Locating video clips and maintaining a video library

Shifts can vary, depending on the program, but Production Assistants can expect to work some long and undesirable hours. Since the position is entry-level, many Production Assistants work late night or early morning shifts, preparing for their shows.

For those who want to make it in television news, particularly as producers, a Production Assistant role is a good beginning. It offers the opportunity to gain experience and learn the ropes from seasoned producers. After several years, Production Assistants come out with a thorough knowledge of broadcasting, as well as ways to troubleshoot issues as they arise. For many, the fast pace and excitement of live news is irreplaceable.

Salaries
Salaries for Production Assistants are quite low, usually beginning around $20,000. According to the 2005 RTNDA (Radio-Television News Directors Association)/Ball State University Annual Survey, the average salary for news assistants (comparable to Production Assistants) was $22,000. In larger markets, Production Assistants may earn slightly more, but low salaries are to be expected as a way of paying your dues.

Employment Prospects
If Production Assistants are serious about launching their careers in television journalism, they must be flexible and

willing to go where the jobs are. Since their jobs are behind the scenes, they have a somewhat better chance of beginning in a larger market than their on-air counterparts. However, Production Assistants must realize that they need to begin at the bottom and no task is too small for them to handle.

Opportunities are often discovered through personal contacts, so internships and networking are key. Positions may also be found through Web sites such as http://www.tvspy.com and http://www.journalismnext.com.

Advancement Prospects
Advancement prospects are good for Production Assistants. Typically, they put in one to three years before moving up the production ranks; assistant or associate producer is usually the next step up. Other Production Assistants may move up to become reporters. They may start out in comparable positions called desk assistants or news assistants.

The more experience and education that a Production Assistant has, the better are his or her chances to advance. Some people work as Production Assistants while completing their degrees, preparing themselves to move up once they graduate. For work as an assistant or associate producer, writing skills are essential.

In television news, advancement also occurs by moving from smaller local markets to larger ones, or markets that may be more national in scope. Production Assistants who develop good experience and can demonstrate tapes of their work may be poised to take a next position in a larger market.

Education and Training
While a college degree is not needed to become a Production Assistant, it is preferred for most positions, required in some markets, and essential for advancement. For those who are looking to become news producers one day, a college degree provides necessary credibility in the field. Many prospective Production Assistants major in journalism, broadcasting, or communications, which can offer a helpful background. However, experience in a newsroom is more important than coursework.

Internships are essential for breaking into television news. Working as a Production Assistant part time while a student may even prepare journalism graduates to begin as producers upon graduation. Studio experience provides exposure not only to the broadcasting equipment necessary to produce a program but also to the fast pace of broadcast news. College television stations can also be a good way to gain experience.

Experience, Skills, and Personality Traits
Production Assistants should be flexible, motivated, and willing to learn. Often serving as the right-hand person to their producers, they must be able to follow directions and

stay organized. Careful attention to detail enables them to troubleshoot and catch mistakes before they become apparent.

Also, Production Assistants looking to succeed as producers should have strong writing and research skills. Through understanding how to write specifically for broadcasting, they can create teasers or copy that fits the tone and style of their program. Research skills allow Production Assistants to gather important background information for their shows. Computer literacy, the ability to use news databases, and familiarity with broadcast equipment are also necessary.

Any Production Assistant who is considering a reporting career must develop his or her on-air skills. Professional appearance, superb verbal communication, and strong presentation skills are required.

Unions and Associations

Production Assistants may belong to a variety of professional associations including the National Association of Broadcasters, the National Academy of Television Arts and Sciences, and the Society of Broadcast Engineers.

Tips for Entry

1. Visit the Web site of the Broadcast Education Association at http://www.beaweb.org/mediasites.html. Here they have excellent links and resources to professional associations, networks, and additional information.
2. Start small. There is a lot more to news than the five national networks you might watch. Conduct research into the variety of broadcast news programs, including local and cable news.
3. Consider cable news networks as another outlet for job opportunities. Visit their Web sites to learn more and find out what type of positions they offer. The Broadcast Education Association site provides links to many national networks.
4. Realize that the majority of positions are never posted. Call local stations about volunteer and internship positions. Network with friends, professors, alumni, and members of professional associations.
5. Check out Mediabizjobs at http://www.mediabizjobs.com/, a good source for broadcasting positions. Read descriptions of what a Production Assistant does in order to better prepare.

ASSIGNMENT EDITOR

CAREER PROFILE

Duties: Manages assignments and schedules for a television news operation, including those of reporters, producers, and photographers

Alternate Title(s): Assigning Editor, Assignment Manager

Salary Range: $25,000 to $60,000 and up

Employment Prospects: Good

Advancement Prospects: Good

Best Geographical Location(s): All

Prerequisites:

Education or Training—Bachelor's degree; journalism, communications, or broadcasting often preferred

Experience—Three to five years or more of prior television newsroom experience

Special Skills and Personality Traits—Excellent managerial skills; strong organizational skills and attention to detail; good news judgment; good editorial and writing skills

CAREER LADDER

```
┌─────────────────────────────────┐
│  Senior Assignment Editor or     │
│      Managing Editor             │
└─────────────────────────────────┘

┌─────────────────────────────────┐
│      Assignment Editor           │
└─────────────────────────────────┘

┌─────────────────────────────────┐
│  Junior/Assistant Assignment     │
│  Editor or other newsroom        │
│      editorial position          │
└─────────────────────────────────┘
```

Position Description

With the vast amount of newsworthy events that happen in a given day, television stations must make sure that all aspects are covered. Furthermore, there are a wide variety of topics a program can choose to handle for longer investigative or feature pieces. Assignment Editors manage the process of assigning these stories and ensuring that all necessary elements are in place and on schedule to get these stories out on time to viewers.

In terms of breaking news, Assignment Editors monitor scanners and wires in order to respond to reports in a timely fashion. Often they are the first to find out about breaking news as it happens. They assign and assemble reporters, producers, and camera crews to go on location, as well as coordinate from the newsroom. In the newsroom, it is often the Assignment Editor who informs the staff about breaking news. Assignment Editors make sure the appropriate reporters, producers, and crew staff each story.

As one journalist put it, Assignment Editors are like the "traffic cops" of the newsroom. They are sticklers for time management, making sure that everyone is on schedule.

Furthermore, Assignment Editors are logistics gurus. They know where reporters and photographers are at any given time. If they need assistance from the field, Assignment Editors provide it, communicating with them from the scene using a two-way radio. They send out the trucks with camera crews to get the necessary footage.

Their master schedule helps to ensure that daily operations run smoothly. Assignment Editors must run a tight ship as managers and supervisors. They direct staff as to where to go and when, so that all beats are covered. Many Assignment Editors maintain daily assignment cards and distribute printed assignment lists out to staff regularly. Simple or elaborate computer systems can be used to maintain this information.

Good news judgment is essential for Assignment Editors. Often, they need to make tough spot decisions about which stories require immediate attention. It is up to them to prioritize and organize coverage. They work with department heads and the news director to coordinate production and planning. Assignment Editors help make sure their station has well-rounded news coverage.

Additionally, Assignment Editors gather information. Throughout the day, they get producers and reporters what they need for their stories, conducting research and working with sources. They may also select producers for particular stories or segments. Assignment Editors work on story planning along with producers and news directors. Series, upcoming events, and features are just some of the types of coverage they may plan for in addition to breaking news.

Writing and editing can also take up some time for Assignment Editors. Frequently, they read and edit news copy, checking for accuracy as well as slander or any libelous material. Other Assignment Editors write copy for producers to be used in different portions of the program. They may be required to edit videotape as well as written material.

Additional duties may include:

- Maintaining current assignment files
- Maintaining files for future feature stories
- Maintaining files of news sources and background information
- Responding to news tip calls
- Developing relationships with sources and community members
- Planning coverage for special events and topics
- Researching information
- Fact-checking
- Developing new story ideas
- Planning and assigning live shots
- Taking tape feeds
- Reviewing news releases
- Monitoring police radios
- Handling a two-way traffic radio
- Handling telephone calls
- Developing and approving ideas for feature stories
- Performing other news writing and editing activities
- Arranging for satellite feeds
- Maintaining schedule logs
- Training new staff members

Assignment Editors handle local news work within their community. They have relationships with people at various city agencies, including the police department, the fire department, the mayor's office, the court system, and the schools. These relationships with sources help their station to be informed about news and to get the scoop on breaking events.

Hours can be long and intense for Assignment Editors. When their programs are aired and news is coming in, they must be there to manage the process. Large stations may have a team of Assignment Editors, managed by a more senior Assignment Editor, which can lead to more flexible shift work.

Salaries

Each year, the Radio-Television News Directors Association (RTNDA) publishes a television and radio salary survey. According to the RTNDA/Ball State University Salary Survey for 2005, Assignment Editors earned an average of $35,500. The survey showed a very large salary range for Assignment Editors—from a minimum of $15,300 to a maximum of $195,800. Salaries tend to vary greatly depending on experience level, market size, and staff size.

Employment Prospects

Employment prospects are relatively good for Assignment Editors, since the position is necessary in order for the news to be delivered. Large stations often employ a team of Assignment Editors. The best opportunities are for those who have already proved themselves in broadcasting. Most positions require between three and five years of prior experience. Willingness to relocate or begin in a small market greatly improves employment prospects.

Advancement Prospects

Assignment Editors can advance by moving to larger markets where they have more direct supervisory experience. Depending on the market, they may supervise staffs of one to two, or five or more. Assignment Editors who are looking to become more seasoned managers will seek out these positions. Others aspire to become managing editors or even news directors.

Education and Training

Assignment Editors hold bachelor's degrees; fields such as journalism, broadcasting, and communications are often preferred. While experience is generally considered to be more important than education in broadcasting, college degrees are required for advancement and are almost a prerequisite to get hired in today's competitive market.

In order to gain necessary experience, insiders advise that the best way to prepare is through on-the-job training as a newsroom intern. Internships and/or working at a local or college television station offers an ideal opportunity to gain writing, editing, reporting, and producing experience, as well as a chance to become familiar with broadcasting operations.

Experience, Skills, and Personality Traits

Assignment Editors should have excellent writing and editing skills. Superb news judgment helps them initiate ideas and create priorities for coverage. They must understand what makes an effective news story and have the ability to staff coverage with the best people.

Furthermore, Assignment Editors need very strong organizational skills. Newsrooms can be crazy places, and they must stay calm under pressure and be logistical thinkers. They should be experts at time management and balancing multiple tasks at once. Good management skills help

Assignment Editors to supervise staff and offer direction to others. Familiarity with technical aspects of broadcasting such as using two-way radio and satellites is also needed to communicate with reporters and crew at a live scene.

Unions and Associations

Assignment Editors belong to a variety of professional associations including the National Association of Broadcasters (NAB), National Federation of Community Broadcasters (NFCB), American Women in Radio and Television, and the National Press Club.

Tips for Entry

1. Visit http://www.assignmenteditor.com, a Web site that serves as a resource for journalists to conduct research on the Internet.

2. Brush up on your organizational and management skills by taking on a leadership role of a club or volunteer organization to which you belong.

3. Gain newsroom experience as an intern or volunteer. Shadow an Assignment Editor to see the multiple facets and responsibilities of this job.

4. Try out different roles in broadcasting to see which is the best fit for you. Since Assignment Editors staff reporters, producers, and photographers, get exposure to each of these areas.

5. Take a news writing course to hone your journalistic writing skills.

6. Assess yourself. The best way to determine your career path is through analyzing your interests, skills, and values. This site offers information about some of the self-assessment tools available on the Internet: http://www.quintcareers.com/career_assessment.html.

NEWS DIRECTOR

CAREER PROFILE	CAREER LADDER

Duties: Leads the news department of a television station, managing news coverage and staff

Alternate Title(s): None

Salary Range: $50,000 to $100,000 and up

Employment Prospects: Fair

Advancement Prospects: Fair

Best Geographical Location(s): All

Prerequisites:

Education or Training—Bachelor's degree, often in journalism, broadcasting, communications, or a related field

Experience—Five to 15 years of progressively responsible newsroom experience

Special Skills and Personality Traits—Excellent news judgment; superior management, leadership, and organizational skills; ability to work well under pressure; knowledge of all aspects of broadcast journalism; good writing, and reporting skills, and presentation skills

CAREER LADDER

```
+------------------------------------------+
| News Director, larger market or          |
| Station Manager                          |
+------------------------------------------+

+------------------------------------------+
| News Director                            |
+------------------------------------------+

+------------------------------------------+
| Assistant News Director,                 |
| Managing Editor, or News Director,       |
| smaller market                           |
+------------------------------------------+
```

Position Description

News Directors are like the CEOs of their newsrooms. They determine the goals, vision, and long-range plans for their newsrooms. At the same time, they are hands-on top managers who oversee day-to-day operations as well. All news coverage goes through them, and News Directors shape the way it is handled.

What we see and hear on our television news is dictated by News Directors. They determine which stories are newsworthy and the angle the station wants to convey. Furthermore, they are involved with hiring, firing, and assigning reporters to stories. By getting the best talent, they strive for news coverage that will meet their goals.

Everything that goes into a news broadcast might be overseen by the News Director. He or she may review the editing, the scripts, and the video footage before it is used. Since the News Director is ultimately responsible for any mistakes in coverage, issues of libel and slander are highly important. News Directors must be knowledgeable about journalistic ethics as well as current FCC guidelines and

more. They make sure their station adheres to appropriate guidelines to prevent lawsuits and fines.

For this reason, News Directors should have expertise in all areas of broadcasting. They must understand news reporting, writing, editing, and producing in order to manage newscasts. Since they are the ones who make final decisions regarding coverage, they often approve written copy and video footage before it is to air. Their experience in all these broadcast journalism areas enables them to know what will make a successful newscast.

News Directors have the final word on personnel management for their programs. This includes hiring, firing, and mentoring reporters, producers, and others who shape the voice of the show. News Directors also look at the tapes for new hopefuls trying to break into broadcast news. They identify future talent and decide who has got what it takes to break into this competitive business.

In addition to handling breaking news, News Directors also plan the long-term vision for their stations. They work on special programming, investigative pieces, feature reports, and other news components that add value for their viewers. This process can include developing story ideas; assembling the teams to staff these projects; and writing, editing, and producing content.

Additional duties may include:

- Sitting in on assignment meetings
- Preparing the news budget
- Writing and editing news stories
- Filling in for staff members if necessary or making other appropriate staffing changes
- Assigning stories and managing coverage
- Preparing or approving schedules
- Reporting on and/or producing segments
- Analyzing and responding to programming requests
- Serving as a liaison to affiliate stations
- Handling performance reviews for employees
- Troubleshooting problems during a live broadcast

News Directors have a large community service aspect to their jobs. In order to have access to breaking news, a station must have good relationships with local agencies such as police, politicians, and school officials. News Directors cultivate and nurture these relationships, maintaining regular contact and ensuring that local coverage will get out to viewers. They often represent their community and its best interests. News Directors also foster these relationships in order to gain exclusive rights to important stories.

Furthermore, they are paramount figures in the business of running a station. News Directors may work with the sales, programming, and advertising departments in order to analyze scheduling and placement. Along with their station manager, they watch their ratings and brainstorm creative programming that will give ratings a boost.

Being a News Director is not a nine to five job. As insiders will tell you, it is a lifestyle choice that can be all consuming. News Directors are constantly on call as major events happen at all times. A passion for news is needed to maintain the energy and ambition to go after stories and bring them to the public.

Salaries

According to an annual salary survey by RTNDA (Radio-Television News Directors Association)/Ball State University, the 2005 figures reported the average salary for a News Director to be $84,400. Earnings ranged from a minimum of $13,000 to a maximum of $300,000. The survey states that, on average, News Directors are the highest paid members of the television newsroom. However, salaries vary greatly depending on the station and market size.

Employment Prospects

Employment prospects are fair for News Directors. The field is extra competitive within the realm of broadcast jour-

nalism since there is only one News Director on a program or station. Positions go to those with the best experience—professionals who have proved themselves with years as top-notch journalists and leaders.

News Directors often start out as reporters or producers; their background usually includes some time spent in a variety of newsroom roles. Many News Director positions also do include reporting, producing, and editing. In order to successfully manage staff and operations, this experience is crucial. News Directors often find out about opportunities through word of mouth, listservs, and professional associations.

Advancement Prospects

News Directors can advance by moving from smaller to larger markets, where they manage bigger staffs and handle news of more major capacity. While station managers supervise News Directors, most News Directors do not look to advance into this role since station manager is a business rather than a journalism position. A high-level position such as News Director is often the result of years of experience, and for a journalist who is looking to be a manager, the pinnacle of his or her career. Some News Directors may teach at journalism schools and/or manage campus television stations.

Education and Training

Because of the level of the position, a bachelor's degree is needed to have credibility as a News Director. Like other broadcasting positions, experience is more important than education; however, in today's market, education usually is what gets one experience to begin with. Journalism and communication degrees are helpful, but News Directors also hold degrees in a range of fields. To start out as a reporter or producer, many schools offer specialties in broadcast journalism and courses on television reporting.

To gain the necessary experience to break into broadcast journalism, insiders advise that the best way to prepare is through internships. On-the-job training as a newsroom intern offers an ideal opportunity to gain on-air reporting experience; editing, writing, and producing exposure; and a chance to become familiar with broadcasting operations.

Furthermore, internships and college broadcasting can be the ideal way through which prospective journalists can develop the demo or audition tapes required for employment.

Experience, Skills, and Personality Traits

To become a successful News Director, one must be an excellent and seasoned journalist. Five to 15 years of experience in many areas of broadcasting are needed, including writing, editing, reporting, producing, and familiarity with technical aspects. News Directors must be investigative and analytical, with strong news judgment. A passion for news is required to understand what makes a valuable story and how to best convey its message to viewers.

In addition to being first-rate journalists, News Directors must also be adept leaders. They draw on their experience to supervise, mentor, and challenge staff to be excellent journalists themselves. Furthermore, they use this knowledge to make wise hiring decisions. In evaluating tapes of new reporters, News Directors bring in staff who will take the quality of news delivery to the next level for their station.

Moreover, News Directors must be well organized. Flexible and adaptable, they must be able to balance multiple tasks at once and switch gears as soon as news breaks. Also, they must stay calm under extreme pressure and focus on the details required for a broadcast to run smoothly. Good communication skills and charisma help News Directors build community relationships.

Unions and Associations

The main professional association for News Directors is the Radio-Television News Directors Association (RTNDA), the world's largest and only professional organization exclusively serving the electronic news profession.

Tips for Entry

1. Explore the RNTDA Web site at http://www.rtnda. org/. It contains valuable information such as journalism salaries, awards and scholarships, and how to get involved in student chapters.

2. TVSpy.com offers an executive directory of News Directors in different markets throughout the country at http://www.tvspy.com/researchdb/research.cfm?page=4&PARENT_CAT_ID=210. This can be an excellent resource for networking and informational interviewing.

3. No one begins in the broadcast journalism field as a news director. Start by gaining experience as a reporter or producer. Hone your communication and presentation skills through course work if you are interested in on-air work.

4. For fun, rent the movie *Up Close and Personal,* starring Robert Redford and Michelle Pfeiffer, about the television news industry.

5. Get the scoop on television industry gossip at http://www.newsblues.com/.

6. Check out NewsLab, a nonprofit resource center for television and radio newsrooms, focused on training and research, at http://www.newslab.org/.

TAPE EDITOR

CAREER PROFILE

Duties: Edits the videotape for use in broadcasts, assuring quality of sound, visual images, length, and other components

Alternate Title(s): Videotape Editor, Video Editor

Salary Range: $18,000 to $40,000 and up

Employment Prospects: Fair

Advancement Prospects: Fair

Best Geographical Location(s): All

Prerequisites:

Education or Training—Bachelor's degree preferred for most positions; fields include broadcasting, photography, or film; video training needed

Experience—One to three years of video editing exposure or experience

Special Skills and Personality Traits—Excellent visual skills; strong attention to detail; good news judgment and understanding of broadcast journalism; ability to work well under pressure

CAREER LADDER

```
┌─────────────────────────────────────┐
│   News Photographer or Producer      │
└─────────────────────────────────────┘

┌─────────────────────────────────────┐
│            Tape Editor               │
└─────────────────────────────────────┘

┌─────────────────────────────────────┐
│   Tape Editor, smaller market or     │
│              Assistant               │
└─────────────────────────────────────┘
```

Position Description

Tape Editors take the video footage shot by news photographers and transform it into the seamless broadcast that we see in our living rooms at home. They work directly with the videotapes and edit their content to ensure that they fit the broadcast. Tape Editors pay attention to details such as sound, quality, and length to make each newscast the best it can be.

Most editing is performed via computer on a standard video editing system. Tape Editors watch footage and check different components. Firstly, they make sure sound is audible and coherent. They may perform nonlinear editing, which involves editing via disk, which allows random access to all video, audio, and images during the editing process. This relatively new advance streamlines the editing process so that edits within the program can be changed at any time without having to recreate the entire edit. Once the tape is reassembled, Tape Editors watch it back to make final corrections.

Tape Editors also edit for time, where their news judgment comes into play. If a reporter completes a story in 12 minutes that must fit into 10, the Tape Editor uses his or her judgment to determine which footage is nonessential to the piece and can be cut. They may work with producers and/or reporters during this process.

Additionally, Tape Editors are often responsible for maintaining videotapes for the newsroom. These archives are very important, as requests may come in from a variety of sources for past material. Tape Editors may arrange these archival files into a system that is easy to use. While in the past, VHS tapes were organized, most archives are now done digitally.

Their duties may include:

- Editing live feeds
- Editing from the studio and remote locations
- Linking feeds to and from news gathering agencies
- Editing voice-overs, sound bytes, and other aspects of the news package
- Tuning in microwave, satellite, and helicopter shots
- Setting up ENG (electric news gathering) vans for live remotes

- Setting up lights, microwave signals, and running cables
- Maintaining and caring for equipment
- Operating microwave trucks
- Working with reporters to edit packages
- Coordinating visual images with sound

Some Tape Editors are also news photographers and vice versa. There are advantages and disadvantages to being the one responsible for editing the work that you actually shot. On the positive side, you are intimately involved with the whole process, having been on the scene and knowing which moments best capture the heart of the story. However, on the other hand, it may be more difficult to view the footage objectively and determine where to make changes and cuts. At any rate, Tape Editors who also have news photography skills can make themselves more marketable.

Tape Editors may need a valid driver's license to operate remote trucks or vans on location for news stories. They may work inside and outside, sometimes in adverse weather conditions. Furthermore, Tape Editors should be comfortable spending portions of their time driving.

The ability to operate technical electronic news gathering equipment such as chip and tube cameras, live microwave gear, and broadcast videotape editing equipment is required. Furthermore, Tape Editors should be familiar with both standard and computer-based editing stations, broadcast lighting equipment, tripods, audio gear, various communications gear such as radios, and newsroom computers. Physical stamina might be need to lift cameras and other heavy equipment weighing more than 50 pounds.

Long hours are required for Tape Editors to prepare material for airing. Since the position is frequently an entry-level one, late night hours or graveyard shifts can be common.

Salaries
According to an annual salary survey by RTNDA (Radio-Television News Directors Association)/Ball State University, the 2005 figures reported the average salary for a Tape Editor to be $27,600. Earnings ranged from a minimum of $6,000 to a maximum of $78,000. Like other broadcasting salaries, the range can vary greatly depending on the station and market size.

Employment Prospects
Employment prospects are fair for Tape Editors. The position can be a good way for someone with good newsroom computer skills to start out in the field. Students should get news photography and editing experience through campus broadcasting and internships. Experience behind the camera can help, as many positions are for joint Tape Editors/news photographers. Producing experience can also be valuable as one sees how the entire finished product is put together.

Aspiring Tape Editors should be willing to relocate and start in small markets to get hired. Freelance work is another way to break into the field and gain valuable technical skills.

Advancement Prospects
Tape Editors can advance in several ways. Many are interested in becoming news photographers, and a next step can be a position that allows them to get behind the camera. Others want to produce and decide to go that route. Like others in journalism, Tape Editors may move from smaller to larger markets to find bigger and more lucrative opportunities. Also, Tape Editors may move from broadcast news to other areas of media such as Internet or film.

Education and Training
While a college degree is not required, most Tape Editors entering the field today hold bachelor's degrees in a variety of subjects. Studying journalism, film, or broadcasting often provides a background that enables students to gain experience while in school through internships. Furthermore, journalism training often offers the opportunity to use newsroom computers and editing systems. Although much hands-on training comes on the job, some prior technical expertise is expected.

Experience, Skills, and Personality Traits
Good eyesight is needed as Tape Editors sit in front of their computers and watch playbacks of tapes. They need excellent attention to detail so as not to miss any inaccuracies. Knowledge of nonlinear editing is helpful, and knowledge of video editing systems is required. Tape Editors must be well versed in the technical aspects of video. Some news photography skills can also be valuable, although some people really enjoy the process of assembling more than the actual filming.

Pressure is a constant fact of life for Tape Editors. They must be able to multitask and meet tight deadlines. Their news judgment helps them make editing decisions and good communication skills enable them to work well with news photographers, reporters, producers, and crew members. Physical strength and stamina is required to handle heavy and cumbersome equipment.

Unions and Associations
Tape Editors may belong to professional associations including the Guild of Television Cameramen, the Society of Camera Operators, the National Association of Broadcasters, and the Society of Motion Picture and Television Engineers.

Tips for Entry
1. Gaining newsroom experience is crucial; this is where you can learn how to use video-editing sys-

tems. Volunteer your time at the campus television station or your local network. Spend time watching the Tape Editors and becoming familiar with the systems.

2. You can practice editing by learning to spruce up your own videotapes. Invest in video editing software to edit your home movies. Sites such as http://stream.uen.org/medsol/digvid/html/5D_editsoftware.html and http://www.promax.com/Products/?utm_id=111&src=GoogleAdWords&gclid=CLn1m8fZr4MCFRMyGgodrz3hFQ can give you ideas about some of the software available.

3. The more diverse your skill set, the better opportunity you have for finding that first job. Take broadcast journalism courses that expose you to reporting, producing, editing, and news writing. Entry-level jobs may require you to wear many hats.

4. Shadow a Tape Editor and news photographer out on a shoot if you can. Become familiar with the equipment and the process of transmitting information back to the station via satellite.

5. Visit the Web sites of local television stations to see if they include job listings. Read more about the job descriptions for Tape Editors.

NEWS PHOTOGRAPHER

CAREER PROFILE

Duties: Shoots video footage out in the field for a television news program; operates camera; may also perform some editing and/or producing

Alternate Title(s): Cameraperson (cameraman or camerawoman), Electric News Gathering (ENG) Photographer or Specialist, Photographer, Chief Photographer, Photojournalist, Truck Operator, Videojournalist

Salary Range: $20,000 to $50,000 and up

Employment Prospects: Fair

Advancement Prospects: Fair

Best Geographical Location(s): All

Prerequisites:

Education or Training—Many News Photographers have bachelor's degrees and/or specific technical training.
Experience—Can be entry-level to more advanced
Special Skills and Personality Traits—Excellent visual skills and camera operating ability; strong knowledge of broadcast journalism; good news judgment; creativity

CAREER LADDER

```
┌─────────────────────────────────────┐
│      Chief Photographer or News      │
│     Photographer, larger market      │
└─────────────────────────────────────┘

┌─────────────────────────────────────┐
│         News Photographer            │
└─────────────────────────────────────┘

┌─────────────────────────────────────┐
│    News Photographer, smaller        │
│  market or freelance; Assistant News │
│    Photographer; or Tape Editor      │
└─────────────────────────────────────┘
```

Position Description

News Photographers are visual storytellers. Using video as their medium, they use a camera to collect video and audio footage out in the field. Working together with reporters and field producers, they create the image of a news story that gets remembered by their viewers.

News Photographers must be quick and able to think on their feet. When out on a news scene, getting the best live shot requires journalistic intuition and good judgment. It involves knowing what the story behind the story is, and which visual image will best capture the emotion or situation at hand. Additionally, News Photographers understand which footage will work most effectively along with the reporter's verbal account of what is happening.

Accompanying reporters and field producers to cover breaking news, a day in the life of a News Photographer is determined by what happens in the world (or local community). As they go on the scene to film what is happening, they are involved with the process of "feeding a story"—reporting, videotaping, and sending it back by satellite to a local station. News Photographers may operate the location trucks, which have capabilities for satellite transmissions to bring live reports from the scene back to the studio. Different News Photographers may be sent out on different assignments by assignment editors, news directors, and producers depending on their individual strengths.

In addition to breaking news, News Photographers also film all other types of news coverage. Features can involve making sure that all human-interest aspects of the story are being filmed, including portraying interview subjects as well as scenes in the way they are meant to be shown. Some News Photographers may specialize in areas such as sports, while others find that their coverage is mixed on a daily basis.

Capturing the heart of a news story on video also involves technical aspects. News Photographers must be masters of video, understanding how to use the appropriate lighting, camera angles, and close-ups to get the best footage. They must know their craft in order to work the camera and know what to look for. Their visual image must tell its own story to go along with the words.

Furthermore, editing is also a big part of the job. News Photographers often put their stories together on a computer editing system. This can involve nonlinear editing, which consists of the computer-assisted editing of video without the need to assemble it in linear sequence; this is done digitally and has vastly improved the editing process over the past few years. News Photographers also coordinate the visual components with the sound, which is often done digitally. Editing requires good journalistic judgment, as what is and is not included in the final piece determines much about its intent and overall meaning.

Additional duties may include:

- Shooting and editing a variety of footage
- Setting up ENG (electric news gathering) vans for live remotes
- Interviewing subjects as needed
- Producing and/or reporting in some positions
- Listening to news wires and police/fire scanners
- Setting up lights, microwave signals, and running cables
- Working in cooperation with anchors, reporters, and the assignment desk
- Maintaining and caring for equipment
- Operating microwave trucks
- Working with reporters to edit packages
- Contributing to story ideas

According to insiders, being a News Photographer requires tremendous passion for the work. It can be physically draining, calling for hours spent outside in the freezing cold or blistering heat, as well as at the scenes of crimes, crises, and even wars. However, those who make a career out of news photography by and large love their jobs. The excitement of being on location as the news happens and determining a way to visually interpret the emotion and feelings of a moment for their viewers is well worth the long hours and difficult work.

The hours for News Photographers are some of the hardest in broadcast journalism. Because television is a visual medium, getting the live shot is a crucial part of a news story. News Photographers, especially those in larger markets, must travel to where the news is in order to get the footage. They need to be flexible and willing to put themselves in difficult settings at a moment's notice.

Some jobs require a valid driver's license, as well as the ability to carry heavy equipment—up to 50 pounds worth of cameras, microphones, batteries, and tapes. News Photographers may need to travel on helicopters; a sense of adventure is necessary.

Salaries

According to an annual salary survey by RTNDA (Radio-Television News Directors Association)/Ball State University, the 2005 figures reported the average salary for a News Photographer to be $29,200. Earnings ranged from a minimum of $12,000 to a maximum of $80,000. Like other broadcasting salaries, the range can vary greatly depending on the station and market size.

Employment Prospects

Employment prospects are fair for News Photographers. Full-time positions are very competitive and many News Photographers start out in part-time or freelance positions where they can prove themselves and their video skills. Working as an intern or volunteer for no pay can be an excellent way to break into the field. Networking is one of the best ways to find a job.

Tapes of previous work are required for employment, with DVD becoming more common as the preferred format. Offering to do it all—including lugging equipment, and even reporting and producing if you have the skills—makes candidates more marketable.

Advancement Prospects

News Photographers can advance in a number of ways; it is easier to advance within the field than it is to break in from the outside. Many try to move to larger markets where they have more diverse and exciting coverage. Others aspire to production or management positions. Still other News Photographers move outside of television news, into other industries such as film.

Education and Training

Most News Photographers entering the field today hold bachelor's degrees in a variety of subjects. While experience is more important than education, studying journalism, film, or broadcasting often provides a background that enables students to gain experience while in school through internships. Many undergraduate and graduate journalism schools offer courses in broadcast news photography and photojournalism.

Experts advise that the best training is through videotaping experience. However, the experience should be related to taping news, rather than making movies, if you are interested in news photography.

Experience, Skills, and Personality Traits

If you read job descriptions for News Photographers, one quality you will see mentioned over again is good storytelling skills. News Photographers must be able to tell a story with visual images, as photojournalists. This is why a journalism background and understanding, including writing and reporting skills, can be so valuable. Creativity is also essential.

News Photographers need high energy and the ability to take initiative. As good communicators, they work well with others and can take direction when needed about their filming style and editing. Good instincts and news judgment enable them to get the best coverage. Being a team player helps News Photographers to work with reporters and producers for a seamless broadcast.

Working well under pressure is a key element of being a successful News Photographer. One must be able to stay calm in difficult situations, whether filming inclement weather, local car crashes, natural disasters, the funeral of a public figure, or a war. Physical strength and stamina is required to handle heavy and cumbersome equipment. Additionally, News Photographers must know the technical aspects of video inside and out. Shooting in DVC Pro—a type of digital videotape—is frequently expected.

Unions and Associations

News Photographers belong to professional associations including the Guild of Television Cameramen, the Society of Camera Operators, the National Association of Broadcasters, the National Press Photographers Association, and the Society of Motion Picture and Television Engineers.

Tips for Entry

1. Don't just watch the news—study it. Tape coverage of the same event on different channels to see how they handle it differently. In your own filming practice, experiment with different styles to see which are most effective.
2. See the Web site http://www.tvcameramen.com, which shares information and experiences from News Photographers throughout the world.
3. The National Press Photographers Association has a wealth of information on their Web site (http://www.nppa.org). They offer courses such as news/video workshops, as well as an entire section devoted to students.
4. Visit the Web site http://www.b-roll.net for information about television photography. It includes job listings, tips and tricks, market information, and a freelance directory, among other resources.
5. If you do not already have one, get yourself a video camera and become an expert on its operation. Speak to local news stations and News Photographers to find out which ones they recommend.

NEWS WRITER

CAREER PROFILE

Duties: Writes and edits scripts to be read on air by anchors; may write and edit some reporter scripts; writes bridges and other materials to be used in broadcasts

Alternate Title(s): Writer, Script Writer

Salary Range: $20,000 to $50,000 and up

Employment Prospects: Fair

Advancement Prospects: Fair

Best Geographical Location(s): All

Prerequisites:

  Education or Training—Bachelor's degree; fields such as journalism, communications, and English helpful

  Experience—One to several years of prior newsroom experience, depending on the position

  Special Skills and Personality Traits—Excellent writing skills and ability to write for broadcasting; good editing, spelling, punctuation, grammar, and usage skills; strong research and organizational skills; ability to work well under pressure

CAREER LADDER

```
┌─────────────────────────────┐
│    Reporter, Producer,       │
│  Managing Editor, or other   │
│      newsroom position       │
└─────────────────────────────┘

┌─────────────────────────────┐
│        News Writer           │
└─────────────────────────────┘

┌─────────────────────────────┐
│       News Assistant         │
└─────────────────────────────┘
```

Position Description

Behind the scenes, a lot goes into making a successful news broadcast or program. The repartee between the anchors, the ease of interviews, and the clear bridges between elements all appear natural in a good show. However, many of these aspects are carefully constructed by News Writers, who develop the scripts that are used by anchors, reporters, guests, and announcers on air.

Many reporters and anchors write much of their own copy to use in their broadcasts. Producers also write scripts to use in the segments or programs they produce. Yet there is still much writing to be done in a newsroom and News Writers fill in the gaps. They write clear and factual copy that fits both the tone of their program and the personalities of those who will be speaking.

In addition to news scripts for anchors and reporters, News Writers may also write the bridges to be used between segments, introductions, and conclusions. They may determine interview questions for hosts to ask program guests, as well as scripts to help guests determine their focus. The

"teasers" that serve to entice viewers to watch the upcoming news program, as well as advertising promotions, are often written by News Writers as well. Good research skills come into play as News Writers gather background information in order to write the best scripts possible.

News writing is a specific skill within journalism. Being a good writer is not enough; one must understand how to write specifically for an on-air broadcast. Words that sound good on paper may not necessarily translate the same when spoken, and News Writers must know how to determine the difference. They pay attention to style, grammar, and usage, keeping with a format that is appropriate for their program.

Additionally, News Writers must be well informed about current events. They often monitor the news feeds and conduct Internet research to find out about breaking news. In order to write well about it, they must be able to understand the news intelligently and clearly. Self-described "news junkies" who love to write about news but do not want to be on-air themselves do well as News Writers.

News Writers are often responsible for preparing news packages, which are reports that are produced and edited prior to broadcast time. They may produce aspects, as well as edit the reporter or anchor script in addition to writing copy. The finished package is then ready for voicing by anchors and reporters.

Additional duties may include:

- Producing segments
- Booking guests for live interviews
- Researching story information
- Assisting the producer with script and videotape organization
- Monitoring story development throughout its various stages
- Acting as a backup producer
- Setting up and field producing special reports
- Checking out news stories by telephone
- Logging video tapes
- Reading wires for late breaking stories

The position of News Writer can be entry-level, more advanced, or somewhere in between. At some stations, it may be the next step up from a news assistant role for aspiring reporters before they go on air. In other settings, a News Writer will need several years of experience and it becomes a niche area for someone who has honed his or her broadcast writing skills.

Furthermore, many News Writer positions entail dual roles, most frequently combined with producing. Since both responsibilities are off camera but require excellent journalism skills and are critical to organizing the broadcast, many News Writers are also producers. They might produce and write specific segments of a program. Additionally, News Writers may also be line producers who are responsible for the selection of elements of the show. They decide how much time to devote to each element.

Like others in broadcasting, News Writers are often required to work long hours, including evenings, holidays, and weekends. Although they are not on air, they write for those who are, and their shifts reflect the nonstop fast pace of broadcast news work.

Salaries

Each year, the Radio-Television News Directors Association (RTNDA) conducts a salary survey. According to the RTNDA/Ball State University for 2005, figures reported the average salary for a News Writer to be $30,500. Earnings ranged from a minimum of $18,000 to a maximum of $75,000. Compared to others in the newsroom, salaries might start higher, but they don't have the potential to go up as much. However, salaries vary greatly depending on the station and market size.

Employment Prospects

Employment prospects are fair for News Writers. Usually, News Writers are employed in markets large enough to justify the need for them, making positions limited. The most plentiful opportunities may be positions that combine other broadcasting roles, especially producing.

Advancement Prospects

News Writers have a number of options for advancement, depending on their position. If they are using the position as an entry-level springboard into broadcast journalism, advancement often occurs in the form of a producer role. Other News Writers transition to become reporters or editors. In these cases, it is important for the News Writer to make the transition early in his or her career, before getting pigeonholed. Yet others may move from television to radio or print journalism. Their writing skills can be applied in a variety of settings.

Education and Training

News Writers hold bachelor's degrees in different subjects, including English, communications, and liberal arts. Journalism study can be particular useful for News Writers, since they need to be able to write in a broadcast style. Most journalism schools offer courses in news writing; the Electronic Journalism Writing course at Miami University in Oxford, Ohio (http://www.units.muohio.edu/cwe/Courses.html) is just an example. Liberal arts courses round out the important grammar, style, usage, and research skills needed to be a News Writer as well.

Internships are an important way to gain newsroom experience. Since opportunities to be on-air are highly competitive, interns often spend much time developing their news writing skills.

Experience, Skills, and Personality Traits

Above all, News Writers need excellent writing skills. The ability to write in clear, concise English, keeping all the while in broadcast style, is paramount. News Writers must adapt their writing to fit the style of the program as well as the reporters/anchors for whom they are writing. Since News Writers may write for general news reporters/anchors, weathercasters, and/or sportscasters, flexibility in writing style is key. Furthermore, they must be able to write quickly and under pressure.

News Writers must be computer literate and adept at many types of research, including Internet research. Good organizational skills help them to prioritize and keep track of assignments. Additionally, the ability to work well with others is important. News Writers should have good relationships with others in the newsroom and must be able to accept criticism in order to improve their writing if necessary.

Unions and Associations

News Writers may belong to professional associations including the National Association of Broadcasters, the National Writers Union, and the Society of Professional Journalists.

Tips for Entry

1. How much do you know about journalism terms? Check out this test at http://users.chartertn.net/gpotter/tests/newst2.htm.

2. Learn more about the study of news writing through this syllabus for a past News Writing and Reporting class at the Philip Merrill College of Journalism of the University of Maryland. It is posted online at http://jclass.umd.edu/cars/Chinoy201/syllabus.htm.

3. Knowledge of AP (Associated Press) Style is crucial. Make sure you have resources such as *The Associated Press Stylebook and Libel Manual* and *The Elements of News Writing* by James W. Kershner, published in 2005, as well as a good dictionary.

4. An online article that provides an introduction to the basics of news writing can be found at http://www.cfnaonline.com/articles/newsrel.html.

5. One-day courses in news writing are also available as part of different programs throughout the country. These courses are designed for people who are trying to break into the field. Mediabistro.com lists a seminar held in Beverly Hills, California, by a current reporter. See http://www.mediabistro.com/courses/cache/crs1113.asp for more information.

MANAGING EDITOR

CAREER PROFILE

Duties: Supervises day-to-day newsroom operations and editorial content; approves scripts and other written materials

Alternate Title(s): None

Salary Range: $40,000 to $80,000 and up

Employment Prospects: Fair

Advancement Prospects: Fair

Best Geographical Location(s): All

Prerequisites:

Education or Training—Bachelor's degree or higher; subjects such as journalism, broadcasting, or communications helpful

Experience—Typically, five years or more in broadcast journalism, especially at the assignment desk

Special Skills and Personality Traits—Excellent organizational skills; good management and leadership skills; strong writing, reporting, and editing skills; solid news judgment; analytical skills

CAREER LADDER

```
┌─────────────────────────┐
│      News Director       │
└─────────────────────────┘

┌─────────────────────────┐
│     Managing Editor      │
└─────────────────────────┘

┌─────────────────────────┐
│    Assignment Editor     │
└─────────────────────────┘
```

Position Description

Under the supervision of the news director, Managing Editors run broadcast newsrooms on a daily basis. They handle operations including leading regular staff meetings, overseeing assignments, and confirming that news is being covered. Furthermore, they make sure that the stories are being covered in ways that meet the goals of the station.

Managing Editors work with reporters on story selection and script writing. They ensure that the format is correct and the style and angle appropriate. Often, they act as liaisons between reporters, producers, and the assignment desk. By confirming that the right staff member is being assigned to each story, Managing Editors help their newscasts succeed.

Additionally, Managing Editors organize and approve all copy that is to be used in a newscast. They develop new ideas and brainstorm ways to make existing ideas better. Managing Editors use their strong news judgment to determine which stories will best appeal to their target viewers. Their experience guides them to pass on those feature stories that will not add value to their program.

As managers in the newsroom, most Managing Editors have personnel responsibilities. While the news director may have final say about hiring decisions, it is the Managing Editor who organizes and oversees the process. News directors often delegate such tasks as performance appraisals, interviewing, promotions, and scheduling. Managing Editors work with staff on training and professional development. Furthermore, they often develop the newsroom budget.

Managing Editors work closely with assignment editors to make sure all breaking news is covered. Together, they might determine daily coverage as well as plan ahead for future programming goals. Beyond breaking news, stations have flexibility in terms of the type of features and special reports they want to present. Managing Editors use their journalistic skills to develop informative and engaging ideas.

Their duties may include:

• Developing the editorial calendar
• Filling in the newsroom as needed
• Training new staff members

- Planning special events coverage
- Determining new feature stories
- Staffing assignments
- Researching information and checking facts
- Reviewing news releases
- Writing and editing copy
- Overseeing the digital and technical aspects of editing
- Working on special projects
- Producing segments

Managing Editors work long hours to get newscasts out; their time at the station reflects the never-ending aspect of news. Additionally, because of their management role, they must be there to troubleshoot problems. Managing Editors also build relationships with their local communities. They may serve as representatives for their station, answer questions, and address concerns. For this reason, they must be well aware of and interested in local news and personalities.

As second-in-command to the news director, a Managing Editor must have good relationships with his or her boss. The news director and Managing Editor may work together to devise a vision for their station and assemble the team to carry it out. Managing Editors must be leaders but also have the ability to take direction and implement the goals set by the news director.

Salaries

According to the annual Radio-Television News Directors Association (RTNDA)/Ball State University Salary Survey for 2005, Managing Editors in television earned an average of $63,800. The survey demonstrated a large range for Managing Editors, from a low of $25,000 to a high of $150,000. After news directors and assistant news directors, Managing Editors reported the highest newsroom salaries. Furthermore, their low figure of $25,000 was the highest of all job titles in the survey.

Employment Prospects

Employment prospects are fair for Managing Editors. This leadership position goes to those journalists with considerable newsroom experience who have proved their skills as managers. Promotion often comes from within, and through networking. Some smaller stations may combine the position with that of the assignment editor. Having a diverse set of skills, including reporting, producing, and editing, makes one more marketable. Aspiring Managing Editors must be willing to relocate to find job opportunities.

Advancement Prospects

Advancement prospects are also fair. The next step up for a Managing Editor is a typically a news director position. This usually requires seven to 10 years of experience or more.

Managing Editors in small markets may seek positions in larger markets before looking to become news directors. Others may go on to positions in other areas of media; some might become journalism professors.

Education and Training

A minimum of a bachelor's degree is usually required to be a Managing Editor. Although experience is more important than formal education, in the current market, education usually is what gets one experience to begin with. Journalism, communication, and broadcasting degrees are helpful. Many Managing Editors start out as reporters or producers.

Broadcasting internships, as well as broadcast journalism courses, can help provide the necessary training to be a Managing Editor. Furthermore, since Managing Editor is a high-level position, most professionals learn the necessary management skills by working their way up the ranks on the job.

Experience, Skills, and Personality Traits

Managing Editors must be excellent and experienced journalists. They need strong writing, editing, and reporting skills, as well as sharp news judgment. They must understand what makes a good broadcast, as well as have the ability to write and analyze successful news copy. Creativity helps them to develop fresh and innovative ideas.

Moreover, Managing Editors must be good leaders. From running editorial meetings to mentoring new reporters, they need to command respect. They should be able to challenge and motivate their staff to work hard and strive for the best.

Also, Managing Editors must be well organized, as well as flexible. While making schedules, they must be able to adapt as news occurs. Good communication skills help them work with colleagues, supervisors, and the community. Managing Editors must be familiar with the digital technology of a multimedia newsroom. Furthermore, knowledge of media laws and ethics helps to prevent inaccuracies and libelous material in broadcasts.

Unions and Associations

Managing Editors may belong to professional associations including the National Association of Broadcasters, the Radio-Television News Directors Association, and the National Press Club.

Tips for Entry

1. Keep up on news about the journalism world by reading publications such as the Columbia Journalism Review (http://www.cjr.org/) and the American Journalism Review (http://www.ajr.org).

2. Go to the Web site for Poynter Online at http://www.poynter.org. The Poynter Institute is a school for journalists, future journalists, and teachers of journalists, and their site offers information about their programs and seminars.
3. Read job listings and career articles about Managing Editors on sites such as http://www.tvspy.com, http://www.journalismjobs.com, and http://www.journalismnext.com.

4. Take courses in broadcast journalism to hone your newsroom skills. Learning how to write a news script is a valuable skill for a Managing Editor.
5. Do not be afraid to start at the bottom. Positions as production assistants, news assistants, or desk assistants are valuable ways to learn the ropes for a broadcast journalism career.

FIELD PRODUCER

Duties: Producing an individual television newscast or program from out in the field; gathering the necessary elements to be used in a broadcast; accompanying reporters in the field

Alternate Title(s): None

Salary Range: $20,000 to $50,000 and up

Employment Prospects: Fair to good

Advancement Prospects: Fair to good

Best Geographical Location(s): All

Prerequisites:

Education or Training—Bachelor's degree preferred and/or required for most positions; journalism or broadcasting major helpful

Experience—Can be entry-level or more senior, requiring one to five years of experience or more

Special Skills and Personality Traits—Excellent writing and reporting skills; flexibility; ability to work well under pressure; good organizational skills

```
┌─────────────────────────────────────┐
│  Executive Producer, Supervising     │
│  Producer, or News Producer          │
└─────────────────────────────────────┘

┌─────────────────────────────────────┐
│  Field Producer                      │
└─────────────────────────────────────┘

┌─────────────────────────────────────┐
│  Field Producer, smaller market or   │
│  Production Assistant                 │
└─────────────────────────────────────┘
```

Position Description

Instead of managing an entire newscast from the station or studio, Field Producers coordinate and gather the various components used in a broadcast from the field. In a sense, they do it all—write, report, produce, and edit. They play a very hands-on role in their broadcast from beginning to end.

In a sense, Field Producers function as behind-the-scenes reporters. Frequently, they do everything a reporter does, ranging from background research to conducting interviews and writing scripts. However, once the script is complete, Field Producers pass it off to the reporters who will track it and present it on-air. It can be a great role for those who like all the journalistic elements of being a reporter—the fast pace, inquisitive nature, and nose for news—but do not feel comfortable on-air.

Many different elements come together to create successful and seamless broadcasts. Field Producers act as the organizers and managers, ensuring that all components occur at the right time. Whether they write scripts themselves or assign them to other producers or writers, they confirm that scripts as well as other written material such as teasers and bridges are complete. Field Producers may prepare people before interviews and/or conduct some interviews themselves. Staying on schedule is essential, and Field Producers keep newscasts moving along at the appropriate pace. They also coordinate video and audio elements, making sure that they work well with the piece.

Field Producers both complete assigned stories and also generate ideas for their own broadcasts. They participate in brainstorming meetings with the news team to come up with creative and innovative programming. Also, they may participate in daily meetings to determine how breaking news coverage will be handled that day.

Both for breaking news stories and preplanned features, Field Producers accompany reporters on the scene. Here they gather the different components for the broadcast, including sound bites and reporter packages. In addition to working with reporters, Field Producers may also go on the scene with the camera crew to get additional footage for a story. He or she will use journalistic judgment to decide which images and footage will work best with the piece.

Because television is so fast-paced, Field Producers often handle a wide variety of coverage. In a typical day, they may handle both live breaking news and taped longer feature pieces. As breaking news happens, Field Producers must be ready to go on location along with reporters and handle spot news. Most Field Producers produce broadcasts on a combination of issues and are involved with developing their own pieces, based on their individual strengths and interests.

Their duties may include:

- Filling in on the assignment desk
- Writing and editing scripts in the newsroom
- Conducting background research for stories
- Developing relationships with sources and community members
- Working with news directors, photographers, camera crew, and reporters
- Investigating story leads
- Planning coverage for special events
- Working on investigative and enterprising reports
- Reviewing background information
- Attending daily planning/story meetings
- Keeping up on local, national, and international current events
- Writing news copy and scripts to accompany pieces
- Editing audio and video content
- Monitoring the live feeds
- Selecting video and graphics for a particular program
- Determining the flow of newscasts

Field Producers often work long hours to handle news as it happens, including early mornings, late nights, weekends, and holidays. Travel may also be required as they go on location with reporters to cover various newsworthy events.

As off-air reporters, Field Producers seek out news stories and the best way to bring them into the homes of their viewers. Although they may not get the recognition that reporters do, they also do not have the pressure that comes with being on air such as attention to personal appearance, voice tone, wardrobe, hair, and makeup. Field Producers are able to focus on the best ways to tell their story without having to present it themselves.

Salaries

Salaries for Field Producers can vary greatly depending on their level of experience and the size of their market. According to the annual Radio and Television Salary Survey by RTNDA (Radio-Television News Directors Association)/ Ball State University for 2005, news producers (which could include Field Producers) earned an average of $31,600. The range reported by the survey was very large—from a minimum of $15,600 to a maximum of $90,000. Market and staff size also play a major role in determining salary.

Employment Prospects

Employment prospects are fair to good for Field Producers. The position can vary from an entry level role as an assistant to reporters and other producers to a more senior role producing major and high-profile pieces. Field Producers may start out as production assistants or Field Producers in smaller markets. Some may move directly into a Field Producer role from undergraduate or graduate school with significant related experience through internships and campus broadcasting. As with others in journalism, Field Producers must be willing to relocate if necessary and begin in small markets to maximize their opportunities.

Advancement Prospects

Field Producers can advance in several ways. One way is by moving to larger markets to have responsibility for bigger programs with more diverse and interesting coverage. Another is through becoming executive or supervising producers, where they oversee many programs for a station. Field Producers may choose to become other types of producers such as news producers, line producers, or segment producers. They can also move into other areas such as new media, commercial television, or film.

Some movement may also occur between Field Producers and reporters. Since their jobs can be so similar, with the main difference being the on-air component, people who begin in one role may find that they are better suited for the other. Field Producers who decide they are interested in being on-air reporters can hone their presentation skills through voice lessons and practicing on-camera skills. On the other hand, reporters who realize they are better suited for behind-the-scenes work may transition to become Field Producers.

Education and Training

A bachelor's degree is preferred for most positions and required by most. While a degree is definitely necessary for advancement, experience does count more than formal education in broadcasting. However, studying journalism as an undergraduate can provide valuable exposure to news writing, as well as networking opportunities with professors and classmates.

To gain essential preparation and training, newsroom internships and campus media experience are ideal ways to break into the field. Working for a campus television station or completing an internship offers hands-on exposure to broadcast journalism. Aspiring Field Producers can get specific experience producing a news program that will help them when they apply for jobs. Since tapes of past programs one has produced are required for many positions, this can be a good way to build a video portfolio.

Experience, Skills, and Personality Traits

Field Producers should have outstanding journalistic and communication skills. Strong reporting ability is essential for developing stories and reports that reach their viewers. Excellent news judgment and investigative minds drive Field Producers to dig deep into their stories with ethics and integrity. Good writing and editing skills help create lively and interesting scripts. As skilled verbal communicators, Field Producers develop a rapport with reporters and interview subjects alike, putting them at ease.

Flexibility and the ability to work well under pressure are also important for Field Producers. As they move around on location, they must stick with their schedules, as well as go with the flow. Staying calm and objective enables them to work under sometimes adverse conditions during difficult stories. Field Producers need to be visionaries who have an eye toward the finished product of their program, as well as detail-oriented enough to manage the immediate operations.

Knowledge of the technical aspects of television broadcasting, such as newsroom computers, Internet, satellite, and microwave news gathering is also essential. Field Producers may work on programs that include coverage from helicopters, news trucks, and more—they need to be familiar with how to handle these elements.

Unions and Associations

Field Producers belong to a variety of professional associations including the National Association of Broadcasters (NAB), National Federation of Community Broadcasters (NFCB), the National Association of Broadcast Employees and Technicians, American Women in Radio and Television, and the National Press Club.

Tips for Entry

1. Learn more about broadcast journalism by visiting the Web site of the National Association of Broadcasters at http://www.nab.org.
2. Take a course in television news production to become familiar with the process. For example, the Annenberg School for Communication at the University of Southern California in Los Angeles offers a Production Core as part of their broadcast journalism major http://www.usc.edu/dept/publications/cat2004/schools/communication/jour_undergraduate.html.
3. Explore the Web site of Broadcasting & Cable: The Business of Television at http://www.broadcastingcable.com.
4. Public broadcasting is another area of television journalism to consider. Current.org lists jobs in public television and radio at http://www.current.org/jobs.
5. While demo tapes are often a necessary element for employment, you cannot land an internship that will allow you to create a demo tape without a strong résumé. Visit sites such as http://www.jobweb.com/Resumes_Interviews/default.htm and http://www.damngood.com/jobseekers/tips.html for ideas.
6. If you are interested in transitioning into reporting, honing your on-air presence is a necessity. Take a look at the book *Sound and Look Professional on Television and the Internet: How to Improve Your On-Camera Presence,* by Michelle McCoy, for tips.

SEGMENT PRODUCER

CAREER PROFILE

Duties: Produces a small production-intensive portion of a television broadcast

Alternate Title(s): None

Salary Range: $20,000 to $50,000 and up

Employment Prospects: Fair

Advancement Prospects: Fair to good

Best Geographical Location(s): All

Prerequisites:

Education or Training—Bachelor's degree preferred and/or required for most positions; journalism or broadcasting major helpful

Experience—Varies; can range from one to five years of experience or more

Special Skills and Personality Traits—Excellent writing, editing, and storytelling skills; creativity; good organizational and time management skills

CAREER LADDER

```
┌─────────────────────────────────────┐
│  Executive Producer, Supervising     │
│  Producer, or News Producer          │
└─────────────────────────────────────┘

┌─────────────────────────────────────┐
│  Segment Producer                    │
└─────────────────────────────────────┘

┌─────────────────────────────────────┐
│  Producer, smaller market or         │
│  Production Assistant                 │
└─────────────────────────────────────┘
```

Position Description

During a news program, whether a morning show like *Good Morning America* or an evening feature program such as *20/20,* there are specific segments that stand out. These segments can be as diverse as a feature piece on fall fashions bringing in magazine editors and models, or an exposé of a health insurance scam occurring at a small-town clinic. Segment Producers develop and produce these particular broadcasts.

While other types of producers focus on an entire newscast, Segment Producers are specialists. They are responsible for small, production-intensive segments appearing in a program. Involved with every aspect of these segments from conception to execution, Segment Producers develop story ideas that fit with the tone of the overall program and appeal to their target audience.

As one Segment Producer described it through this example, a Segment Producer might be in charge of a celebrity chef component of a morning news program. His or her role includes getting the chef everything he or she needs, such as cooking ingredients, cooking implements, etc. The Segment Producer also makes sure that the chef and the anchors have their scripts, which he or she has frequently written. Furthermore, the Segment Producer also coordinates the rest of the broadcast, ensuring that the graphics department has what they need to put the recipe on the screen. In this way, Segment Producers make sure that their portions of the broadcast go off without a hitch.

When their segment requires guests or other types of interviewees, Segment Producers handle selecting and booking these individuals. They often conduct extensive background research. When an anchor interviews a guest, the audience is often impressed by how much the anchor seems to know in advance about the guest. Frequently, it is the Segment Producer who provides the anchor with this necessary information, helping to dictate the questions and direction to take the interview to meet the goal of the story.

Like other types of producers, Segment Producers organize and manage their particular broadcast from start to finish. They ensure that schedules are being adhered to and that all elements are in place. Much, if not all, of the writing for their segments is their own, including scripts, interview questions, and other items. Additionally, Segment Producers may prepare people before interviews and/or conduct some interviews themselves. They also coordinate video and audio elements, making sure that they work well with the piece.

While some Segment Producers specialize in particular areas such as health or politics, most handle a wide variety of coverage. Segment Producers produce broadcasts on a combination of issues and generate ideas for their own pieces based on their individual strengths and interests. They also may produce segments as assigned by their news director. For some pieces, Segment Producers go out into the field with reporters where they act as field producers, handling the segment from the location rather than the studio.

Their duties may include:

- Identifying potential topics for segments
- Handling special projects
- Participating in regular editorial meetings
- Logging and editing scripts
- Conducting background research for stories
- Working with news directors, photographers, camera crew, and reporters
- Working on investigative and enterprising reports
- Reviewing background information
- Keeping up on local, national, and international current events
- Writing news copy and scripts to accompany pieces
- Editing audio and video content
- Selecting video and graphics for a particular program
- Determining the flow of newscasts

Segment Producers often work long hours, including early mornings, late nights, weekends, and holidays. If they work on a live morning show, this can involve arriving in the studio as early as 4 A.M. Segments may be live or pre-taped, which can affect hours. Travel may also be required to produce segments in various domestic and international locations.

As many Americans tune in to news programs to learn more about the world, Segment Producers use their creativity to develop stories that will inform, enlighten, and entertain their audience. They also enjoy spending more time with their pieces than other types of producers who typically handle immediate news. Although many Segment Producers adapt their schedules to accommodate breaking news, they frequently focus on features that they have slightly more time to explore and develop. Segment Producers also work on investigative or enterprise stories, uncovering hidden issues and sharing them with viewers.

Salaries

According to the annual Radio and Television Salary Survey by RTNDA (Radio-Television News Directors Association)/ Ball State University for 2005, news producers (which can include Segment Producers) earned an average of $31,600.

The range reported by the survey was very large—from a minimum of $15,600 to a maximum of $90,000.

However, salaries for Segment Producers can vary greatly depending on their level of experience and the size of their market. Market and staff size also play a major role in determining salary.

Employment Prospects

Employment prospects are fair for Segment Producers. Because their work is specialized, they may find fewer opportunities than other types of producers. The position can be at different levels and require different types of experience, depending on the size of the market. Segment Producers may begin as production assistants or producers in smaller markets. Often, they gain general news production experience before focusing in to handle segments. As with others in journalism, Segment Producers must be willing to relocate if necessary and begin in small markets to maximize their opportunities.

Advancement Prospects

Segment Producers can advance in several ways. One way is by moving to larger markets to have responsibility for bigger programs with more diverse and interesting coverage. Another is through becoming executive or supervising producers, where they oversee many programs for a station. Segment Producers may choose to become other types of producers such as news producers, line producers, or field producers. They can also move into other areas such as new media, commercial television, or film.

Some Segment Producers work as freelancers, producing different segments for several stations. This can be a niche area for those who develop feature specialties.

Education and Training

While there is not one educational path that determines success as a Segment Producer, certain courses of study will make the road easier. A bachelor's degree is preferred for most positions and required by many. Although experience tends to count more than formal education in broadcasting, a degree is definitely necessary for advancement. Studying journalism can provide valuable exposure to news writing and producing, as well as networking opportunities with professors and classmates that can lead to first breaks.

To gain essential preparation and training, newsroom internships and campus media experience are ideal ways to break into the field. Working for a campus television station or completing an internship offers hands-on exposure to broadcast journalism. Aspiring Segment Producers can get specific experience that will help them when they apply for jobs. Since tapes of past programs one has produced are required for many positions, this can be a good way to build a video portfolio.

Experience, Skills, and Personality Traits

Creativity is essential for Segment Producers, as are strong writing and storytelling skills. In features, the ability to tell a story well and reach out to viewers determines success. Segment Producers who develop interesting features and present them in visually appealing ways win over their audience, thus earning the respect of their news directors and colleagues. Excellent writing and editing skills help create lively scripts.

Furthermore, Segment Producers need strong journalistic and verbal communication skills. They must be able to develop rapport with reporters and interview subjects alike, being able to put them at ease. Furthermore, as they select and book guests for their segments, Segment Producers take advantage of good persuasive skills to convince them (or their publicists) that appearing on their program would be a good idea.

Excellent news judgment is important as well. The ability to work well under pressure and manage multiple projects at once is critical. Segment Producers must pay attention to the small details of producing their segment yet look toward the big picture to make sure their piece has overall flow and meets its goals.

Knowledge of the technical aspects of television broadcasting, such as newsroom computers, Internet, satellite, and microwave news gathering is also essential. Segment Producers may work on programs that include coverage from helicopters, news trucks, and more—they need to be familiar with how to handle these elements.

Segment Production offers a good opportunity for journalists who find themselves drawn to the human-interest side of production. While they can cover hard news in terms of investigative pieces, many stories are feature driven and can be entertaining as well as informative.

Unions and Associations

Segment Producers belong to a variety of professional associations including the National Association of Broadcasters (NAB), National Federation of Community Broadcasters (NFCB), American Women in Radio and Television, and the National Press Club.

Tips for Entry

1. What types of feature programming interest you? As you watch a news program, pay attention to the various segments and all the elements involved.
2. Type "Segment Producer" into a search engine such as Google or Yahoo to see if you can find job descriptions.
3. Conduct an informational interview with a Segment Producer at a local station. How is his or her job different from that of other producers? Find out how he or she got started in the field.
4. How familiar are you with the technical aspects of a newsroom? Volunteer and/or arrange a tour at a local station to get an idea of how it all works.
5. Internships are crucial for getting your first break. Many stations offer a variety of internship programs. See ABC News internships at http://abcnews.go.com/Reference/story?id=141275&page=1 and the Radio-Television News Directors Association Internships at http://www.rtnda.org/asfi/internships/internships.shtml to get some ideas.

RADIO

NEWS DIRECTOR

CAREER PROFILE

Duties: Directs news reporting for a radio station, including assigning stories, supervising reporters, and working with management; may also do some reporting

Alternate Title(s): News and Public Affairs Director

Salary Range: $40,000 to $70,000 and up

Employment Prospects: Poor to Fair

Advancement Prospects: Fair

Best Geographical Location(s): All

Prerequisites:

Education or Training—Bachelor's degree; fields such as journalism and communications very helpful

Experience—At least five years of prior radio reporting experience

Special Skills and Personality Traits—Excellent reporting, writing, and editing skills; strong communication skills; good news judgment; leadership and management competence

CAREER LADDER

News Director, larger market
or Program Director

News Director

Reporter

Position Description

News Directors manage news operations for a radio station. As supervisors and leaders, they oversee a reporting staff that can range from one or two reporters to 15 or more at larger stations. Not only do they develop ideas for news coverage, but they are also involved in overall radio program planning and vision for the news department.

In both public and commercial news radio, News Directors make decisions about programming. They ensure that a capable reporting team covers spot news. Knowing their reporters and their strengths enables them to decide who should handle each story. At small stations, they determine assignments, while in larger markets, News Directors may delegate this task to an assignment editor. Furthermore, News Directors might look for interesting human-interest stories for feature broadcasts.

As managers, News Directors mentor, supervise, and coach reporters. A good News Director will help develop the strengths of the reporters on his or her team, challenging them to constantly improve their skills. Frequently, they run daily meetings to discuss coverage for the day. Along with

news editors, they edit reporters' copy and make suggestions for improvement. Also, News Directors are responsible for evaluating the performance of reporters.

In many settings, News Directors perform some reporting themselves. This is appealing to many that miss the on-air excitement now that they are in management. While it will depend on the size of the station, News Directors may report on special high-profile cases, interview high-profile guests, or serve as news anchors. They may present a combination of live and taped broadcasts.

News Directors plan for the long-term goals of their station. Often, they handle special news coverage, such as elections and other major events. Not only do they decide who will go where and cover what, but they also determine how the coverage will be structured. Furthermore, they generate ideas for new and creative programming. News Directors conduct research and tap into their communities to help develop programming ideas.

News Directors analyze their audience and their station's mission in order to provide the type of coverage that listeners want and expect when they tune in. Making sure that coverage is fair and balanced, they work to uphold journalistic integrity and make sure listeners are happy. News Directors project the image of their station with its news coverage, angles, reporters, and story selection.

Depending on the size of the station, News Directors often have some editing and producing roles as well. They ensure that news content is uniform, with reporters using the same beginning and ending format in all broadcasts. Furthermore, they can ensure quality of sound, proper placement of programs, and appropriate time lengths for stories. News Directors may also oversee other news components such as sports or entertainment.

Their duties may include:

- Setting and monitoring the news budget
- Hosting specific programs as needed
- Participating in special events and public appearances
- Preparing and presenting reports
- Hiring and firing news staff
- Working with their national network
- Producing segments or other content
- Participating in fund-raising (in public radio)
- Monitoring the wire service
- Keeping up with current news and events
- Identifying important community news issues
- Arranging schedules for reporters
- Making substitutions when needed

News Directors often work long and irregular hours. As news keeps going around the clock, News Directors plan and account for programming times. Heavy programming usually coincides with morning and evening commuting hours, when people are in their cars and radio usage is at its peak.

News Directors may supervise more than one station for a network. For example, they may work at a state bureau where they manage several local affiliates. News Directors perform the same role at all the stations they manage, overseeing reporters, news coverage, and programming.

Salaries

According to the 2005 RTNDA (Radio-Television News Directors Association)/Ball State University Annual Survey, the average salary for News Directors was $35,900. The survey included a range from a minimum of $6,000 to a maximum of $110,000. However, like other journalism positions, salaries vary greatly depending on the size of the market. Insiders say that most News Directors earn between $40,000 and $70,000 per year, based on experience.

Employment Prospects

Overall, employment prospects are poor to fair for News Directors. At many smaller stations, News Directors wear multiple hats, serving as reporters, anchors, producers, and editors all together. However, larger stations may have more than 10 reporters, but only one News Director. The best opportunities are for those who have proved themselves as capable reporters and have networked well within their stations. By developing good relationships with their News Directors when they are reporters, jobs can open up when the current News Director leaves.

News Directors may work in public or commercial radio. While the vast majority of jobs are at local affiliates, they may also work for state or national broadcasting networks.

Advancement Prospects

Advancement prospects are also fair for News Directors. Some may advance within radio to become News Directors at larger stations, or to become program directors with greater management responsibility. Other News Directors seek positions outside of radio, with television broadcasting or public relations as a common choice. Additional career areas for News Directors to transfer into include media communications, corporate communications, and teaching/education.

Education and Training

The vast majority of News Directors hold bachelor's degrees; it is considered an essential credential for anyone who has recently entered the profession. Fields such as journalism and communications are very helpful but not required. Radio news professionals say that courses in writing, journalism and communications, and social sciences are all very useful.

Even more important than education is the on-the-job training needed to break into radio. To start out as a reporter, internships are essential. On-air experience can be gained through college radio stations. Demo tapes of on-air broadcasts are needed for employment.

Experience, Skills, and Personality Traits

News Directors must be excellent leaders and managers. They need to be able to motivate and evaluate staff, inspiring reporters to achieve high quality in their coverage. Through at least five years of prior reporting experience, they have developed strong news judgment and writing, editing, and reporting expertise. Good organizational skills help News Directors handle scheduling and assigning.

Time pressure is a constant issue in news journalism. News Directors must be able to work well under stress and be on top of breaking news. They must be able to figure out how to get to the heart of a story in a small time segment. Excellent communication and presentation ability is also needed for on-air and taped broadcasts.

Additionally, News Directors should be comfortable with the technical aspects of a radio newsroom. Digital editing experience and familiarity with newsroom computer systems is very helpful.

Unions and Associations

The main professional association for News Directors is the Radio-Television News Directors Association. Learn more by visiting their Web site at http://www.rtnda.org. Those in public radio may belong to the Public Radio News Directors Incorporated. Others may be members of the National Association of Broadcasters.

Tips for Entry

1. There are virtually thousands of radio stations throughout the country. Be willing to start out in any market that is hiring, in order to gain valuable experience and make yourself marketable.
2. College radio is the ideal setting in which to try out a News Director role. After gaining experience as a reporter, work your way up to a management role.
3. Go onto the Web site of a news radio station such as WCBS 880 (http://www.newsradio88.com/). Read bios of their news team to learn more about the background needed to find a job in such a market.
4. Public radio provides many interesting options for News Directors, including the chance to be involved with niche interest, public-issue based programming. Visit National Public Radio's (NPR) Web site at http://www.npr.org and Public Radio News Directors Incorporated's Web site at http://www.prndi.org/.
5. Listen to news radio. Conduct an informational interview with a News Director at your favorite local station to learn more about the position.

REPORTER

CAREER PROFILE

Duties: Develops and delivers news and feature stories for a radio station

Alternate Title(s): Correspondent, Broadcaster, Newscaster, News Reporter, News Analyst, Anchor

Salary Range: $20,000 to $60,000 and up

Employment Prospects: Poor to Fair

Advancement Prospects: Fair

Best Geographical Location(s): All

Prerequisites:

Education or Training—While there are no formal requirements, a bachelor's degree is considered essential in today's market; fields such as journalism and communication are helpful

Experience—Several years of radio work through internships or full-time jobs

Special Skills and Personality Traits—Excellent communication and public speaking skills; investigative mind; good research and writing skills; ability to work well under pressure

CAREER LADDER

```
┌─────────────────────────────────────┐
│  Senior Reporter/Correspondent or    │
│           News Director              │
└─────────────────────────────────────┘

┌─────────────────────────────────────┐
│              Reporter                │
└─────────────────────────────────────┘

┌─────────────────────────────────────┐
│  Production Assistant, Intern, or    │
│         expert in other field        │
└─────────────────────────────────────┘
```

Position Description

Throughout our country, many people in spend a large portion of their time in their cars. No matter how much time is spent on the Internet and watching television at home, for the vast majority radio is our main source of information while we are driving. Radio Reporters keep us informed about local and national news while we are on the road.

Reporters at radio stations often handle a wide range of stories. Like their print counterparts, general assignment Reporters work on covering a combination of stories assigned to them by their news director, as well as generating their own story ideas. They scan the local and national media, including newspapers, magazines, television, and the Internet for ideas. Radio stations subscribe to various news wire services, such as the Associated Press for news and Reuters for business, which constantly update them on breaking news. Furthermore, they also receive press releases with information about different stories.

Breaking news is a key component of radio work and Reporters must be ready to go on location if needed and handle spot news. Engineers or other technical staff who handle the taping may accompany them. Breaking news also may be reported on directly from the station. Insiders say that their broadcasts are a combination of live and taped coverage. Coverage may include some reporting live from the scene with taped introductions and other comments inserted at the studio.

Once Reporters have their stories, they are responsible for writing their own pieces. They choose the angle they want to take as well as the ideas they want to highlight. Spot news stories are done on a daily basis, while feature stories may take several days or even weeks to write. Features may also consist of a series of broadcasts on similar topics, such as health. After writing their stories, Reporters edit their own work as well as share them with a news editor or news director for additional editing and direction.

Unlike television reporters, radio Reporters don't need to deal with hair, makeup, and wardrobe pressures when they go on air. Since the audience can hear but not see them, they can read their notes directly from paper rather than using a teleprompter. However, excellent public speaking skills are required to deliver a smooth broadcast.

For the most part, radio news is locally based. Some Reporters work for local affiliates of national news stations such as WCBS. As Reporters work on their stories, they pay attention to the local angle in a national news piece. For example, if a prominent politician passes away, they may seek comments from local politicians or relatives to somehow connect the two for their listeners.

Their duties may include:

- Conducting live and studio interviews
- Preparing and presenting reports
- Researching and writing stories
- Operating a broadcast console, digital sound editor, and other radio/satellite equipment
- Working with news directors, engineers, and producers
- Traveling when necessary
- Assisting with special programming
- Investigating story leads
- Producing segments
- Keeping up on special events
- Pitching ideas to the news director

Reporters may work in commercial or public radio. Public radio serves its community by providing in-depth, human-interest reporting where issues of importance to its listeners are highlighted. Unlike their commercial news counterparts, Reporters working in public radio rarely deliver traffic or weather reports, or relay the latest local events. While they may cover some breaking news on occasion, their main goal is focused on original programming that gets to the heart of issues and provides discussion and analysis of perspectives.

Some Reporters working in public radio may host their own programs at regularly scheduled times. They may interview guests or take phone calls from listeners. Call-in shows require collaboration with producers, booking agents, and other broadcasting professionals.

Flexibility is a must for Reporters in radio. They must be prepared to cover a story on short notice, while facing intense deadline pressure. Other Reporters serve as anchors, where they present news from the station and introduce clips from live, on-the-scene reporting. Furthermore, in addition to reporting, they must be aware of the radio-specific components of a news broadcast, such as the sound, the length of time, and the tape quality.

In this age, most recording is done digitally, through the use of minidiscs. Everything is downloaded onto a computer in an instant, making editing a lot easier, and a big change from the days of eight-track tapes. Hours for Reporters can be long and difficult, including weekends, evenings, and holidays, since the news never stops. However, for most Reporters, the challenge and excitement of being on-air and sharing a story make the long hours worthwhile.

Salaries

Salaries for Reporters can vary depending on their level of experience. According to the annual 2005 Radio and Television Salary Survey by RTNDA (Radio-Television News Directors Association)/Ball State University, news Reporters earned an average of $24,900 in 2004. The survey demonstrated a range from a minimum of $8,000 to a maximum of $48,000. However, most Reporters specify their salaries to be in the $30,000 to $45,000 range. Public radio often pays less than commercial news radio.

Employment Prospects

Employment prospects are poor to fair for Reporters in radio. Since opportunities are so competitive, those who are starting out must be willing to go where the jobs are—small towns and small markets. Furthermore, internships are a crucial way to break into the field. Working for free pays off in the end, as news directors are more likely to hire someone who has already proven his or her abilities.

Demo or audition tapes are often required for employment. These tapes demonstrate a Reporter's ability to present a newscast or program. Many prospective Reporters develop these tapes through courses, internships, or college radio experience.

Advancement Prospects

Advancement prospects are also fair, although it is easier to advance within radio than it is to break in from the outside. Reporters may move up to become news directors, where they have management responsibility. They can also seek opportunities in larger markets or move from local to national affiliates. Some Reporters advance to become more senior correspondents, handling specific stories or topics from start to finish, such as election coverage. Others may move to public radio where they can host their own programs and have more autonomy over content.

Education and Training

Insiders say that radio is a field where experience is more important than education. However, virtually all Reporters getting hired today have bachelor's degrees in a variety of fields. Journalism and communication degrees are helpful, but Reporters also hold degrees in a range of liberal arts fields. Furthermore, Reporters with specialties such as finance or politics may hold degrees in business or political science.

Internships are an essential part of the training process for Reporters. College radio offers an ideal opportunity to gain on-air reporting experience. Interns may or may not get the opportunity to be on-air, performing producing, technical, writing, and administrative tasks until they have proven themselves.

Through college radio experience or internships, prospective Reporters can develop demo or audition tapes that can be required for employment. By hearing the tapes of candidates on-air, news directors can evaluate reporting style, voice tone, and overall presentation.

Experience, Skills, and Personality Traits

Reporters on the radio must be excellent journalists, with inquisitive minds and a curiosity for both news and people. They must think on their feet, with the ability to work well under time pressure and meet tight deadlines. Also, Reporters should be good writers who can develop interesting perspectives on their news stories.

Additionally, radio Reporters must be superb communicators. They need to be articulate and well-spoken to command attention on-air. Precise diction, projection, and a good speaking voice are essential. Professionalism is key, as is the ability to handle the challenge of live broadcasts. Staying calm in difficult situations enables them to go on location when needed and retain composure, reassuring listeners. Communication skills are also utilized when conducting interviews and working with the public.

It is also important for Reporters to understand the medium of radio, including operating equipment, editing, and producing to some degree. They must be able to work within time constraints, such as keeping their story to fit in a certain time slot.

Unions and Associations

Reporters may belong to professional associations including the Radio-Television News Directors Association & Foundation, the National Association of Broadcasters, American Women in Radio and Television, the American Federation of Television and Radio Artists, and the Public Radio Programmer's Association, Inc.

Tips for Entry

1. Be persistent. To get ahead in a competitive field such as radio, you need a thick skin and a tenacious attitude. Remember that starting small is a good way to gain experience. Do not hesitate to send out dozens of audition tapes and to contact news directors several times until they give you a chance.

2. Explore public radio as an option for Reporters. Go on the Web site of National Public Radio (NPR) at http://www.npr.org and listen to their programming through your local afflilate.

3. Be an avid listener of radio news. Identify the different styles of various reporters and be attuned to feature stories versus spot news.

4. Volunteer at a radio station during a busy time such as election night. Although you will not get on-air experience, it can be a great way to make contacts and learn more about how radio stations operate.

5. Many journalism schools offer specializations or courses in radio broadcasting. Research the programs that interest you and speak to faculty with expertise in this area. One such program is at the Columbia Graduate School of Journalism in New York City; see http://www.jrn.columbia.edu/studentwork/radio/ for information.

PRODUCER

CAREER PROFILE

Duties: Produces news segments and programs for a radio station

Alternate Title(s): Executive Producer, Associate Producer, News Producer, Audio Producer

Salary Range: $40,000 to $60,000 and up

Employment Prospects: Fair

Advancement Prospects: Fair

Best Geographical Location(s): All

Prerequisites:

Education or Training—Bachelor's degree for most positions; fields such as journalism, broadcasting, and communications helpful

Experience—Several years of radio news experience

Special Skills and Personality Traits—Ability to operate technical radio equipment; knowledge of digital editing and audio; strong reporting, writing, and editing skills; good communication skills; ability to work well under pressure and multitask

CAREER LADDER

```
┌─────────────────────────────┐
│   Executive Producer or     │
│    other leadership role    │
└─────────────────────────────┘

┌─────────────────────────────┐
│          Producer           │
└─────────────────────────────┘

┌─────────────────────────────┐
│      Assistant Producer     │
└─────────────────────────────┘
```

Position Description

When you turn on your radio to listen to the news, many elements are at work to bring you that broadcast. Producers aim to ensure the quality of that broadcast, with regard to both sound and content.

Producers often have roles that have both audio and news components. Audio Producers are responsible for the overall sound of a broadcast. This can include taking calls from reporters out in the field, recording a story, putting it onto the computer, and preparing it for on-air broadcast. While technicians may make sure it is recording properly, Producers work with reporters to advise them about how it sounds and where to make changes. Furthermore, they ensure technical quality both in the station and in the field, making sure that equipment is functioning properly. Audio Producers may develop Standard Operating Procedures (SOPs) to keep broadcasts uniform.

News Producers focus on developing and producing innovative and creative news content and formats. They translate programming ideas into technical terms when nec-

essary and determine the best ways to make these broadcasts successful. In some settings, news Producers report, anchor, and edit as well. While it will depend on the size of the station, news Producers may report on breaking news or feature stories, research ideas, and write news copy. They may present a combination of live and taped broadcasts on-air. Additionally, they may edit individual elements of the program to provide consistency.

Producers may work in the production department or the newsroom, depending on their station. They are often responsible for directing newsroom broadcasts, including running rehearsals or tapings in the studio. Producers provide the necessary organization for a radio program. This can include arranging the elements of the show into a format for use by both reporters and technicians. Computer-based rundowns, as well as printed copies, may be used.

Producers are also responsible for designing the sound and style for their programs. Working together with the production team, they may create and/or oversee the musical bridges or other sound effects that introduce or conclude programs, as well as fill the space between them. Additionally, they may select and edit other audio materials. It is crucial that Producers are well versed in the digital editing and recording procedure, where minidisks are loaded onto the computer for editing.

Producers may supervise assistant or associate producers, as well as technicians and engineers, especially in an executive producer role. They may run daily meetings and provide technical assistance. Producers also work closely with the news team of directors, editors, and reporters to make sure that weekly coverage goals are being fulfilled. They may provide materials for newscasts and select stories for airing or editing.

Their duties may include:

- Taking calls from reporters and/or accompanying them out on location
- Managing audio equipment
- Planning out news programs
- Directing rehearsals for specific programs when applicable
- Listening to pieces for sound quality
- Altering sound quality or rerecording when necessary
- Organizing the broadcast, including the order of pieces
- Providing music bridges and other sound elements
- Directing flow of pieces from reporter to studio
- Preparing printed rundowns of tasks
- Loading pieces into studio computers
- Operating a control board
- Keeping up with current news and events
- Producing or updating Web content
- Performing some editing and reporting as needed

Planning and goal setting for their station is also part of a Producer's role. They may generate ideas for new and creative programming. Producers develop a vision for presenting the news in a format that will work for their listeners. They take all components into consideration, including sound, timing, and reporting style in order to create a dynamic broadcast format.

Some Producers work on specific programs for their station, such as a morning show. These Producers work closely with the hosts/anchors and are very involved with the show's content. They may research ideas, preinterview or prepare guests, and develop/edit content.

Like others in radio, Producers often work long and irregular hours. Evening, weekend, and holiday shifts are typical. A Producer's hours also may coincide with morning and evening commuting hours, when people are in their cars and radio usage is at its peak.

Salaries
According to the 2005 RTNDA (Radio-Television News Directors Association)/Ball State University Annual Survey, the average salary for news Producers was $35,800. The survey showed a range from a minimum of $13,000 to a maximum of $55,000. However, like other journalism positions, salaries vary greatly depending on the size of the market. Insiders say that most Producers earn between $40,000 and $50,000 per year, based on experience.

Employment Prospects
Employment prospects are fair overall for Producers. Many smaller stations do not hire employees specifically to be Producers. Reporters and news directors may perform the work of Producers, with engineers and technicians handling the equipment. However, larger stations in big markets do hire Producers. The best opportunities are for those with several years of prior radio experience. Since some Producers serve as reporters, anchors, producers, and editors all together, a diverse range of experience is ideal.

Producers may work in public or commercial radio. While the vast majority of jobs are at local affiliates, they may work for state or national broadcasting networks.

Advancement Prospects
Producers face fair advancement prospects within radio. Some may advance to become Producers at larger stations, or to become executive producers or program directors with greater management responsibility. Others seek positions outside of radio, moving into other areas of broadcasting where their production skills are useful, such as Web production or television.

Education and Training
According to insiders, experience is more important than education in radio. However, in today's competitive market, it is difficult to gain experience without a degree. Most Producers have a bachelor's degree in fields such as broadcasting, journalism, or communications. For Producers who also have writing and reporting responsibilities, the degree can be more important than for those who have purely technical roles.

Practical on-the-job training is needed to break into radio. To start out, internships are essential. On-air experience can be gained through college radio stations. Demo tapes of on-air broadcasts are needed for employment.

Experience, Skills, and Personality Traits
Because of the technical component of their jobs, Producers must have extensive knowledge of broadcast computer systems including digital audio workstations, digital on-air systems, and recording equipment and automated network switching systems. They should be able to operate audio processing equipment, microphones, consoles, audio storage devices, and telecommunications equipment including satellite and other technology. Experience recording in many acoustic environments can also be helpful for creating optimum sound.

Producers also must be able to take charge of a situation. As they may supervise assistant producers and technicians, they should be good managers. Furthermore, they need to exercise authority when they direct rehearsals or newscasts. Excellent news judgment, as well as attention to sound and other details, is very important.

Prior radio experience gives many Producers writing, editing, and reporting expertise as well. Strong organizational skills enable them to create consistent broadcasts and timely schedules. Working well under pressure is a must for Producers. They frequently need to troubleshoot during a live broadcast, while staying calm and professional. Also, they must be flexible to adapt to breaking news.

Unions and Associations

Producers may belong to a variety of professional associations including the National Association of Broadcasters, the Radio-Television News Directors Association, and American Women in Radio and Television.

Tips for Entry

1. Take time to learn about the technical side of radio. Volunteer or intern as a technician or engineer at a local station to learn about digital recording and other equipment.

2. Also, hone your skills as a journalist. Take broadcasting courses; anything specifically related to radio is a plus. A writing, reporting, and editing background increases marketability.

3. Consider public radio as an arena to produce innovative types of news programming. Visit National Public Radio's (NPR) Web site at http://www.npr.org and listen to your local affiliate.

4. Read job listings for radio Producers on sites such as http://www.journalismnext.com and http://www.nab.org.

5. Arrange an informational interview with a Producer at your favorite local station to learn more about the position. Get his or her tips for how to prepare and plan for such a career.

6. If you are a woman looking to get involved with radio broadcasting, visit the Web site of American Women in Radio and Television at http://www.awrt.org. This organization can provide an excellent outlet to find a mentor and gain support and insight.

NEWS EDITOR

CAREER PROFILE

Duties: Edits news copy and taped broadcasts for a radio station; may also be involved with writing, reporting, and producing

Alternate Title(s): Editor, Assigning Editor, Managing Editor, Supervising Editor, Associate Editor

Salary Range: $30,000 to $60,000 and up

Employment Prospects: Poor to Fair

Advancement Prospects: Fair

Best Geographical Location(s): All

Prerequisites:

Education or Training—Bachelor's degree; major in journalism or communications helpful

Experience—Several years of prior reporting/editing/producing experience for radio

Special Skills and Personality Traits—Excellent writing and editorial skills; good reporting skills; management and organizational ability; understanding of radio format; strong listening skills

CAREER LADDER

```
┌─────────────────────────────────────┐
│   Senior Editor or News Director     │
└─────────────────────────────────────┘

┌─────────────────────────────────────┐
│            News Editor               │
└─────────────────────────────────────┘

┌─────────────────────────────────────┐
│         Assistant Editor,            │
│  Assistant Producer, or Reporter     │
└─────────────────────────────────────┘
```

Position Description

While listening to the radio, have you ever noticed that each news story fits into its exact time slot? Weather and traffic are repeated on the minute or hour they are supposed to be, without news ever running over or interfering. News Editors fine-tune radio broadcasts to ensure that each story is not only engaging and accurate but also on time, audible, and seamless.

The job of a News Editor often has both traditional editorial and technical components, depending on the station. News Editors edit copy, just as they do in print journalism settings. After reporters finish a story on paper for a taped broadcast, it might go on to the News Editor, who will read it for content, grammatical errors, and style. Unlike print journalism, spelling is not important. However, editing the copy so that it reads well is crucial. News Editors make changes and suggestions to copy, working with reporters to create an ideal finished product.

Then comes the editing, which requires excellent listening skills. Just as newspaper editors must make articles fit within the space confines of a page, News Editors at radio stations have a similar challenge. They must make each story fit within its allotted amount of time. They listen to taped broadcasts and determine where content can be cut. For example, a story may need to fit into a seven-minute time slot. This slot can include not only the story but also the lead-in, a live tag, and a conclusion. News Editors also listen to sound, determining how the broadcast will play to listeners. They make sure the format is uniform between different reporters.

There is other copy that must be written for radio broadcasts. This is the copy that is not already recorded by reporters and anchors when they give their news reports. News Editors often write introductions and conclusions. They may determine interview questions, prepare cues for reporters, and write copy for breaks. All the while, News Editors work to keep consistency in style and tone. Good writing skills are key in order to adapt the content to fit the goals and format of the program.

Furthermore, News Editors work on the big picture for the news department as well. They may determine placement for different features of a news program, such as when the weather will come on, or how long the traffic report will be. Part of their role involves organization and coordinating how pieces will be grouped.

Their duties may include:

- Researching and writing stories
- Operating production and studio equipment
- Producing content and segments
- Working on special programming
- Generating news story and programming ideas
- Reporting as necessary
- Participating in creative aspects of programming
- Substituting for other news staff
- Editing a Webcast or other online content for the station
- Preparing copy for reporters or program hosts
- Supervising script writing
- Keeping current with news and local events

The job of a News Editor will vary depending on the station. At small stations, their responsibilities often include reporting and producing as well. As members of the news team, News Editors attend regular news meetings with reporters and news directors where story and program ideas are brainstormed and goals are set.

Hours can be long, including shifts over nights, weekends, and holidays to handle news editing as news happens. Some News Editors focus in on specific areas of news such as sports, politics, or features.

Salaries

Salaries for News Editors depend on the size of their station and market, as well as their years of experience. Insiders say that a typical range is between $30,000 to $50,000. Salaries may be higher for News Editors that also do some reporting or producing.

Employment Prospects

Employment prospects are poor to fair for News Editors. Many stations do not have the budget for News Editors and their job might absorbed by various news directors and reporters. Opportunities are greater in positions that combine News Editor with a reporting or producing component. Another growing area can be positions that also have an online editing component. News Editors should be willing to be geographically flexible and go where the jobs are.

Advancement Prospects

Advancement prospects are fair for News Editors. They may advance within radio to larger stations in bigger markets, or they may move up to become senior editors or news directors. Other News Editors move into other journalism roles, such as television editing or new media.

Education and Training

Most News Editors have bachelor's degrees in a variety of subjects. Fields such as journalism and communications are very helpful but not required. English and writing courses that hone language and grammatical skills are also valuable. Course work in politics and/or the social sciences develops a good understanding of different newsworthy issues.

In radio, experience and training is more important than education. News Editors work for several years as reporters or assistants before finding these positions. To begin as a reporter, internships are essential for training. On-air experience can be gained through working at college radio stations. In this setting, Future News Editors can create demo tapes of on-air broadcasts that are needed for employment.

Experience, Skills, and Personality Traits

News Editors need excellent editorial skills to perform their jobs well. They must have a strong grasp of language, including grammar, style, and usage. Furthermore, they need a good ear for language as well as an eye. As they listen to broadcasts to make suggestions, News Editors need the listening skills to understand what sounds good and why from a news standpoint.

Through several years of prior experience, News Directors develop their reporting and presentation skills as well. Their news judgment is keen, as well as their natural curiosity and interest in current and world events. In their editing, News Directors know how to keep the focus on the heart of the story. Organizational skills enable them to structure programs and broadcasts well.

News Editors must be able to thrive under pressure and balance many tasks at once. They should be comfortable with the technical aspects of a radio newsroom. Digital editing experience and familiarity with newsroom computer systems is very helpful. Additionally, Web editing experience can be valuable since some jobs may require online content editing.

Unions and Associations

News Editors may belong to a variety of professional associations, including the National Association of Broadcasters, the Radio-Television News Directors Association, and American Women in Radio and Television.

Tips for Entry

1. Learn more about jobs in radio by viewing listings on Web sites such as the California Chicano News Media Association at http://www.ccnma.org/Radio_Jobs.htm and Current.org at http://www.current.org/jobs/.
2. National Public Radio (NPR) has job listings on their Web site as well, including a category for editorial positions. Public radio provides many edi-

torial opportunities, since they offer a wide variety of news-related programming. Take a look at http://www.npr.org/about/jobs/positions.html#Editorial%20Positions.

3. Try out a radio internship. About.com lists some internship programs on their site for radio at http://radio.about.com/cs/latestradionews/a/aa010604a.htm. Also, contact local news stations to find out what they have available.

4. Another helpful feature on About.com's radio site discusses how to make an audition tape: http://radio.about.com/c/ht/02/07/How_Create_Audition_Tape1027450146.htm?terms=make+a+demo+tape.

5. Take courses to hone your journalism, writing, communications, and editing skills.

6. See North American Network's Radio Space, a site with links to much radio news and information at http://www.radiospace.com/.

PROGRAM DIRECTOR

CAREER PROFILE

Duties: Manages an entire on-air program/programming for a radio station

Alternate Title(s): None

Salary Range: $40,000 to 70,000 and up

Employment Prospects: Fair

Advancement Prospects: Fair

Best Geographical Location(s): All

Prerequisites:

Education or Training—Typically, a bachelor's degree; major in broadcasting, business, or communications helpful

Experience—Three to 10 years or more of prior reporting/editing/producing experience for radio

Special Skills and Personality Traits—Excellent leadership and management skills; writing, editorial, and reporting skills; good business and journalistic sense; strong news judgment; good organizational skills

CAREER LADDER

```
┌─────────────────────────────────────┐
│  Station Owner, General Manager, or  │
│           Station Manager            │
└─────────────────────────────────────┘

┌─────────────────────────────────────┐
│          Program Director            │
└─────────────────────────────────────┘

┌─────────────────────────────────────┐
│           News Director              │
└─────────────────────────────────────┘
```

Position Description

Program Directors oversee programming for their radio station from conception to broadcast. Serving as the link between journalism and business, they seek to develop programming with strong journalistic integrity that also achieves the ratings needed for success. Program Directors may be responsible for all programming on a station including news, music, special reports, and features, or they may focus on one or several areas.

The vision and sound of the station is determined by the Program Director. He or she considers the big picture and works with the news director to hire reporters and other on-air talent who can enhance the station. Program Directors manage the production process and scheduling, both of the staff and the programming. Scheduling is important to the success of various programs. Program Directors analyze a station's lineup and determine the best placement for different features.

Program Directors are responsible for attracting target audiences to their stations. They develop business objectives to make this happen and achieve their ratings goals. In commercial radio, they work to develop successful sales and promotions; in public radio, Program Directors may work closely with sponsors and fund-raising. They largely shape the overall format for the station.

Furthermore, Program Directors look to bring new and innovative programming to their station lineup. They may conduct demographic research or evaluate results of research studies of their target audience. Program Directors often cultivate relationships, and they might meet with members of the listening community to hear their voice with regard to programming objectives.

All station features can fall under the realm of the Program Director. Music, morning shows, traffic, weather, and news are just some of the areas. Program Directors who come from a news reporting background use their journalistic skills as managers. They shape news coverage in order to ensure it is fair and accurate. While the news director can focus solely on the news, Program Directors must look at the big picture and determine how the news can fit station objectives and needs of listeners.

Their duties may include:

- Maintaining an operations budget
- Managing day-to-day operations
- Evaluating and analyzing demographic and market research data
- Some writing, producing, editing, or reporting on-air in some positions
- Training staff members
- Looking for new syndicated programs
- Working as a liaison with the press and providing programming information
- Keeping current with news and local events
- Operating audio equipment
- Developing and producing local programs
- Enforcing FCC regulations
- Coordinating program schedules
- Deciding on different time slots for programming
- Serving as the face of their station to the community

As managers, Program Directors supervise a large number of staff members. These can include news directors, editors, reporters, producers, announcers, hosts, disc jockeys, and engineers. Usually, they conduct regular meetings with the heads of each department to set long-term goals as well as follow up on daily objectives. While they do not necessarily tell each department what to do, Program Directors certainly influence all major decisions. They report to management—a station/general manager or owner.

Hours are long for Program Directors, including many evenings, weekends, and holidays. However, the job is a good fit for a radio journalist with business savvy, looking for a management role.

Salaries
Salaries for Program Directors depend on the size of their station and market, as well as their years of experience. Insiders say that a typical range is between $40,000 and $70,000.

Employment Prospects
Employment prospects are fair for Program Directors. Radio is a competitive business, and a management position can be difficult to achieve. The best opportunities go to those who have networked extensively and gained at least five years of experience.

For Program Directors who are journalists, public radio can offer the opportunity to flex writing and reporting skills. Public radio tends to offer diverse programming for a Program Director to oversee. News stations like to hire Program Directors with a journalism background as well.

Advancement Prospects
Advancement prospects are also fair for Program Directors. Advancement typically involves moving to larger sta-

tions in bigger markets. Some Program Directors look to become general managers of stations. Other Program Directors apply their skills outside of radio to other broadcasting outlets such as television or new media.

Education and Training
There is not one specific educational path required to become a Program Director in news radio. While experience tends to matter more than education, radio journalists often have bachelor's degrees in journalism, broadcasting, media studies, or communications. Business courses are useful for the business component of the job, and writing courses help hone the writing skills needed in a news role.

Program Directors work for several years in radio to gain the necessary training—this can be between three and 10 years, depending on the size of the station and market. To begin in radio, internships are the best way to break into the field. On-air and behind-the-scenes experience can be gained through college radio stations; this is also a good way to create demo tapes of previous broadcasts that can be required for employment.

Experience, Skills, and Personality Traits
Program Directors should be strong managers and leaders. As they supervise staff members, they must be able to bring out their strengths for the station to work up to its best capacity. They need a vision for their station's programming needs and the technical and journalistic savvy to bring it to life.

Furthermore, Program Directors need an excellent understanding of radio. A good business sense helps drive ratings in commercial radio and fund-raising in public radio. Program Directors need not only attention to detail but also the ability to see the big picture in order to make decisions that will bring their station success.

Program Directors that come from news director roles have excellent writing, reporting, and editing skills. They are in touch with their audience and they know what makes an effective news story. Strong presenters, they are able to represent their station in the community when necessary. Like others in broadcasting, they must be able to work well under pressure and multitask. Familiarity with all radio technical equipment has been developed through past experience.

Unions and Associations
Program Directors may belong to a variety of professional associations, including the National Association of Broadcasters, the Radio-Television News Directors Association, and American Women in Radio and Television.

Tips for Entry
1. Learn more about creating a radio audition tape. The radio site on About.com is a good way to get started:

http://radio.about.com/c/ht/02/07/How_Create_
Audition_Tape1027450146.htm.

2. Contact a Program Director at a local radio station. Although they are very busy, speaking with one will give you a good idea not only about what he or she does but also about how to get hired in radio.

3. A campus radio station is an excellent way to get experience as a Program Director. If you are not currently a college student, visit the Web sites of different schools and find the links to their radio stations for more information.

4. Read about jobs in public radio at http://www.current. org/jobs/ and other radio positions at http://www.ccnma. org/Radio_Jobs.htm.

5. Listen to your favorite news or public radio station and list all the programs that you hear. Think about how a Program Director decided on the different time slots. Why do you think they do work or do not work well?

TRAFFIC REPORTER

CAREER PROFILE

Duties: Reports on local traffic conditions for a radio station

Alternate Title(s): Traffic Anchor, Traffic Manager

Salary Range: $20,000 to $60,000 and up

Employment Prospects: Poor to Fair

Advancement Prospects: Fair

Best Geographical Location(s): All

Prerequisites:

Education or Training—While there are no formal requirements, a bachelor's degree is considered essential in today's market; fields such as journalism and communication are helpful.

Experience—Several years of radio work through internships or full-time jobs

Special Skills and Personality Traits—Excellent communication and public speaking skills; investigative mind; interest in and knowledge of traffic conditions; ability to work well under pressure

CAREER LADDER

```
┌─────────────────────────────────────┐
│  Traffic Director or Traffic Manager │
└─────────────────────────────────────┘

┌─────────────────────────────────────┐
│           Traffic Reporter           │
└─────────────────────────────────────┘

┌─────────────────────────────────────┐
│           Traffic Assistant          │
└─────────────────────────────────────┘
```

Position Description

Nothing ruins a morning commute like traffic. A leisurely Saturday drive to the country can prove to be tremendously stressful when an accident backs up the highway for miles. If only you had taken a different route! Thanks to Traffic Reporters, some of these hassles can be alleviated.

Traffic Reporters inform listeners about local traffic conditions on the major roadways in their listening area. While it is not required for them to be local natives, most Traffic Reporters are, since they must demonstrate familiarity with the local roads. If they are from out of town, they must prove the knowledge necessary to perform their jobs well.

Traditionally, Traffic Reporters split their time between the morning and evening commutes. Morning commute can begin as early as 5 A.M. and run until 11 A.M.; evening may begin at 4 P.M. and go until 8 P.M. Holidays or other major traffic days will extend these hours. Traffic Reporters may work one or both of these shifts, depending on the station. Typical shifts range from five to seven hours. Some news radio stations offer traffic reports every 10 minutes throughout the day; Traffic Reporters in these settings must constantly monitor the situation. The heaviest commuting times are usually reserved for the Traffic Reporters with the most experience.

Although television stations and Web sites also may include major traffic updates, traffic reporting is a unique feature of radio in that people are frequently listening while they are in their cars. Traffic Reporters help listeners to make split second decisions about which road to take based on current conditions. Many factors must be taken into account that affect traffic. These can include accidents, weather conditions, and construction, among others.

In order to determine current traffic conditions, Traffic Reporters may have to literally fly above the scene in a helicopter. Fear of heights cannot be an issue as they gathering information from their vantage point looking down on the roads. They report on what they see, such as an overturned tractor-trailer or a six-car accident. Traffic Reporters may also observe traffic from vehicles, such as cars, vans, or trucks, on the roadways. Engineers or other technical staff who handle the taping may accompany them. Traffic Reporters get additional information about traffic conditions from public transportation agencies, news wires, and listener call-ins.

While general reporters may deliver their newscasts from both the field and the station, most traffic reports are live, which adds an increased element of stress and pressure. Traffic Reporters may conduct some research and writing in advance, but they often go on air without a script. Their reporting is determined by the conditions of the day. Excellent public speaking skills are required to deliver a smooth broadcast. Since traffic broadcasts can be dry or dull, Traffic Reporters use their communication skills to make their reports interesting and easy to follow for their listeners.

Additional duties may include:

- Monitoring police, fire, and traffic scanners
- Maintaining traffic records
- Updating traffic conditions on a corresponding Web site
- Preparing reports in advance as well as presenting them live
- Reading commercials and public service announcements
- Operating a broadcast console, digital sound editor, and other radio/satellite equipment
- Working with news directors, engineers, and producers
- Assisting with special programming
- Producing segments
- Making public appearances to represent the radio station

Traffic Reporters may be considered local personalities who represent their radio station. As people hear them in their cars each day, the reporters can develop a following among listeners. Along with other reporters and disc jockeys, they may attend or become involved in community events.

Traffic Reporters can expect long and difficult hours. Weekends, early mornings and/or evenings, and especially holidays can cause traffic news. Additionally, some Traffic Reporters must be "on-call" for their stations, ready to go on the scene of an accident or other major traffic event at all times.

Salaries

Salaries for Traffic Reporters can vary depending on their level of experience. According to the annual 2005 Radio and Television Salary Survey by RTNDA (Radio-Television News Directors Association)/Ball State University, news reporters earned an average of $24,900 in 2004. The survey demonstrated a range from a minimum of $8,000 to a maximum of $48,000. Although these figures are not specific to Traffic Reporters, they can provide a general idea.

Employment Prospects

Employment prospects are poor to fair for Traffic Reporters. Since opportunities are so competitive, those who are starting out must be willing to go where the jobs are—small towns and small markets. Furthermore, they can also expect to work during the least desirable shifts to pay their dues.

Internships are an essential way to break into the field. Experience in college radio or working for free at a small local station helps Traffic Reporters to prove their competence and get a feel for the work. These experiences also can provide an opportunity to develop the demo or audition tapes that are required for employment.

Advancement Prospects

Advancement prospects are also fair, although it is easier to advance within radio than it is to break in from the outside. Traffic Reporters may advance to become traffic directors or managers for their stations, supervising Traffic Reporters working a variety of shifts and determining the focus for coverage. Others may move into other areas of radio such as general assignment reporting, production, or sports; some Traffic Reporter positions include general reporting or producing as well. Traffic Reporters can also seek opportunities in larger markets that offer both higher profiles and salaries.

Education and Training

While experience is considered more important than education to break into radio, most Traffic Reporters getting hired today have bachelor's degrees in a variety of fields. Journalism and communication degrees are helpful, particularly in broadcasting or television/radio arts. Developing knowledge of traffic patterns is also very valuable. Understanding and following traffic reports for your local community, as well as how to make this information accessible to the public, provides good training. During internships or college radio experience, gaining exposure to the traffic reporting staff can be key.

Experience, Skills, and Personality Traits

Traffic Reporters must be excellent communicators, with superb presentation skills. They need to be articulate and well spoken to command attention on-air. Precise diction, projection, and a good speaking voice are essential. Professionalism is essential, as is the ability to handle the challenge of live broadcasts. Staying calm in difficult situations enables them to go on location; comfort with different types of travel such as helicopters is also needed.

Moreover, Traffic Reporters must be well versed with the constraints of radio broadcasting. They must be able to fit their comments into a specific time slot, conveying as much information as possible within a short time. Some Traffic Reporters may need to edit or produce portions of their broadcasts as well. They must be familiar with the particular computer software programs used by their station, such as Wicks VT-Visual Traffic.

Unions and Associations

While there is not a professional association specifically for Traffic Reporters, they may belong to other associations, including the Radio-Television News Directors Association & Foundation, the National Association of Broadcasters, American Women in Radio and Television, and the American Federation of Television and Radio Artists.

Tips for Entry

1. Take a look at Traffic411, a nationwide online traffic resource. Here you can see traffic reports, as well as learn to speak the lingo of a traffic reporter: http://www.traffic411.com/. You can also help report traffic incidents and get a feel at SmarTraveler.com, a site that partners with local transportation agencies: http://www.smartraveler.com/.

2. See job listings in radio at sites such as http://tvandradiojobs.com and http://www.journalismjobs.com.

3. Listen to the traffic reports on a variety of stations. On news stations that report on traffic every 10 minutes, see how the reports vary over a two-hour time period.

4. Are you familiar with the major roads and commuting patterns in your local area? This can include bridges, tunnels, and popular routes that people take to work. Spend time studying maps; this can be especially important when applying for a job in a specific community.

5. Gain on-air experience through radio internships. Practice your communication skills through courses in public speaking where you can hone your speaking voice.

NEW MEDIA

CONTENT WRITER

CAREER PROFILE

Duties: Writes online content for a Web site or Internet publication

Alternate Title(s): Staff Writer, Writer, Reporter

Salary Range: $20,000 to $60,000 and up

Employment Prospects: Fair to Good

Advancement Prospects: Fair to Good

Best Geographical Location(s): All, with the best opportunities in major cities or through freelance work

Prerequisites:

Education or Training—Bachelor's degree in journalism, communication, or related fields; some computer or technical coursework or training helpful

Experience—Entry-level to several years of writing experience, either print or online

Special Skills and Personality Traits—Excellent writing and editing skills; strong computer skills and willingness to learn; good organizational skills and ability to adhere to tight deadlines

CAREER LADDER

```
┌─────────────────────────────────────┐
│    Senior Writer, Editor,            │
│  Community Manager, or Producer      │
└─────────────────────────────────────┘

┌─────────────────────────────────────┐
│         Content Writer               │
└─────────────────────────────────────┘

┌─────────────────────────────────────┐
│  Production Assistant, Intern,       │
│  Assistant, or other entry-level position │
└─────────────────────────────────────┘
```

Position Description

Plain and simple, Web sites are made up of words. Whether the site is for a small business or huge corporation promoting its products and services or an online version of a print publication, sites serve similarly. No matter what the purpose—to sell, enlighten, or inform—content must be written in order for these goals to be achieved. Content Writers create this copy for Web sites.

Content Writers may be journalists who report on breaking news or writers that create copy for the Web sites of businesses, nonprofits, and other organizations. They use their writing skills to create content that fits the tone of the Web site they write for and meet the needs of readers.

Content can vary tremendously. Some Content Writers focus on articles, while others write columns and personal opinion pieces. There is also much content writing that focuses on advertising and marketing. Content Writers may also write technical copy that helps users to navigate the Web site.

Content Writers may work on even tighter deadlines than traditional newspaper and magazine writers, since the Internet is a constantly updated medium. If news breaks, they must get their story in within a matter of minutes or hours. Content Writers who are not reporters also must make updates on short time notice. If a program or service in their organization changes, they must make sure that the Web site reflects the current status.

Some Content Writers may have additional responsibilities that include editing, producing, and managing a community. Community managers monitor discussion boards and chat rooms, interacting with the site's target community and developing content accordingly. Others may be responsible for certain sections of the Web site where they determine the goals and content for that specific area.

Writing for the Web is different than writing for a newspaper or magazine. Content Writers not only vary their tone and style for an online audience, but also make sure to capture their attention quickly before they jump to another page. Furthermore, they consider where appropriate links will occur, as readers click to find additional information.

While most Content Writers are not expected to have advanced technical skills, basic HTML and Photoshop can be extremely helpful and even required for some positions. An understanding of computer technology helps Content Writers to be thinking broadly, as to where to link and expand.

Their duties may include:

- Updating content
- Editing articles or other copy
- Collaborating with editors and producers
- Generating ideas
- Monitoring and watching the news wires for breaking news
- Working with Webmasters and designers on page layout
- Selecting page content
- Working with outside sources
- Identifying most pressing stories
- Producing multimedia and interactive content
- Monitoring message boards
- Writing articles
- Coordinating links such as statistics, photographs, and links to other related articles

Some Content Writers also write for the print version of their newspaper or magazine, if applicable. However, print media is moving toward having Web-only features and articles.

Similarly to other journalism settings, hours can be long and nontraditional. Since the Internet is a 24-hour medium, shift work is essential to ensure constant coverage. However, since many positions are freelance, some Content Writers have the freedom to make their own schedules and/or work from home.

Salaries

Salaries for Content Writers vary depending on the level of their position. A typical range may be from $25,000 to $45,000. Sites with the largest markets and many employees tend to pay more. Those Content Writers working on a freelance basis may get paid per hour, word, article, or project. Per-word compensation for an article can range from $.10 a word or less to $2.00 a word and more.

Employment Prospects

Many journalists feel that the future of the field is through online media. As newspapers and magazines consolidate and downsize, people turn to the Internet to get their information. Therefore, as content is needed to help Web sites grow, so will the need for Content Writers.

However, job security may be hard to come by. Many of the opportunities for Content Writers are on a freelance basis with staff positions competitive and difficult to find. In-house positions often entail other responsibilities such as editing or producing as well. Some Content Writers move from print media to online media, while others begin directly at Web sites after completing their education.

Advancement Prospects

Advancement prospects are also fair to good. Content Writers can move up on the content track to become editors, producers, or community managers, having responsibility for content vision and direction in addition to writing. They may try to move from freelance positions to staff positions, or vice versa if they feel their freelance career can offer more flexibility and opportunity. Larger sites may offer more money and writing responsibility.

With their strong writing skills, Content Writers may move to print media, such as newspapers or magazines, or electronic media such as radio or television. Many writers try out several of these mediums throughout their career. Others may focus in on technical writing.

Education and Training

Content Writers can have a variety of backgrounds. Many hold bachelor's degrees in journalism, English, or related fields. A journalism degree may be needed for those who write for online newspapers or news sites. Business, marketing, and public relations coursework is helpful for those who write content with an advertising spin. Furthermore, technical coursework is also very valuable across the board.

To work in new media, Content Writers must be computer savvy. While they receive training on the job, their education often includes computer coursework and experience with Web publishing. Having his or her own Web page is a good way for a Content Writer to demonstrate his or her writing and computer abilities.

Experience, Skills, and Personality Traits

Creativity is one of the key skills that a Content Writer must have. In addition to strong editing and reporting skills, Content Writers must be flexible and able to develop content that serves a multitude of purposes. Working well under time pressure is highly important in new media, as things are constantly changing.

Writing skills are paramount, as well as an understanding of grammar, spelling, style, and usage. A Content Writer who juggles several freelance assignments may handle marketing and advertising copy, news articles, and informational or "how to" text all at once. Knowledge of language and the ability to write clearly in a user-friendly tone is needed.

Additionally, Content Writers often need an entrepreneurial spirit to market themselves and their talents. Those who pursue freelance opportunities must be persistent and ambitious to seek out the best opportunities. They also need strong self-discipline and motivation to complete their assignments on their own time.

Among the computer programs and technical areas helpful for Content Writers to know are Photoshop and HTML.

Unions and Associations

Content Writers may belong to the Online News Association (ONA), which is open around the world to journalists who produce news on the Internet. In addition, some Content Writers belong to the Online-Publishers Association, the Editorial Freelancers Association, and the National Writers Union.

Tips for Entry

1. One way to showcase your writing talents in a computer-savvy way is by developing your own Web site. Whether it is to market yourself as a freelancer or to highlight your writing portfolio, your Web site will demonstrate to employers that you are successful at online writing.

2. Check out popular new media sites such as CyberJournalist.net (http://www.cyberjournalist.net), a news and resource site that focuses on how the Internet and new technologies are changing the media.

3. Take a look at Wired Magazine at http://www.wired.com, which covers new media issues.

4. Visit the online counterparts of your favorite magazines and newspapers. Do you see any articles or features that say "Internet only?"

5. As you surf the Web, pay attention to the different content that comprises a Web site. For which type would you be interested in writing and why?

6. View freelance writing job listings at sites such as http://www.writersweekly.com and http://www.freelancewriting.com and view staff Content Writer jobs at sites such as http://www.journalismjobs.com.

ONLINE EDITOR

CAREER PROFILE

Duties: Oversees, conceptualizes, designs, and plans copy for an Internet news publication or a Web site; assigns projects to writers and producers

Alternate Title(s): Managing Editor, News Editor, Deputy Editor, Executive Editor, Editor in Chief

Salary Range: $30,000 to $80,000 and up

Employment Prospects: Fair to Good

Advancement Prospects: Fair to Good

Best Geographical Location(s): All, with most opportunities in major cities

Prerequisites:

Education or Training—Bachelor's degree or higher in journalism or related field; some technical/computer coursework or knowledge

Experience—Several years of writing and editing experience, either print or online

Special Skills and Personality Traits—Excellent writing, reporting, and editing skills; knowledge of Internet journalism; computer skills; strong management and leadership skills; good organizational skills and ability to adhere to tight deadlines

CAREER LADDER

```
┌─────────────────────────────┐
│  Executive Producer or      │
│  Executive Editor           │
└─────────────────────────────┘

┌─────────────────────────────┐
│  Online Editor              │
└─────────────────────────────┘

┌─────────────────────────────┐
│  Assistant Editor, Associate│
│  Editor, or Reporter        │
└─────────────────────────────┘
```

Position Description

Online journalism is constantly growing and changing. As more newspapers go online each week, the industry is redefining itself as much of the public turns to their computer as their first source of news each day. People tune in at their desks at work, at school, and at home, often leaving news portals up for constant updates. As we all know, the Internet is a 24/7 medium, unlike newspapers and magazines, which must be printed by a specific deadline for distribution. On many sites, news gets posted as it happens, making the World Wide Web the quickest source for breaking news.

At this time, newspapers are still deciding how to handle this dual coverage: print and online. Many papers utilize the same reporting and editorial staff for both their print and online editions. However, others have developed their online content to include breaking news and updates, requir-

ing different staff to run the process. Online Editors manage this original "Web-only" content that enhances their print editions.

There are a number of roles and job titles for Online Editors within new media. It can be difficult to pin down these exact job titles, since roles and responsibilities can vary greatly depending on the setting. Following are a sampling of some of the Online Editors involved with Internet news journalism:

- Executive editor: Runs the entire Web site, including long-term strategy and vision; works with top management at the paper, if applicable
- Editor in chief, editor, managing editor: Oversees the day-to-day operations, including advertising, human resources, and other business functions in addition to editorial

- News editor/deputy editor: Runs the news desk, with a focus on the home page and breaking news
- Copy editor: Writes headlines and reviews copy for grammar, punctuation, and style

Online Editors are responsible for coordinating content and assigning stories to writers. Most work with a combination of in-house and freelance reporters. Furthermore, many Online Editors also assign projects to producers, who handle getting the content online and creating the pages.

At newspaper Web sites, the Online Editors who are responsible for specific sections or desks (i.e., Features or Sports) work closely with the editors in these areas at the paper. They coordinate to discuss what each is planning to cover that day. While content may vary, style and format will be the same.

In addition to the Web versions of print newspapers, Online Editors may also work for news Web sites that do not have print counterparts. They may have broadcast counterparts instead, such as CNN (http://www.cnn.com) or global news wires such as the Associated Press (http://www. ap.org), or they may be stand-alone sites. Another big market is in news or consumer magazines. Furthermore, Online Editors can work for Web sites representing various corporations and nonprofit organizations. In these settings, they can write, edit, organize, and monitor content including Web copy, newsletters, marketing/advertising material, and other internal/external publications.

Most Online Editors (except for copy editors) do not do as much physical editing as their newspaper or magazine counterparts, say insiders in the field. Rather, they are more concerned with the overall coverage and look. The home page is a big editorial issue, as important as the front page of a newspaper. Depending on what people see right away, they will decide whether or not to continue reading. Furthermore, determining where to link will also help retain an audience.

Their duties may include:

- Monitoring and watching the news wires for breaking news
- Collaborating with staff at newspaper headquarters
- Working with Webmasters and designers on page layout
- Selecting page content
- Working with outside sources
- Working with staff writers and reporters
- Updating content
- Generating new ideas
- Identifying most pressing stories
- Producing multimedia and interactive content
- Monitoring message boards
- Writing articles
- Coordinating links such as statistics, photographs, and links to other related articles
- Responding to freelance pitches

Online Editors in new media strive to distinguish their site both from the print version of their publication (if applicable) and/or its competition. They comb the wires, looking for the most engaging news stories, and assign the best people to cover them. Also, they consider how to make their site aesthetically pleasing so that people will get their news in the most reader-friendly format possible.

Hours can be long and nontraditional, similar to other journalism settings. Since the Internet is a 24-hour medium, shift work is essential to ensure constant coverage.

Salaries

Salaries for Online Editors vary depending on the level of their position. Copy Editors may earn $30,000 to $40,000 per year, while Deputy Editors and Executive Editors can earn $70,000 to $100,000 or more. Sites with the largest markets and many employees tend to pay more.

Employment Prospects

Employment prospects for Online Editors in new media are fair to good, and they are constantly growing. More newspapers and magazines are recognizing the importance of building up their Web sites to be more than merely an online replica of their publication each day. Furthermore, outside of the publishing realm, Web sites spring up frequently that need Online Editors. One example of opportunity for Online Editors can be found in local entertainment news portals that contain information about restaurants and cultural events.

Some Online Editors move from print media to online media, while others begin directly at Web sites after completing their education.

Advancement Prospects

Advancement prospects are also fair to good. Depending on the level of their position, Online Editors can move up the editorial ladder to become the top editors of their site. Also, they can move to larger sites where they have more managerial responsibility.

Education and Training

Like other editors at more traditional publications, most Online Editors hold bachelor's degrees in journalism or related fields. Many hold master's degrees in journalism as well, particular in upper level editorial positions. Technical coursework is also very valuable.

However, one difference between print and new media journalism is that Online Editors must be extremely computer savvy. While they receive training on the job, their education often includes computer coursework and experience with Web publishing. Some Online Editors may have certificates in Web publishing or training in programs such as Photoshop and Dreamweaver.

Experience, Skills, and Personality Traits

The new media setting does not change the fact that Online Editors must be seasoned journalists. They have the excellent editing, writing, and reporting skills that led them to journalism and the flexibility to use them in a different way. Furthermore, Online Editors should be good leaders and managers. Many Online Editors supervise large staffs of producers, writers, reporters, freelancers, and other editors; they must be able to lead with ease. Staying calm under pressure and adhering to tight deadlines is even more important in new media, as things are constantly changing. Being an editor in this setting is for those who thrive on stress and enjoy an extremely fast-paced atmosphere. According to Online Editors, there is always something going on, so adaptability is key.

In addition to journalism skills, Online Editors in new media must also have the technical expertise needed to perform their jobs. They need a good visual sense to position text, including font size and story length. Also, they must understand HTML coding in order to enable site content searches. An eye for design and graphics is important for creating pages with flair.

Among the computer programs and technical areas helpful for Editors to know are Cold Fusion, Photoshop, HTML, Dreamweaver, and Flash. Knowledge of AP (Associated Press) style is also needed at a news site.

Unions and Associations

The Online News Association (ONA) is the main professional association for Online Editors in new media. Founded in 1999, it is open to journalists around the world who produce news on the Internet. In addition, some Online Editors may belong to associations such as the Newspaper Guild or the American Association of Newspaper Editors.

Tips for Entry

1. See the Web site of the Online News Association at http://www.onlinenewsassociation.org. It contains valuable information such as ongoing discussions, conferences, and tips for those interested in the field.
2. Get experience with online journalism as early as possible. Consider internships with news Web sites. If you are already working or interning in print journalism, find out how you can also contribute to their online companion sites.
3. Make sure your technical skills are up to speed. Take courses in Web publishing and learn programs such as HTML, Photoshop, and Dreamweaver.
4. Speak to Online Editors to learn about their career paths. Did they work in print and move over, or did they begin in new media? What advice do they have for someone trying to start out in the field?
5. Search job listings at sites such as http://www.journalismjobs.com. This site has a job search category specifically for online media.

PRODUCER

CAREER PROFILE

Duties: Oversees the direction and content for a specific section of a Web site

Alternate Title(s): Content Producer, Web Producer, Multimedia Producer

Salary Range: $40,000 to $70,000 and up

Employment Prospects: Fair

Advancement Prospects: Fair

Best Geographical Location(s): All

Prerequisites:

Education or Training—Bachelor's degree; helpful fields can include journalism, communications, graphic design, or computer science, depending on the position

Experience—Three to five years of Web production experience

Special Skills and Personality Traits—Excellent computer/technical skills and knowledge of specific multimedia programs; good writing and editing skills; graphic design, video, and/or photography skills; creativity; ability to work well under pressure and multitask

CAREER LADDER

```
┌─────────────────────────────────┐
│  Senior Producer, Editor, or     │
│      Executive Producer          │
└─────────────────────────────────┘

┌─────────────────────────────────┐
│           Producer               │
└─────────────────────────────────┘

┌─────────────────────────────────┐
│  Assistant or Associate Producer │
└─────────────────────────────────┘
```

Position Description

Web sites are comprised of a variety of sections. Each section may have written content, graphics/photographs, links, and multimedia images such as video or sound. Producers manage the big picture for the section for which they are responsible.

Producers ensure that their section appears as it should at all times. This includes brainstorming and determining content for the home page and other areas. They may assign and receive content from writers and put them onto a template for production. Furthermore, on news sites, they watch the wires for stories and may send them directly to the template. Overall, they ensure that news is getting to readers immediately as it happens.

The content they produce is not limited to writing. Producers also publish articles, photos, polls, audio/visual and interactive content, often on a daily basis. They must coordinate with editors, writers, graphic designers, and other staff to keep the site up to date. Producers also may perform some writing and editing, including headlines and summaries. They decide how the Web pages should look.

For a Web site to be successful, viewers expect different types of multimedia to add to its appeal. With the rapid growth of broadband, sites have the capabilities to feature multimedia. This can be known as "rich media," referring to the visual richness that includes animation, sound, and video rather than just text. If a Web site does not have this rich media, readers will often go to another site that does.

Multimedia Producers are responsible for creating this rich media. They shoot, produce, and post video footage, putting it online. They must be comfortable with writing, editing, audio, video, and photography to perform their jobs. Many of the features they produce are Flash-based, so they need the technical skills required.

Their duties may include:

- Gathering media from the field
- Managing multimedia projects
- Updating content throughout the day
- Working with freelance writers
- Assigning and scheduling projects

- Creating and laying out pages
- Gathering background information
- Editing video and audio using digital software
- Moderating online discussions
- Reviewing and posting reader comments
- Brainstorming new content ideas
- Working with advertising and product development teams

Producers often work long hours to reflect the immediate nature of the Internet. They may work in shifts to make sure all hours are covered. Producers should be well organized in order to supervise both projects and staff members; they must also be able to troubleshoot problems that arise.

Salaries

Salaries for Producers vary depending on their work setting. Average ranges are between $40,000 and $50,000. Some Producers work on a freelance basis, getting paid per project. For Producers at high-profile Web sites, or for those who have built a strong freelance reputation, salaries can be higher.

Employment Prospects

Employment prospects are fair for Producers. Many new Web sites start up all the time; however, many also fail every day. Opportunity may be good in the online equivalents of magazines or newspapers, since their relevance and importance in journalism today is expanding. Furthermore, education is an area where the use of multimedia is growing, and Producers may be needed for educational sites or projects.

Advancement Prospects

Producers can advance in a number of ways, depending on their goals. Some Producers aspire to continue up the production ladder to senior or executive producer, where they have full responsibility for producing a site. Others transition to other areas that make use of their best skills such as editing, writing, or graphic design. Producers may transition from freelance to in-house positions or vice versa.

Education and Training

Most Producers hold bachelor's degrees; helpful subjects vary depending on the position. For some Producer roles, degrees in computer science, Web development, or graphic design are valued. At news-oriented Web sites where writing is also a component of the job, journalism or communications degrees might be needed.

Much of the training comes on the job and through internships. Aspiring Producers can gain experience with multimedia technologies by working at Internet companies while in school.

Experience, Skills, and Personality Traits

Producers need a range of skills in order to perform the many components of their jobs well. For some positions, graphic design and Web programming skills are necessary. For others, writing and editing skills are crucial. Regardless of the position, strong communication abilities and creativity are needed.

Additionally, Producers should be excellent problem solvers. They must be able to work well under pressure and multitask, handling details and big picture issues. If content is incorrect, they must fix it, and everything must be done in a timely fashion. Project management skills are also valuable, as well as supervisory skills for those who manage other staff members.

Among the specific technical skills needed by Producers are Macromedia Flash, Photoshop, HTML, JavaScript, CSS, XML, DHTML, Freehand, Dreamweaver, and Illustrator. These may not all be required by each position, but knowledge of and familiarity with as many of these programs as possible helps Producers to be more marketable and expand their options.

Unions and Associations

Producers in new media may belong to a variety of professional associations including the Online News Association, the National Multimedia Association of America, and the Interactive Media Association.

Tips for Entry

1. Courses in multimedia production are available at a variety of schools across the country. Check out the programs at Columbus State Community College in Columbus, Ohio (http://www.cscc.edu/DOCS/MMPTDES.htm) and the University of Texas at San Antonio (http://multimedia.utsa.edu/info-mp.html).
2. If you live in the New York area, see the job listings posted by the New York New Media Association at http://jobsnetwork.nynma.org/.
3. How good are your technical skills? You can find free tutorials online to help you learn different programs. Try http://graphicssoft.about.com/od/photoshop/l/bllps5out.htm for Photoshop, http://www.learnthat.com/computers/learn-362-dreamweaver_mx_2004.htm for Dreamweaver, and http://www.trainingtools.com/ for a variety of courses.
4. Get an internship for a new media news site. The Producer in this setting is somewhat like an electronic journalism producer who manages an entire newscast. Regardless of your role as an intern, make sure you speak to different Producers about their jobs and get their tips.
5. Take courses in a variety of subjects, including computer graphics, business, and English, to round out your education. As a Producer, you may benefit from studying many different subjects.

WEBMASTER

CAREER PROFILE

Duties: Develops, manages, and maintains a Web site; oversees programming and content for the site

Alternate Title(s): Web Site Administrator, Web Developer, Web Producer, Web Site Manager

Salary Range: $40,000 to $70,000 and up

Employment Prospects: Fair

Advancement Prospects: Fair

Best Geographical Location(s): All, especially major cities

Prerequisites:

Education or Training—Bachelor's degree in computer science preferred, but not required; knowledge of computer programming

Experience—Related experience creating and managing Web sites through full-time work or internships

Special Skills and Personality Traits—Excellent computer programming skills; understanding of Internet and online communication technologies; strong organizational skills; ability to meet deadlines and work well under pressure; knowledge of graphic design

CAREER LADDER

```
┌─────────────────────────────────────┐
│   Webmaster, larger organization     │
└─────────────────────────────────────┘

┌─────────────────────────────────────┐
│            Webmaster                 │
└─────────────────────────────────────┘

┌─────────────────────────────────────┐
│  Web Page Designer or Programmer     │
└─────────────────────────────────────┘
```

Position Description

Webmasters create and implement Internet visions for online news sites. Starting from scratch, they strategize as to what will make a successful Web site for their company, whether it is a companion Web site to a newspaper or magazine, or other type of organization. They gather information from all the departments and key players to determine the overall structure of the site. Their aim is to command the attention of visitors and to make them want to linger on the site. In the case of companion sites, the Web site should offer features that the print edition does not. A user-friendly site can mean a considerable difference in success.

The job of a Webmaster is often defined differently at varying sites. It may include programming, graphic design, and determining the appearance of the site, content development, and production. Most Webmasters continuously maintain and update their sites after development, troubleshooting problems. They create the links that visitors use to navigate the site. Also, they record the "hits" so they know the parts of the site people most often visit and whether or not they complete any online registrations.

Additionally, Webmasters may work on both the back end and the front end of a Web site. The back end involves the database and hardware infrastructure that supports the site, requiring the Webmaster to be skilled at programming. The front end relates to the aspects that users can see, such as design and navigation tools, needing the Webmaster to be up to speed on graphics and content development. Webmasters must decide on the hardware needed to build the site and the software needed to make it work properly.

Webmasters must continuously communicate with reporters, editors, and other staff members at their organizations to make sure that the information on the Web site is up to date and reflects the most current news. Information gets outdated in the blink of an eye, so they must be on top of all new developments. They work with all departments employed by the Web site, and sometimes the corresponding print staff, if applicable. Usually, they serve as internal liaisons and do little work with external vendors.

Furthermore, Webmasters create the documents—Web pages—that comprise the site. They may supervise the content writers and computer programmers that develop the text and graphics. Always, they are guided both by what will work as well as what will look aesthetically pleasing. Web design and Web development may also be components of the Webmaster's job. Web design involves the visual art and graphic design that defines the look of the site. Web development focuses more on the site's structure and interactivity.

Their duties may include:

- Setting up and managing internal and external listservs
- Fixing software bugs
- Brainstorming ideas
- Adding new features such as discussion boards and registration capabilities
- Researching Web sites of similar organizations
- Writing code
- Responding to visitor feedback
- Supporting users nationwide and worldwide
- Posting content pages
- Editing and reviewing content
- Testing the links on the site to make sure they work properly
- Dealing with security issues

Although most Webmasters are not journalists in the traditional sense, they are able to use their technical skills to make news and information accessible to the public. However, good writing and editing skills can also be crucial in addition to technical capabilities as the job continues to grow and evolve. Most Webmasters are passionate about the Internet and are very involved in their work, getting paid to indulge in one of their favorite hobbies. Since the Internet does not function on a nine to five schedule, nor does the news, neither do most Webmasters. Their jobs may involve long, nontraditional hours to enable sites to go live, fix any problems, and keep up with the demands of breaking news.

Salaries

Salaries of Webmasters vary based on where they work, as well as the job responsibilities. As the position continues to change and get redefined in new media, salaries will differ. Typical ranges can be anywhere from $40,000 to $70,000 and up for those with considerable experience. These figures demonstrate the large range for these types of positions.

Employment Prospects

Within the field of journalism, employment prospects for Webmasters are fair. However, growth is promising as many newspapers and magazines are building and expanding their Web sites. Sometimes, the Webmaster role is combined with that of a producer or other specialist. Opportunities are the best for those with a wide range of skills including programming, writing, management, and graphic design. Some Webmasters work on a freelance basis, which may be a good way to gain experience in the field.

Advancement Prospects

Webmasters may advance by moving to larger companies with more complex Web sites. They may seek out positions that enable them to build more online features such as registrations and discussion boards, and even cutting-edge technologies such as streaming videos or live chats. Webmasters at larger organizations can earn higher salaries. Webmasters may also decide to become self-employed, working as new media consultants. Those who have built experience working in Internet journalism can develop a niche area for themselves, working specifically to build up newspaper or magazine Web sites.

Education and Training

While formal education is less important for Webmasters than having the required skill sets, most position listings require bachelor's degrees. Fields such as computer science, programming, or information technology are especially helpful. Some positions require additional skills, such as writing and graphic design.

The best training for the field comes from actually doing the work. Most Webmasters gain experience through internships and part-time jobs while they are students. As they design Web sites for campus organizations or companies, they receive the valuable training needed to perform this job on a regular basis. Furthermore, constant training is needed to keep skills up-to-date with new technologies.

Experience, Skills, and Personality Traits

Excellent computer skills are required to become a Webmaster. Depending upon the position, different programming languages may be needed. Some common requirements may include HTML, XML, CGL, SQL, Java, JavaScript, ASP, Cold Fusion, and C++. Web development and design tools such as Acrobat, Dreamweaver, Flash Animation, and Photoshop can also be required. Webmasters should be experienced and familiar with Internet technologies, having already had the experience of personally building and maintaining several Web sites in order to get hired.

In addition to technical skills, Webmasters need to be excellent organizers. They need to have creative vision combined with the ability to manage projects, meet deadlines, and work well under pressure. Those Webmasters who write and develop content should have strong writing skills as well.

Unions and Associations

Webmasters may belong to a variety of professional associations including the World Organization of Webmasters and the Internet Society, as well as regional groups. Others who are involved with online news may belong to the Online News Association. New associations are frequently forming since the field is still so new.

Tips for Entry

1. Volunteer to create and maintain the Web site for a student organization on campus. This will provide firsthand experience on the work of a Webmaster.

2. Visit the Web sites of several newspapers and magazines that interest you. Notice what features they all have in common, as well as their design and layout.

3. Take courses that will help you enhance your computer skills. In addition to those offered by local universities, there are hundreds of online tutorials. Conduct a search engine query for the programs you want to learn to explore the options.

4. Apply for a formal internship in Web development. This will provide you with skills, as well as mentors who may be able to help you find a job.

5. Learn more about the job of a Webmaster and other careers in Web site development by visiting links such as http://www.wetfeet.com/asp/careerprofiles_overview. asp?careerpk=45 and http://www.course.com/careers/dayinthelife/webdev_jobdesc.cfm

STRATEGIC
COMMUNICATION

COPYWRITER

CAREER PROFILE	CAREER LADDER

Duties: Writes advertising copy for an agency or client including print and broadcast media, as well as Internet copy and other promotional material

Alternate Title(s): Advertising Copywriter

Salary Range: $20,000 to $80,000 and up

Employment Prospects: Fair

Advancement Prospects: Good

Best Geographical Location(s): East and west coasts; other major cities such as Chicago

Prerequisites:

Education or Training—Bachelor's degree or higher; courses in copywriting, advertising, marketing, journalism, English, and writing helpful

Experience—Prior experience through internships and portfolio needed

Special Skills and Personality Traits—Creativity; excellent writing skills; good editing skills; strong communicator and presenter; knowledge of advertising

---

Senior Copywriter or Creative Director

Copywriter

Junior Copywriter

Position Description

Advertising is a pervasive part of American culture. We all remember commercials, billboards, or magazine pages that have touched our hearts, made us laugh, or raised controversy. Each advertising campaign is devised by a multitude of professionals from those who work with the clients to those who plan the budgets. However, it is ultimately the creative team that comes up with the language used in the ads.

As members of the creative team, Copywriters write advertising copy. They are responsible for the jingles that we hum and the slogans that leap off the pages. Their writing skills must be top-notch not only to devise catchy phrases but also to tailor their message according to the client needs. Copywriters may write copy used for print or Internet publication as well as for broadcast media.

Whether they are promoting products, services, or a mission, Copywriters use language to get their message across. As a journalism career choice, Copywriters also seek to impart information. Each ad devised by a Copywriter helps people to make decisions and can influence the way they think. Ads can make political or social statements as well as use humor to diffuse difficult topics.

A creative director who directs both writers and artists to create a coordinated approach for each ad manages the creative department. The creative team develops a viable concept and brainstorms ideas for how to make it into a reality. Copywriters and the art team work closely together to construct a seamless visual and verbal strategy. Furthermore, Copywriters also work with account executives and marketing staff to create targeted approaches for clients.

Strategy is a big part of being a Copywriter. With any given product, there are many features that can be highlighted. Copywriters consider which are the most important and what type of campaign will be most successful at piquing the interest of consumers. Furthermore, since each client is different, so is the message they want to get across. Even with similar products or services, Copywriters must think of ways to make each client's campaign unique. Market research and focus groups may help to develop the best methods for each ad.

Advertising is about being persuasive, whether the goal is to convince its audience to buy a product, support a program, or use a service. Copywriters participate in other types of persuasive writing in addition to print and broadcast media ads. They may devise names for products, as well as sales pitches, proposals, and articles. Also, some Copywriters develop what is known as "collateral marketing"—brochures, direct mail, inserts, and other promotional materials for a company. Taglines, the slogans that companies become known for (such as Nike's "Just Do It"), are written by Copywriters. They are adept at portraying an image that is consistent with their client's goals.

The best work of Copywriters consists of descriptive writing that appeals to people's senses and generates a buzz, as those in the industry say. Getting consumers to talk about their product is a goal for most clients. With sales being the bottom line, Copywriters play a large part in the financial success of a product. This stress drives many Copywriters constantly to strive for excellence and be at the top of their game.

Yet some Copywriters feel conflicted about the business aspect of their job. Insiders say that client's wishes will dictate campaigns, even if they hamper the Copywriter's creativity. Furthermore, like other advertising professionals, Copywriters may need to promote products that they do not support. Most Copywriters are able to reconcile these issues, and those who feel conflicted may go on to work for nonprofit organizations where they are promoting a mission rather than a product.

Their duties may include:

- Meeting with clients and interviewing them about how to best promote their products
- Presenting ideas to clients
- Editing, proofreading, and rewriting copy
- Responding to client feedback and reworking campaigns
- Keeping up on advertising trends
- Staying abreast of popular culture
- Attending creative team meetings
- Writing press releases
- Writing direct mail material
- Analyzing market data
- Maintaining relationships with clients
- Attending photo or video shoots

Copywriters often work long hours, especially as deadlines draw close. A 50-hour workweek is typical, with extended days during busy times. Meetings with clients may take place during evenings and weekends.

However, the long hours are often part of the glamour and intrigue of copywriting work. Attending launch parties for new products and campaigns and other events may

be part of the job for some Copywriters. They might travel frequently and enjoy free merchandise and other perks of working for large corporate clients.

Some Copywriters specialize in writing copy for particular types of organizations or industries, such as financial firms, fashion, or nonprofits. Others may specialize by product types.

Salaries

Copywriters often experience a large salary range during the course of their careers. Entry-level salaries for junior Copywriters can be very low, beginning in the low $20,000 range or even less. However, with experience they can earn considerably more. According to an annual *Advertising Age* salary survey, Copywriters earned an average base salary of $59,000 in 2004.

Geographic location also influences salary. The same survey shows the average base salary for Copywriters on the East Coast as $73,000, the West Coast as $61,000, the South as $55,000, and the Midwest as $53,000. Salaries are also higher for Copywriters working for large agencies.

Another salary survey, the AIGA/Aquent Survey of Design Salaries 2005, conducted by AIGA—the Professional Association for Design, showed the average total cash compensation for Copywriters to be $55,000. The range was from $40,800 in the 25th percentile to $70,000 in the 75th percentile.

As Copywriters continue to advance, their salary range goes up. As creative directors, average salaries are typically over $100,000. Furthermore, Copywriters may receive bonuses based on the success of the agency in a given year.

Employment Prospects

Jobs for Copywriters are very competitive. The creative side of advertising is difficult to break into. Experts recommend being persistent and discourage aspiring Copywriters from taking entry-level positions on the business/account side of advertising because it may be difficult to transition. Internships are crucial and can greatly improve chances of getting hired as an entry-level Copywriter.

A portfolio is a prerequisite for creative employment. The portfolio consists of sample ads that the candidate has created for a variety of products and services. College courses in advertising, as well as independent copywriting and advertising courses can help with portfolio development. Other writing samples are not pertinent.

Although copywriting differs from traditional journalism, it is not uncommon for journalists with several years of experience to transition to copywriting. Both positions require analyzing the environment, imparting information, and writing. Media contacts and reporting experience help make the change, as do copywriting training programs.

As the job market gets tighter, freelancing becomes an increasingly viable way to break into the field. Working for hire on specific projects can be a good way to get your work known, develop a portfolio, and make valuable contacts. Some freelancers become so successful that they make a career of freelance work.

Advancement Prospects

As Copywriters become more advanced in their careers, their responsibilities grow and change. Rather than carrying out the vision handed down by their creative director and focusing on the words, senior Copywriters are able to shape and develop their own concepts for clients. Some Copywriters advance to become creative directors themselves or aspire to open their own agencies.

Other Copywriters may move into freelance work to have more control over their careers. Unlike those who use freelancing as a way to break in, experienced Copywriters have networks of contacts and can pick and choose their projects. Copywriters may also move out of advertising into magazine or newspaper journalism, as well as other types of writing such as creative fiction or screenplays.

Education and Training

Copywriters must have a minimum of a bachelor's degree. Majors can vary, but coursework in advertising, copywriting, marketing, business, journalism, and English, as well as some liberal arts are valuable. Exposure to and knowledge of the advertising industry through internships and/or coursework is essential.

Specific advertising and copywriting schools help people assemble portfolios. There are many programs online and through local schools; they vary in terms of their reputation. While a Google search for "Copywriting classes" will yield numerous results, speak to professionals in the field to determine which are the best programs.

Experience, Skills, and Personality Traits

Creativity is the most essential attribute for Copywriters. They need not only outstanding writing skills but also the ability to generate fresh ideas with humor and wit. Verbal communication skills are also critical. Copywriters must be able to articulate their ideas to clients and supervisors. They should be extroverts who enjoy working with people. Additionally, they must be open to feedback and criticism.

Copywriters should also be computer literate, and it can be helpful to know design programs such as Quark Xpress and Adobe Photoshop. They must be able to meet tight deadlines, manage their time, and juggle multiple projects with high demands at once. High energy enables Copywriters to meet the demands of their job and keep a sense of humor. Flexibility is also important for Copywriters to balance different types of ads—print, radio, and television—as well as varying personalities and work styles of clients.

Unions and Associations

Copywriters may belong to the American Association of Advertising Agencies, the American Advertising Federation, the Art Directors Club, and AIGA—the Professional Association for Design.

Tips for Entry

1. Internships in advertising are the best way to gain related experience. Explore the largest advertising agencies such as BBDO Worldwide (http://www.bbdo.com/), Young & Rubicam (http://www.yr.com/yr/), and Saatchi & Saatchi (http://www.saatchi.com/worldwide/index1.html).
2. See this article "The 21 Most Powerful Copywriting Rules of All Time," by Joe Vitale: http://advertising.about.com/gi/dynamic/offsite.htm?zi=1/XJ&sdn=advertising&zu=http%3A%2F%2Fwww.mrfire.com%2Farticles%2F0013.html.
3. Become familiar with *Advertising Age,* the main publication for the advertising industry. Read the digital version at http://www.adage.com/.
4. Keep a folder of print advertisements you admire. Analyze the strategy, the words, and the visual affect. As a Copywriter, what approach might you have taken? Watch commercials and listen to radio ads with the same critical thinking.
5. Speak to Copywriters and other creative professionals in advertising. Gain their advice for how to get started in the field.
6. Take courses in journalism and other subjects that enable you to hone your writing skills.

CORPORATE COMMUNICATIONS SPECIALIST

CAREER PROFILE

Duties: Creates, writes, edits, and/or oversees communications for a company or nonprofit organization; may be responsible for one specific area such as newsletters, Internet copy, or public relations; or might manage overall communication strategy

Alternate Title(s): Public Information Officer, Speechwriter, Corporate Communicator, Staff Writer, Consultant, Communications Specialist, Media Relations Officer

Salary Range: $40,000 to $85,000 and up

Employment Prospects: Good

Advancement Prospects: Good

Best Geographical Location(s): All

Prerequisites:

Education or Training—Bachelor's degree; helpful fields include communications, English, journalism, public relations, media studies, or business

Experience—Positions range from entry-level assistants to senior-level managers

Special Skills and Personality Traits—Excellent writing and editing skills; strong verbal communications, media savvy; persuasive skills; good attention to detail and ability to be organized

CAREER LADDER

```
┌─────────────────────────────────────┐
│ Corporate Communications Director/   │
│ Manager or Vice President            │
└─────────────────────────────────────┘

┌─────────────────────────────────────┐
│ Corporate Communications Specialist  │
└─────────────────────────────────────┘

┌─────────────────────────────────────┐
│ Corporate Communications Assistant   │
└─────────────────────────────────────┘
```

Position Description

Companies and organizations use writing to get their message across in a variety of ways. Externally, a Web site promotes its products, services, and mission. It may offer information to investors, share job descriptions as a recruiting tool, or encourage people to register for programs. Corporations also may have additional external written material including newsletters and brochures, as well as communications to be shared verbally such as speeches, presentations, and proposals. On the internal side, many organizations have presentations as well. Particularly at large companies, there are internal newsletters, memos, and other communications. Corporate Communications Specialists are involved with writing and promoting this material.

The job of a Corporate Communications Specialist can involve public relations—activities and communications designed to enhance their company's image. They may be responsible for helping define their company's image through written material. This means that Corporate Communications Specialists must understand their employers inside and out. They must be on board with their mission and fully know the goals and objectives they are trying to convey through communications. Every type of writing, from memos to Web copy, must promote the same image and goals.

Corporate Communications Specialists frequently spend much time writing. Some have specific responsibilities, such as writing and editing an internal newsletter. This can include brainstorming content, assigning material to other staff members, working on layout, and editing the finished product. Other Corporate Communications Specialists handle writing Internet copy or marketing material such as brochures or advertising information. Writing skills are key here, for regardless of the material, catchy and persuasive content is necessary.

In addition to written materials, many Corporate Communications Specialists handle the verbal aspect of communications. They may write speeches and presentations for top management to use internally or externally. Furthermore, they may represent their organization to the media, acting as spokespeople and putting a positive spin on recent events. In this way, their communication strategies can directly affect their company's success.

Some Corporate Communications Specialists work directly for the CEO or president of their organization. Especially at a large company, the communication approach of this leader is crucial to their image. The Corporate Communications Specialist might write letters, memos, and other correspondence on the president's behalf. In addition to writing speeches, he or she may also advise on overall communication strategy. It can be almost like being a White House speechwriter, who targets and projects a cultivated image.

Although the most frequent job title is "Corporate" Communications Specialist, nonprofits often offer good opportunities for these types of professionals. At a nonprofit organization, Corporate Communications Specialists focus on fund-raising and promoting the mission as the bottom line, rather than sales. In addition to some of the similar writing they would do at a company, they may also write grant proposals, develop curriculum, and design program materials.

Additional duties may include:

- Running publicity campaigns
- Building community relationships
- Offering trainings and seminars
- Writing press releases
- Organizing media tours
- Creating media and analyst pitches
- Developing collateral marketing materials
- Coaching other staff members with regard to communication strategy
- Overseeing Internet copy and making updates
- Coordinating interviews
- Conducting research
- Organizing and planning special events
- Enforcing brand compliance
- Serving as a liaison with the news media
- Developing diversity initiatives

Corporate Communications Specialists in leadership positions have much supervisory and management responsibility. They often manage a department and oversee both professional and support staff in several communications areas that can include public relations, media, community/philanthropic relations, employee relations, publications, marketing, advertising, and others. Moreover, they participate in the overall communications vision and strategy for their organization at an upper level.

While different from traditional journalism, the field of corporate communications offers a different work environment for those with journalism skills. Journalists who get tired of the pressure of the newsroom and want more steady hours with perhaps higher pay might transition to corporate communications. It offers an opportunity to write and persuade as well, in a different context.

Salaries

Salaries vary for Corporate Communications Specialists depending on the level of their position. Entry-level positions or those requiring one to three years of experience may pay in the $40,000 range, while management positions can pay considerably more. A corporate communications manager with more than five years of experience and supervisory responsibility can earn an average of $70,000. Surveys say that a typical salary for an experienced Corporate Communications Specialist is between $60,000 and $85,000 per year.

Employment Prospects

Employment prospects are generally good for Corporate Communications Specialists. As competition and public expectation increases, companies seek ways to make themselves stand out, as well as to improve and safeguard their image. Corporate Communications Specialists help them enhance the way they are seen by the public. Furthermore, as the Internet continues to grow as another media outlet for organizations, more Corporate Communications Specialists will be needed to write, edit, and promote this content.

Advancement Prospects

Corporate Communications Specialists bring with them and further develop a skill set that can be used in a variety of areas. Writing, editing, research, public relations, and marketing skills can be applied in a number of ways. Some Corporate Communications Specialists advance by moving into management positions such as communications director or vice president. Others become specialized in one area such as public relations, new media content writing, or speechwriting.

Education and Training

Corporate Communications Specialists hold bachelor's degrees in variety of fields. As one might expect, communications fields are particular helpful, including communications, journalism, public relations, and English, as well as business and marketing.

Some schools offer specific programs in corporate communications. Courses hone strategic writing, persuasive writing, and presentation skills. These degree programs include Mercy College in White Plains, N.Y. (http://www.mercy.edu/AcaDivisions/litlangcomm/CorporateCommunications/careers.htm) and Hawaii Pacific University in Honolulu (http://www.hpu.edu/index.cfm?contentID=170&siteID=1).

Experience, Skills, and Personality Traits

Successful Corporate Communications Specialists must be skilled at writing. They must know how to use words to persuade and catch people's attention. In addition to good use of language, they also need editing skills to review their own work, as well as the work of others, and research skills to validate their material.

Prior relationships with the media also can be helpful for Corporate Communications Specialists. For this reason, it may be a common career transition for journalists who are looking to use their writing skills in a different venue. Others come to the field from public relations firms. Those who enter corporate communications directly from school usually begin in assistant-level positions where they can learn the ropes.

Corporate Communications Specialists must be team players. The business world emphasizes teamwork and they must be able to lead, as well as work independently. Additionally, their verbal communication skills must be top notch as well, as they build relationships and manage projects.

Unions and Associations

There are a variety of professional associations to which Corporate Communications Specialists may belong, depending on their specialty. These include the Association for Business Communication, the International Association of Business Communicators, the National Council for Marketing and Public Relations, the Public Relations Society of America, and the Association for Women in Communications.

Tips for Entry

1. Learn more about corporate communications by visiting the following Web site about marketing careers: http://marketing.about.com/od/exploremarketingcareers/l/blcommang.htm.
2. Joining a professional association is an excellent way to network in the field. See the Web sites of the Association for Business Communication (http://www.businesscommunication.org/) and the International Association of Business Communicators (http://www.iabc.com/). Both list membership information, conferences, and job boards.
3. Get exposure to the corporate world. Intern in the public relations or corporate communications department of a large company to get a feel for the work.
4. Learn more about educational opportunities in corporate communications by searching for classes. Typing "courses in corporate communications" into a search engine such as Google will yield results that include degree programs, classes, and training.
5. Writing a strong cover letter is critical for job searching success. In a field such as communications, your writing skills matter more than ever. See sites such as http://resume.monster.com/archives/coverletter/ and http://www.quintcareers.com/covers.html for tips.

PUBLIC RELATIONS SPECIALIST

CAREER PROFILE

Duties: Manages relationships between a company, organization, or client and their public

Alternate Title(s): Public Affairs Specialist/Manager, Communications Specialist/Manager, Media Relations Specialist/Manager, Community Relations Specialist/Manager, Publicist

Salary Range: $30,000 to $75,000 and up

Employment Prospects: Good

Advancement Prospects: Good

Best Geographical Location(s): All, but major cities have most opportunities

Prerequisites:

Education or Training—Bachelor's degree; major in journalism, communications, public relations, or related fields very helpful

Experience—One to three years and up of related internship or work experience

Special Skills and Personality Traits—Excellent verbal communication skills; strong writing and editing ability; media savvy; planning and organizational skills; networking and building relationships

CAREER LADDER

```
┌─────────────────────────────────────┐
│  Senior Public Relations Executive,  │
│    Vice President, or Director of     │
│  Public Relations/Communications      │
└─────────────────────────────────────┘

┌─────────────────────────────────────┐
│      Public Relations Specialist      │
└─────────────────────────────────────┘

┌─────────────────────────────────────┐
│    Assistant Account Executive,       │
│    Assistant Media Planner, or        │
│    Public Relations Assistant         │
└─────────────────────────────────────┘
```

Position Description

According to the Public Relations Society of America, public relations (also known as PR) involves helping an organization and its publics adapt mutually to each other. Every company, organization, or client that interfaces with the public has a particular angle they want to portray. They have programs, products, or other aspects of their work that they want the public to understand. Public relations is crucial to organizations because it is the medium through which their message comes across. It can affect their mission, their profits, and their overall success in meeting their goals.

Public Relations Specialists are masters of image. It is up to the Public Relations Specialist to help hone their client's image and make the public aware of their strengths and offerings. By acting as a liaison to the media and the public, Public Relations Specialists tell the story of their organization to garner support and involvement. Because they bridge the gap between their organization and the public, they must fully understand their client and its goals. Furthermore, they must be equally attuned to the public and their needs, as they seek to improve communication and foster relationships.

The "public" refers to many different groups. On the business end, it can consist of corporations, nonprofit organizations, or the government. On the people end, "public" might generally refer to the American public of all ages, or it can target specific demographics such as adolescent girls, Latino males over age 30, senior citizens, or professionals with master's degrees or higher. Because the public is so diverse, so is the process of managing these relationships.

The nature of public relations varies among organizations. It may include such components as public information, corporate/community relations, public affairs, corporate communications, employee relations, marketing or product publicity, consumer service/customer relations, managing publications, special events, public speaking, and fund-raising. However, regardless of the specifics, communication is always the key factor. Public Relations Specialists must be able to effectively communicate the goals of their organization through writing, speaking, and visual images. Developing a communications strategy is integral to PR work.

Writing is a major component of being a Public Relations Specialist. Materials such as press releases, which inform the media about breaking news and information, as well as brochures, newsletters, advertisements, and more need to be written on a regular basis. Public Relations Specialists use their journalism skills to craft documents that portray their clients in a positive light. They know how to impart information in the most effective way, with attention to tone, style, and key points. Furthermore, they are able to translate industry jargon into language that people can understand.

Once they have written their material, Public Relations Specialists find the appropriate outlets for distribution. These outlets can be internal such as newsletters or external such as brochures and Web sites. Additionally, Public Relations Specialists may try to get radio or television spots for their clients, as well as newspaper and magazine articles, in order to promote their services.

Verbal communication is equally important. Public Relations Specialists may represent their organization at meetings, at press conferences, and even on radio or television. Those in director roles may serve as the face of their organization, controlling what information is shared. Journalism training helps Public Relations Specialists to ask the right questions. They are able to put others at ease and get them talking as well, resulting in a mutually beneficial dialogue.

Their duties may include:

- Serving as media liaisons
- Attending meetings and making presentations
- Managing newsletters and other publications
- Coordinating community relations
- Writing speeches
- Planning and running special events
- Lobbying for their organization or issue
- Handling broadcast communications
- Conducting outreach to various public groups
- Representing their organization at events
- Writing Web copy
- Developing written materials for media distribution
- Managing a PR budget
- Using e-mail and telephone conversations to communicate their messages
- Creating marketing pieces to help sell projects, services, or ideas

One way that Public Relations Specialists can quantify their results is by measuring public opinion. They may be involved with creating surveys and conducting research that lets them know how effective their efforts have been. Additionally, they can measure the expectations of the public. Through research and evaluation, Public Relations Specialists can also help organizations assess and define their goals and programs accordingly. They are strategists who manage the short-term as they plan for the long-term.

Public Relations Specialists work closely with other communication professionals, such as specialists in advertising, marketing, and editing. They may work as part of a public relations, communications, or advertising department, reporting to a director of public relations or communications. Furthermore, Public Relations Specialists can work for corporations, public relations firms, nonprofit organizations, the government, or private individuals. While a Public Relations Specialist employed by a public relations firm performs PR work for outside clients, a Public Relations Specialist employed by another type of organization (such as an investment bank or a museum) usually performs PR for that organization itself.

Hours will vary depending on the work setting. High-powered positions can be quite demanding, requiring workweeks of 45 to 50 hours and more. Some travel might be necessary to attend meetings with clients, and evening work might be needed for special events.

Salaries

According to the Bureau of Labor Statistics (BLS), median annual earnings for salaried Public Relations Specialists were $41,710 in 2002. The middle 50 percent earned between $31,300 and $56,180; the lowest 10 percent earned less than $24,240, and the top 10 percent earned more than $75,100. The BLS Web site also shows additional information coming from a joint survey conducted by the International Association of Business Communicators and the Public Relations Society of America. This survey states that the median annual income for a Public Relations Specialist in 2002 was $66,800.

Furthermore, the Public Relations Society of America states that entry-level salaries in public relations are in the $18,000 to $22,000 range. With experience at a middle level, a typical salary might be between $35,000 and $60,000, depending on the size of the firm. At a vice president level, Public Relations Specialists may earn $75,000 and more.

Employment Prospects

According to the BLS, employment of Public Relations Specialists is expected to increase faster than the average for all occupations through 2012. With keen competition between companies for products and services, a good public relations strategy can affect the bottom line. Businesses and nonprofits alike cannot afford *not* to hire PR firms or in-house staff. For this reason, jobs in public relations are expected to grow.

However, even though employment prospects are good, entry-level jobs remain very competitive. Qualified college graduates go head to head for positions at top firms. A degree in journalism or communications can be a big help in getting started. Because of their close working relationships with traditional journalists, a number of Public Relations Specialists have a journalism background and have transitioned from the field. Seasoned journalists with reporting or broadcasting experience will usually enter at the mid-level.

Advancement Prospects

Advancement prospects are also good for Public Relations Specialists. They acquire a set of core communications skills that can be used in a variety of settings. Public Relations Specialists may advance within their own company or join larger firms. They may specialize in different areas of PR such as corporate communications or media relations. Additionally, they may specialize related to an interest area such as fashion or health-care PR.

The next step for Public Relations Specialists can be as directors, managers, vice presidents, or consultants. Yet others explore different areas within journalism and communications, going to magazines, new media companies, or broadcasting.

Education and Training

Bachelor's degrees are required for Public Relations Specialists, with the most valuable majors including journalism, communications, or English. Some colleges and universities offer public relations courses, minors, or majors, which can also be helpful. Additionally, some undergraduate and graduate journalism programs offer courses or specializations in public relations. This curriculum helps hone the writing and communication skills that are so critical on the job. A business background may also be useful for its training in marketing and strategy.

While most Public Relations Specialists report that much of their training comes on the job and through internships, additional training is available to help professionals advance to the next level. The Public Relations Society of America accredits Public Relations Specialists with at least five years of experience in the field. For this voluntary accreditation, they must pass a comprehensive six-hour examination. Furthermore, the International Association of Business Communicators also has an accreditation program for professionals in the communication field, including Public Relations Specialists. Through this program, which also requires a minimum of five years of experience, qualified professions receive the Accredited Business Communicator (ABC) designation.

Experience, Skills, and Personality Traits

A Public Relations Specialist must be a people person. He or she should be articulate and professional, with the ability to speak to large groups of people with ease. Top-notch communication and writing skills are a necessity. Public Relations Specialists should be able to work well under pressure, maintaining calm and projecting confidence for their clients even in difficult situations. Creativity enables them to create new and innovative PR campaigns. Flexibility, energy, and ambition drive Public Relations Specialists to be successful.

Public Relations Specialists can handle adversity. They seek out press opportunities and are savvy enough to know how to put a positive spin on a bad situation. As strategic thinkers as well as journalists, they help shape public opinion by understanding what makes a good news story. Public Relations Specialists are aware of the connection between image and perception. As keen observers of human nature, they can tap into the hearts and minds of the public. They are able to build relationships with corporate leaders, community members, and media professionals alike.

Unions and Associations

Public Relations Specialists may belong to a variety of professional associations including the Public Relations Society of America, the International Association of Business Communicators, and Women Executives in Public Relations.

Tips for Entry

1. Spend time on the Web site of the Public Relations Society of America. Read their career information, their job listings, and their definitions of different PR functions, while you learn about their programs for students at http://www.prsa.org.
2. Public relations internships are crucial for a career as a Public Relations Specialist. Visit sites such as http://www.internships.com, speak with your campus career center, and search your yellow pages for local PR firms to get some ideas.
3. Explore the Web sites of some of the nation's largest PR firms such as Burson-Marsteller (http://www.bm.com), Ketchum (http://www.ketchum.com), and Edelman (http://www.edelman.com/).
4. Learn more about public relations by visiting Online Public Relations at http://www.online-pr.com/. The site is designed for PR professionals and helps them to deliver better services.
5. Take courses in journalism, communications, and public relations. Speak to journalism professors who have specializations and/or experience working in PR-related fields.

EDUCATION

JOURNALISM TEACHER (GRADES 6–12)

CAREER PROFILE

Duties: Teaches journalism to middle school or high school students

Alternate Title(s): English Teacher

Salary Range: $30,000 to $50,000 and up

Employment Prospects: Good

Advancement Prospects: Good

Best Geographical Location(s): All

Prerequisites:

Education or Training—Bachelor's degree in education or other field; master's degree in education required for many positions

Experience—Completion of educational requirements including student teaching; may also have some professional journalism experience

Special Skills and Personality Traits—Excellent written and verbal communication skills; knowledge of teaching methods and classroom management; understanding of journalism; patience; leadership skills

Special Requirements—All 50 states require teachers to be licensed in order to teach in the public school system. Journalism Teachers working in private schools may not need certification or licensure.

CAREER LADDER

```
┌─────────────────────────────┐
│      Department Head         │
└─────────────────────────────┘

┌─────────────────────────────┐
│     Journalism Teacher       │
└─────────────────────────────┘

┌─────────────────────────────┐
│   Student Teacher or Intern  │
└─────────────────────────────┘
```

Position Description

Many journalists will tell you that high school, or even earlier in middle school, is when their interest in the profession was sparked. Through work on the campus newspaper, they get bitten by the bug that drives them to uncover the truth and share it with the public. In order to gain the skills that will enable them to report on breaking stories, edit copy, and design pages, courses in journalism early on are extremely helpful. At some schools, there are Journalism Teachers who can provide this early education.

Journalism Teachers are often part of another department within their school systems. There are two main reasons for this. One is that many schools do not have the budget for a journalism program; the other is that journalism education is not offered in all teacher education training and certification programs.

The most common department for Journalism Teachers to be part of is English, but they may also teach government, history, social studies, and others. While these are the fields that they study, they also have knowledge of journalism. This knowledge usually comes from a combination of journalism coursework and practical experience, either through full-time work or student journalism involvement.

Journalism Teachers can teach up to eight classes per day, in journalism and their other field of specialty. Classes may be mixed in terms of age of the students or may be specific such as a senior journalism seminar. Journalism courses at the grade 6–12 level are designed to help students understand the basics of writing and reporting. They are taught how to write news and feature stories, often completing practical assignments. Generating story ideas and conducting interviews are also important.

In addition to learning writing and reporting, journalism courses can include much more. Topics such as advertising, design, editing, photography, and sports are often represented. Broadcast journalism may also be taught. Furthermore, no journalism curriculum can be complete without a discussion of ethics and legal ramifications. Journalism Teachers need to understand laws and liabilities, as well as impart to students the ethics that guide the profession and the consequences of violating them.

Many Journalism Teachers are also faculty advisers to the student newspaper. This can include selecting the editorial staff, working with the editor in chief and leadership team on content and vision, and advising students about any controversial coverage. Other Journalism Teachers serve as advisers to school television or radio stations, or literary magazines.

Along with the knowledge of journalism they bring, Journalism Teachers also are skilled educators. They develop curriculum and syllabi, prepare assignments, and determine grades. Each has a different teaching style and uses different methods for class presentations and to engage students to participate. Good Journalism Teachers are aware of their students' abilities. They inspire a diverse group of students to pay attention and learn.

Additional duties may include:

- Bringing in guest speakers to their classrooms
- Taking students on field trips to see professional journalism in action
- Developing class projects
- Designing course materials
- Attending faculty meetings
- Participating in conferences and teacher training activities
- Meeting individually with students, parents, and administrators
- Participating in school events such as graduation and pep rallies
- Coaching sports
- Identifying students with special needs and making appropriate referrals
- Writing college recommendations for students

Typically, Journalism Teachers work seven to eight hours per day based on school schedules such as 8 A.M. to 3 P.M. Extra hours may be required to work with student clubs such as the newspaper. Most Journalism Teachers enjoy a traditional 10-month year with several vacations while school is on break, as well as the summer months off.

Salaries

According to a salary survey by the American Federation of Teachers (AFT), the 2002–03 average teacher salary was $45,771. Beginning teachers with bachelor's degrees earned an average of $29,564 during the 2002–03 school year. A press release by the AFT estimates that the average beginning salary for 2003–04 went up to $30,496. The AFT also reports that growing health insurance costs are preventing salaries from rising at a higher rate. As a union, the AFT lobbies for higher teacher salaries.

Both average and entry-level salaries vary depending on the particular school district and geographic location. States such as California, Michigan, and Connecticut are at the high end of the spectrum, with North Dakota, Oklahoma, and South Dakota bringing up the rear. Journalism Teachers in well-paying districts can earn upward of $90,000 after 20 years.

Generally speaking, private school teachers earn less than public school teachers do. However, some well-known private schools may have the funding to pay Journalism Teachers salaries comparable to those in public schools.

Employment Prospects

Employment prospects for Journalism Teachers are good. Overall, there is a growing effort to encourage more recent graduates to enter the teaching field, through better salaries and training programs that include student loan forgiveness.

However, as enrollment slows down and budgets are cut, opportunities will be best for those Journalism Teachers who are flexible, both academically and geographically. Inner-city schools may have more openings since teachers are harder to retain, but they often do not have journalism programs. Journalism Teachers who are bilingual or who can teach a variety of other subjects may have the greatest job prospects.

Journalism Teachers may work in public or private schools. Private schools are not governed by the same regulations as public schools, and teachers in these settings can benefit from greater freedom in curriculum and style. There are several resources for finding private school jobs such as the Council for American Private Education (http://www.capenet.org/).

Advancement Prospects

Journalism Teachers in public schools can obtain tenure after a probationary period of teaching, usually three years. According to the Bureau of Labor Statistics (BLS), most states have tenure laws that prevent teachers from being fired without just cause and due process.

After receiving tenure, Journalism Teachers can advance to become department heads. They may also apply for special scholarships to initiate new programs at their schools.

Education and Training

All Journalism Teachers hold a minimum of a bachelor's degree, usually in education, English, communications, or journalism. In addition to the bachelor's degree, all states also require public school teachers to have completed an approved teacher training program with a specific number of subjects and education credits, as well as a supervised practice teaching internship.

According to the BLS, a number of states require that teachers obtain a master's degree in education within a specified period after they begin teaching.

The BLS also reports that many States offer alternative licensure programs for teachers who have bachelor's degrees in the subject they will teach, but who lack the necessary education courses required for a regular license. These teachers may begin teaching under provisional licensure while they receive supervision and take education classes.

Many schools do not offer degrees in journalism education. However, the specialization is becoming more common and can be seen at schools such as the University of Missouri (http://mudirect.missouri.edu/degrees/jour_ed.htm, Indiana University (http://www.journalism.indiana.edu/academics/MAT.html), and the University of Texas at the Permian Basin (http://www.utpb.edu/educ/cert/cert.html#fields). Coursework includes a combination of teaching methodologies and journalism skills. It is expected that an applicant to such a program would have an undergraduate major or minor in journalism, or some coursework at the least.

Even if journalism certification is not available, there are often specializations in journalism through many teacher education programs. It can be through English, communications, mass media, or related fields.

Requirements for teaching in private schools are not as stringent. Journalism Teachers may hold master's degrees in journalism or have experience working as professional journalists.

Special Requirements
The BLS states that all 50 States and the District of Columbia require public school teachers to be licensed. Licensure is not required for teachers in private schools. Usually licensure is granted by the State Board of Education or a licensure advisory committee. Each individual state board of education is the contact for more information. Journalism Teachers who are planning to relocate should review requirements for different states.

Furthermore, voluntary certification for Journalism Teachers is available through the Journalism Education Association. This professional group seeks to promote professionalism in scholastic journalism. They offer credentials such as a Certified Journalism Educator (CJE) and Master Journalism Educator (MJE). See http://www.jea.org/certification/cert.html for more information.

Experience, Skills, and Personality Traits
It is helpful for Journalism Teachers to have experience with journalism outside the classroom. Whether it is through several years at a multimedia Web site, a 15-year career at a television station, or an internship at a school newspaper, the practical experience they get from these settings is invaluable.

Journalism Teachers should be inquisitive, curious, and aware. They need excellent communication skills to both manage their classrooms and engage their students. Creativity helps guide assignments and lesson planning. With strong writing and reporting skills, they set an example and guide their students to learn their craft. Furthermore, their good command of language enables them to be conscientious editors.

Also important is understanding education and the art of teaching, including methodologies, philosophy, evaluation, and classroom management. This goes hand in hand with a thorough knowledge of their subject matter—journalism. Journalism Teachers need to know the history and practice, as well as ethics and information laws. Furthermore, knowledge of applicable computer programs for layout and design such as Adobe Photoshop and photography is helpful as well.

Unions and Associations
There are a number of different professional associations to which Journalism Teachers may belong. One that is specifically related to journalism education is the Journalism Education Association. Another organization for educators in journalism is the National Scholastic Press Association http://studentpress.journ.umn.edu/nspa/.

In terms of teaching associations, the American Federation of Teachers is an affiliated international union of the AFL-CIO that represents the economic, social, and professional interests of classroom teachers. Other Journalism Teachers may belong to the National Education Association as well.

Tips for Entry
1. The High School Journalism Web site (http://www.highschooljournalism.org), presented by the American Society of Newspaper Editors has excellent resources for Journalism Teachers. It includes teaching tips and advising ideas, among many other resources.
2. Check out http://www.jteacher.com/, a Web site for high school journalism teachers and students set up by a teacher in Houston. It has much useful information, such as lesson plans, teaching materials, and links.
3. Another great site for high school journalism is from the American Press Institute at http://www.americanpressinstitute.org/content/3930.cfm.

4. If you are interested in teaching broadcast journalism, take a look at this program of the Radio-Television News Directors Association and Foundation: http://www.rtnda.org/resources/highschool.shtml. It offers high school teachers the opportunity to attend an all-expense paid summer institute where they will learn how to begin a broadcast journalism program on their campus.

5. The Dow Jones Newspaper Fund also offers great information for high school teachers, including fellowship programs. View their Web site at http://djnewspaperfund.dowjones.com/fund/hst_teachers.asp.

6. Contact the Board of Education in your home state to find out about teaching job listings. Also see sites such as http://www.k12jobs.com/ and http://www.educationjobs.com/ for jobs in both public and private schools.

JOURNALISM PROFESSOR

CAREER PROFILE

Duties: Serves on the faculty of a college or university, teaching courses to undergraduates and/or graduate students; may also conduct research and/or publish scholarly works

Alternate Title(s): Adjunct Instructor, Lecturer, Faculty Member, English Professor, Communications Professor

Salary Range: $30,000 to $125,000 and above

Employment Prospects: Fair

Advancement Prospects: Fair to Good

Best Geographical Location(s): All (especially college towns and schools that offer journalism programs)

Prerequisites:

Education or Training—Typically a master's degree in journalism is the minimum credential; professionals with extensive journalism accomplishments may have only a bachelor's degree; Ph.D. required at some colleges and universities

Experience—At least five years of work as a professional journalist or combination of graduate education, completed dissertation, and experience

Special Skills and Personality Traits—Excellent writing, reporting, and editing skills; strong research background; good communication skills; teaching ability

CAREER LADDER

```
┌─────────────────────────────────┐
│  Tenured Journalism Professor;   │
│   Department Head; or Dean,      │
│      School of Journalism        │
└─────────────────────────────────┘

┌─────────────────────────────────┐
│      Journalism Professor        │
└─────────────────────────────────┘

┌─────────────────────────────────┐
│     Professional Journalist      │
└─────────────────────────────────┘
```

Position Description

Journalism Professors are responsible for teaching, training, and mentoring the journalists of the future. Spanning the journalism disciplines such as print, broadcast, and new media, they impart their reporting, writing, and editing expertise to students in order to prepare them for professional journalism careers.

Being a professor in a specific field such as journalism can be somewhat different from the traditional path of an academic. By and large, Journalism Professors are current or former journalists. Whether their specialty is in broadcasting, newspapers, magazines, or new media, they have had experience and accomplishments out in the field. Since journalism is a professional discipline more than a purely academic one, Journalism Professors need to understand the profession from the inside out.

While all schools teach advanced writing, reporting, and editing, journalism schools may offer concentrations or specializations in the following areas:

- Newspapers
- Magazines
- Broadcast
- New media
- Health, science, and environment
- Photojournalism
- International affairs
- Public affairs

- Strategic communication
- Advertising
- Public relations
- Design
- Media management

Usually, curricula also include courses on mass media, journalism ethics and law, graphic design, and research methods.

Depending on what they studied when they were students and the trajectory of their career following their education, Journalism Professors often specialize in one of these areas. They teach core courses in addition to their specialty. Some Journalism Professors work at colleges or universities that do not have separate journalism schools or even majors. They may be part of a college of arts and sciences and/or departments of communication or English.

Journalism Professors may teach exclusively undergraduate students or graduate students, or a combination of both. They have an assigned course load per semester, usually about 12–16 teaching hours per week. In addition to the actual teaching of these courses, Journalism Professors prepare extensively for them. Developing curriculum and syllabi, selecting texts and reading material, designing tests and assignments, and determining grades are all part of the process. In the classroom, Journalism Professors are able to draw from their experience and use their creativity to devise the most effective methods of teaching their subject according to their own personal style.

Additional duties may include:

- Serving as academic advisers to undergraduate or graduate students
- Supervising teaching assistants
- Writing grant proposals to fund research
- Participating in faculty meetings
- Holding office hours for students
- Writing textbooks or other publications
- Teaching online courses
- Serving as faculty advisers to campus newspapers, magazines, radio stations, or TV stations
- Collaborating with campus administrators

Many Journalism Professors still work in some capacity as professional journalists, writing regular or occasional articles, columns, or editorials. With teaching schedules usually not taking up more than 16 hours per week, they are able to use their time flexibly, often grading papers, conducting research, and writing during the evenings and weekends. Many Journalism Professors also enjoy reduced course loads or no course assignments over the summer months and during school breaks.

Salaries

Salaries for Journalism Professors can vary greatly depending not only on the school at which they teach but also according to their own professional background. Well-known schools of journalism may use money as a way to recruit high-profile journalists to come and teach in their program, while those professors at other institutions will follow the traditional academic salary scales.

According to a 2003–04 survey by the American Association of University Professors, salaries for full-time faculty with doctorates averaged $75,863. By rank, the average was $100,682 for professors, $68,640 for associate professors, $58,576 for assistant professors, $39,476 for instructors, and $45,763 for lecturers. At the master's level, the average salary for all types of professors combined was $59,400.

Generally speaking, faculty at private four-year institutions earn higher average salaries than those teaching at community colleges or state colleges and universities.

In addition to their base salaries, Journalism Professors often earn additional income from writing, consulting, or speaking engagements. They may also receive special university benefits such as tuition for dependents, housing allowances, and other perks.

Employment Prospects

Seasoned journalists who are looking for a change, as well as a more regular schedule, often covet positions as Journalism Professors. After the demands of a newsroom, the hours of freedom between course loads and lack of evening work can be very attractive. Because of this, competition for positions, especially at prestigious schools of journalism, can be very tight.

Furthermore, the more prestigious the school, the higher the expectations are for the Journalism Professor's accomplishments. At the top schools, Journalism Professors come from the main networks, the biggest newspapers, and the most cutting-edge magazines.

Another area of opportunity for Journalism Professors is through work as an adjunct instructor. Adjunct instructors are not full-time employees of their institutions. While common at two-year colleges, community colleges, and smaller colleges and universities, it is also frequent at larger institutions when a working journalist only wants to teach one course. This is cost-effective for the school, as they do not have to pay for overall salary and benefits and the Journalism Professor is only paid per class taught.

Working as an adjunct instructor can be a good way for a journalist to gain teaching experience as an entry to a full-time professorship or a way for otherwise-employed professionals to share their skills and teach on the side. Unfortunately, adjunct work alone is not usually financially feasible for most people looking to support themselves.

The job-search process for full-time Journalism Professors is very grueling. Interviews are extensive, and a candidate's past writing and research is scrutinized. A selection committee makes final decisions after candidates fully explain their teaching methodologies, journalistic accomplishments, and writing philosophies.

For those who are determined to find a position as a Journalism Professor, it is necessary to be geographically flexible. Positions may open up in small towns, and opportunities that get passed up may not come again.

Advancement Prospects

Advancement for Journalism Professors, as with other university professors, is usually through the tenure process. The time frame for tenure review varies by school but often occurs approximately seven years under contract. At this point, the instructor's accomplishments are reviewed and tenure may be awarded.

What this means is that those granted tenure essentially enjoy job stability for the rest of their lives, if they so desire. Journalism Professors with tenure can feel free to explore new ideas and controversial topics without fear of losing their jobs for being unpopular.

Once granted tenure, Journalism Professors can advance to become department heads or even deans of journalism schools.

Education and Training

Unlike professors in other fields, education for Journalism Professors will vary. At many schools, career accomplishments are valued more highly than educational credentials. Journalism Professors may hold bachelor's degrees, master's degrees, or doctoral degrees. However, those working specifically in schools of journalism also may have experience out in the field as journalists.

At colleges and universities without journalism schools, professors from a variety of disciplines may teach journalism and journalism-related courses. Professors in the English, communications, or media studies department may teach journalism courses. These professors usually have the traditional academic background of a Ph.D. degree, although they may have professional nonacademic work experience as well.

The Ph.D. typically takes six to eight years beyond the bachelor's degree, culminating in a significant original research paper called a dissertation. Coursework may take up half the time, and the research and writing of the dissertation the other half.

Experience, Skills, and Personality Traits

In order to teach their subject well, Journalism Professors need experience and expertise in professional journalism.

For most, this comes from years of work in the field; for others, particularly those with more of a communications or English focus, it can come from internship and research experience.

To train future journalists, Journalism Professors must be expert communicators. Impeccable writing, reporting, editing, research, and speaking skills are vital. In addition to having these skills, Journalism Professors must also be good teachers and have the ability to impart their knowledge to others. They need to motivate students to succeed and must be able to assess their work fairly and objectively.

Furthermore, Journalism Professors are curious, flexible, and creative. They are driven and work well independently, having the discipline to work on their own schedules. For those who come from the newsroom, their experience adhering to tight deadlines serves them well in an academic setting.

Unions and Associations

Some Journalism Professors may belong to academic professional associations such as the American Association of University Professors, the Association of American Colleges and Universities, and the American Association of Community Colleges. Others may belong to journalism associations such as the Newspaper Association of America, Investigative Reporters and Editors, the Society of Professional Journalists, the National Association of Broadcasters, and the Magazine Publishers of America.

Tips for Entry

1. Columbia University, in New York, N.Y., has one of the top journalism schools in the country. In 2005 they instituted a new program offering a Master of Arts (MA) in journalism, designed to teach journalists more about their subject matter. Check out the program at http://www.jrn.columbia.edu/admissions/apply/ma-program/index.asp.

2. Consider working as a teaching assistant for a journalism, communications, or English course. This will provide valuable experience with standing up in front of a class, devising assignments, and working on grading methods.

3. Speak to your journalism professors about their career path. How did they come to academia? Where did they work before and for how long? Take the opportunity to benefit from their valuable advice.

4. Take a look at the Web site for the *Chronicle of Higher Education* (http://www.chronicle.com), the leading publication in the academic world. Look at their job listings for Journalism Professors to learn more about requirements.

EDUCATION REPORTER

CAREER PROFILE

Duties: Covers education for a newspaper, magazine, Web site, or other publication; reports on all issues relating to education

Alternate Title(s): Education Writer

Salary Range: $25,000 to $60,000 and up

Employment Prospects: Fair

Advancement Prospects: Fair

Best Geographical Location(s): All

Prerequisites:

Education or Training—Bachelor's degree in journalism or related field helpful; may also have educational background in teaching

Experience—Several years as a reporter; teaching or educational administration experience may also be a plus

Special Skills and Personality Traits—Excellent writing, reporting, and editing skills; good communication and interviewing skills; understanding of issues pertinent to education and educational systems

CAREER LADDER

```
┌─────────────────────────────────────────┐
│  Education Reporter, larger paper;        │
│  Education Editor; News, Features, or      │
│           Managing Editor                  │
└─────────────────────────────────────────┘

┌─────────────────────────────────────────┐
│           Education Reporter               │
└─────────────────────────────────────────┘

┌─────────────────────────────────────────┐
│  Beat Reporter or Education Reporter,     │
│            smaller paper                   │
└─────────────────────────────────────────┘
```

Position Description

Education is an important topic in journalism today. Although it is not one of the more stereotypically glamorous beats, education reporting keeps people aware of what is happening in their local schools, their state universities, and in national trends. Education Reporters handle this coverage and report on issues that matter to the public.

Parents and taxpayers have a vested interest in what goes on in the schools; their children and/or their money are going into the system. Education Reporters keep them informed and hold schools accountable. They balance breaking news with enterprise stories that dig deeper into events, policies, personalities, and politics.

There are a variety of topics that Education Reporters may cover. Some serve as beat reporters at newspapers, responsible for daily or weekly copy about education. Education Reporters in these settings generate stories about whatever information they can find through phone calls, meetings, and interviews. These stories often center on school board meetings and the local public elementary, middle, and sec-

ondary schools. Issues as diverse as a superintendent who has resigned to students who have been selected to compete in a trivia competition to school lunches show the range of stories an Education Reporter may write.

Other Education Reporters write longer, feature or investigative pieces. They delve into controversial issues such as guns in schools and test scores. They spend extensive time interviewing people and conducting background research. These stories often serve to drive educational reform and advocacy.

Furthermore, some Education Reporters specifically handle higher education. They can focus on community, state, and/or private colleges and universities. Discussions of tuition costs, fundraising, faculty recruiting, and student life are among some of the issues. Also, Education Reporters focusing on higher education may also cover changes and issues related to college admissions such as college entrance exams like the SAT.

On the national level, Education Reporters handle the political scene, including programs such as the No Child

Left Behind Act and others. Education can be a very politically charged topic and the cornerstone of an election campaign. Education Reporters may cover the federal budget process as well as legislation, policy, and programs. Focusing on Capitol Hill, the White House, unions and trade associations, advocacy groups, and lobbyists, they portray stories from a number of angles using a variety of sources.

A challenge for Education Reporters is to weigh the competing interests of all constituents. Children, parents, teachers, and administrators all play a role and their needs must be represented. Their stories should be objective and ethical, yet interesting to readers. Education Reporters need to understand the educational system in order to explain actions and their consequences to readers.

Their duties may include:

- Covering grant-seeking and educational fund-raising issues
- Reading and reporting on budgets
- Reporting on general news assignments
- Attending school board meetings
- Working with other departments such as news or features to prevent overlap
- Conducting interviews with students, teachers, and administrators
- Reading through public records
- Attending meetings with editors to brainstorm story ideas
- Interpreting test scores and other data

Education Reporters may work for managing editors or editors in news or features. In a publication with a major focus on education, there may be a specific education editor as well. Usually, Education Reporters generate story ideas as well as receive assignments from their editors.

Hours for Education Reporters can vary depending on their specific focus. Interviews may need to be conducted after school hours, and meetings often occur in the evening. Like other reporters, they work shifts in order to ensure that breaking news gets covered. Some local or state travel may be required.

Salaries

Education Reporters experience a wide range in salary depending on their employment setting as well as their level of experience.

The Inland Press Association conducts an annual Newspaper Industry Compensation Survey, which is the authoritative "industry standard" for newspaper industry compensation planning. According to the survey, entry level reporters earned an average of $28,162 per year in 2004 in total direct compensation. With considerable experience, that average went up to $43,292. The range for reporters was from a low of $10,042 to a high salary of $163,926 at the experienced level. While these figures are for general

reporters and are not particular to education, they can be used as a guide.

Furthermore, Education Reporters working for magazines and Web sites earn comparable ranges. They may work as freelancers for several types of publications.

Employment Prospects

Employment prospects are fair for Education Reporters. Because their topic is specialized, there are not as many opportunities as exist for generalists. However, their niche can make them marketable for the jobs that do come up.

Education Reporters may work for newspapers, magazines, Web sites, or a combination of the three. Many Education Reporters hold primary jobs at newspapers but also serve as contributing writers to other publications based on their expertise. Some make their career out of freelancing, which can offer a variety of writing assignments but no guaranteed stability.

As is the case with all reporting jobs, aspiring Education Reporters should expect to start at the bottom at small papers covering any available beat. Geographic flexibility is necessary to get started. After proving themselves as reporters, they can look to focus some articles on education and develop a specialty.

Advancement Prospects

Advancement for Education Reporters can happen in several ways. Firstly, they can advance to become editors at the publications at which they work. At a newspaper, they may work their way up to becoming managing editors or features editors. Some papers may even have specific editors responsible for education.

Also, Education Reporters can advance by moving to larger and more prominent publications. They can cover more extensive beats and issues of national attention. By developing a following through their insight and writing style, they may write columns, freelance articles, or even books.

Education and Training

Most Education Reporters hold bachelor's degrees in journalism or related fields. Some may also have degrees in other subjects including liberal arts and education, but some journalism course work or training as well. Other Education Reporters may hold master's degrees in journalism.

It is not required for Education Reporters to have formal education or training in the education field; they must be journalists first with mastery over writing and reporting. However, while most do not, there are a number of Education Reporters who have some training as teachers or administrators. This can help them to better understand the educational system and its players.

Experience, Skills, and Personality Traits

Excellent writing and reporting skills are essential for Education Reporters. They need creativity and curiosity to generate interesting and informative stories. Also, strong communication skills are needed to conduct interviews and speak to a variety of people. They must be comfortable talking to groups ranging from kindergartners to superintendents to policy makers. The ability to gain people's trust and put them at ease adds to good reporting. Furthermore, Education Reporters must be passionate about education. They must be knowledgeable about their beat and interested in the topics it covers. Ambitious and savvy, they can go after difficult stories and adhere to tight deadlines.

Additionally, some Education Reporters may be responsible for copyediting or page design, particularly those working at smaller newspapers. Knowledge of computer programs such as QuarkXPress is helpful, as is the ability to understand and interpret complicated data such as test scores.

Unions and Associations

The Education Writers Association is the national professional association for Education Reporters. Founded in 1947, it has more than 1,000 members and supports all types of education coverage. Education Reporters may also belong to associations such as the National Education Technology Writers Association, the National Writers Union, and the American Society of Journalists and Authors.

Tips for Entry

1. Spend some time on the Web site for the Education Writers Association at http://www.ewa.org/. They have specific resources for Education Reporters covering preschool through higher education, as well as information about conferences and membership.
2. Which area of education interests you the most? Gain experience covering an education beat for your campus or local paper to get a feel for the work.
3. Think about which topics in education are/were most important to you as a student. How would you like them to be covered and why?
4. Browse through a local weekly paper, a local daily paper, and a national daily paper. Find articles about education in each. Think about the differences in coverage depending on the scope of the publication.
5. In addition to journalism courses, take a class on the history of education. It can help to give you a better understanding of the major issues facing schools both past and present.

APPENDIXES

APPENDIX I
EDUCATIONAL PROGRAMS

A. ACCREDITED PROGRAMS IN JOURNALISM AND MASS COMMUNICATION

According to their Web site (http://www.ku.edu/~acejmc/), the Accrediting Council on Education in Journalism and Mass Communications (ACEJMC) is "the agency responsible for the evaluation of professional journalism and mass communications programs in colleges and universities." As of 2004–05, ACEJMC accredited 104 programs in journalism and mass communications at colleges and universities in the United States and one at a university outside of the United States. Under each listing, it is specified whether the school offers an undergraduate degree, a graduate degree, or both. The list of accredited programs follows. A complete up-to-date list can be found online at http://www.ku.edu/~acejmc/STUDENT/PROGLIST. SHTML. Dates in parentheses refer to year program accreditation was given.

ALABAMA

Auburn University
Department of Communication and
    Journalism
Auburn University, AL 36849-5206
William Dale Harrison, chair
B.A. Journalism; B.A. Public Relations.
    (2000)
Phone: (334) 844-5166
Fax: (334) 844-4573
E-mail: harriwd@auburn.edu
http://www.auburn.edu/academic/liberal_
    arts/cmjn

University of Alabama
College of Communication and
    Information Sciences
P.O. Box 870172
Tuscaloosa, AL 35487-0172
E. Culpepper Clark, dean. [Advertising
    and Public Relations; Journalism;
    Telecommunication and Film]
B.A. Communication & Information
    Sciences; M.A. Communication &
    Information Sciences. (2003)
Phone: (205) 348-4787
Fax: (205) 348-3836
E-mail: cclark@ccom.ua.edu
http://www.ccom.ua.edu

ALASKA

University of Alaska–Anchorage
Department of Journalism and Public
    Communications
3211 Providence Drive
Anchorage, AK 99508
Fred Pearce, chair
B.A. Journalism and Public
    Communications. (2002)
Phone: (907) 786-4180
Fax: (907) 786-4190
E-mail: fpearce@jpc.alaska.edu
http://jpc.uaa.alaska.edu

University of Alaska–Fairbanks
Department of Journalism
P.O. Box 756120
101 Bunnell
Fairbanks, AK 99775-6120
Elinor Burkett, chair
B.A. Journalism. (2003)
Phone: (907) 474-6249
Fax: (907) 474-6326
E-mail: ffecb@uaf.edu
http://www.uaf.edu/journal

ARIZONA

Arizona State University
Walter Cronkite School of Journalism and
    Mass Communication
P.O. Box 871305
Tempe, AZ 85287-1305
Stephen Doig, interim director
B.A. Journalism and Mass
    Communication; M.M.C. Mass
    Communication. (1999)
Phone: (480) 965-5011
Fax: (480) 965-7041
E-mail: (undergraduate) cronkiteinfo@
    asu.edu; (graduate) masscomm@asu.
    edu
http://cronkite.asu.edu

University of Arizona
Department of Journalism
Tucson, AZ 85721-0158
Jacqueline Sharkey, head
B.A. Journalism. (2000)
Phone: (520) 621-7556
Fax: (520) 621-7557
E-mail: journal@w3.arizona.edu
http://journalism.arizona.edu

ARKANSAS

Arkansas State University
College of Communications
P.O. Box 540
State University, AR 72467-0540
Russell E. Shain, dean. [Journalism,
    Radio-Television]
B.S. Journalism, Radio-TV. (2003)
Phone: (870) 972-2468
Fax: (870) 972-3856
E-mail: comm@astate.edu
http://comm.astate.edu

University of Arkansas–Fayetteville
Walter J. Lemke Department of Journalism
Fayetteville, AR 72701-1201
Patsy Watkins, chair
B.A. Journalism. (2004)
Phone: (479) 575-3601

Fax: (479) 575-4314
E-mail: pwatkins@uark.edu
http://www.uark.edu/depts/jourinfo/
  public_html

CALIFORNIA

California State University–Chico
Department of Journalism
207 Tehama Hall
Chico, CA 95929-0600
Katherine J. Milo, chair
B.A. Journalism. (2004)
Phone: (530) 898-4779
Fax: (530) 898-4839
E-mail: kmilo@csuchico.edu
http://www.csuchico.edu/jour

California State University–Fullerton
Department of Communications
800 N. State College Boulevard
Fullerton, CA 92834-6846
Wendell Crow, chair
B.A. Communications. (2003)
Phone: (714) 278-3517
Fax: (714) 278-2209
E-mail: wcrow@fullerton.edu
http://communications.fullerton.edu

California State University–Northridge
Department of Journalism
18111 Nordhoff Street
Northridge, CA 91330-8311
R. Kent Kirkton, chair
B.A. Journalism. (2004)
Phone: (818) 677-3135
Fax: (818) 677-3438
E-mail: kent.kirkton@csun.edu
http://jour.csun.edu

San Francisco State University
Department of Journalism
1600 Holloway Avenue
San Francisco, CA 94132
John Burks, chair
B.A. Journalism. (2002)
Phone: (415) 338-1689/2663
Fax: (415) 338-2084
E-mail: jburks@sfsu.edu
http://www.journalism.sfsu.edu

San Jose State University
School of Journalism and Mass
  Communications
San Jose, CA 95192-0055
Dennis Wilcox, director
B.S. Journalism; B.S. Advertising;
  B.S. Public Relations; M.S. Mass
  Communications. (2002)

Phone: (408) 924-3249 or (408) 924-
  3240
Fax: (408) 924-3229
E-mail: dwilcox@casa.sjsu.edu or
  jmcinfo@casa.sjsu.edu
http://www.jmc.sjsu.edu

University of California–Berkeley
Graduate School of Journalism
121 North Gate Hall #5860
Berkeley, CA 94720-5860
Orville Schell, dean
M.J. Journalism. (2000)
Phone: (510) 642-3383
Fax: (510) 643-9136
E-mail: schell@uclink.berkeley.edu
http://journalism.berkeley.edu

University of Southern California
Annenberg School for Communication
3502 Watt Way, ASC 325
Los Angeles, CA 90089-0281
Michael Parks, director
B.A. Broadcast Journalism; B.A. Print
  Journalism; B.A. Public Relations;
  M.A. Journalism (emphases in
  Broadcast Journalism, Online
  Journalism, Print Journalism); M.A.
  Strategic Public Relations. (1999)
Phone: (213) 740-3914
Fax: (213) 740-8624
E-mail: mparks@usc.edu
http://annenberg.usc.edu

COLORADO

Colorado State University
Department of Journalism and Technical
  Communication
Fort Collins, CO 80523
Garrett O'Keefe, chair
B.A. Technical Journalism. (1999)
Phone: (970) 491-6310
Fax: (970) 491-2908
E-mail: Garrett.OKeefe@colostate.edu
http://www.colostate.edu/depts/tj

University of Colorado
School of Journalism and Mass
  Communication
478 UCB
Boulder, CO 80309-0478
Paul Voakes, dean [Advertising;
  Broadcast News; Broadcast
  Production Management; News-
  Editorial; Media Studies; M.A.
  Newsgathering]
B.S. Journalism; M.A. Journalism. (1999)
Phone: (303) 492-4364

Fax: (303) 492-0969
E-mail: SJMCdean@colorado.edu
http://www.colorado.edu/journalism

CONNECTICUT

University of Connecticut
Department of Journalism
337 Mansfield Road, U-1129
Storrs, CT 06269-1129
Maureen Croteau, head
B.A. Journalism. (2003)
Phone: (860) 486-4221
Fax: (860) 486-3294
E-mail: Maureen.Croteau@UConn.edu
http://www.journalism.uconn.edu

DISTRICT OF COLUMBIA

American University
School of Communication
Washington, DC 20016-8017
Larry Kirkman, dean. [Journalism; Public
  Communication]
B.A. Communication: Journalism;
  B.A. Communication: Public
  Communication; M.A. Journalism
  and Public Affairs; M.A. Public
  Communication. (2003)
Phone: (202) 885-2058
Fax: (202) 885-2099
E-mail: kristipg@american.edu
http://www.soc.american.edu

Howard University
John H. Johnson School of
  Communication
Washington, DC 20059
Jannette Dates, dean [Journalism; Radio-
  TV-Film]
B.A. Journalism, B.A. Broadcast
  Production and Telecommunications
  Management. (2004)
Phone: (202) 806-7694
Fax: (202) 232-8040
E-mail: jdates@howard.edu or jcolbert@
  howard.edu
http://www.soc.howard.edu

FLORIDA

Florida A&M University
Division of Journalism
Tallahassee, FL 32307
James E. Hawkins, dean, School
  of Journalism and Graphic
  Communication
B.S.J. Journalism. (2000)

Phone: (850) 599-3718
Fax: (850) 599-3086
E-mail: james.hawkins@famu.edu
http://www.sjgc.net

Florida International University
School of Journalism and Mass
    Communication
North Miami, FL 33181
Lillian Lodge Kopenhaver, interim dean
B.S. Communication; M.S. Mass
    Communication. (2003)
Phone: (305) 919-5625
Fax: (305) 919-5203
E-mail: sjmc@fiu.edu
http://jmc.fiu.edu/sjmc

University of Florida
College of Journalism and
    Communications
Gainesville, FL 32611-8400
Terry Hynes, dean
B.S. Journalism; B.S. Advertising;
    B.S. Telecommunication; B.S.
    Public Relations; M.A. Mass
    Communication. (2000)
Phone: (352) 392-0466
Fax: (352) 392-3919
E-mail: thynes@jou.ufl.edu
http://www.jou.ufl.edu

University of Miami
School of Communication
P.O. Box 248127
Coral Gables, FL 33124
Edward J. Pfister, dean. [Advertising
    and Public Relations; Broadcasting,
    Broadcast Journalism and Media
    Management; Journalism and
    Photography]
B.S. Communication; M.A. Journalism.
    (2004)
Phone: (305) 284-3420
Fax: (305) 284-2454
E-mail: epfister@umiami.ir.miami.edu
http://www.miami.edu/com

University of South Florida
School of Mass Communications
4202 East Fowler Avenue – CIS 1040
Tampa, FL 33620
Edward Jay Friedlander, director
B.A. Mass Communications; M.A. Mass
    Communications. (2001)
Phone: (813) 974-2591
Fax: (813) 974-2592.
E-mail: mcom@cas.usf.edu
http://www.cas.usf.edu/mass_com/index.
    html

**University of South Florida–
    St. Petersburg**
Department of Journalism and Media
    Studies
40 Seventh Avenue South
St. Petersburg, FL 33701
G. Michael Killenberg, director
B.A.; M.A. (2004)
Phone: (727) 553-4174
Fax: (727) 553-4034
E-mail: killenbe@stpt.usf.edu
http://jmc.fiu.edu/sjmc

GEORGIA

University of Georgia
Henry W. Grady College of Journalism
    and Mass Communication
Athens, GA 30602-3018
John Soloski, dean
A.B.J. Journalism; M.A. Journalism and
    Mass Communication; M.M.C Master
    of Mass Communication.(2000)
Phone: (706) 542-1704
Fax: (706) 542-2183
E-mail: jsoloski@uga.edu
http://www.grady.uga.edu

ILLINOIS

Eastern Illinois University
Department of Journalism
600 Lincoln Avenue
Charleston, IL 61920-3099
L. R. Hyder, chair
B.A. Journalism (2000)
Phone: (217) 581-6003
Fax: (217) 581-7188
E-mail: journal@eiu.edu
http://www.eiu.edu/%7Ejournal

Northwestern University
Medill School of Journalism
Fisk Hall, 1845 Sheridan Road
Evanston, IL 60208
Loren Ghiglione, dean
B.S.J. Journalism; M.S. Integrated
    Marketing Communications; M.S.J.
    Journalism. (1999)
Phone: (847) 491-2045
Fax: (847) 491-5565
E-mail: ghiglion@northwestern.edu
http://www.medill.northwestern.edu

**Southern Illinois University–
    Carbondale**
School of Journalism
Carbondale, IL 62901-6601

Walter Jaehnig, director
B.S. Journalism. (2001)
Phone: (618) 536-3361
Fax: (618) 453-5200
E-mail: jschool@siu.edu
http://journal.siu.edu

**University of Illinois at
    Urbana-Champaign**
College of Communications
810 S. Wright Street
Urbana, IL 61801
Ron Yates, dean
B.S. Advertising; B.S. Media Studies;
    B.S. Journalism including Broadcast
    Journalism; M.S. Advertising; M.S.
    Journalism including Broadcast
    Journalism. (2001)
Phone: (217) 333-2350
Fax: (217) 333-9882
E-mail: ccomm@uiuc.edu
http://www.comm.uiuc.edu

INDIANA

Ball State University
Department of Journalism
Muncie, IN 47306
Marilyn A. Weaver, chair
B.A. Journalism; B.S. Journalism;
    B.A. Advertising; B.S. Advertising;
    B.A. Public Relations; B.S. Public
    Relations. (2004)
Phone: (765) 285-8200
Fax: (765) 285-7997
E-mail: bsujourn@bsu.edu
http://www.bsu.edu/journalism

Indiana University
School of Journalism
Bloomington, IN 47405
Trevor R. Brown, dean
B.A. Journalism. (2002)
Phone: (812) 855-9249
Fax: (812) 855-0901
E-mail: sojweb@indiana.edu
http://www.journalism.indiana.edu

University of Southern Indiana
Department of Communications
Evansville, IN 47712-3596
Dal M. Herring, chair [Journalism;
    Public Relations/Advertising; Radio/
    Television]
Phone: (812) 465-7079
Fax: (812) 465-7152
E-mail: dherring@usi.edu
http://www.usi.edu/libarts/comm

IOWA

Drake University
School of Journalism and Mass
    Communication
Des Moines, IA 50311
Charles Edwards, Jr., dean
B.A. Journalism and Mass
    Communication. (1999)
Phone: (515) 271-3194
Fax: (515) 271-2798
E-mail: Charles.Edwards@drake.edu
http://www.drake.edu/journalism

**Iowa State University of Science and
    Technology**
Greenlee School of Journalism and
    Communication
101A Hamilton Hall
Ames, IA 50011
Michael Bugeja, director. [Advertising;
    Journalism and Mass Communications]
    B.A. Journalism and Mass
    Communication (including Electronic
    Media Studies); B.A. Advertising;
    B.S. Journalism and Mass
    Communication (including Science
    Communication). (2004)
Phone: (515) 294-4342
Fax: (515) 294-5108
E-mail: greenlee@iastate.edu
http://www.jlmc.iastate.edu

University of Iowa
School of Journalism and Mass
    Communication
100 Adler Journalism Building Room E305
Iowa City, IA 52242-2004
Pamela J. Creedon, director
B.A. Journalism; B.S. Journalism; M.A.
    Professional. (1998)
Phone: (319) 335-3486
Fax: (319) 335-3502
E-mail: journalism-admin@uiowa.edu
http://www.uiowa.edu/%7Ejournal

KANSAS

Kansas State University
A.Q. Miller School of Journalism and
    Mass Communications
Manhattan, KS 66506-1501
Angela Powers, director
B.A. Mass Communications; B.S. Mass
    Communications. (2002)
Phone: (785) 532-6890
Fax: (785) 532-5484
E-mail: journalism@ksu.edu
http://jmc.ksu.edu

University of Kansas
William Allen White School of
    Journalism and Mass Communications
1435 Jayhawk Boulevard
Lawrence, KS 66045-7575
Ann Brill, interim dean
B.S. Journalism; M.S. Journalism. (1999)
Phone: (785) 864-4755
Fax: (785) 864-5318
E-mail: abrill@ku.edu
http://www.journalism.ku.edu

KENTUCKY

Murray State University
Department of Journalism and Mass
    Communications
114 Wilson Hall
Murray, KY 42071-3311
Jeanne Swan Scafella, chair
B.A.; B.S. Journalism, Advertising, Public
    Relations and Electronic Media. (2004)
Phone: (270) 762-2387
Fax: (270) 762-2390
E-mail: journalism@murraystate.edu
http://www.murraystate.edu/journalism

University of Kentucky
School of Journalism and
    Telecommunications
Lexington, KY 40506-0042
Beth E. Barnes, director
B.A. or B.S. Communications
    (Journalism; Integrated
    Strategic Communication;
    Telecommunications). (2003)
Phone: (859) 257-1730
Fax: (859) 323-3168
E-mail: bbarnes@uky.edu
http://www.uky.edu/CommInfoStudies/JAT

Western Kentucky University
School of Journalism and Broadcasting
Bowling Green, KY 42101-3576
Pam McAllister Johnson, director.
    [Advertising, Broadcasting, News/
    Editorial Journalism, Photojournalism,
    Public Relations]
B.A. Advertising; B.A. Photojournalism;
    B.A. News/Editorial Journalism; B.A.
    Public Relations. (2004)
Phone: (270) 745-4144
Fax: (270) 745-5835
E-mail: Pam.Johnson@wku.edu
http://www.wku.edu/Journalism

LOUISIANA

Grambling State University
Department of Mass Communication

P.O. Box 45
Grambling, LA 71245
Rama M. Tununguntla, head
B.A. Mass Communication. (1999)
Phone: (318) 274-2403/2189
Fax: (318) 274-3194
E-mail: tununguntla@gram.edu
http://www.gram.edu/Colleges_Schools/
    Liberal%20Arts/Mass%20Comm/
    index.htm

Louisiana State University
Manship School of Mass Communication
Baton Rouge, LA 70803
John Maxwell Hamilton, dean
B.A.M.C.; M.M.C. (2004)
Phone: (225) 578-2002
Fax: (225) 578-2125
E-mail: jhamilt@lsu.edu
http://www.manship.lsu.edu

Nicholls State University
Department of Mass Communication
Thibodaux, LA 70310
James Stewart, head
B.A. Mass Communication. (2000)
Phone: (985) 448-4586
Fax: (985) 448-4577
E-mail: james.stewart@nicholls.edu
http://www.nicholls.edu/maco

Northwestern State University
Department of Journalism
P.O. Box 5273
Natchitoches, LA 71497
Steve Horton, head
B.A. Journalism. (2003)
Phone: (318) 357-4425
Fax: (318) 357-4434
E-mail: journalism@nsula.edu
http://www.nsula.edu/journalism/default.asp

Southern University
Department of Mass Communications
Baton Rouge, LA 70813
Ted White, chair
B.A. Journalism; M.A. Journalism. (2000)
Phone: (225) 771-5790
Fax: (225) 771-4943
E-mail: ted_white@cxs.subr.edu
http://www.subr.edu

University of Louisiana at Lafayette
Department of Communication
P.O. Box 43650
Lafayette, LA 70504-3650
T. Michael Maher, head
B.A. Mass Communication; M.S. Mass
    Communication. (2000)

Phone: (337) 482-6103
Fax: (337) 482-6104
E-mail: tmm8088@louisiana.edu
http://comm.louisiana.edu

University of Louisiana at Monroe
Mass Communications Program
Monroe, LA 71209-0322
Bette J. Kauffman, head
B.A. Mass Communications. (2000)
Phone: (318) 342-1406
Fax: (318) 342-1422
E-mail: kauffman@ulm.edu
http://www.ulm.edu/masscomm

MARYLAND

University of Maryland
Philip Merrill College of Journalism
College Park, MD 20742
Thomas Kunkel, dean
B.A. Journalism; M.A. Journalism; M.J.
    Journalism. (2004)
Phone: (301) 405-2383
Fax: (301) 314-1978
E-mail: tkunkel@jmail.umd.edu
http://www.journalism.umd.edu

MICHIGAN

Central Michigan University
Department of Journalism
Mount Pleasant, MI 48859
Maria B. Marron, chair
B.A. Journalism, B.S. Journalism. (2003)
Phone: (989) 774-3196
Fax: (989) 774-7114
E-mail: jrndept@cmich.edu
http://journalism.cmich.edu

Michigan State University
School of Journalism
East Lansing, MI 48824-1212
Jane Briggs-Bunting, director
B.A. Journalism. (2002)
Phone: (517) 355-1520
Fax: (517) 355-7710
E-mail: JBB@msu.edu
http://www.jrn.msu.edu

MINNESOTA

St. Cloud State University
Department of Mass Communications
St. Cloud, MN 56301-4498
Roya Akhavan-Majid, chair
B.S. Mass Communications; M.S. Mass
    Communications. (1999)
Phone: (320) 308-3293

Fax: (320) 308-2083
E-mail: comm@stcloudstate.edu
http://www.stcloudstate.edu/
    masscommunications

University of Minnesota
School of Journalism and Mass
    Communication
111 Murphy Hall, 206 Church Street S.E.
Minneapolis, MN 55455-0418
Albert Tims, director
B.A. Journalism-Professional Program.
    (2001)
Phone: (612) 625-1338
Fax: (612) 626-8251
E-mail: achar001@umn.edu
http://sjmc.umn.edu

MISSISSIPPI

Jackson State University
Department of Mass Communications
P.O. Box 18590
Jackson, MS 39217
John Sullivan, acting chair
B.S. Mass Communications. (2003)
Phone: (601) 979-7022
Fax: (601) 979-5800
E-mail: john.m.sullivan@jsums.edu
http://www.jsums.edu/~jsumasscom

University of Mississippi
Department of Journalism
University, MS 38677-1848
Samir Husni, interim chair
B.A. Journalism. (1999)
Phone: (662) 915-7146
Fax: (662) 915-7765
E-mail: hsamir@olemiss.edu
http://www.olemiss.edu/depts/journalism

University of Southern Mississippi
School of Mass Communication and
    Journalism
P.O. Box 5121
Hattiesburg, MS 39406-5121
David Davies, interim director. [Journalism,
    Advertising, Broadcast Journalism,
    Radio-Television Production]
B.A. Journalism; B.A. Advertising.
    (Provisional 2004)
Phone: (601) 266-4258
Fax: (601) 266-6473
E-mail: dave.davies@usm.edu
http://www.usm.edu/mcj

MISSOURI

University of Missouri–Columbia
School of Journalism

120 Neff Hall
Columbia, MO 65211
Dean Mills, dean
B.J. Journalism; M.A. Journalism. (1999)
Phone: (573) 882-6686
Fax: (573) 884-5400
E-mail: journalism@missouri.edu
http://journalism.missouri.edu

MONTANA

The University of Montana
School of Journalism
Missoula, MT 59812
Jerry Brown, dean
B.A. Journalism, options in print
    journalism and photojournalism; B.A.
    Radio-Television, options in broadcast
    news and radio-television production;
    M.A. Journalism, options in print,
    photojournalism and broadcast. (2000)
Phone: (406) 243-4001
Fax: (406) 243-5369
E-mail: jerry.brown@umontana.edu
http://www.umt.edu/journalism

NEBRASKA

University of Nebraska
College of Journalism and Mass
    Communications
147 Andersen Hall
Lincoln, NE 68588-0443
Will Norton, dean
B.A. Advertising; Broadcasting; News/
    Editorial. M.A. Journalism. (2004)
Phone: (402) 472-3041
Fax: (402) 472-8597
E-mail: wnorton1@unl.edu
http://journalism.unl.edu

NEVADA

University of Nevada–Reno
Donald W. Reynolds School of
    Journalism
Reno, NV 89557-0040
Cole C. Campbell, dean
B.A. Journalism; M.A. Journalism. (2002)
Phone: (775) 784-6531
Fax: (775) 784-6656
E-mail: cole@unr.edu
http://www.unr.edu/journalism

NEW MEXICO

New Mexico State University
Department of Journalism and Mass
    Communications

MSC 3J, P.O. Box 30001
Las Cruces, NM 88003-8001
Frank Thayer, head
B.A. Journalism. (1999)
Phone: (505) 646-1034
Fax: (505) 646-1255
E-mail: nanhowel@nmsu.edu
http://www.nmsu.edu/~journali

NEW YORK

Columbia University
Graduate School of Journalism
New York, NY 10027
Nicholas Lemann, dean
M.S. Journalism. (2001)
Phone: (212) 854-3572
Fax: (212) 854-3939
E-mail: nick@jrn.columbia.edu
http://www.jrn.columbia.edu

Hofstra University
Department of Journalism and Mass
    Media Studies
318 Dempster Hall
Hempstead, NY 11549-1110
Barbara Kelly, chair
Phone: (516) 463-4100
Fax: (516) 463-4866
E-mail: jrnbmk@hofstra.edu
http://www.hofstra.edu/Academics/
    SOC/Journalism/index_Journalism.
    cfm

Iona College
Department of Mass Communication
715 North Avenue
New Rochelle, NY 10801-1890
Orly Shachar, chair
B.A. Mass Communication; M.A.
    Communication; M.S. Journalism.
    (2003)
Phone: (914) 633-2229
Fax: (914) 637-2797
E-mail: oshachar@iona.edu
http://www.iona.edu/academic/
    arts_sci/departments/mass_com/
    deptofmasscomm.htm

Syracuse University
S.I. Newhouse School of Public
    Communications
Syracuse, NY 13244
David Rubin, dean
B.S. Public Communications; M.A.
    Public Communications; M.S. Public
    Communications. (2004)
Phone: (315) 443-2301
Fax: (315) 443-3946

E-mail: newhouse@syr.edu or dmrubin@
    syr.edu
http://newhouse.syr.edu

NORTH CAROLINA

University of North Carolina
School of Journalism and Mass
    Communication
Chapel Hill, NC 27599-3365
Richard R. Cole, dean
A.B. Journalism and Mass
    Communication; M.A. Journalism and
    Mass Communication. (2003)
Phone: (919) 962-1204
Fax: (919) 962-0620
E-mail: richard_cole@unc.edu
http://www.jomc.unc.edu

OHIO

Bowling Green State University
Department of Journalism
Bowling Green, OH 43403
Terry Rentner, chair
B.S. Journalism. (Provisional 2004)
Phone: (419) 372-2076/2079
Fax: (419) 372-0202
E-mail: rfirsdo@bgnet.bgsu.edu
http://www.bgsu.edu/departments/
    journalism

Kent State University
School of Journalism and Mass
    Communication
Kent, OH 44242-0001
Jeff Fruit, director
B.S. Journalism and Mass
    Communication. (2003)
Phone: (330) 672-2572
Fax: (330) 672-4064
E-mail: jfruit@kent.edu
http://www.jmc.kent.edu

Ohio University
E.W. Scripps School of Journalism
Athens, OH 45701
Thomas S. Hodson, director
B.S.J. Journalism; M.S.J. Journalism.
    (2001)
Phone: (740) 593-2590
Fax: (740) 593-2592
E-mail: hodson@ohio.edu
http://www.scrippsjschool.org

OKLAHOMA

Oklahoma State University
School of Journalism and Broadcasting

Stillwater, OK 74078-0195
Tom Weir, director
B.S. and B.A. Journalism. (2002)
Phone: (405) 744-6357
Fax: (405) 744-7104
E-mail: tweir@okstate.edu
http://ok4h.fourh.dasnr.okstate.edu/sjb/
    SJBindex.php

University of Oklahoma
Gaylord College of Journalism and Mass
    Communication
Norman, OK 73019
Charles Self, dean
B.A. Journalism; M.A. Journalism and
    Mass Communication. (2003)
Phone: (405) 325-2721
Fax: (405) 325-7565
E-mail: cself@ou.edu
http://jmc.ou.edu

OREGON

University of Oregon
School of Journalism and Communication
1275 University of Oregon
Eugene, OR 97403-1275
Tim Gleason, dean
B.A. Journalism; M.A. Communications.
    (2000)
Phone: (541) 346-3739
Fax: (541) 346-0682
E-mail: tgleason@oregon.uoregon.edu
http://jcomm.uoregon.edu

PENNSYLVANIA

Pennsylvania State University
College of Communications
201 Carnegie Building
University Park, PA 16802
Douglas A. Anderson, dean
B.A. Journalism; B.A. Film/Video; B.A.
    Advertising/Public Relations; B.A.
    Telecommunications; B.A. Media
    Studies; M.A. Telecommunications
    Studies. (2001)
Phone: (814) 863-1484
Fax: (814) 863-8044
E-mail: doug-anderson@psu.edu
http://www.psu.edu/dept/comm

Temple University
Department of Journalism
2020 N. 13th Street
Philadelphia, PA 19122
Bonnie S. Brennen, chair
B.A. Journalism. (2001)
Phone: (215) 204-7433

Fax: (215) 204-1974
E-mail: journ@temple.edu
http://www.temple.edu/journalism

SOUTH CAROLINA

University of South Carolina
School of Journalism and Mass
    Communications
Columbia, SC 29208
Shirley Staples Carter, director
B.A. Journalism; M.M.C. (1999)
Phone: (803) 777-3324
Fax: (803) 777-4103
E-mail: sscarter@gwm.sc.edu
http://www.jour.sc.edu

Winthrop University
Department of Mass Communication
Rock Hill, SC 29733-0001
J. William Click, chair
B.A. Broadcasting; B.A. Journalism; B.S.
    Integrated Marketing Communication.
    (2003)
Phone: (803) 323-2121
Fax: (803) 323-2464
E-mail: clickw@winthrop.edu
http://www.winthrop.edu/masscomm

SOUTH DAKOTA

South Dakota State University
Department of Journalism and Mass
    Communication
Brookings, SD 57007
Mary Peterson Arnold, head
B.S. Journalism; B.A. Journalism.
    (2000)
Phone: (605) 688-4171
Fax: (605) 688-5034
E-mail: mary_arnold@sdstate.edu
http://www3.sdstate.edu/Academics/
    CollegeOfArtsAndScience/
    JournalismandMassCommunication/
    Index.cfm

University of South Dakota
Department of Contemporary Media and
    Journalism
Vermillion, SD 57069-2390
Ramon Chavez, chair
B.A. Mass Communication; B.S. Mass
    Communication. (2003)
Phone: (605) 677-5477
Fax: (605) 677-4250
E-mail: jskotvol@usd.edu
http://www.usd.edu/cmj

TENNESSEE

East Tennessee State University
Department of Communication
Johnson City, TN 37614-0667
Charles Roberts, chair. [advertising,
    broadcasting, journalism, public
    relations]
B.A. Mass Communications; B.S. Mass
    Communications. (2001)
Phone: (423) 439-4491
Fax: (423) 439-7540
E-mail: robertsc@mail.etsu.edu
http://www.etsu.edu/cas/comm/index.htm

Middle Tennessee State University
College of Mass Communication
Murfreesboro, TN 37132
Anantha Babbili, dean
B.S. Mass Communication; M.S. Mass
    Communication. (1999)
Phone: (615) 898-5872
Fax: (615) 898-5682
E-mail: ababbili@mtsu.edu
http://www.mtsu.edu/~masscomm

University of Memphis
Department of Journalism
Room 300, Meeman Journalism Building
Memphis, TN 38152
Jim Redmond, chair
B.A. Journalism; M.A. Journalism.
    (2001)
Phone: (901) 678-2401
Fax: (901) 678-4287
E-mail: cphilpot@memphis.edu
http://www.people.memphis.edu/
    ~jourlib

University of Tennessee
College of Communication and
    Information
Knoxville, TN 37996-0332
Faye D. Julian, interim dean
B.S. Communications; M.S.
    Communications. (1999)
Phone: (865) 974-3031
Fax: (865) 974-3896
E-mail: fjulian@utk.edu
http://excellent.com.utk.edu

**University of Tennessee at
    Chattanooga**
Department of Communication
Chattanooga, TN 37403-2598
S. Kittrell Rushing, head
Phone: (423) 425-4400
Fax: (423) 425-4695

E-mail: kit-rushing@utc.edu
http://www.utc.edu/Academic/
    Communication

University of Tennessee at Martin
Department of Communications
Martin, TN 38238-5099
Robert Nanney, chair
Phone: (731) 587-7546
Fax:(731) 587-7550
E-mail: rnanney@utm.edu
http://www.utm.edu/departments/comm

TEXAS

Abilene Christian University
Department of Journalism and Mass
    Communication
P.O. Box 27892, ACU Station
Abilene, TX 79699
Cheryl M. Bacon, chair
B.S. Journalism; B.S. Integrated
    Marketing Communication; B.S.
    Electronic Media. (2001)
Phone: (325) 674-2812
Fax: (325) 674-2139
E-mail: cheryl.bacon@jmc.acu.edu
http://www.acu.edu/academics/cas/jmc.
    html

Baylor University
Department of Journalism
P.O. Box 97353
Waco, TX 76798-7353
Douglas Ferdon, chair. [News-Editorial,
    Public Relations]
B.A. Journalism. (2003)
Phone: (254) 710-3261
Fax: (254) 710-3363
E-mail: Doug_Ferdon@baylor.edu
http://www.baylor.edu/journalism

Texas Christian University
Department of Journalism
TCU Box 298060
Ft. Worth, TX 76129
Tommy Thomason, chair
B.A. News-Editorial Journalism,
    International Communication;
    B.S. News-Editorial Journalism,
    Advertising-Public Relations,
    Broadcast Journalism. (Provisional
    2004)
Phone: (817) 257-7425
Fax: (817) 257-7322
E-mail: t.thomason@tcu.edu
http://www.jou.tcu.edu

Texas State University–San Marcos
Department of Mass Communication
San Marcos, TX 78666-4616
Bruce L. Smith, chair
B.A. Mass Communication-Advertising;
    B.A. Mass Communication-Electronic
    Media; B.A. Mass Communication-
    General Mass Communication;
    B.A. Mass Communication-
    Print Journalism; B.A. Mass
    Communication-Public Relations.
    (2003)
Phone: (512) 245-2656
Fax: (512) 245-7649
E-mail: bs20@txstate.edu
http://www.masscomm.txstate.edu

Texas Tech University
College of Mass Communications
Lubbock, TX 79409-3082
Jerry Hudson, dean
B.A. Journalism; B.A. Advertising; B.A.
    Public Relations; B.A. Electronic
    Media; B.A.Photocommunications.
    (2004)
Phone: (806) 742-3385
Fax: (806) 742-1085
E-mail: jerry.hudson@ttu.edu
http://www.depts.ttu.edu/mcom

University of North Texas
Department of Journalism and Mayborn
    Graduate Institute of Journalism
P.O. Box 311460
Denton, TX 76203-1460
Susan Zavoina, chair
B.A. Journalism; M.A. Journalism; M.J.
    Journalism. (Provisional 2004)
Phone: (940) 565-2205
Fax: (940) 565-2370
E-mail: zavoina@unt.edu
http://www.jour.unt.edu

University of Texas
School of Journalism
Austin, TX 78712
Lorraine Branham, director
B.J. Journalism. (2003)
Phone: (512) 471-1845
Fax: (512) 471-7979
E-mail: jbrandon@mail.utexas.edu
http://journalism.utexas.edu

UTAH

Brigham Young University
Department of Communications
Room E509

Harris Fine Arts Center
Provo, UT 84602-6404
Edward Adams, chair. [Advertising and
    Marketing Communications; Print
    and Broadcast Journalism; Public
    Relations; Communication Studies]
B.A. Communications. (2003)
Phone: (801) 422-2997
Fax: (801) 422-0160
E-mail: ed_adams@byu.edu
http://cfac.byu.edu/com

University of Utah
Department of Communication
255 S. Central Campus Drive,
    Room 2400
Salt Lake City, UT 84112
Ann Darling, chair. [Mass Communication]
B.S. Mass Communication; B.A. Mass
    Communication. (1999)
Phone: (801) 581-5324
Fax: (801) 585-6255
E-mail: duignan@admin.comm.utah.edu
http://www.communication.utah.edu

VIRGINIA

Hampton University
Scripps Howard School of Journalism and
    Communications
Hampton, VA 23668
Christopher Campbell, director
B.A. Journalism and Communications.
    (2000)
Phone: (757) 727-5405
Fax: (757) 728-6011
E-mail: shsjc@hamptonu.edu
http://www.hamptonu.edu/arts_edu/arts_
    humn/mass_media

Norfolk State University
Department of Mass Communications
    and Journalism
Norfolk, VA 23504
Emmanuel Onyedike, chair
B.S. Mass Communications; B.A.
    Journalism. (1999)
Phone: (757) 823-8330
Fax: (757) 823-9119
E-mail: eonyedike@nsu.edu
http://www.nsu.edu/mcjr

Washington and Lee University
Department of Journalism and Mass
    Communications
Lexington, VA 24450
Brian E. Richardson, head
Phone: (540) 458-8432

Fax: (540) 458-8845
E-mail: journalism@wlu.edu
http://journalism.wlu.edu

WASHINGTON

University of Washington
Department of Communication
P.O. Box 353740
Seattle, WA 98195-3740
Gerald Baldasty, chair. [Journalism]
B.A. Arts and Sciences. (2003)
Phone: (206) 543-2660
Fax: (206) 616-3762
E-mail: ndosmann@u.washington.edu
http://www.com.washington.edu/
    Program/index.html

WEST VIRGINIA

Marshall University
W. Page Pitt School of Journalism and
    Mass Communications
One John Marshall Drive
Huntington, WV 25755-2622
Corley Dennison, interim dean
B.A. Journalism; M.A. Journalism. (2003)
Phone: (304) 696-2360
Fax: (304) 696-2732
E-mail: sojmc@marshall.edu
http://www.marshall.edu/sojmc

West Virginia University
Perley Isaac Reed School of Journalism
1511 University Avenue
P.O. Box 6010
Morgantown, WV 26506-6010
Maryanne Reed, acting dean
B.S.J. Advertising, Broadcast News, News-
    Editorial, Public Relations. (2004)
Phone: (304) 293-3505 (×5413)
Fax: (304) 293-3072
E-mail: pireed@mail.wvu.edu or
    maryanne.reed@mail.wvu.edu
http://journalism.wvu.edu

WISCONSIN

Marquette University
College of Communication
Milwaukee, WI 53201-1881
William R. Elliott, dean
B.A. Advertising, Broadcast and
    Electronic Communication,
    Journalism, Public Relations; M.A.
    Advertising, Broadcast and Electronic
    Communication, Journalism, Public
    Relations. (2004)

Phone: (414) 288-7133
Fax: (414) 288-5227
E-mail: coc@marquette.edu
http://www.marquette.edu/comm/index.html

University of Wisconsin–Eau Claire
Department of Communication and
    Journalism
Eau Claire, WI 54702-4004
Karen Kremer, chair. [Mass
    Communication Advertising;
    Broadcast Journalism; Print
    Journalism; Mass Communication
    Public Relations]
Phone: (715) 836-2528
Fax: (715) 836-3820
E-mail: kremerkm@uwec.edu
http://www.uwec.edu/COMMJOUR

University of Wisconsin–Oshkosh
Department of Journalism
Oshkosh, WI 54901-8696
James Tsao, chair
B.A. Journalism; B.S. Journalism. (2004)
Phone: (920) 424-1042
Fax: (920) 424-7146
E-mail: tsao@uwosh.edu
http://www.uwosh.edu/journalism

University of Wisconsin–River Falls
Department of Journalism
410 South Third
River Falls, WI 54022
Colleen Callahan, chair
B.A. Journalism; B.S. Journalism. (2001)
Phone: (715) 425-3169
Fax: (715) 425-0658

E-mail: colleen.a.callahan@uwrf.edu
http://www.uwrf.edu/journalism/
    welcome.html

INTERNATIONAL

**Pontificia Universidad Católica de
    Chile**
School of Journalism
Alameda 340
Santiago, Chile
Maria-Elena Gronemeyer, director
Licentiate in journalism; professional title
    in journalism. (2004)
Phone: (011) 56-2-686-2029
Fax: (011) 56-2-354-2054
E-mail: mgroneme@puc.cl
http:///www.per.puc.cl

B. OTHER JOURNALISM PROGRAMS

In addition to accredited programs, there are also a number of non-accredited journalism programs. A comprehensive list of programs, created by the Department of Journalism and Media Studies at the University of South Florida at St. Petersburg, includes journalism departments, schools, and programs. For an updated list, see http://www1.stpt.usf.edu/journalism/j-schools.html.

Yet another list is compiled by Highschooljournalism.org, a Web site presented by the American Society of Newspaper Editors. This site is a clearinghouse for journalism information for high school students, their teachers, and professional journalists. On their site, http://highschooljournalism.org/Students/Students.cfm?id=52, they provide a comprehensive list of journalism programs, both accredited and non-accredited. Furthermore, they discuss the merits and importance of accreditation.

The following list, representing information from both of these sources, includes journalism programs not accredited by ACEJMC. However, contact the schools directly for changes in accreditation.

ALABAMA

Alabama State University
Department of Communications
915 South Jackson Street
Levi Watkins Learning Center/5th
    Floor/#531
Montgomery, AL 36101-0271
Phone: (334) 229-4493
Fax: (334) 229-4976
http://www.alasu.edu/College_of_Arts_
    and_Sciences/default.aspx?id=5

Jacksonville State University
College of Education and Professional
    Studies
Department of Communication
700 Pelham Road North
Jacksonville, AL 36265
Phone: (256) 782-5300
Fax: (256) 782-8175
http://www.jsu.edu/depart/edprof/comm

Samford University
Department of Journalism and Mass
    Communications
800 Lakeshore Drive
Birmingham, AL 35229
Phone: (205) 726-2011
http://www.samford.edu/schools/artsci/jmc

University of South Alabama
Department of Communication
1000 University Commons
Mobile, AL 36688
Phone: (251) 380-2800
Fax: (251) 380-2850
http://comm.southalabama.edu

ARKANSAS

Arkansas Tech University
Department of Speech, Theatre, &
    Journalism

Wilson 127, Arkansas Tech University
Russellville, AR 72801
Phone: (479) 964-0890
Fax: (479) 964-0899
http://lfa.atu.edu/stj

Harding University
Department of Communication
900 E. Center
Searcy, AR 72149
Phone: (501) 279-4445
http://www.harding.edu/communication/
    index.html

Henderson State University
Department of Communication & Theatre
    Arts
HSU Box 7760
Arkadelphia, AR 71999
Phone: (870) 230-5469
Fax: (870) 230-5144
http://www.hsu.edu/content.aspx?id=1539

John Brown University
Division of Communication
2000 W. University Street
Siloam Springs, AR 72761
Phone: (479) 524-9500
http://www.jbu.edu/academics/
    communication

University of Central Arkansas
Department Mass Communication and
    Theatre
201 Donaghey Avenue
Stanley Russ Hall 216
Conway, AR 72035
Phone: (501) 450-3162
Fax: (501) 852-2375
http://www.uca.edu/cfac/mct

CALIFORNIA

California Lutheran University
Communication Department
Spies-Bornemann Center for Educational
    Technology
Mail Code 3600
60 West Olsen Road
Thousand Oaks, CA 91360-2787
Phone: (805) 493-3850
http://lupine.clunet.edu/Academic_
    Programs/Departments/
    Communication

California Polytechnic State University
College of Liberal Arts
Journalism Department
San Luis Obispo, CA 93407
Phone: (805) 756-2508
http://cla.calpoly.edu/jour

**California State Polytechnic University,
    Pomona**
Communication Department
3801 West Temple Avenue
Pomona, CA 91768
Phone: (909) 869-7659
http://www.csupomona.edu/~comdept

**California State University, Dominguez
    Hills**
Department of Communications
1000 E. Victoria Street
Carson, CA 90747
Phone: (310) 243-3696
http://www.csudh.edu/communications/
    index.htm

California State University, East Bay
College of Letters, Arts, and Social
    Sciences

Department of Communication
Meiklejohn Hall 3011
25800 Carlos Bee Boulevard
Hayward, CA 94542
Phone: (510) 885-3292
Fax: (510) 885-4099
http://class.csueastbay.edu/
    communication

California State University, Fresno
Mass Communication & Journalism
McKee Fisk Building, Room 238
2225 E. San Ramon Avenue
M/S MF10
Fresno, CA 93740-8029
Phone: (559) 278-2087
Fax: (559) 278-4995
http://www.csufresno.edu/MCJ

California State University, Long Beach
Department of Journalism, SSPA-024
1250 Bellflower Boulevard
Long Beach, CA 90840-4601
Phone: (562) 985-4981
Fax: (562) 985-5300
http://www.csulb.edu/depts/journalism

California State University, Los Angeles
Department of Communication Studies
5151 State University Drive
Los Angeles, CA 90032-8111
Phone: (323) 343-4200
Fax: (323) 343-6467
http://www.calstatela.edu/academic/
    comstud

**California State University,
    Sacramento**
Communication Studies Department
Mendocino Hall 5014
6000 J Street
Sacramento, CA 95819
Phone: (916) 278-6688
Fax: (916) 278-7216
http://www.asn.csus.edu/coms

Humboldt State University
Department of Journalism and Mass
    Communication
Bret Harte House 52
Arcata, CA 95521
Phone: (707) 826-4775
http://www.humboldt.edu/~jnhsu/contact.
    html

Menlo College
Mass Communication Program
1000 El Camino Real
Atherton, CA 94027

Phone: (800) 556-3656
http://www.menlo.edu/academics/degree.
    htm

Pacific Union College
Communication Department
One Angwin Avenue
Angwin, CA 94508
Phone: (707) 965-6437
Fax: (707) 965-6624
http://www.puc.edu/PUC/academics/
    Academic_Departments/Comm_Dept

Pepperdine University
Communication Division
24255 Pacific Coast Highway
Malibu, CA 90263
Phone: (310) 506-4211
Fax: (310) 456-3083
http://seaver.pepperdine.edu/
    communication

Point Loma Nazarene University
Department of Communication &
    Theatre
Cabrillo Hall
3900 Lomaland Drive
San Diego, CA 92106
Phone: (619) 849-2605
http://www.ptloma.edu/communication

Saint Mary's College of California
Communication Department
P.O. Box 3101
Moraga, CA 94575-3101
Phone: (925) 631-4048
http://www.stmarys-ca.edu/academics/
    undergraduate/programs_by_name/
    academics.php?Department='Comm
    unication'

San Diego State University
School of Communication
College of Professional Studies and Fine
    Arts
5500 Campanile Drive
San Diego, CA 92182-4561
Phone: (619) 594-5450
Fax: (619) 594-6246
http://www-rohan.sdsu.edu/dept/
    schlcomm/index.html

Santa Clara University
Communication Department
500 El Camino Real
Santa Clara, CA 95053-0277
Phone: (408) 554-2798
Fax: (408) 554-4913
http://www.scu.edu/comm

Stanford University
Department of Communication
450 Serra Mall
Stanford, CA 94305-2050
Phone: (650) 723-1941
Fax: (650) 725-2472
http://communication.stanford.edu/index.
html

University of San Francisco
Department of Communication Studies
2130 Fulton Street
San Francisco, CA 94117-1080
Phone: (415) 422-6680
Fax: (415) 422-5680
http://artsci.usfca.edu/servlet/
DeptWelcome?deptID=3

University of the Pacific
Communication Department
3601 Pacific Avenue
Stockton, CA 95211
Phone: (209) 946-2505
http://www1.pacific.edu/cop/
communication/index.html

COLORADO

Adams State College
Department of Communications
208 Edgemont Boulevard
Alamosa, CO 81102
Phone: (719) 587-7011
Fax: (719) 587-7522
http://artsandletters.adams.edu/comm/
index.html

Mesa State University
Humanities & Social Sciences—Mass
Communications
1100 North Avenue
Grand Junction, CO 81501
Phone: (970) 248-1687
http://www.mesastate.edu/schools/shss/
llc/masscomm/index.htm

Metropolitan State College of Denver
Communication Arts and Sciences
Department
Campus Box 34
P.O. Box 173362
Denver, CO 80217-3362
Phone: (303) 556-3033
Fax: (303) 556-3013
http://www.mscd.edu/~cas/journalism.
htm

University of Denver
School of Communication

2490 South Gaylord Street
Denver, CO 80208
Phone: (303) 871-2088
Fax: (303) 871-4949
http://soc.du.edu

University of Northern Colorado
Department of Journalism and Mass
Communication
Candelaria Hall 1265
Campus Box 114
Greeley, CO 80639
Phone: (970) 351-2726
Fax: (970) 351-2519
http://www.unco.edu/jmc

CONNECTICUT

Quinnipiac University
School of Communications
275 Mount Carmel Avenue
Hamden, CT 06518-1940
Phone: (203) 582-8974
http://www.quinnipiac.edu/×216.xml

Southern Connecticut State University
Journalism Department
501 Crescent Street
New Haven, CT 06515
Phone: (203) 392-5800
http://www.southernct.edu/undergrad/
schcomm/JRN

University of Bridgeport
Department of Mass Communications
126 Park Avenue
Bridgeport, CT 06604
Phone: (203) 576-4966; (800) EXCEL-UB
Fax: (203) 576-4967
http://www.bridgeport.edu/mass/index.html

University of Hartford
School of Communication
200 Bloomfield Avenue
Harry Jack Gray Center, Room E210
West Hartford, CT 06117
Phone: (860) 768-4633
Fax: (860) 768-4096
http://uhaweb.hartford.edu/cmm

DELAWARE

University of Delaware
Department of Communication
250 Pearson Hall
Newark, DE 19716
Phone: (302) 831-8041
Fax: (302) 831-1892
http://www.udel.edu/communication

DISTRICT OF COLUMBIA

The George Washington University
School of Media and Public Affairs
805 21st Street NW
Suite 400
Washington, DC 20052
Phone: (202) 994-6227
Fax: (202) 994-5806
http://www.gwu.edu/~smpa

FLORIDA

Edward Waters College
Communications Program
1658 Kings Road
Jacksonville, FL 32209
Phone: (888) 898-3191
http://www.ewc.edu/default.html

Flagler College
Communication Department
P.O. Box 1027
St. Augustine, FL 32085-1027
Phone: (904) 819-6247
http://www.flagler.edu/academics/d_
comdept.html

Florida Southern College
Communication Department
111 Lake Hollingsworth Drive
Lakeland, FL 33801-5698
Phone: (863) 680-4169
http://www.flsouthern.edu/academics/
comm/index.htm

University of Central Florida
Nicholson School of Communication
4000 Central Florida Boulevard
Orlando, FL 32816
Phone: (407) 823-2681
http://www.cas.ucf.edu/communication

University of West Florida
Department of Communication Arts
Building 36
11000 University Parkway
Pensacola, FL 32514-5750
Phone: (850) 474-2874
Fax: (850) 474-3153
http://uwf.edu/commarts/home.htm

GEORGIA

Berry College
Journalism Program, Department of
Communication
2277 Martha Berry Highway NW
Mount Berry, GA 30149

Phone: (706) 233-4073
http://www.berry.edu/academics/majors.
　asp?major=journalism

Brenau University
Mass Communication Program
One Centennial Circle
Gainesville, GA 30501
Phone: (770) 538-4707
Fax: (770) 538-4558
http://www.brenau.edu/sbmc/masscomm/
　default.htm

Clark Atlanta University
Department of Mass Media Arts
223 James P. Brawley Drive SW
Atlanta, GA 30314
Phone: (404) 880-8304
http://www.cau.edu/acad_prog/mass_
　media/media_right.html

Georgia Southern University
Department of Communication Arts
P.O. Box 8091
Statesboro, GA 30460
Phone: (912) 681-5138
Fax: (912) 681-0822
http://class.georgiasouthern.edu/
　commarts

Georgia State University
Department of Communication
P.O. Box 3965
Atlanta, GA 30302-3965
Phone: (404) 651-3200
http://communication.gsu.edu

Mercer University
Department of Communication and
　Theatre Arts
1400 Coleman Avenue
Macon, GA 31207-0001
Phone: (800) MERCER-U
http://www.mercer.edu/cta

Toccoa Falls College
School of Communication
P.O. Box 125
Toccoa Falls, GA 30598
Phone: (706) 282-5270
http://www.toccoafalls.edu/academics/
　Schools/school%20of%20communicat
　ion/scom.htm

HAWAII

Chaminade University
3140 Waialae Avenue
Honolulu, HI 96816-1578

Phone: (808) 735-4727, ext. 727
Fax: (808) 440-4249
http://www.chaminade.edu/catalog

University of Hawai'i at Manoa
College of Social Sciences
School of Communications
2550 Campus Road
Crawford Hall 320
Honolulu, HI 96822-2217
Phone: (808) 956-8881
Fax: (808) 956-5396
http://www.communications.hawaii.edu

IDAHO

Boise State University
Department of Communication
1910 University Drive
Boise, ID 83725-1920
Phone: (208) 426-3320
Fax: (208) 426-1069
http://comm.boisestate.edu

University of Idaho
School of Journalism and Mass Media
P.O. Box 443178
Moscow, ID 83844-3178
Phone: (208) 885-6458
Fax: (208) 885-6450
http://www.class.uidaho.edu/jamm

ILLINOIS

Bradley University
Slane College of Communication and
　Fine Arts
Department of Communication
1501 W. Bradley Avenue
Peoria, IL 61625
Phone: (309) 677-2354
http://gcc.bradley.edu/com/home.html

Columbia College Chicago
Journalism Department
600 South Michigan Avenue
Chicago, IL 60605
Phone: (312) 344-8900
http://www.colum.edu/undergraduate/
　journalism/index.html

DePaul University
Department of Communication
2320 North Kenmore Avenue
Chicago, IL 60614
Phone: (773) 325-7585
Fax: (773) 325-7584
http://communication.depaul.edu

Illinois College
Department of Communication Studies
1101 West College Avenue
Jacksonville, IL 62650
Phone: (217) 245-3030
http://www.ic.edu/academics/
　communications.asp

Illinois State University
School of Communication
Normal, IL 61790-4480
Phone: (309) 438-3671
http://www.communication.ilstu.edu/dept

Loyola University–Chicago
Department of Communication
Lake Shore Campus, Loyola Hall
1110 W. Loyola Avenue
Chicago, IL 60626
Phone: (773) 508-3730
Fax: (773) 508-8821
http://www.luc.edu/communication

Northern Illinois University
Department of Communication
DeKalb, IL 60115
Phone: (815) 753-1563
Fax: (815) 753-7109
http://www.comm.niu.edu

Roosevelt University
Department of Communication
430 S. Michigan Avenue
Chicago, IL 60605
Phone: (312) 341-3500
http://www.roosevelt.edu/cas/comm/
　journalism.htm

University of St. Francis
Mass Communication Department
500 Wilcox Street
Joliet, IL 60435
Phone: (800) 735-7500
http://www.stfrancis.edu/masscomm

Western Illinois University
Department of English & Journalism
1 University Circle
Macomb IL 61455-1390
Phone: (309) 298-1103
Fax: (309) 298-2974
http://www.wiu.edu/users/mieng

INDIANA

Anderson University
Department of Communication
1100 East Fifth Street
Anderson, IN 46012

Phone: (800) 428-6414
http://www.anderson.edu/academics/
    cmun/index.html

Butler University
Eugene S. Pulliam School of Journalism
218 Fairbanks Center
4600 Sunset Avenue
Indianapolis, IN 46208
Phone: (317) 940-9708
Fax: (317) 940-9252
http://www.butler.edu/journalism

Calumet College of St. Joseph
English and Professional Writing Program
2400 New York Avenue
Whiting, IN 46394
Phone: (219) 473-4215
http://www.ccsj.edu/academics/programs/
    eng/index.html

Depauw University
Communication and Theatre Department
101 East Seminary Street
Greencastle, IN 46135-0037
Phone: (800) 447-2495; (765) 658-4006
http://www.depauw.edu/acad/
    communication/index.htm

Franklin College
Pulliam School of Journalism
101 Branigin Boulevard
Franklin, IN 46131
Phone: (317) 738-8200
http://psj.franklincollege.edu

Goshen College
Communication Department
1700 South Main Street
Goshen, IN 46526
Phone: (574) 535-7745
Fax: (574) 535-7660
http://www.goshen.edu/communication

Indiana State University
Department of Communication
Erickson Hall
200 North Seventh Street
Terre Haute, IN 47809-9989
Phone: (812) 237-3430
Fax: (812) 237-3217
http://www.communication.indstate.edu

Purdue University
Beering Hall of Liberal Arts and
    Education, Room 2114
Department of Communication
100 North University Street
West Lafayette, IN 47907-2098

Phone: (765) 494-3429
Fax: (765) 496-1394
http://www.cla.purdue.edu/academic/
    comm

Saint Mary-of-the-Woods College
Department of English, Journalism and
    Languages
Saint Mary-of-the-Woods, IN 47876
Phone: (812) 535-5151
http://www.smwc.edu/acad/ejl_dept/jour/
    index.shtml

Taylor University
Communication Arts Department
236 West Reade Avenue
Upland, IN 46989-1001
Phone: (765) 998-5255
Fax: (765) 998-4810
http://www.taylor.edu/academics/
    acaddepts/commarts

University of Evansville
Department of Communciation
1800 Lincoln Avenue
Evansville, IN 47722
Phone: (800) 423-8633
http://communication.evansville.edu/
    index.htmlhttp://communication.
    evansville.edu/about.html

University of Indianapolis
Department of Communication
1400 East Hanna Avenue
Indianapolis, IN 46227
Phone: (317) 788-3280
http://communication.uindy.edu

University of Notre Dame
Department of American Studies
Journalism Program
314 O'Shaughnessy Hall
Notre Dame, IN 46556
Phone: (574) 631-7316
Fax: (574) 631-4268
http://www.nd.edu/~amst/journalism/
    index.shtml

Valparaiso University
Department of Communication
Valparaiso, IN 46383-6493
Phone: (219) 464-5271
http://www.valpo.edu/comm

Vincennes University
Journalism Program
1002 North First Street
Vincennes, IN 47591

Phone: (812) 888-4551; (812) 888-4480
Fax: (812) 888-5531
http://www.vinu.edu/academicresources/
    majors/factsheet.aspx?fsh_lKey=89

IOWA

Clarke College
Communication Department
1550 Clarke Drive
Dubuque, IA 52001
Phone: (563) 588-6300; (800) 383-2345
http://www.clarke.edu/academics/
    departments/communication/index.htm

Grand View College
Communication Department
1200 Grandview Avenue
Des Moines, IA 50316
Phone: (515) 263-2810; (800) 444-6083,
    ext. 2810
Fax: (515) 263-2974
http://www.gvc.edu/aspx/audience/
    audience.aspx?pageid=131

University of Northern Iowa
Department of Communication Studies
326 Lang Hall
Cedar Falls, IA 50614-0139
Phone: (319) 273-2217
Fax: (319) 273-7356
http://www.chfa.uni.edu/comstudy/about

KANSAS

Baker University
Department of Communication and
    Theatre Arts
P.O. Box 65
Baldwin City, KS 66006-0065
Phone: (785) 594-6451
http://www.bakeru.edu/departments/com_
    theater/academic_theatrearts.htm

Fort Hays State University
Department of Communication Studies
102 Malloy Hall
600 Park Street
Hays, KS 67601-4099
Phone: (785) 628-5365
http://www.fhsu.edu/communication

Pittsburg State University
Department of Communication
Grubbs Hall 434
Pittsburg, KS 66762
Phone: (620) 235-4716
http://www.pittstate.edu/comm

Washburn University
Department of Mass Media
Henderson Learning Center, Third Floor
Topeka, KS 66621
Phone: (785) 231-1010, ext. 1836
http://www.washburn.edu/cas/massmedia

Wichita State University
Elliott School of Communication
Wichita, KS 67260
Phone: (316) 978-3185
http://webs.wichita.edu/?u=elliott&p=/
index

KENTUCKY

Asbury College
Department of Communication Arts
One Macklem Drive
Wilmore, KY 40390
Phone: (859) 858-3511
http://www.asbury.edu/academics/
communication/index.cfm

Eastern Kentucky University
Department of Communication
Alumni Coliseum 108
Richmond, KY 40475
Phone: (859) 622-1871
http://www.masscomm.eku.edu

Morehead State University
Department of Communication and
Theatre
150 University Boulevard
Morehead, KY 40351
Phone: (800) 585-6781
http://www.morehead-st.edu

Northern Kentucky University
Department of Communication
134 Landrum Academic Center
Nunn Drive
Highland Heights, KY 41099
Phone: (859) 572-5435
Fax: (859) 572-6187
http://www.nku.edu/~communicate

University of Louisville
Department of Communication
Louisville, KY 40292
Phone: (502) 852-6976
Fax: (502) 852-8166
http://comm.louisville.edu

LOUISIANA

McNeese State University
The Department of Mass Communication

P.O. Box 90335
Lake Charles, LA 70609
Phone: (337) 475-5430
Fax: (337) 475-5291
http://www.mcneesemcom.com

Louisiana State University in Shreveport
Department of Communications
Bronson Hall, Room 330
Shreveport, LA 71115
Phone: (318) 797-5375
Fax: (318) 797-5132
http://www.lsus.edu/la/communications

Louisiana Tech University
Journalism Program
P.O. Box 3178
Ruston, LA 71272
Phone: (318) 257-3036; (800) LATECH-1
http://eb.journ.latech.edu

Loyola University–New Orleans
Department of Communications
6363 St. Charles Avenue
New Orleans, LA 70118
Phone: (504) 865-3430
http://www.loyno.edu/communications

Southeastern Louisiana University
Department of Communication
Hammond, LA 70402
Phone: (985) 549-2105
Fax: (985) 549-5407
http://www.selu.edu/communication

University of New Orleans
Department of Film, Theatre, and
Communication Arts
2000 Lakeshore Drive
New Orleans, LA 70148
Phone: (504) 280-6000
http://ftca.uno.edu

Xavier University of Louisiana
Communications Department
1 Drexel Drive
Campus Box 93
New Orleans, LA 70125-1098
Phone: (504) 520-5092
Fax: (504) 520-7919
http://www.xula.edu/communications

MAINE

University of Maine
Department of Communication and
Journalism
5724 Dunn Hall, Room 420
Orono, ME 04469

Phone: (207) 581-1283
Fax: (207) 581-1286
http://www.cmj.umaine.edu

MARYLAND

Bowie State University
Department of Communications
14000 Jericho Park Road
Bowie, MD 20715-9465
Phone: (301) 860-3700/3709
Fax: (301) 860-3728
http://www.bowiestate.edu/community/
communications.asp

Defense Information School
Journalism Program
6500 Mapes Road
Ft. George G. Meade, MD 20755-5620
Phone: (301) 677-2968
http://www.dinfos.osd.mil/index.asp

Hood College
English and Communication Arts
Department
401 Rosemont Avenue
Frederick, MD 21701
Phone: (301) 663-3131
http://www.hood.edu/academic/english

Loyola College in Maryland
Department of Communication
4501 N. Charles Street
Baltimore, MD 21210
Phone: (800) 221-9107
http://www.loyola.edu/communication/
index.htm

Towson University
Department of Mass Communication and
Communication Studies
8000 York Road
Towson, MD 21252-0001
Phone: (410) 704-3431
Fax: (410) 704-3656
http://wwwnew.towson.edu/mccs

MASSACHUSETTS

Boston University
College of Communication, Department
of Journalism
640 Commonwealth Avenue
Boston, MA 02215
Phone: (617) 353-3450
http://www.bu.edu/com

Emerson College
Department of Journalism

120 Boylston Street
Boston, MA 02116-4624
Phone: (617) 824-8500
http://www.emerson.edu/journalism

Northeastern University
School of Journalism
102 Lake Hall
360 Huntington Avenue
Boston, MA 02115
Phone: (617) 373-3236
Fax: (617) 373-8773
http://www.journalism.neu.edu

Simmons College
Department of Communications
300 The Fenway
Boston, MA 02115
Phone: (617) 521-2838
Fax: (617) 521-3136
http://www.simmons.edu/academics/
    undergraduate/communications/index.
    html

Stonehill College
Department of Communication
320 Washington Street
Easton, MA 02357
Phone: (508) 565-1000
http://www.stonehill.edu/cta/index.htm

Suffolk University
Department of Communication and
    Journalism
41 Temple Street
Boston, MA 02108
Phone: (617) 573-8500
Fax: (617) 742-6982
http://www.cas.suffolk.edu/geisler/Web/
    index.html

University of Massachusetts–Amherst
Journalism Department
108 Bartlett Hall
Amherst, MA 01003
Phone: (413) 545-1376
http://www.umass.edu/journal/
    UMAJournalism/index.html

MICHIGAN

Alma College
Department of Communication
614 W. Superior Street
Alma, MI 48801
Phone: (989) 463-7111
http://newmedia.alma.edu/
    communication/default.html

Calvin College
Communication Arts & Sciences
DeVos Communication Center
1810 East Beltline SE
Grand Rapids, MI 49546
Phone: (616) 526-6283
Fax: (616) 526-6601
http://www.calvin.edu/academic/cas

Eastern Michigan University
Department of English Language and
    Literature Journalism Program
612 Pray-Harrold
Ypsilanti, MI 48197
Phone: (734) 487-4220
http://www.emich.edu/public/english/
    journalism/index.html

Grand Valley State University
School of Communications
290 Lake Superior Hall
Allendale, MI 49401
Phone: (616) 331-3668
Fax: (616) 331-2700
http://www.gvsu.edu/soc

Madonna University
Journalism/Public Relations and
    Journalism/English Program
36600 Schoolcraft Road
Livonia, MI 48150
Phone: (734) 432-5339; (800) 852-4951
Fax: (734) 432-5393
http://www.madonna.edu/pages/jrn.cfm

Oakland University
Department of Journalism
317 Wilson Hall
Rochester, MI 48309-4401
Phone: (248) 370-4120
http://www2.oakland.edu/jrn

University of Detroit Mercy
Department of Communication Studies
4001 W. McNichols Road
Detroit, MI 48221-3038
Phone: (313) 993-3250
http://liberalarts.udmercy.edu/
    commstudies/index.html

University of Michigan
Department of Communication Studies
2020 Frieze Building
105 South State Street
Ann Arbor, MI 48109-1285
Phone: (734) 764-0420; (734) 647-9723
Fax: (734) 764-3288
http://www.lsa.umich.edu/comm

Wayne State University
Department of Communication
585 Manoogian Hall
Detroit, MI 48201
Phone: (313) 577-2943
http://www.comm.wayne.edu/index2.
    php

Western Michigan University
School of Communication
Kalamazoo, MI 49008
Phone: (269) 387-3130
Fax: (269) 387-3990
http://www.wmich.edu/communication

MINNESOTA

Alcorn State University
Department of Communications
Industrial Technology Building, Room 106
1000 ASU Drive 269
Alcorn State, MS 39096-7500
Phone: (601) 877-6612
Fax: (601) 877-2213
http://www.alcorn.edu/academic/academ/
    comm.htm

Bemidji State University
Department of Mass Communication
206 Bangsberg
1500 Birchmont Drive NE
Bemidji, MN 56601
Phone: (218) 755-3926
http://cal.bemidjistate.edu/masscomm

Minnesota State University, Mankato
Department of Mass Communications
136 Nelson Hall
Mankato, MN 56001
Phone: (507) 389-6417
Fax: (507) 389-5525
http://www.mnsu.edu/masscom

Minnesota State University, Moorhead
Mass Communications Department
1104 7th Avenue South
Moorhead, MN 56563
Phone: (800) 593-7246
http://www.mnstate.edu/masscomm/
    home.html

Saint Mary's University of Minnesota
Media Communications Department
700 Terrace Heights #41
Winona, MN 55987-1399
Phone: (800) 635-5987, ext. 1753
http://www.smumn.edu/sitepages/pid70.
    php

University of St. Thomas
Department of Journalism and Mass
    Communication
460 OEC O'Shaughnessy Educational
    Center
2115 Summit Avenue
St. Paul, MN 55105
Phone: (651) 962-5250
http://www.stthomas.edu/jour

Winona State University
Mass Communication Department
Phelps Hall
Winona, MN 55987-3288
Phone: (507) 457-5474
Fax: (507) 457-5155
http://www.winona.edu/masscomm

MISSISSIPPI

Mississippi State University
Department of Communication
130 McComas Hall
Mail Stop 9574
P.O. Box PF
Mississippi State, MS 39762
Phone: (662) 325-3320
Fax: (662) 325-3210
http://www.msstate.edu/dept/
    communication

Mississippi University for Women
Division of Business & Communication
1100 College St. MUW - 940
Columbus, MS 39701-5800
Phone: (662) 329-7354
Fax: (662) 329-7250
http://www.muw.edu/communication

Mississippi Valley State University
Department of Mass Communications
14000 Highway 82 West
Itta Bena, MS 38941
Phone: (662) 254-9041
http://www.mvsu.edu/mass.html

Rust College
Department of Mass Communications
150 Rust Avenue
Holly Springs, MS 38635
Phone: (662) 252-8000, ext. 4558
Fax: (662) 252-8869
http://www.rustcollege.edu/net/depts/
    humanities/masscomm/index.html

Tougaloo College
Journalism Program
500 West County Line Road
Tougaloo, MS 39174

Phone: (601) 977-7700
http://www.tougaloo.edu/content/
    Academics/divisions/humanities.htm

MISSOURI

Central Missouri State University
Communication Department
136 Martin Building
Warrensburg, MO 64093
Phone: (660) 543-4840
http://www.cmsu.edu/x7023.xml

Culver-Stockton College
Communication Program
One College Hill
Canton, MO 63435
Phone: (573) 288-6000
http://www.culver.edu/academics/
    programs/details.asp?id=4

Evangel University
Department of Communication
1111 North Glenstone
Springfield, MO 65802
Phone: (417) 865-2815 ext. 8412
http://www.evangel.edu/Academics/
    Communication/index.asp

Lincoln University
Division of Humanities, Fine Arts and
    Journalism
820 Chestnut Street
Jefferson City, MO 65101
Phone: (800) 521-5052
http://www.lincolnu.edu/pages/620.asp

Lindenwood University
Communications Division
209 S. Kingshighway
St. Charles, MO 63301
Phone: (636) 949-4949
http://www.lindenwood.edu/academics/
    communications

Maryville University
Communication Program
13550 Conway Road
St. Louis, MO 63141
Phone: (800) 627-9855
http://www.maryville.edu/academics/lp/
    Communications

Missouri Southern State University
Department of Communication
3950 East Newman Road
Joplin, MO 64801-1595
Phone: (417) 625-9580

Fax: (417) 625-9585
http://www.mssu.edu/comm/overview.
    htm

Missouri State University–Springfield
Department of Media, Journalism and
    Film
901 S. National Avenue
Springfield, MO 65804
Phone: (417) 836-5218
http://mjf.missouristate.edu

Missouri Western State University
Department of English, Foreign
    Languages, and Journalism
4525 Downs Drive
St. Joseph, MO 64507
Phone: (816) 271-4310
http://www.mwsc.edu/eflj

Northwest Missouri State University
Mass Communication Department
800 University Drive
Wells Hall #237
Maryville, MO 64468-6001
Phone: (660) 562-1361
Fax: (660) 562-1947
http://info.nwmissouri.edu/~masscom

Saint Louis University
Department of Communication
Xavier Hall 300
3733 West Pine Mall
Saint Louis, MO 63108
Phone: (314) 977-3191
Fax: (314) 977-3195
http://www.slu.edu/colleges/AS/CMM

Stephens College
Department of Mass Media
1200 E. Broadway
Columbia, MO 65215
Phone: (573) 442-2211
http://www.stephens.edu/academics/
    programs/communication

Truman State University
Division of Language and Literature—
    Communication Program
Kirksville, MO 63501
Phone: (660) 785-6004; (660) 785-4188
http://ll.truman.edu/comm.html

University of Missouri–Kansas City
Department of Communication Studies
202 Haag Hall
5120 Rockhill Road
Kansas City, MO 64110

Phone: (816) 235-1337
Fax: (816) 235-5539
http://cas.umkc.edu/comm

University of Missouri–St. Louis
Department of Communication
590 Lucas Hall
One University Boulevard
St. Louis, MO 63121
Phone: (314) 516-5486
Fax: (314) 516-5816
http://www.umsl.edu/divisions/artscience/
  communication

Webster University
School of Communications
470 E. Lockwood Avenue
St. Louis, MO 63119
Phone: (314) 968-6900
http://www.webster.edu/depts/comm

NEBRASKA

Hastings College
Communication Arts, Business, and
  Economics Department
710 N. Turner
Hastings, NE 68901
Phone: (800) 532-7642
http://bronco11.hastings.edu/academic/
  CABE/cabe.html

University of Nebraska at Kearney
Department of Communication
Mitchell Center
Kearney, NE 68849
Phone: (308) 865-8249
Fax: (308) 865-8708
http://www.unk.edu/acad/comm/index.php

University of Nebraska at Omaha
School of Communication
6001 Dodge Street, ASH 140
Omaha, NE 68182
Phone: (402) 554-2600
http://communication.unomaha.edu

NEVADA

University of Nevada, Las Vegas
Hank Greenspun School of Journalism &
  Media Studies
4505 Maryland Parkway
P.O. Box 455007
Las Vegas, NV 89154-5007
Phone: (702) 895-3325
Fax: (702) 895-5189
http://www.unlv.edu/Colleges/Greenspun

NEW HAMPSHIRE

Keene State College
Department of Communication,
  Journalism & Philosophy
229 Main Street
Keene, NH 03435
Phone: (800) KSC-1909
http://academics.keene.edu/comm

University of New Hampshire
English/Journalism Major
Durham, NH 03824
Phone: (603) 862-1360
http://www.unh.edu/ur-engl.html#journ

NEW JERSEY

**Fairleigh Dickinson University–College
  at Florham**
Communication Studies Program
285 Madison Avenue
Madison, NJ 07940
Phone: (973) 443-8716
http://view.fdu.edu/?id=1413

**Fairleigh Dickinson University–
  Metropolitan Campus**
School of Art and Media Studies
1000 River Road
Teaneck, NJ 07666
Phone: (201) 692-2416
http://ucoll.fdu.edu/art/media.html

Rider University
Communication Department
2083 Lawrenceville Road
Lawrenceville, NJ 08648
Phone: (609) 896-5089
http://www.rider.edu/172_1716.htm

Rowan University
College of Communication
201 Mullica Hill Road
Glassboro, NJ 08028
Phone: (856) 256-4000
http://www.rowan.edu/colleges/
  communication

**Rutgers, The State University of
  New Jersey**
Department of Communication,
  Information Technologies, and
  Journalism
Office of University Undergraduate
  Admissions
Room 202
65 Davidson Road
Piscataway, NJ 08854-8097
Phone: (732) 932-INFO
http://admissions.rutgers.edu/030203.asp

**Rutgers, The State University of
  New Jersey, Newark**
Journalism and Media Studies Program
Office of Graduate and Undergraduate
  Admissions
249 University Avenue
Newark, NJ 07102-1896
Phone: (973) 353-5205
http://nwk-web.rutgers.edu/~dvpa/
  journalism/journalism_main.htm

Seton Hall University
Department of Communication
400 South Orange Avenue
South Orange, NJ 07079
Phone: (973) 761-9000
http://artsci.shu.edu/communication

William Paterson University
Department of Communication
Hobart Hall
300 Pompton Road
Wayne, NJ 07470
Phone: (973) 720-2150
http://www.wpunj.edu/coac/
  communication

NEW MEXICO

Eastern New Mexico University
Department of Communicative Arts and
  Sciences
ENMU Station 3
1500 S. Avenue K
Portales, NM 88130
Phone: (505) 562-2130
http://www.enmu.edu/academics/
  undergrad/colleges/las/cas/index.
  shtml

New Mexico Highlands University
Department of Communications and Fine
  Arts
P.O. Box 9000
Las Vegas, NM 87701
Phone: (505) 454-3238
Fax: (505) 454-3241
http://www.nmhu.edu/comfinearts/
  default.php

University of New Mexico
Department of Communication &
  Journalism
C&J Building 115, Room 235
Albuquerque, NM 87131
Phone: (505) 277-5305
Fax: (505) 277-4206
http://www.unm.edu/~cjdept

NEW YORK

Canisius College
Department of Communication Studies
Lyons Hall, Room 314
2001 Main Street
Buffalo, NY 14208
Phone: (716) 888-2115
Fax: (716) 888-3118
http://www.canisius.edu/comm_stud/
    default.asp

Cornell University
Department of Communication
336 Kennedy Hall
Ithaca, NY 14853
Phone: (607) 255-2111
Fax: (607) 254-1322
http://www.comm.cornell.edu/default.htm

Fordham University
Communication and Media Studies
Rose Hill Campus
Bronx, NY 10458
Phone: (718) 817-1000
http://www.fordham.edu/gsas/pcom/
    comm.html

Ithaca College
Roy H. Park School of Communications
311 Park Hall
Ithaca, NY 14850-7250
Phone: (607) 274-1021
Fax: (607) 274-1108
http://www.ithaca.edu/rhp.php

**Long Island University, Brooklyn
    Campus**
Journalism Department
Metcalf (Main) Building, Room 404
Brooklyn, NY 11201-8423
Phone: (718) 488-1153
http://www.brooklyn.liunet.edu/
    journalism

Marist College
School of Communication and the Arts
3399 North Road
Poughkeepsie, NY 12601
Phone: (845) 575-3000, ext. #2678
http://www.marist.edu/commarts/comm/
    journalism/index.html

New York University
Department of Journalism
Arthur Carter Hall
10 Washington Place
New York, NY 10003
Phone: (212) 998-7980
Fax: (212) 995-4148
http://journalism.nyu.edu

Niagara University
Communication Studies
Niagara University, NY 14109
Phone: (716) 285-1212; (800) 778-3450
http://www.niagara.edu/communication

Pace University
Media and Communication Department
861 Bedford Road
Pleasantville, NY 10570
Phone: (914) 773-3790
http://appserv.pace.edu/execute/page.
    cfm?doc_id=3762

Rochester Institute of Technology
School of Photographic Arts and
    Sciences
Photojournalism Program
One Lomb Memorial Drive
Rochester, NY 14623
Phone: (585) 475-2770
http://www.rit.edu/~661www/theschool.
    html

St. Bonaventure University
Russell J. Jandoli School of Journalism
    and Mass Communication
P.O. Box J
St. Bonaventure, NY 14778-2289
Phone: (716) 375-2521
Fax: (716) 375-2588
http://www.sbu.edu/go/academics/jandoli-
    school-of-journalism-and-mass-
    communication/index.htm

St. John Fisher College
Communication/Journalism Program
3690 East Avenue
Rochester, NY 14618
Phone: (585) 385-8000
http://www.sjfc.edu/subsites/commjourn

University at Albany, SUNY
Department of Communication, SS 340
1400 Washington Avenue
Albany, NY 12222
Phone: (518) 442-4871
Fax: (518) 442-3884
http://www.albany.edu/communication/
    index.html

University at Buffalo, SUNY
School of Informatics, Department of
    Communication
528 Baldy Hall
Buffalo, NY 14260-1020
Phone: (716) 645-6481
Fax: (716) 645-3775
http://www.informatics.buffalo.edu/com

University at New Paltz, SUNY
Department of Communication & Media
Coykendall Science Building (CSB) 51
75 S. Manheim Boulevard, Suite 9
New Paltz, NY 12561-2443
Phone: (845) 257-3450
Fax: (845) 257-3461
http://www.newpaltz.edu/comm_media

Utica College
Journalism Studies Program
1600 Burrstone Road
Utica, NY 13502
Phone: (315) 792-3006
Fax: (315) 792-3003
http://www.utica.edu/academic/ssm/
    journalism/index.cfm

NORTH CAROLINA

Appalachian State University
Department of Communication
P.O. Box 32039
Boone, NC 28608-2039
Phone: (828) 262-2221
Fax: (828) 262-2543
http://www.asucom.appstate.edu/index.
    php

Campbell University
Department of Mass Communication
P.O. Box 488
Buies Creek, NC 27506
Phone: (800) 334-4111
http://www.campbell.edu/coas/
    masscomm/index.htm

East Carolina University
School of Communication
102 Joyner East
Greenville, NC 27858-4353
Phone: (252) 328-4227
http://www.ecu.edu/comm

Elon University
School of Communications
2850 Campus Box
Elon, NC 27244-2010
Phone: (336) 278-5724
http://www.elon.edu/jourcomm

Gardner-Webb University
Department of Communication Studies

P.O. Box 997
Boiling Springs, NC 28017
Phone: (704) 406-3803
http://commstud.gardner-webb.edu/index.
    html

Johnson C. Smith University
Communications, Music, and Fine Arts
    Department
100 Beatties Ford Road
Charlotte, NC 28216
Phone: (704) 378-1000, ext. 1196
http://www.jcsu.edu/academics/
    artsandsciences/communication.htm

Lenoir-Rhyne College
Communication Program
625 7th Avenue NE
Hickory, NC 28601
Phone: (828) 328-1741
http://www.lrc.edu/com

University of North Carolina–Asheville
Mass Communication Department
Karpen Hall, CPO # 2120
One University Heights
Asheville, NC 28805
Phone: (828) 232-5027
Fax: (828) 232-2421
http://www.unca.edu/masscom

**University of North Carolina–
    Pembroke**
Department of Mass Communications
P.O. Box 1510
Pembroke, NC 28372-1510
Phone: (910) 522-5723
Fax: (910) 522-5795
http://www.uncp.edu/mc

Wingate University
Communication Studies
P.O. Box 159
Wingate, NC 28174
Phone: (800) 755-5550
http://www.wingate.edu/academics/
    communication

NORTH DAKOTA

North Dakota State University
Department of Communication
321 Minard Hall
P.O. Box 5075
Fargo, ND 58105-5075
Phone: (701) 231-7705
Fax: (701) 231-7784
http://www.ndsu.nodak.edu/
    communication

University of North Dakota
School of Communication
O'Kelly Hall 202
P.O. Box 7169
Grand Forks, ND 58202
Phone: (701) 777-2159
Fax: (701) 777-3090
http://www.und.edu/dept/scomm

OHIO

Cleveland State University
School of Communication
Music & Communication, Room MU233
2121 Euclid Avenue
Cleveland, OH 44115-2214
Phone: (216) 687-4630
Fax: (216) 687-5435
http://www.csuohio.edu/com

Franciscan University of Steubenville
Communication Arts
1235 University Boulevard
Steubenville, OH 43952
Phone: (740) 283-3771
http://www.franciscan.edu/home2/
    Content/Admissions/main.
    aspx?id=549

John Carroll University
Department of Communication
20700 North Park Boulevard
University Heights, OH 44118
Phone: (216) 397-1886
http://www.jcu.edu/communications

Marietta College
Mass Media Department
215 Fifth Street
Marietta, OH 45750
Phone: (740) 376-4802
Fax: (740) 376-4807
http://www.marietta.edu/%7Emass

Ohio State University
School of Communication
3016 Derby Hall
154 North Oval Mall
Columbus, OH 43210-1339
Phone: (614) 292-3400
Fax: (614) 292-2055
http://www.comm.ohio-state.edu

Ohio Wesleyan University
Journalism Program
61 South Sandusky Street
Delaware, OH 43015
Phone: (800) 922-8953
http://journalism.owu.edu

Otterbein College
Department of Communication
One Otterbein College
Westerville, OH 43081-2006
Phone: (614) 823-3380
Fax: (614) 823-3367
http://www.otterbein.edu/dept/COMM/
    index.htm

University of Akron
School of Communication
Kolbe Hall 108
Akron, OH 44325-1003
Phone: (330) 972-7600
http://www3.uakron.edu/schlcomm/page/
    index.htm

University of Cincinnati
Department of Communication
620 Teachers College
M.L. 184
Cincinnati, OH 45221-0184
Phone: (513) 556-4440
Fax: (513) 556-0899
http://asweb.artsci.uc.edu/communication/
    index.htm

University of Dayton
Department of Communication
300 College Park
Dayton, OH 45469
Phone: (937) 229-2028
http://artssciences.udayton.edu/
    Communication

University of Toledo
Department of Communication
University Hall, Room 4600
2801 W. Bancroft Street
Toledo, OH 43606
Phone: (419) 530-2005
http://communication.utoledo.edu/index2.
    html

Wright State University
Department of Communication
425 Millett Hall
3640 Colonel Glenn Hwy
Dayton, OH 45435-0001
Phone: (937) 775-2145
Fax: (937) 775-2148
http://www.cola.wright.edu/Dept/COM

Xavier University
Department of Communication Arts
3rd Floor, Schott Hall
Cincinnati, OH 45207
Phone: (513) 745-3088
http://www.xavier.edu/communication_arts

Youngstown State University
Department of English—Journalism
    Major
Youngstown, OH 44555
Phone: (330) 941-3414
http://www.as.ysu.edu/~english/english.
    htm

OKLAHOMA

East Central University
Department of Communication
1100 E. 14th Street
Ada, OK 74820
Phone: (580) 310-5485
http://www.ecok.edu/academics/schools/
    hss/comm/default.asp

Northeastern State University
Mass Communications Program
600 N. Grand Avenue
Tahlequah, OK 74464
Phone: (918) 456-5511; (800) 722-9614
http://www.nsuok.edu/departments

Oklahoma Baptist University
Department of Journalism and Public
    Relations
500 West University
Shawnee, OK 74804
Phone: (800) 654-3285; (405) 275-2850
http://www.okbu.edu/academics/cas/
    langandlit/departments/journalism.
    html

Oklahoma Christian University
Department of Communication
P.O. Box 11000
Oklahoma City, OK 73136-1100
Phone: (800) 877-5010
http://www.oc.edu/academics/
    arts%5Fsciences/communication

University of Central Oklahoma
Department of Mass Communication
Communications Building 210A
Edmond, OK 73034
Phone: (405) 974-5303
Fax: (405) 974-5125
http://www.libarts.ucok.edu/masscomm

University of Tulsa
Department of Communication
600 South College
Tulsa, OK 74104
Phone: (918) 631-2541
Fax: (918) 631-3809
http://www.cas.utulsa.edu/comm

OREGON

Linfield College
Department of Mass Communication
900 S.E. Baker Street
McMinnville, OR 97128
Phone: (503) 883-2521
http://www.linfield.edu/comm

Southern Oregon University
Department of Communication
1250 Siskiyou Boulevard
Ashland, OR 97520
Phone: (541) 552-6668
http://www.sou.edu/communication/
    index.html

University of Portland
Department of Communication Studies
5000 N. Willamette Boulevard
Portland, OR 97203-5798
Phone: (503) 943-7229; (800) 227-4568
http://college.up.edu/commstudies

PENNSYLVANIA

Bloomsburg University
Department of Mass Communication
1100 McCormick Center
Bloomsburg, PA 17815
Phone: (570) 389-4836
Fax: (570) 389-3983
http://departments.bloomu.edu/
    masscomm/newsite/index.htm

Cabrini College
English and Communication Program
610 King of Prussia Road
Radnor, PA 19087-3698
Phone: (610) 902-8100
http://www.cabrini.edu/default.
    aspx?pageid=355

Duquesne University
Department of Communication &
    Rhetorical Studies
340 College Hall
Pittsburgh, PA 15282
Phone: (412) 396-6460
Fax: (412) 396-4792
http://www.communication.duq.edu

Elizabethtown College
Communications Department
One Alpha Drive
Elizabethtown, PA 17022
Phone: (717) 361-1262
Fax: (717) 361-1180
http://www2.etown.edu/com

Indiana University of Pennsylvania
Department of Journalism
434 Davis Hall
Indiana, PA 15705
Phone: (724) 357-4411
Fax: (724) 357-7845
http://www.chss.iup.edu/journalism

La Salle University
Communication Department
1900 West Olney Avenue
Philadelphia, PA 19141-1199
Phone: (215) 951-1844
Fax: (215) 951-5043
http://www.lasalle.edu/academ/commun/
    home.htm

Lehigh University
Journalism and Communication Program
9 West Packer Avenue
Bethlehem, PA 18015
Phone: (610) 758-4180
http://www3.lehigh.edu/arts-sciences/
    casujournalism.asp

Lock Haven University of Pennsylvania
Communication Media Program
401 N. Fairview Street
Lock Haven, PA 17745
Phone: (570) 893-2011
http://www.lhup.edu/com%5Fphil

Lycoming College
Department of Communication
700 College Place
Williamsport, PA 17701
Phone: (570) 321-4000
http://www.lycoming.edu/comm

Millersville University
Department of Communication &
    Theatre
P.O. Box 1002
Millersville, PA 17551-0302
Phone: (717) 872-3233
Fax: (717) 871-2051
http://muweb.millersville.edu/~comm

Point Park University
Journalism and Mass Communication
    Program
201 Wood Street
Pittsburgh, PA 15222
Phone: (412) 391-4100
http://www.pointpark.edu/default.
    aspx?id=67

Shippensburg University
Department of Communication/Journalism

Wright Hall 103
1871 Old Main Drive
Shippensburg, PA 17257
Phone: (717) 477-1521
http://www.ship.edu/academic/artcom.html

University of Pennsylvania
Annenberg School for Communication
3620 Walnut Street
Philadelphia, PA 19104-6220
Phone: (215) 898-7041
Fax: (215) 898-2024
http://www.asc.upenn.edu/asc/
    application/default.asp

University of Pittsburgh
Department of Communication
1117 Cathedral of Learning
Pittsburgh, PA 15260
Phone: (412) 624-6567
Fax: (412) 624-1878
http://www.pitt.edu/~comm/index.html

Ursinus College
Media and Communication Studies
    Department
P.O. Box 1000
601 East Main Street
Collegeville, PA 19426-1000
Phone: (610) 409-3000
http://www.ursinus.edu/content.
    asp?page=AcademicPrograms/
    MediaCommunicationStudies.htm

RHODE ISLAND

University of Rhode Island
Journalism Department
10 Chafee Road, Suite 7
Kingston, RI 02881
Phone: (401) 874-2195
Fax: (401) 874-4450
http://www.uri.edu/artsci/jor/
    welcomeprosp.htm

SOUTH CAROLINA

Benedict College
English, Foreign Languages, and Mass
    Communication Department
1600 Harden Street
Columbia, SC 29204
Phone: (803) 253-5000
http://www.benedict.edu/divisions/acadaf/
    sch-humanities/eng_fl_mass/bc-eng_
    fl_mass.html

College of Charleston
Department of Communication

5 College Way
Charleston, SC 29401
Phone: (843) 953-7017
Fax: (843) 953-7037
http://www.cofc.edu/communication

Francis Marion University
Department of Communication
P.O. Box 100547
Florence, SC 29501
Phone: (843) 661-1362
http://www.fmarion.edu/academics/-
    1999995959

University of South Carolina–Aiken
Department of Communication
471 University Parkway
Aiken, SC 29801
Phone: (803) 648-6851
http://www.usca.edu/communications/
    index.html

SOUTH DAKOTA

Black Hills State University
Department of Mass Communications
1200 University Street, Unit 9502
Spearfish, SD 57799-9502
Phone: (605) 642-6343
Fax: (605) 642-6254
http://www.bhsu.edu/artssciences/
    masscomm/index.html

TENNESSEE

Austin Peay State University
Department of Communication &
    Theatre
P.O. Box 4446
Clarksville, TN 37044
Phone: (931) 221-7378
Fax: (931) 221-7265
http://www.apsu.edu/comm_thea

Christian Brothers University
English for Corporate Communications
    and Management Department
650 East Parkway
South Memphis, TN 38104
Phone: (901) 321-3000; (877) 321-4CBU
http://www.cbu.edu/Academics/
    englishcorp.html

Tennessee Technological University
Department of English
Henderson Hall Room 320
P.O. Box 5053
Cookeville, TN 38505

Phone: (931) 372-3343
Fax: (931) 372-3484
http://ttuweb.tntech.edu/english

TEXAS

Angelo State University
Department of Communications, Drama,
    and Journalism
2601 W. Avenue N
San Angelo, TX 76909
Phone: (915) 942-2031
http://www.angelo.edu/dept/cdj

Hardin Simmons University
Department of Communication
2200 Hickory, Box 16050
Abilene, TX 79698
Phone: (325) 670-1206
http://www.hsutx.edu/academics/
    communication/pages/index.html

Houston Baptist University
Department of Communications
7502 Fondren Road
Houston, TX 77074-3298
Phone: (281) 649-3520
http://fc.hbu.edu/arts&human/com/dept/
    page01.html

Lamar University
Department of Communication
4400 MLK Boulevard
P.O. Box 10009
Beaumont, TX 77710
Phone: (409) 880-7011
http://dept.lamar.edu/cofac/communication

Midwestern State University
Department of Journalism
3410 Taft Boulevard
Wichita Falls, TX 76308
Phone: (940) 397-4391
Fax: (940) 397-4909
http://finearts.mwsu.edu/journalism/
    index.asp

Prairie View A&M University
Department of Languages &
    Communication
P.O. Box 0156
Prairie View, TX 77446-2257
Phone: (936) 857-2215
Fax: (936) 857-2309
http://www.pvamu.edu/gridold/lang_com/
    index.html

Sam Houston State University
Department of Mass Communication

SHSU Box 2207
Huntsville, TX 77341
Phone: (936) 294-1341
Fax: (936) 294-1888
http://www.shsu.edu/%7Ecom_www

Southern Methodist University
Meadows School of the Arts—Division of
    Journalism
P.O. Box 750113
Dallas, TX 75275-0113
Phone: (214) 768-2775
http://www.smu.edu/meadows/journalism

Stephen F. Austin State University
Department of Communication
P.O. Box 13002 SFA Station
Nacogdoches, TX 75962
Phone: (936) 468-4604
Fax: (936) 468-7215
http://www.sfasu.edu/aas/comm/index.
    html

Texas A&M University–Commerce
Department of Mass Media,
    Communication, & Theatre
P.O. Box 3011
Commerce, TX 75429
Phone: (903) 886-5346
http://www.tamu-commerce.edu/mmct/
    jour-news/default.asp?ID=3

Texas A&M University–Kingsville
Department of Communications and
    Theatre Arts
MSC 178
Kingsville, TX 78363
Phone: (361) 593-3401
Fax: (361) 593-3402
http://www.tamuk.edu/artsci/webuser/as/
    art_science/com_t_art/comwp.html

Texas Lutheran University
Department of English and
    Communication Studies
1000 W. Court Street
Seguin, TX 78155
Phone: (830) 372-8050; (800) 771-8521
http://www.tlu.edu/academics/english/
    default.html

Texas Southern University
Department of Communications
3100 Cleburne Street
Houston, TX 77004
Phone: (713) 313-4287
Fax: (713) 313-7983
http://www.tsu.edu/academics/arts/
    program/communications.asp

Texas Wesleyan University
Mass Communication Department
1201 Wesleyan Street
Fort Worth, TX 76105
Phone: (817) 531-4444
http://web.txwes.edu/masscomm/index.
    html

Trinity University
Department of Communication
One Trinity Place #86
San Antonio, TX 78212-7200
Phone: (210) 999-8113
http://www.trinity.edu/departments/
    communication/index.html

University of Houston
School of Communication
101 Communications Building
Houston, TX 77204-3002
Phone: (713) 743-2873
http://www.hfac.uh.edu/comm

University of Texas at Arlington
Department of Communication
118 Fine Arts Building
P.O. Box 19107
Arlington, TX 76019
Phone: (817) 272-2163
http://www.uta.edu/communication

University of Texas at El Paso
Department of Communication
500 West University Avenue
El Paso, TX 79968
Phone: (915) 747-5129
http://academics.utep.edu/Default.
    aspx?alias=academics.utep.edu/comm

**University of Texas of the Permian
    Basin**
Department of Humanities and Fine Arts
    – Communication Program
4901 East University
Odessa, TX 79762
Phone: (432) 552-2020
http://www.utpb.edu/UTPB_
    Adm/AcademicAffairs/
    CollegeOfArtScience/
    DeptOfHumanitiesFineArts/
    ProgramOfMassCommunications/
    index_frame.htm

University of Texas–Pan American
Department of Communication
1201 West University Drive
Edinburg, TX 78541
Phone: (956) 381-UTPA
http://www.panam.edu/dept/comm

West Texas A&M University
Mass Communication Program
2501 4th Avenue
Canyon, TX 79016-0001
Phone: (806) 651-2000
http://www.wtamu.edu/academic/
    fah/art/MassCommWeb/
    masscommunicationindex.htm

UTAH

Utah State University
The Department of Journalism &
    Communication
4605 Old Main Hill
Logan, UT 84322-4605
Phone: (435) 797-3292
Fax: (435) 797-3973
http://www.usu.edu/communic

Weber State University
Department of Communication
1605 University Circle
Ogden, UT 84408-1605
Phone: (801) 626-8924
Fax: (801) 626-7975
http://weber.edu/communication/default.
    html

VERMONT

Saint Michael's College
Department of Journalism and Mass
    Communication
One Winooski Park
Colchester, VT 05439
Phone: (802) 654-2000
http://academics.smcvt.edu/journalism

VIRGINIA

Emory & Henry College
Mass Communications Department
P.O. Box 947
Emory, VA 24327-0947
Phone: (276) 944-4121
http://admissions.ehc.edu/cgi-bin/
    PPlus?VIEW=/public/academics/view.
    txt&currentdept=1012

James Madison University
School of Media Arts & Design
Harrison Hall 0276
MSC 2104
Harrisonburg, VA 22807
Phone: (540) 568-7007
Fax: (540) 568-7026
http://smad.jmu.edu

Liberty University
Department of Communication Studies
1971 University Boulevard
Lynchburg, VA 24502
Phone: (434) 582-2000
http://www.liberty.edu/academics/
    communications/coms/index.
    cfm?PID=109

Lynchburg College
Communication Studies Program
1501 Lakeside Drive
Lynchburg, VA 24501
Phone: (434) 544-8100
http://www.lynchburg.edu/academic/
    commstud/index.htm

Mary Baldwin College
Communication Department
Staunton, VA 24401
Phone: (540) 887-7019
http://www.mbc.edu/academic/
    departments/comm.asp

Radford University
Media Studies Department
Porterfield Hall 188
P.O. Box 6929
Radford, VA 24141
Phone: (540) 831-5531
Fax: (540) 831-6005
http://www.radford.edu/~mstd-web

Regent University
School of Communication and the Arts
1000 Regent University Drive
Virginia Beach, VA 23464
Phone: (888) 777-7729
Fax: (757) 226-4291
http://www.regent.edu/acad/schcom

University of Richmond
Department of Journalism
28 Westhampton Way
University of Richmond, VA 23173
Phone: (800) 700-1662
http://journalism.richmond.edu

Virginia Commonwealth University
College of Humanities and Sciences
School of Mass Communications
901 West Main Street, Room 2216
P.O. Box 842034
Richmond, VA 23284-2034
Phone: (804) 828-2660
Fax: (804) 828-9175
http://www.has.vcu.edu/mac

**Virginia Polytechnic Institute and
    State University**
Department of Communication
121 Shanks Hall
Mail Code 0311
Blacksburg, VA 24061
Phone: (540) 231-7136
http://www.comm.vt.edu

Virginia Union University
Department of Mass Communication
1500 North Lombardy Street
Richmond, VA 23220
Phone: (804) 257-5600
http://www.vuu.edu

WASHINGTON

Central Washington University
Communication Department
400 E. University Way
Ellensburg, WA 98926-7438
Phone: (509) 963-1066
Fax: (509) 963-1060
http://www.cwu.edu/~comm

Eastern Washington University
Journalism Program
Spokane Center, Room 313
705 West 1st Avenue
Spokane, WA 99201
Phone: (509) 623-4347
Fax: (509) 623-4238
http://www.ewu.edu/x2011.xml

Gonzaga University
Department of Communication Arts
502 E. Boone Avenue
AD Box 22
Spokane, WA 99258
Phone: (509) 323-6662
Fax: (509) 323-5718
http://www.gonzaga.edu/Academics/
    Colleges+and+Schools/
    College+of+Arts+and+Sciences/
    Communication+Arts/default.htm

Pacific Lutheran University
School of the Arts and Communication
Department of Communication and
    Theatre
Tacoma, WA 98447
Phone: (253) 535-7150
http://www.plu.edu/%7Ecoth/comm/
    index.html

Seattle University
Communication Department

901 12th Avenue
P.O. Box 222000
Seattle, WA 98122-1090
Phone: (206) 296-5327
http://www.seattleu.edu/artsci/
    communication

Walla Walla College
Communications Department
204 S. College Avenue
College Place, WA 99324
Phone: (509) 527-2832
Fax: (509) 527-2253
http://www.wwc.edu/academics/
    departments/communications

Washington State University
Edward R. Murrow School of
    Communication
101 Communication Addition
P.O. Box 642520
Pullman, WA 99164-0000
Phone: (509) 335-1556
http://communication.wsu.edu

Western Washington University
Department of Journalism
MS 9161
516 High Street
Bellingham, WA 98225-9161
Phone: (360) 650-3252
Fax: (360) 650-2848
http://www.ac.wwu.edu/~journal

Whitworth College
Communication Studies Department
300 W. Hawthorne Road
MS 0307
Spokane, WA 99251
Phone: (509) 777-4739
Fax: (509) 777-4512
http://www.whitworth.edu/academic/
    Department/CommunicationStudies/
    index.asp

WEST VIRGINIA

Bethany College
Department of Communication
Bethany, WV 26032
Phone: (304) 829-7000
http://www.bethanywv.edu/
    communication

WISCONSIN

University of Wisconsin–La Crosse
Communication Studies Department

346 Center for the Arts
La Crosse, WI 54601-9959
Phone: (608) 785-8519
Fax: (608) 785-6719
http://perth.uwlax.edu/CommStudies

University of Wisconsin–Madison
School of Journalism & Mass
    Communication
5115 Vilas Hall
821 University Avenue
Madison, WI 53706
Phone: (608) 262-3690
Fax: (608) 262-1361
http://www.journalism.wisc.edu

University of Wisconsin–Madison
Life Sciences Communication
College of Agriculture & Life Sciences
440 Henry Mall
Madison, WI 53706

Phone: (608) 262-1464
http://www.wisc.edu/agjourn

University of Wisconsin–Milwaukee
Department of Journalism and Mass
    Communication
117 Johnston Hall
P.O. Box 413
Milwaukee, WI 53201
Phone: (414) 229-4436
Fax: (414) 229-2411
http://www.uwm.edu/Dept/JMC

University of Wisconsin–Stevens Point
College of Fine Arts & Communication
Division of Communication
Noel Fine Arts Center, Room 101
Stevens Point, WI 54481
Phone: (715) 346-4920
http://www.uwsp.edu/comm

University of Wisconsin–Whitewater
College of Arts & Communication
Communication Department
464 Heide Hall
Whitewater, WI 53190
Phone: (262) 472-1034
http://academics.uww.edu/CAC/
    Communication/index.htm

WYOMING

University of Wyoming
Department of Communication and
    Journalism, Department 3904
1000 E. University Avenue
Laramie, WY 82071
Phone: (307) 766-3122
http://uwadmnweb.uwyo.edu/COJO

C. PHOTOJOURNALISM PROGRAMS

The National Press Photographers Association (NPPA) provides the following list of schools that have a program, a course, or special interest in photojournalism. This list is constantly being updated; see http://www.nppa.org/ professional_development/students/schools_and_colleges/ schools.html for more information. However, this is just a sampling of programs. In addition to this list, other schools of journalism also offer photojournalism courses, so be sure to check out any program of interest to determine its curriculum. An Internet search for "photojournalism" can also uncover new and additional programs.

FOUR-YEAR COLLEGES AND UNIVERSITIES

ALABAMA

University of Alabama
College of Communication and
    Information Sciences
Department of Journalism
P.O. Box 870172
Tuscaloosa, AL 35487-0172
Phone: (205) 348-4787
Fax: (205) 348-3836
http://www.ccom.ua.edu

ARIZONA

Northern Arizona University
School of Communication
South San Francisco Street
Flagstaff, AZ 86011
Phone: (928) 523-0460
http://www.comm.nau.edu/; http://www.
    schwepkerphoto.com/nau.html

ARKANSAS

Arkansas State University
Department of Journalism and Printing
Photojournalism Emphasis Program
P.O. Box 1930
State University, AR 72467
Phone: (870) 972-3075
http://www.clt.astate.edu/photojournalism

CALIFORNIA

Brooks Institute of Photography
801 Alston Road
Santa Barbara, CA 93108
Phone: (888) 304-FILM
http://www.brooks.edu

California State Polytechnic University, Pomona
College of Letters, Arts, and Social Sciences
Communication Department
3801 West Temple Avenue
Pomona, CA 91768

Phone: (909) 869-759
http://www.csupomona.edu/~comdept

California State University, Fresno
Mass Communication & Journalism
McKee Fisk Building, Room 238
2225 E. San Ramon Avenue
M/S MF10
Fresno, CA 93740-8029
Phone: (559) 278-2087
Fax: (559) 278-4995
http://www.csufresno.edu/MCJ

California State University, Fullerton
College of Communications
Fullerton, CA 92831
Phone: (714) 278-2011
http://communications.fullerton.edu

San Francisco State University
Department of Journalism,
    Photojournalism Sequence
1600 Holloway Avenue
San Francisco, CA 94132

Phone: (415) 338-1111
http://www.journalism.sfsu.edu/
    departmentinfo/photoseq.htm

San Jose State University
School of Journalism and Mass
    Communications
Photojournalism Program
San Jose, CA 95192-0055
Phone: (408) 924-3245
Fax: (408) 924-3229
http://jmcweb.sjsu.edu/dunleavy/index.html

University of LaVerne
1950 Third Street
La Verne, CA 91750
Phone: Photography: (909) 593-3511,
    ext. 4281; Journalism: (909) 392-2712
http://www.ulv.edu/photo; http://www.
    ulv.edu/communications/majors/
    majors.html

COLORADO

Colorado State University
Department of Journalism and Technical
    Communication
Fort Collins, CO 80523
Phone: (970) 491-6310
Fax: (970) 491-2908
http://www.colostate.edu/depts/tj

University of Colorado
School of Journalism and Mass
    Communication
478 UCB
Boulder, CO 80309-0478
Phone: (303) 492-4364
Fax: (303) 492-0969
http://www.colorado.edu/journalism

DISTRICT OF COLUMBIA

American University
    School of Communication
4400 Massachusetts Avenue NW
Washington, DC 20016
Phone: (202) 885-2060
Fax: (202) 885-2019
http://www.soc.american.edu

Corcoran College of Art and Design
Photography Department
500 Seventeenth Street NW
Washington, DC 20006-4804
Phone: (202) 639-1801
http://www.corcoran.edu/departments/
    index.asp?bc=p2&Dept_ID=2

FLORIDA

University of Central Florida
Department of Journalism
2070 Weimer Hall
P.O. Box 118400
Gainesville, FL 32611-8400
Phone: (352) 392-0500
http://www.jou.ufl.edu/default.asp

University of Florida
College of Journalism and
    Communications
Gainesville, FL 32611-8400
Phone: (352) 392-0466
Fax: (352) 392-3919
http://www.jou.ufl.edu

University of Miami
School of Communication
Frances L. Wolfson Communication
    Building
5100 Brunson Drive
Coral Gables, FL 33146
Phone: (305) 284-2265
http://www.miami.edu/com

GEORGIA

University of Georgia
Henry W. Grady College of Journalism
    and Mass Communication
Athens, GA 30602-3018
Phone: (706) 542-1704
Fax: (706) 542-2183
http://www.grady.uga.edu

ILLINOIS

Columbia College Chicago
Photography Department
600 South Michigan Avenue
Chicago, IL 60605-1996
Phone: (312) 344-7230
http://www.colum.edu/undergraduate/
    photo/contact/contact.php

Eastern Illinois University
Department of Journalism
600 Lincoln Avenue
Charleston, IL 61920-3099
Phone: (217) 581-6003
Fax: (217) 581-7188
http://www.eiu.edu/%7Ejournal

Southern Illinois University,
    Carbondale
School of Journalism

Department of Cinema and Photography
Carbondale, IL 62901-6601
Phone: (618) 536-3361
Fax: (618) 453-5200
http://cp.siu.edu

INDIANA

Ball State University
College of Communication, Information,
    and Media
Art and Journalism #300
Muncie, IN 47306-0485
Phone: (765) 285-8200
Fax: (765) 285-7997
http://www.bsu.edu/journalism/
    academicprogram/photojournalism

Indiana University
School of Journalism and Henry Radford
    Hope School of Fine Arts
940 E. Seventh Street; 1201 E. Seventh
    Street, Room 123
Bloomington, IN 47405
Phone: (812) 855-9247;
    (812) 855-7766
Fax: (812) 855-0901; (812) 855-7498
http://www.journalism.indiana.edu/;
    http://www.fa.indiana.edu

KANSAS

Kansas State University
A.Q. Miller School of Journalism and
    Mass Communications
Manhattan, KS 66506-1501
Phone: (785) 532-6890
Fax: (785) 532-5484
http://jmc.ksu.edu/

Pittsburg State University
Department of Photojournalism
Grubbs Hall 434
Pittsburg, KS 66762
Phone: (620) 235-4716
http://www.pittstate.edu/comm/pages/
    photoj.html

KENTUCKY

Western Kentucky University
School of Journalism and Broadcasting
Photojournalism Program
216 Mass Media & Technology Hall
1906 College Heights Boulevard #1070
Bowling Green, KY 42101
Phone: (270) 745-4144
Fax: (270) 745-5835
http://www.wku.edu/Journalism/Photo/
    index.htm

MASSACHUSETTS

Boston University
College of Communication
Photojournalism Program
640 Commonwealth Avenue
Boston, MA 02215
Phone: (617) 353-3450
http://www.bu.edu/com/jo/photo.html

MICHIGAN

Michigan State University
School of Journalism
East Lansing, MI 48824-1212
Phone: (517) 355-1520
Fax: (517) 355-7710
http://www.jrn.msu.edu

MISSOURI

University of Missouri
Missouri School of Journalism
Programs in Photojournalism
120 Neff Hall
Columbia, MO 65211-1200
Phone: (573) 882-1908
Fax: (573) 884-5400
http://journalism.missouri.edu

MONTANA

University of Montana
School of Journalism
Missoula, MT 59812
Phone: (406) 243-2238
http://www.umt.edu/journalism/academic_
    programs/photo_option.html

NEBRASKA

University of Nebraska–Lincoln
College of Journalism and Mass
    Communications
P.O. Box 880443
Lincoln, NE 68588-0443
Phone: (402) 472-3041
Fax: (402) 472-8597
http://journalism.unl.edu

NEW YORK

Rochester Institute of Technology
School of Photographic Arts and
    Sciences
Photojournalism Program
One Lomb Memorial Drive
Rochester, NY 14623

Phone: (585) 475-2411
http://www.rit.edu/~661www/
    departments/pj_photo.html

Syracuse University
S.I. Newhouse School of Public
    Communications
Syracuse, NY 13244
Phone: (315) 443-2301
Fax: (315) 443-3946
http://newhouse.syr.edu

NORTH CAROLINA

Gardner-Webb University
Department of Communication Studies,
    Photojournalism Sequence
P.O. Box 817
Boiling Springs, NC 28017
Phone: (704) 406-4000
http://commstud.gardner-webb.edu/
    photoj.html

**University of North Carolina at
    Chapel Hill**
School of Journalism and Mass
    Communication
Campus Box #3365
Chapel Hill, NC 27599-3365
Phone: (919) 962-1204
Fax: (919) 962-0620
http://www.jomc.unc.edu

NORTH DAKOTA

University of North Dakota
School of Communication
O'Kelly Hall 202
P.O. Box 7169
Grand Forks, ND 58202
Phone: (701) 777-4785
Fax: (701) 777-3090
http://www.und.edu/dept/scomm

OHIO

Kent State University
School of Journalism and Mass
    Communication
Undergraduate Photojournalism
    Program
Kent, OH 44242-0001
Phone: (330) 672-8725
Fax: (330) 672-4064
http://www.jmc.kent.edu/students/
    prospective/mjr09.htm

Ohio University
School of Visual Communication

301 Siegfred Hall
Athens, OH 45701
Phone: (740) 593-4898
Fax: (740) 593-0190
http://www.commcoll.ohiou.edu

PENNSYLVANIA

Pennsylvania State University
College of Communications
201 Carnegie Building
University Park, PA 16802
Phone: (814) 863-1484
Fax: (814) 863-8044
http://www.psu.edu/dept/comm

TENNESSEE

Middle Tennessee State University
School of Journalism
1301 East Main Street
Murfreesboro, TN 37132-0001
Phone: (615) 898-2300
http://www.mtsu.edu/~jour

TEXAS

Abilene Christian University
College of Arts and Sciences
Department of Journalism and Mass
    Communication
ACU Box 27892
Abilene, TX 79699-7892
Phone: (325) 674-2296
http://www.acu.edu/academics/cas/jmc.
    html

Baylor University
Department of Journalism
P.O. Box 97353
Waco, TX 76798-7353
Phone: (254) 710-3261
Fax: (254) 710-3363
http://www.baylor.edu/journalism

San Antonio College
Journalism-Photography Program
1300 San Pedro Avenue
San Antonio, TX 78212-4299
Phone: (210) 733-2870
Fax: (210) 733-2868
http://www.accd.edu/sac/j-p/jlsm.html

University of North Texas
Department of Journalism
P.O. Box 311277
Denton, TX 76203
Phone: (940) 565-2205
http://www.jour.unt.edu

The University of Texas at Austin
School of Journalism
Photojournalism Program
1 University Station A1000
Austin, TX 78712
Phone: (512) 471-1845
Fax: (512) 471-7979
http://journalism.utexas.edu/areas/
    photojournalism.html

VERMONT

Lyndon State College
Digital and Graphic Arts Department
1001 College Road
P.O. Box 919
Lyndonville, VT 05851
Phone: (802) 626-6200
http://www.lyndonstate.edu/dga

University of Oregon
School of Journalism and Communication
1275 University of Oregon
Eugene, OR 97403-1275
Phone: (541) 346-3738
Fax: (541) 346-0682
http://jcomm.uoregon.edu

COMMUNITY COLLEGES

CALIFORNIA

Pierce College
6201 Winnetka Avenue
Woodland Hills, CA 91371
Phone: (818) 719-6401
http://www.piercecollege.edu

MARYLAND

**Defense Information School (United
    States Military Training)**
6500 Mapes Road
Ft. George G. Meade, MD 20755-5620

Phone: (301) 677-2968
http://www.dinfos.osd.mil

MICHIGAN

Lansing Community College
2301 – Visual Arts and Media
    Department
208A Academic and Office Facility
315 North Grand Avenue
Lansing, MI 48933
Phone: (517) 483-9651
Fax: (517) 483-1050
http://www.lansing.cc.mi.us/vam/photo

NEW YORK

LaGuardia Community College
Commercial Photography Program
31-10 Thomson Avenue
Long Island City, NY 11101
Phone: (718) 349-4028
http://www.lagcc.cuny.edu/humanities/
    visart/photo/foto.details.html

NORTH CAROLINA

Randolph Community College
629 Industrial Park Avenue
P.O. Box 1009
Asheboro, NC 27204-1009
Phone: (336) 633-0285
http://www.randolph.cc.nc.us/edprog/
    curr/phjour.html

INTERNATIONAL PROGRAMS

CANADA

Loyalist College
Photojournalism Program
Wallbridge-Loyalist Road, P.O. Box 4200
Belleville, Ontario, Canada K8N 2B9

Phone: (613) 969-1913
Fax: (613) 962-1376
http://www.loyalistc.on.ca/Loyalist/
    index_e.aspx?DetailID=230

**Southern Alberta Institute of
    Technology**
Information & Communications
    Department
Photojournalism Major
1301 – 16th Avenue Northwest
Calgary, Alberta, Canada T2M 0L4
Phone: (403) 284-8543
http://www.sait.ca/calendars/daycalendar/
    courses/aja.htm

DENMARK

The Danish School of Journalism
Phone: (+45) 89 440 440
E-mail: info@djh.dk
http://afdelinger.djh.dk/international

NETHERLANDS

The Hogeschool van Utrecht (HvU)
School of Journalism
International Office
P.O. Box 13272
3507 LG Utrecht
The Netherlands
Phone: 011 +31 (0)30 2758928
Fax: 011 +31 (0)30 2586448
E-mail: io@hvu.nl
http://www.hvu-international.com/;
http://svj.intranet.fcj.hvu.nl/index.
    cfm?actie=infopagina&CNr=1233&R
    Nr=4074

D. OTHER CERTIFICATE AND TRAINING PROGRAMS

American Press Institute
11690 Sunrise Valley Drive
Reston, Virginia 20191-1498
Phone: (703) 620-3611
Fax: (703) 620-5814
E-mail: info@americanpressinstitute.org
http://www.americanpressinstitute.org

Journalism Training.org
c/o Society of Professional Journalists

3909 N. Meridian Street
Indianapolis, IN 46208
Phone: (317) 927-8000
Fax: (317) 920-4789
http://www.journalismtraining.org/action/
    home

**Knight Center for Specialized
    Journalism**
University of Maryland

1117 Cole Field House
College Park, MD 20742-1024
Phone: (301) 405-4817
E-mail: knight@umd.edu

National Endowment for the Arts
National Initiative: Journalism Institutes
1100 Pennsylvania Avenue NW
Washington, DC 20506
http://www.nea.gov/national/aji/index.html

National Institute for Computer-Assisted Reporting (part of Investigative Reporters and Editors, Inc. and the Missouri School of Journalism)
http://www.nicar.org

The Poynter Institute
801 Third Street South
St. Petersburg, FL 33701
Phone: (888) 769-6837
http://www.poynter.org

Robert C. Maynard Institute for Journalism Education
1211 Preservation Park Way
Oakland, CA 94612
Phone: (510) 891-9202
Fax: (510) 891-9565
E-mail: mije@maynardije.org
http://www.maynardije.org

Society of Professional Journalists
SPJ/Bloomberg Journalism Training Program

Eugene S. Pulliam National Journalism Center
3909 N. Meridian Street
Indianapolis, IN 46208
Phone: (317) 927-8000
Fax: (317) 920-4789
http://www.spj.org/spj_training.asp

APPENDIX II
PROFESSIONAL ASSOCIATIONS

A. NEWSPAPERS

American Association of Sunday and Features Editors (AASFE)
AASFE Executive Director
College of Journalism
1117 Journalism Building
University of Maryland
College Park, MD 20742
Phone: (301) 314-2631
E-mail: aasfe@jmail.umd.edu
http://www.aasfe.org

American Society of Newspaper Editors
11690B Sunrise Valley Drive
Reston, VA 20191
Phone: (703) 453-1122
Fax: (703) 453-1133
E-mail: asne@asne.org
http://www.asne.org

Association of Alternative Newsweeklies
1020 Sixteenth Street NW, 4th Floor
Washington, DC 20036-5702
Phone: (202) 822-1955
Fax: (202) 822-0929
E-mail: aan@aan.org
http://aan.org/gyrobase/Aan

Association of Opinion Page Editors
http://www.psu.edu/dept/comm/aope

Inland Press Association/Inland Press Foundation
701 Lee Street
Suite 925
Des Plaines, IL 60016

Phone: (847) 795-0380
Fax: (847) 795-0385
http://www.inlandpress.org

International Society of Weekly Newspaper Editors
Institute of International Studies
Missouri Southern State University
3950 E. Newman Road
Joplin, MO 64801-1595
Phone: (417) 625-9736
Fax: (417) 659-4445
http://www.mssu.edu/iswne

National Newspaper Association
P.O. Box 7540
Columbia, MO 65205-7540
Phone: (800) 829-4NNA (4662); (573) 882-5800
Fax: (573) 884-5490
http://www.nna.org

National Society of Newspaper Columnists
1345 Fillmore Street
Suite 507
San Francisco, CA 94115
Phone: (415) 563-5403
Fax: (415) 563-5403
http://www.columnists.com

Newspaper Association of America
1921 Gallows Road
Suite 600
Vienna, VA 22182

Phone: (703) 902-1600
Fax: (703) 917-0636
http://www.naa.org

The Newspaper Guild
501 Third Street NW, 6th Floor
Washington, DC 20001
Phone: (202) 434-7177
Fax: (202) 434-1472
http://www.newsguild.org

Southern Newspaper Publishers Association
Mailing address:
P.O. Box 28875
Atlanta, GA 30358
Street address:
Southern Newspaper Publishers Association
5775 Peachtree-Dunwoody Road
Building G, Suite 100
Atlanta, GA 30342
Phone: (404) 256-0444
Fax: (404) 252-9135
http://www.snpa.org

World Association of Newspapers
7 Rue Geoffroy St. Hilaire
75005 Paris, France
Phone: (33-1) 47 42 85 00
Fax: (33-1) 47 42 49 48
E-mail: contact_us@wan.asso.fr
http://www.wan-press.org

B. MAGAZINES

American Society of Magazine Editors
Part of the Magazine Publishers of America
810 Seventh Avenue, 24th Floor
New York, NY 10019
Phone: (212) 872-3700
http://www.magazine.org/Editorial

City and Regional Magazine Association
4929 Wilshire Boulevard,
   Suite 428

Los Angeles, CA 90010
Phone: (323) 937-5514
Fax: (323) 937-0959
http://www.citymag.org

International Federation of the Periodical Press (FIPP)
Queens House
55-56 Lincoln's Inn Fields
London WC2A 3LJ United Kingdom

Phone: 011 +44 (0) 20 7404 4169
Fax: 011 +44 (0) 20 7404 4170
E-mail: info@fipp.com
http://www.fipp.com

C. BROADCASTING

American Sportscasters Association
225 Broadway
Suite 2030
New York, NY 10007
Phone: (212) 227-8080
Fax: (212) 571-0556
http://www.americansportscasters.com

**American Women in Radio and
Television**
8405 Greensboro Drive
Suite 800
McLean, VA 22102
Phone: (703) 506-3290
Fax: (703) 506-3266
http://www.awrt.org

**Association of Independents in Radio
(AIR)**
328 Flatbush Avenue, #322
Brooklyn, NY 11238
Phone: (888) 937-2477
http://www.airmedia.org

**The Broadcast Film Critics
Association**
http://www.bfca.org

**National Association of Broadcast
Employees and Technicians**
http://www.nabetcwa.org/about

National Association of Broadcasters
1771 N Street NW
Washington, DC 20036
Phone: (202) 429-5300
Fax: (202) 429-4199
http://www.nab.org

**National Federation of Community
Broadcasters (NFCB)**
1970 Broadway
Suite 1000
Oakland, CA 94612
Phone: (510) 451-8200
Fax: (510) 451-8208
http://www.nfcb.org

**Public Radio News Directors,
Incorporated**
http://www.prndi.org

**Public Radio Program Directors
Association, Inc. (PRPD)**
517 Ocean Front Walk
Suite 10
Venice, CA 90291
Phone: (310) 664-1591
Fax: (310) 664-1592
http://www.prpd.org

**Radio-Television News Directors
Association and Foundation**
1600 K Street NW
Suite 700
Washington, DC 20006-2838
Phone: (202) 659-6510
Fax: (202) 223-4007
http://www.rtnda.org

D. NEW MEDIA

The Internet Press Guild
http://www.netpress.org/index.html

The Online News Association
P.O. Box 30702
Bethesda, MD 20824
Phone: (617) 450-7023

Fax: (617) 450-2974
http://www.onlinenewsassociation.org

Online Publishers Association
500 Seventh Avenue, 14th Floor
New York, NY 10018
Phone: (212) 600-6342

Fax: (212) 600-6349
http://www.online-publishers.org/
?pg=contact

E. EDITING, WRITING, AND REPORTING: GENERAL AND SPECIALTIES

**American Copy Editors Society
(ACES)**
P.O. Box 250239
Columbia University Station
New York, NY 10025
Fax: (703) 620-4557
http://www.copydesk.org

**American Society of Business
Publication Editors**
214 North Hale Street
Wheaton, IL 60187
Phone: (630) 510-4588
Fax: (630) 510-4501

E-mail: info@asbpe.org
http://www.asbe.org

**American Society of Journalists and
Authors**
1501 Broadway
Suite 302
New York, NY 10036
Phone: (212) 997-0947
Fax: (212) 937-2315
http://www.asja.org

Associated Press Managing Editors
450 West 33rd Street

New York, NY 10001
Phone: (212) 621-1838
Fax: (212) 506-6102
E-mail: apme@ap.org
http://www.apme.com

Associated Press Sports Editors
http://apse.dallasnews.com

**The Association of American Editorial
Cartoonists (AAEC)**
P.O. Box 37669
Raleigh, NC 27627
Phone: (919) 329-8129

Fax: (919) 772-6007
http://info.detnews.com/aaec/index.cfm

**Association of Capitol Reporters and
Editors**
http://www.capitolbeat.org

Association of Food Journalists
http://www.afjonline.com

**Association of Health Care Journalists
(AHCJ)**
Missouri School of Journalism
10 Neff Hall
Columbia, MO 65211
Phone: (573) 884-5606
Fax: (573) 884-5609
http://www.healthjournalism.org

The Canadian Association of Journalists
Algonquin College
1385 Woodroffe Avenue, B224
Ottawa, ON K2G 1V8
Phone: (613) 526-8061
Fax: (613) 521-3904
http://www.eagle.ca/caj

Committee to Protect Journalists (CPJ)
330 7th Avenue, 11th Floor
New York, NY 10001
Phone: (212) 465-1004
Fax: (212) 465-9568
http://www.cpj.org

**Council for the Advancement of
Science Writing**
P.O. Box 910
Hedgesville, WV 25427
Phone: (304) 754-5077
http://www.casw.org

Criminal Justice Journalists
720 Seventh Street NW, Third Floor
Washington, DC 20001
Phone: (202) 448-1717
http://reporters.net/cjj/index.html

Editorial Freelancers Association
71 West 23rd Street
Suite 1910
New York, NY 10010-4181
Phone: (212) 929-5400; (866) 929-5400
Fax: (212) 929-5439; (866) 929-5439
info@the-efa.org
http://www.the-efa.org

Education Writers Association
2122 P Street NW
Suite 201
Washington, DC 20037
Phone: (202) 452-9830

Fax: (202) 452-9837
E-mail: ewa@ewa.org
http://www.ewa.org

International Center for Journalists
1616 H Street NW, Third Floor
Washington, DC 20006
Phone: (202) 737-3700
Fax: (202) 737-0530
E-mail: editor@icfj.org
http://www.icfj.org

**The International Federation of Film
Critics**
http://www.fipresci.org

International Federation of Journalists
IPC-Residence Palace, Bloc C
Rue de la Loi 155
B-1040 Brussels
Belgium
Phone: 011-32-2-235 22 00
Fax: 011-32-2-235 22 19
E-mail: ifj@ifj.org
http://www.ifj.org

**International Food Wine & Travel
Writers Association (IFW&TWA)**
1142 South Diamond Bar Boulevard #177
Diamond Bar, CA 91765-2203
Phone: (877) 439-8929
Fax: (877) 432-8929
http://www.ofwtwa.org

Investigative Reporters & Editors
National Institute for Computer-Assisted
Reporting
138 Neff Hall
Missouri School of Journalism
Columbia, MO 65211
Phone: (573) 882-2042
Fax: (573) 882-5431
E-mail: info@ire.org
http://www.ire.org

The Midwest Travel Writers Association
http://www.mtwa.org/index.html

**National Association of Science Writers
(NASW)**
P.O. Box 890
Hedgesville, WV 25427
Phone: (304) 754-5077
Fax: (304) 754-5076
http://www.nasw.org

National Conference of Editorial Writers
3899 N. Front Street
Harrisburg, PA 17110
Phone: (717) 703-3015
Fax: (717) 703-3014

E-mail: ncew@pa-news.org
http://www.ncew.org

National Press Club
529 14th Street NW, 13th Floor
Washington, DC 20045
Phone: (202) 662-7500
http://www.press.org

National Writers Union
113 University Place, Sixth Floor
New York, NY 10003
Phone: (212) 254-0279
Fax: (212) 254-0673
http://www.nwu.org
nwu@nwu.org

**North American Travel Journalists
Association (NATJA)**
531 Main Street #902
El Segundo, CA 90245
Phone: (310) 836-8712
Fax: (310) 836-8769
http://www.natja.org

The Online Film Critics Society
http://ofcs.rottentomatoes.com

Organization of News Ombudsmen
c/o Gina Lubrano
Executive Secretary
P.O. Box 120191
San Diego, CA 92112
Phone: (619) 293-1525
E-mail: ono@uniontrib.com
http://www.newsombudsmen.org

**Outdoor Writers Association of
California**
http://www.owac.org

Regional Reporters Association
Ben Franklin Station
P.O. Box 254
Washington, DC 20044
Phone: (202) 408-2705
E-mail: president@rra.org
http://www.rra.org

Religion Newswriters Association
P.O. Box 2037
Westerville, OH 43086
Phone: (614) 891-9001
Fax: (614) 891-9774
http://www.rna.org

**The Reporters Committee for Freedom
of the Press**
1101 Wilson Boulevard
Suite 1100
Arlington, VA 22209

Phone: (800) 336-4243; (703) 807-2100
E-mail: rcfp@rcfp.org
http://www.rcfp.org

Society of American Business Editors and Writers
Missouri School of Journalism
134 Neff Annex
Columbia, MO 65211-1200
Phone: (573) 882-7862
Fax: (573) 884-1372
E-mail: sabew@missouri.edu
http://www.sabew.org

Society of American Travel Writers (SATW)
1500 Sunday Drive, Suite 102
Raleigh, NC 27607
Phone: (919) 861-5586

Fax: (919) 787-4916
http://www.satw.org/satw/index.asp

Society of Environmental Journalists
P.O. Box 2492
Jenkintown, PA 19046
Phone: (215) 884-8174
Fax: (215) 884-8175
E-mail: sej@sej.org
http://www.sej.org

Society of Professional Journalists
Eugene S. Pulliam National Journalism Center
3909 N. Meridian Street
Indianapolis, IN 46208
Phone: (317) 927-8000
Fax: (317) 920-4789
http://www.spj.org

Special Library Association—News Division
331 South Patrick Street
Alexandria, VA 22314-3501
Phone: (703) 647-4900
Fax: (703) 647-4901
http://www.ibiblio.org/slanews/sland.htm

Washington Independent Writers
220 Woodward Building
733 15th Street NW
Washington, DC 20005
Phone: (202) 737-9500
Fax: (202) 638-7800
E-mail: info@washwriter.org
http://www.washwriter.org

F. SPECIAL INTEREST GROUPS

Asian American Journalists Association
1182 Market Street
Suite 320
San Francisco, CA 94102
Phone: (415) 346-2051
Fax: (415) 346-6343
E-mail: National@aaja.org
http://www.aaja.org

Association for Women in Communications
780 Ritchie Highway
Suite 28-S
Severna Park, MD 21146
Phone: (410) 544-7442
Fax: (410) 544-4640
http://www.womcom.org

Association for Women in Sports Media (AWSM)
E-mail: Info@awsmonline.org
http://www.awsmonline.org

The Association of Young Journalists
University of Maryland Philip Merrill College of Journalism
1117 Journalism Building
College Park, MD 20742-7111
http://www.youngjournos.org

California Chicano News Media Association
USC Annenberg School of Journalism

One California Plaza
300 S. Grand Avenue
Suite 3950
Los Angeles, CA 90071-8110
Phone: (213) 437-4408
Fax: (213) 437-4423
E-mail: ccnmainfo@ccnma.org
http://www.ccnma.org

Criminal Justice Journalists
Jerry Lee Center of Criminology
720 Seventh Street NW, Third Floor
Washington, DC 20001
http://reporters.net/cjj/index.html

Journalism and Women Symposium
10 Brainerd Road
Summit, NJ 07901
Phone: (908) 608-0976
http://www.jaws.org

National Arab American Journalists Association
http://www.journalismandthearabworld.com/index.php?option=content&pcontent=1&task=view&id=39&Itemid=44
http://www.hanania.com/caajc/caajc.htm

National Association for Multi-Ethnicity in Communications (NAMIC), Inc.
336 West 37th Street
Suite 302
New York, NY 10018

Phone: (212) 594-5985
Fax: (212) 594-8391
http://www.namic.com

National Association of Black Journalists
University of Maryland
8701-A Adelphi Road
Adelphi, MD 20783-1716
Phone: (301) 445-7100
Fax: (301) 445-7101
E-mail: nabj@nabj.org
http://www.nabj.org

National Association of Hispanic Journalists
1000 National Press Building
529 14th Street NW
Washington, DC 20045-2001
Phone: (202) 662-7145
Fax: (202) 662-7144
E-mail: nahj@nahj.org
http://www.nahj.org

National Association of Minority Media Executives
1921 Gallows Road
Suite 600
Vienna, VA 22182
Phone: (703) 893-2410; (888) 968-7658
Fax: (703) 893-2414
info@namme.org
http://www.namme.org

National Federation of Press Women
P.O. Box 5556
Arlington, VA 22205
Phone: (800) 780-2715
Fax: (703) 812-4555
http://www.nfpw.org

National Lesbian and Gay Journalists
Association
1420 K Street NW
Suite 910
Washington, DC 20005
Phone: (202) 588-9888
Fax: (202) 588-1818
E-mail: info@nlgia.org
http://www.nlgja.org

National Newspaper Publishers
Association (The Black Press of
America)
3200 13th Street NW
Washington, DC 20010
Phone: (202) 588-8764
http://www.nnpa.org/news/default.asp

Native American Journalists Association
555 Dakota Street
Al Neuharth Media Center
Vermillion, SD 57069
Phone: (605) 677-5282
Fax: (866) 694-4264
E-mail: info@naja.com
http://www.naja.com

Newswomen's Club of New York
15 Gramercy Park South
New York, NY 10003
Phone: (212) 777-1610
Fax: (212) 353-9569
http://www.newswomensclubnewyork.com

South Asian Journalists Association
Columbia Graduate School of Journalism
2950 Broadway
New York, NY 10027
Phone: (212) 854-5979
E-mail: saja@columbia.edu
http://www.saja.org

G. PHOTOGRAPHY, ART, AND DESIGN

American Institute of Graphic Arts
(AIGA)
164 Fifth Avenue
New York, NY 10010
Phone: (212) 807-1990
http://www.aiga.org

The Art Directors Club
106 West 29th Street
New York, NY 10001
Phone: (212) 643-1440
Fax: (212) 643-4266
E-mail: info@adcglobal.org
http://www.adcglobal.org

Association of Art Editors
Phil Freshman, President
3912 Natchez Avenue South
St. Louis Park, MN 55416
Phone and Fax: (952) 922-1374
http://www.artedit.org

National Press Photographers
Association
3200 Croasdaile Drive
Suite 306
Durham, NC 27705
Phone: (919) 383-7246
Fax: (919) 383-7261
E-mail: info@nppa.org
http://www.nppa.org

Society for News Design
1130 Ten Rod Road
Suite F-104
North Kingstown, RI 02852-4177
Phone: (401) 294-5233
Fax: (401) 294-5238
http://www.snd.org

Society of Illustrators
128 East 63rd Street
New York, NY 10021-7303
Phone: (212) 838-2560

Fax: (212) 838-2561
http://www.societyillustrators.org

Society of Publication Designers
475 Park Avenue South
Suite 2200
New York, NY 10016
Phone: (212) 532-7527
Fax: (212) 268-1867
http://www.spd.org

Type Directors Club
127 West 25th Street, 8th Floor
New York, NY 10001
Phone: (212) 633-8943
Fax: (212) 633-8944
E-mail: director@tdc.org
http://www.tdc.org

White House News Photographers'
Association
http://www.whnpa.org

H. EDUCATION

American Journalism Historians
Association
http://www.berry.edu/ajha

Association for Education
in Journalism and Mass
Communication (AEJMC)
234 Outlet Pointe Boulevard
Columbia, SC 29210-5667
Phone: (803) 798-0271
Fax: (803) 772-3509
http://aejmc.org

Broadcast Education Association
c/o Executive Director
1771 N Street NW
Washington, DC 20036-2891
Phone: (202) 429-3935
http://www.beaweb.org

Journalism Education Association
Kansas State University
103 Kedzie Hall
Manhattan, KS 66506-1505

Phone: (785) 532-5532
http://www.jea.org

National Scholastic Press Association
Associated Collegiate Press
2221 University Ave SE
Suite 121
Minneapolis, MN 55414
Phone: (612) 625-8335
Fax: (612) 626-0720
http://www.studentpress.org/contact.html

I. ASSOCIATIONS FOR STUDENTS

ASNE (American Society of Newspaper Editors) High School Journalism Initiative
11690B Sunrise Valley Drive
Reston VA 20191-1409
Fax: (703) 453-1139
http://www.highschooljournalism.org

Associated Collegiate Press Association
http://studentpress.journ.umn.edu/acp/index.html

College Media Advisers
http://www.collegemedia.org

Columbia Scholastic Press Association (CSPA)
Columbia University Mail Code 5711
New York, NY 10027-6902
Phone: (212) 854-9400
Fax: (212) 854-9401
http://www.columbia.edu/cu/cspa

Quill and Scroll Society
International Honorary Society for High School Journalists
The University of Iowa
School of Journalism and Mass Communication
100 Adler Journalism Building, Room E346
Iowa City, IA 52242
Phone: (319) 335-3457
Fax: (319) 335-3989
http://www.uiowa.edu/~quill-sc

J. OTHER

American Business Media
675 Third Avenue
New York, NY 10017-5704
Phone: (212) 661-6360
Fax: (212) 370-0736
E-mail: info@abmmail.com
http://www.americanbusinessmedia.com

American Communication Association
http://www.americancomm.org

International Association of Business Communicators
One Hallidie Plaza
Suite 600
San Francisco, CA 94102
Phone: (415) 544-4700; (800) 776-4222
Fax: (415) 544-4747
http://www.iabc.com

Newsletter & Electronic Publishers Association
1501 Wilson Boulevard
Suite 509
Arlington, VA 22209
Phone: (703) 527-2333; (800) 356-9302
Fax: (703) 841-0629
E-mail: nepa@newsletters.org
http://www.newsletters.org

Society for Technical Communication
901 North Stuart Street
Suite 904
Arlington, VA 22203
Phone: (703) 522-4114
Fax: (703) 522-2075
E-mail: stc@stc.org
http://www.stc.org

APPENDIX III
INDUSTRY PUBLICATIONS, INTERNSHIPS, FELLOWSHIPS AND SCHOLARSHIPS, OTHER RESOURCES, AND JOB LISTINGS

A. PUBLICATIONS

The American Editor
The American Society of Newspaper
    Editors
11690B Sunrise Valley Drive
Reston, VA 20191-1409
Phone: (703) 453-1122
http://www.asne.org/kiosk/editor/tae.htm

American Journalism Review
University of Maryland, 1117 Journalism
    Building
College Park, MD 20742-7111
Phone: (301) 405-8803
Fax: (301) 405-8323
E-mail: editor@ajr.umd.edu
http://www.ajr.org

Black Journalism Review
P.O. Box 570
Washington, DC 20044-0570
Phone: (202) 298-9519
http://www.blackjournalism.com

The Business Journalist
(Published by the Society of American
    Business Editors and Writers, Inc.)
http://www.sabew.org/

Columbia Journalism Review
Journalism Building
2950 Broadway
Columbia University
New York, NY 10027
Phone: (212) 854-1881
Fax: (212) 854-8580
http://www.cjr.org

Communicator
(Published by the Radio-Television News
    Directors Association)
http://www.rtnda.org/communicator/
    archive.shtml

CyberJournalist.net
(Published by the Online News Association)
http://www.cyberjournalist.net

Digital Journalist
http://digitaljournalist.org

Editor & Publisher
770 Broadway
New York, NY 10003-9595
Phone: (800) 336-4380
Fax: (646) 654-5370
http://www.editorandpublisher.com/eandp

Folio Magazine
33 South Main Street
Norwalk, CT 06854
Phone: (203) 854-6730
Fax: (203) 854-6735
http://www.foliomag.com

Online Journalism Review
http://www.ojr.org

Presstime
(Published by the Newspaper Association
    of America)
http://www.naa.org/presstime

The St. Louis Journalism Review
Webster University
470 E. Lockwood, Room 414
St. Louis, MO 63119
Phone: (314) 968-5905
Fax: (314) 963-6104
E-mail: review@webster.edu
http://www.stljr.org

B. INTERNSHIPS

Internships are one of the major keys to launching a journalism career. The following list is just a sampling of the many newspaper, magazine, television, radio, and new media programs available. For the best results, contact any publication or station that interests you. Check their Web site to see if they have information available. Even if there is nothing on their Web site, call to find out if there is an opportunity. Most organizations are very receptive to having eager aspiring journalists volunteer their time. Professional associations often have valuable internship information as well.

**The American Society of Newspaper
    Editors**
Newspaper Newsroom Internship Database
http://www.asne.org/index.cfm?id=3749

The Associated Press
Various Internships
http://www.ap.org/apjobs/internship.
    html

CBS News Internship Program
524 West 57th Street
New York, NY 10019
Fax: (212) 975-6699

E-mail: internships@cbsnews.com
http://www.cbsnews.com/
    stories/2004/04/26/broadcasts/
    main613839.shtml

Dow Jones Newspaper Fund
P.O. Box 300
Princeton, NJ 08543-0300
Phone: (609) 452-2820
Fax: (609) 520-5804
E-mail: newsfund@wsj.dowjones.com
http://djnewspaperfund.dowjones.com/
    fund/cs_internships.asp

Magazine Publishers of America
810 Seventh Avenue, 24th Floor
New York, NY 10019
Phone: (212) 872-3700
http://www.magazine.org/careers/
    Internships

Meredith Corporation
1716 Locust Street
Department MSIP

Des Moines, IA 50309-3023
http://www.meredith.com

Minority Editorial Training Program (METPRO)
E-mail: webmaster@metpronews.com
http://www.metpronews.com

National Public Radio
Human Resources Department
635 Massachusetts Avenue NW
Washington, DC 20001
Fax: (202) 513-3047
E-mail: internship@npr.org.
http://www.npr.org/about/jobs/intern

NBC Internship Program
http://www.nbc.com/NBC_Career_
    Opportunities/Internship_Program.
    html

Radio-Television News Directors Association
Internship programs

http://www.rtnda.org/asfi/internships/
    internships.shtml

Turner Broadcasting Systems
http://www.turner.com/careers/
    internships.html

The Washington Post
Attention: Newsroom Summer Internship
    Program
1150 15th Street NW
Washington, DC 20071
Phone: (202) 334-6765
http://washpost.com/news_ed/summer_
    internships

WGBH (Boston Public Television)
Human Resources Department
125 Western Avenue
Boston, MA 02134
http://careers.wgbh.org/internships/
    internships.html

C. FELLOWSHIPS AND SCHOLARSHIPS

Chips Quinn Scholars
http://www.chipsquinn.org

Dow Jones Newspaper Fund
P.O. Box 300
Princeton, NJ 08543-0300
Phone: (609) 452-2820
Fax: (609) 520-5804
E-mail: newsfund@wsj.dowjones.com
http://djnewspaperfund.dowjones.com/fund

Fund for Investigative Journalism
P.O. Box 60184
Washington, DC 20039-0184
Phone: (202) 362-0260
Fax: (301) 422-7449
E-mail: fundfij@aol.com.
http://fij.org

George Washington Williams Fellowship
Independent Press Association
65 Battery, 2nd Floor
San Francisco, CA 94111
Phone: (415) 445-0230, ext. 116 or 107
E-mail: gww@indypress.org
http://www.indypress.org/site/programs/
    gwwfellow.html

International Journalism Exchange
International Center for Journalists

1616 H Street NW, Third Floor
Washington, DC 20006
Phone: (202) 737-3700
Fax: (202) 737-0530
E-mail: ije@icfj.org
http://www.icfj.org/ije.html.

Investigative Reporters and Editors
Fellowships and Scholarships
http://www.ire.org/training/fellowships.
    html

The National Association of Broadcasters
List of internships and scholarships
http://www.nab.org/BCC/jobbank/
    Scholarships

National Press Club
Awards and Scholarships
529 14th Street NW
Washington, DC 20045
http://npc.press.org/programs/awards.cfm

The National Press Foundation
1211 Connecticut Avenue NW
Suite 310
Washington, DC 20036
Phone: (202) 663-7280
http://www.nationalpress.org

Phillips Foundation Journalism Fellowship Program
Attention: John Farley
7811 Montrose Road
Potomac, MD 20854
Phone: (301) 340-7788, ext. 6090
E-mail: jfarley@phillips.com.
http://www.thephillipsfoundation.org

Society of Environmental Journalists Fellowship Program
P.O. Box 2492
Jenkintown, PA 19046
Phone: (215) 884-8174
Fax: (215) 884-8175
E-mail: sej@sej.org
http://www.sej.org

Sundance Documentary Fund
http://institute.sundance.org/jsps/site.
    jsp?resource=pag_ex_programs_sdf_
    generalinfo&sk=98uhZrJ5CgztwXfd

D. OTHER JOURNALISM RESOURCES

The Associated Press
450 West 33rd Street
New York, NY 10001
Phone: (212) 621-1500
http://www.ap.org

**The Foundation for American
Communications**
85 South Grand Avenue
Pasadena, CA 91105
Phone: (626) 584-0010
Fax: (626) 584-0627
http://www.facsnet.org

NewsLab (resource for television and
radio news)
5510 Western Avenue #100
Chevy Chase, MD 20815

Phone: (301) 652-4881
Fax: (301) 652-4881
http://www.newslab.org

NewsLink
(Links to U.S. newspapers and radio/
television stations worldwide)
http://newslink.org

Newswise (research resource)
http://www.newswise.com

The Pulitzer Prizes
Columbia University
709 Journalism Building
2950 Broadway
New York, NY 10027
Phone: (212) 854-3841

Fax: (212) 854-3342
E-mail: pulitzer@www.pulitzer.org
http://www.pulitzer.org

**The Reporters Committee for Freedom
of the Press**
1101 Wilson Boulevard
Suite 1100
Arlington, VA 22209
Phone: (800) 336-4243; (703) 807-2100
E-mail: rcfp@rcfp.org
http://www.rcfp.org

E. JOB LISTINGS

These are just some of the many sites out there for journalism job listings. Don't forget to check additional professional associations, as well as the individual Web sites of organizations of interest.

General

The E.W. Scripps Company: http://jobs.scripps.com
JournalismJob.com: http://www.journalismjob.com
JournalismJobs: http://www.journalismjobs.com
Journalism Jobs: http://journalism_jobs.tripod.com
The Journalist's Toolbox: http://www.journalliststoolbox.com/newswriting/jobs.html
Mass Media Jobs: http://massmediajobs.com
MediaBistro: http://www.mediabistro.com
Reuters: http://about.reuters.com/careers
Tribune Company: http://www.tribune.com/employment
The Write Jobs: http://www.writejobs.com/jobs
Writing and Journalism Jobs: http://www.quintcareers.com/writing/writing_jobs.html

Special Interest Groups

JournalismNext: http://www.journalismnext.com
California Chicano News Media Association: http://www.ccnma.org

South Asian Journalist's Association Job Bank: http://www.saja.org/jobs.html
Journalism & Women Symposium Job Bank: http://www.jaws.org/jobs

Broadcasting

Current.org (public television and radio): http://www.current.org
TvSpy.com: http://www.tvspy.com
TvJobs.com: http://www.tvjobs.com
Tv and Radio Jobs: http://www.tvandradiojobs.com
The Rundown: http://www.tvrundown.com/resource.html

Freelance Writing

Craig's List: http://www.craigslist.com
E-lance: http://www.elance.com
FreelanceWriting.com: http://www.freelancewriting.com
Freelance Writing at About.com: http://freelancewrite.about.com/?once=true&
WritersWeekly: http://www.writersweekly.com

Newspapers

Knight Ridder Job Board: http://careers-kri.com/kri/jobboard

The National Diversity Newspaper Job Bank: http://www.newsjobs.com
Editor & Publisher Classifieds: http://www.editorandpublisher.com/eandp/classifieds/index.jsp
Associated Press Sports Editors Job Board: http://apse.dallasnews.com/job_board/apse_job_board.html
Associated Press Jobs: http://www.ap.org/apjobs
Multiple listings from the Detroit Free Press Jobs Board: http://www.freep.com/legacy/jobspage/links/jobboard.htm

New Media

I Want Media: http://www.iwantmedia.com/jobs
New York New Media Association: http://jobsnetwork.nynma.org
Tech Job Center: http://jobs.internet.com

Strategic Communications

Talent Zoo: http://jobs.internet.com
Creative Central: http://www.creativecentral.com/central.htm
OnlinePRjobs: http://www.online-pr.com/prjobs.htm

PRWeek Jobs: http://www.prweekjobs.com

Workinpr.com: http://www.workinpr.com/index.asp

O'Dwyer's Public Relations News: http://www.odwyerpr.com

Education

HigherEdJobs: http://www.higheredjobs.com

Academic360.com: http://www.academic360.com

The Chronicle of Higher Education: http://www.chronicle.com

TeacherJobs: http://www.teacherjobs.com

APPENDIX IV
COMPANY LISTINGS

A. LARGEST NEWSPAPERS

The following is a list of the top 100 daily newspapers in the United States by circulation. As you can see, they are located across the country. As you consider opportunities in journalism, look at these different papers to see the contrasts in their news coverage and overall style. You can also use this list as a potential employment and networking resource.

(Source: Editor & Publisher International Year Book 2004—according to infoplease.com)

1. *USA Today* **(circ. 2,154,539)**
7950 Jones Branch Drive
McLean, VA 22108-0605
Phone: (703) 854-3400
http://www.usatoday.com

2. *The Wall Street Journal*
      (circ. 2,091,062)
Dow Jones & Company
1 World Financial Center
200 Liberty Street
New York, NY 10281
Phone: (212) 416-2000
http://online.wsj.com/public/us

3. *The New York Times* **(circ. 1,118,565)**
The New York Times Company
229 West 43rd Street
New York, NY 10036
Phone: (212) 556-1234
http://www.nytimes.com

4. *The Los Angeles Times* **(circ. 914,584)**
202 W. 1st Street
Los Angeles, CA 90012
Phone: (213) 237-5000
http://www.latimes.com

5. *The Washington Post* **(circ. 732,872)**
1150 15th Street NW
Washington, DC 20071
Phone: (202) 334-6000
http://www.washingtonpost.com

6. *The New York Daily News*
      (circ. 729,124)
450 West 33rd Street
New York, NY 10001
Phone: (212) 949-1500
http://www.nydailynews.com

7. *The Chicago Tribune* **(circ. 680,879)**
435 N. Michigan Avenue
Chicago, IL 60611

Phone: (312) 222-3232
http://www.chicagotribune.com

8. *The New York Post* **(circ. 652,426)**
1211 Avenue of the Americas
New York, NY 10036-8790
Phone: (212) 930-8000
http://www.nypost.com

9. *Newsday* **(circ. 580,069)**
235 Pinelawn Road
Melville, NY 11747-4250
Phone: (516) / (631) 843-4000
http://www.newsday.com

10. *Houston Chronicle* **(circ. 553,018)**
801 Texas Avenue
Houston, TX 77002
Phone: (713) 220-7171
http://www.chron.com

11. *The San Francisco Chronicle*
       (circ. 512,640)
901 Mission Street
San Francisco, CA 94103
Phone: (415) 777-1111
http://www.sfgate.com/chronicle

12. *The Dallas Morning News*
       (circ. 510,133)
P.O. Box 655237
Dallas, TX 75265-5237
Phone: (214) 977-8222
http://www.dallasnews.com

13. *The Chicago Sun-Times*
       (circ. 481,798)
401 N. Wabash
Chicago, IL 60611
Phone: (312) 321-3000
http://www.suntimes.com

14. *The Boston Globe* **(circ. 450,538)**
135 Morrissey Boulevard
Boston, MA 02107

Phone: (617) 929-2000
http://www.boston.com

15. *The Arizona Republic* **(circ. 432,284)**
200 E. Van Buren Street
Phoenix, AZ 85004
Phone: (602) 444-8000; (800) 331-9303
http://www.azcentral.com/arizonarepublic

16. *The Star-Ledger* **(Newark) (circ.
       408,672)**
Star-Ledger Plaza
Newark, NJ 07102-1200
Phone: (973) 392-4141
http://www.nj.com/news/ledger

17. *Minneapolis–St. Paul Star Tribune*
       (circ. 380,354)
425 Portland Avenue South
Minneapolis, MN 55488
Phone: (612) 673-4000
http://www.startribune.com

18. *Philadelphia Inquirer*
       (circ. 376,493)
P.O. Box 8263
Philadelphia, PA 19101
Phone: (215) 854-2000
http://www.philly.com/mld/philly

19. *Atlanta Journal-Constitution*
       (circ. 371,853)
P.O. Box 4689
Atlanta, GA 30302
Phone: (404) 526-5151; (800) 846-6672
http://www.ajc.com

20. *Cleveland Plain Dealer*
       (circ. 365,288)
Plain Dealer Plaza
1801 Superior Avenue
Cleveland, OH 44114
Phone: (216) 999-4800
http://www.cleveland.com

21. *Detroit Free Press* (**circ. 352,714**)
600 W. Fort
Detroit, MI 48226
Phone: (313) 222-6600
http://www.freep.com

22. *The Oregonian* (**circ. 334,783**)
1320 S.W. Broadway
Portland, OR 97201
Phone: (503) 221-8327
http://www.oregonlive.com

23. *St. Petersburg Times* (**circ. 334,742**)
490 First Avenue South
St. Petersburg, FL 33701
Phone: (727) 893-8111
http://www.sptimes.com

24. *San Diego Union-Tribune*
    (**circ. 328,531**)
P.O. Box 120191
San Diego, CA 92112-0191
Phone: (619) 299-3131
http://www.signonsandiego.com

25. *The Miami Herald* (**circ. 315,850**)
One Herald Plaza
Miami, FL 33132
Phone: (305) 350-2111; (800)
    HERALD5
http://www.miami.com/mld/miamiherald

26. *The Orange County Register*
    (**circ. 302,864**)
625 N. Grand Avenue
Santa Ana, CA 92701
Phone: (877) 469-7344
http://www.ocregister.com

27. *The Baltimore Sun* (**circ. 301,186**)
501 N. Calvert Street
P.O. Box 1377
Baltimore, MD 21278
Phone: (410) 332-6000
http://www.sunspot.net

28. *The Sacramento Bee* (**circ. 289,905**)
P.O. Box 15779
Sacramento, CA 95852
Phone: (916) 321-1000
http://www.sacbee.com

29. *The Denver Post* (**circ. 288,937**)
1560 Broadway
Denver, CO 80202
Phone: (303) 820-1201
http://www.denverpost.com

30. *Rocky Mountain News*
    (**circ. 288,889**)
100 Gene Amole Way
Denver, CO 80204

Phone: (303) 892-5000
http://www.rockymountainnews.com

31. *St. Louis Post-Dispatch*
    (**circ. 285,869**)
900 N. Tucker Boulevard
St. Louis, MO 63101
Phone: (314) 340-8000; (800) 365-0820
http://www.stltoday.com

32. *San Jose Mercury News*
    (**circ. 271,997**)
750 Ridder Park Drive
San Jose, CA 95190
Phone: (408) 920-5000
http://www.mercurynews.com/mld/
    mercurynews/news

33. *Kansas City Star* (**circ. 267,273**)
1729 Grand Boulevard
Kansas City, MO 64108
Phone: (816) 234-4636
http://www.kansascity.com/mld/
    kansascitystar

34. *The Orlando Sentinel* (**circ. 257,222**)
633 N. Orange Avenue
Orlando, FL 32801
Phone: (407) 420-5000
http://www.orlandosentinel.com

35. *New Orleans Times-Picayune*
    (**circ. 253,610**)
3800 Howard Avenue
New Orleans, LA 70125-1429
Phone: (504) 826-3300; (800) 925-0000
http://www.nola.com/t-p

36. *The Columbus Dispatch*
    (**circ. 252,564**)
34 S. 3rd Street
Columbus, OH 43215
Phone: (614) 461-5000
http://www.dispatch.com

37. *The Indianapolis Star* (**circ. 249,891**)
P.O. Box 145
Indianapolis, IN 46206
Phone: (317) 444-4000; (800) 669-7827
http://www.indystar.com

38. *Milwaukee Journal Sentinel*
    (**circ. 244,288**)
P.O. Box 661
Milwaukee, WI 53201
Phone: (414) 224-2000
http://www.jsonline.com

39. *Pittsburgh Post-Gazette*
    (**circ. 242,546**)
34 Boulevard of the Allies
Pittsburgh, PA 15222

Phone: (412) 263-1100
http://www.post-gazette.com

40. *The Boston Herald* (**circ. 241,457**)
One Herald Square
P.O. Box 55843
Boston, MA 02205
Phone: (617) 426-3000
http://www.bostonherald.com

41. *Fort Lauderdale Sun-Sentinel*
    (**circ. 233,634**)
200 E. Las Olas Boulevard
Fort Lauderdale, FL 33301
Phone: (954) 356-4000
http://www.sun-sentinel.com

42. *The Seattle Times* (**circ. 231,505**)
P.O. Box 70
Seattle, WA 98111
Phone: (206) 464-2111
http://seattletimes.nwsource.com/html/
    home

43. *The Detroit News* (**circ. 227,392**)
615 W. Lafayette Boulevard
Detroit, MI 48226
Phone: (313) 222-2300
http://www.detroitnews.com

44. *The Charlotte Observer*
    (**circ. 226,849**)
600 S. Tryon Street
Charlotte, NC 28202
Phone: (704) 358-5000
http://www.charlotte.com/mld/observer

45. *The Tampa Tribune* (**circ. 224,220**)
P.O. Box 191
Tampa, FL 33601
Phone: (813) 259-7600
http://www.tampatrib.com

46. *San Antonio Express-News*
    (**circ. 222,536**)
400 3rd Street
San Antonio, TX 78287-2171
Phone: (210) 250-3000; Job Line (210)
    554-0500, category 7210
http://www2.mysanantonio.com/aboutus/
    expressnews

47. *Investor's Business Daily*
    (**circ. 215,788**)
12655 Beatrice Street
Los Angeles, CA 90066
Phone: (310) 448-6000
http://www.investors.com

48. *Fort Worth Star-Telegram* (**circ.
    215,452**)
400 West 7th
Fort Worth, TX 76102

Phone: (817) 335-4837
http://www.dfw.com/mld/dfw

**49. *Louisville Courier-Journal*
(circ. 213,176)**
525 W. Broadway
P.O. Box 740031
Louisville, KY 40201-7431
Phone: (502) 582-4011
http://www.courier-journal.com

50. *The Buffalo News* (circ. 207,989)
One News Plaza
P.O. Box 100
Buffalo, NY 14240
Phone: (716) 849-4444
http://www.buffalonews.com

51. *The Oklahoman* (circ. 207,538)
P.O. Box 25125
Oklahoma City, OK 73125
Phone: (405) 478-7171
http://www.newsok.com

52. *The Virginian-Pilot* (circ. 201,141)
150 West Brambleton Avenue
Norfolk, VA 23510
Phone: (757) 446-2000
http://www.hamptonroads.com/
pilotonline

**53. *Omaha World-Herald*
(circ. 192,075)**
World-Herald Square
Omaha, NE 68102
Phone: (402) 444-1000
http://www.omaha.com

**54. *St. Paul Pioneer Press*
(circ. 190,392)**
345 Cedar Street
St. Paul, MN 55101
Phone: (651) 222-1111; Job Line: (651)
228-5008
http://www.twincities.com/mld/
pioneerpress

**55. *Richmond Times-Dispatch*
(circ. 188,540)**
300 E. Franklin Street
Richmond, VA 23219
Phone: (804) 649-6000; (800) 468-3382
http://www.timesdispatch.com

**56. *The Hartford Courant* (circ.
185,570)**
285 Broad Street
Hartford, CT 06115
Phone: (860) 525-5555
http://www.ctnow.com

**57. *Riverside Press-Enterprise*
(circ. 183,974)**
P.O. Box 792
Riverside, CA 92502-0792
Phone: (909) 684-1200
http://www.pe.com/index.html

**58. *Arkansas Democrat-Gazette*
(circ. 183,343)**
121 East Capitol Avenue
Little Rock, AR 72201
Phone: (501) 378-3400
http://www.ardemgaz.com

**59. *The Austin American-Statesman*
(circ. 183,312)**
P.O. Box 670
Austin, TX 78767
Phone: (512) 445-3500
http://www.statesman.com

60. *Contra Costa Times* (circ. 182,541)
2640 Shadelands Drive
Walnut Creek, CA 94598
Phone: (925) 935-2525
http://www.contracostatimes.com/mld/
cctimes

**61. *The Cincinnati Enquirer*
(circ. 182,176)**
312 Elm Street
Cincinnati, OH 45202
Phone: (513) 721-2700
http://www.enquirer.com/today

**62. *The Record* (Bergen County, NJ)
(circ. 179,270)**
North Jersey Media Group Inc.
150 River Street
Hackensack, NJ 07601-7172
Phone: (201) 646-4100
http://www.bergen.com

**63. *Los Angeles Daily News*
(circ. 178,360)**
P.O. Box 4200
Woodland Hills, CA 91365
Phone: (818) 713-3000; (800) 346-6397
http://www.dailynews.com

**64. *Rochester Democrat and Chronicle*
(circ. 173,900)**
55 Exchange Boulevard
Rochester, NY 14614
Phone: (585) 232-7100
http://www.democratandchronicle.com

**65. *The Nashville Tennessean*
(circ. 172,149)**
1100 Broadway
Nashville, TN 37203

Phone: (615) 259-8300
http://www.tennessean.com

**66. *The Palm Beach Post*
(circ. 168,147)**
Mailing address:
P.O. Box 24700
West Palm Beach, FL 33416
Main office:
2751 S. Dixie Highway
West Palm Beach, FL 33405
Phone: (561) 820-4663; (800) 926-POST
http://www.palmbeachpost.com

**67. *The Jacksonville Times-Union*
(circ. 167,851)**
P.O. Box 1949
Jacksonville, FL 32231
Phone: (904) 359-4111
http://www.jacksonville.com

**68. *The Providence Journal*
(circ. 167,609)**
75 Fountain Street
Providence, RI 02902
Phone: (401) 277-7000
http://www.projo.com

**69. *The Asbury Park Press*
(circ. 167,284)**
3601 Highway 66
P.O. Box 1550
Neptune, NJ 07754
Phone: (732) 922-6000
http://www.app.com/apps/pbcs.dll/
frontpage

**70. *Raleigh News & Observer*
(circ. 163,769)**
P.O. Box 191
Raleigh, NC 27602
Phone: (919) 829-4700
http://www.news-observer.com

**71. *The Las Vegas Review-Journal*
(circ. 160,391)**
1111 W. Bonanza Road
P.O. Box 70
Las Vegas, NV 89125
Phone: (702) 383-0211
http://www.reviewjournal.com

72. *The Fresno Bee* (circ. 158,651)
1626 E Street
Fresno, CA 93786
Phone: (559) 441-6363
http://www.fresnobee.com

**73. *Memphis Commerical Appeal*
(circ. 157,820)**
495 Union Avenue
Memphis, TN 38103

Phone: (901) 529-2345
http://www.gomemphis.com

**74. The Des Moines Register
(circ. 152,885)**
P.O. Box 957
Des Moines, IA 50304-0957
Phone: (515) 284-8000
http://www.dmregister.com

**75. Seattle Post-Intelligencer
(circ. 150,851)**
P.O. Box 1909
Seattle, WA 98111-1909
Phone: (206) 448-8000
http://seattlepi.nwsource.com

76. Chicago Daily Herald (circ. 150,364)
Mailing address:
P.O. Box 280
Arlington Heights, IL 60006-0280
Office address:
155 E. Algonquin Road
Arlington Heights, IL 60005
Phone: (847) 427-4300
http://www.dailyherald.com

**77. The Birmingham News (circ.
148,938)**
P.O. Box 2553
Birmingham, AL 35202
Phone: (205) 325-2222
http://www.al.com/birmingham

**78. The Philadelphia Daily News
(circ. 143,631)**
P.O. Box 7788
Philadelphia, PA 19101
Phone: (215) 854-2000
http://www.philly.com/mld/dailynews

**79. The Journal News (Westchester
County, NY) (circ. 142,873)**
One Gannett Drive
White Plains, NY 10604
Phone: (914) 694-9300
http://www.thejournalnews.com/apps/
   pbcs.dll/frontpage

**80. The Honolulu Advertiser
(circ. 142,025)**
P.O. Box 3110
Honolulu, HI 96802
Phone: (808) 525–8090
http://www.honoluluadvertiser.com

81. The Toledo Blade (circ. 139,520)
541 N. Superior Street
Toledo, OH 43660

Phone: (419) 724-6000
http://www.toledoblade.com/apps/pbcs.
   dll/frontpage

82. The Tulsa World (circ. 139,383)
318 S. Main
Tulsa, OK 74103
Phone: (918) 583-2161
http://www.tulsaworld.com

**83. The Grand Rapids Press
(circ. 138,620)**
155 Michigan Street NW
Grand Rapids, MI 49503
Phone: (616) 222-5400
http://www.gr-press.com

**84. The Salt Lake Tribune
(circ. 134,985)**
P.O. Box 867
Salt Lake City, UT 84110
Phone: (801) 257-8742
http://www.sltrib.com

**85. Akron Beacon Journal
(circ. 134,401)**
44 East Exchange Street
P.O. Box 640
Akron, OH 44309-0640
Phone: (330) 996-3135
http://www.ohio.com/mld/ohio

**86. Tacoma News Tribune
(circ. 128,511)**
1950 South State Street
Tacoma, WA 98405
Phone: (253) 597-8742
http://www.thenewstribune.com

87. Dayton Daily News (circ. 126,642)
45 S. Ludlow Street
Dayton, OH 45402
Phone: (937) 222-5700; (888) 397-6397
http://www.daytondailynews.com

88. La Opinion (circ. 124,692)
700 S. Flower Street
Suite 3100
Los Angeles, CA 90017
Phone: (213) 622-8332
http://www.laopinion.com

**89. Syracuse Post-Standard
(circ. 120,701)**
Clinton Square
P.O. Box 4915
Syracuse, NY 13221-4915
Phone: (315) 470-0011
http://www.post-standard.com

**90. Greensburg Tribune Review
(circ. 119,646)**
622 Cabin Hill Drive
Greensburg, PA 15601
Phone: (724) 834-1151
http://www.pittsburghlive.com/x/tribune-
   review/trib

**91. Wilmington News Journal
(circ. 116,398)**
P.O. Box 15505
Wilmington, DE 19850
Phone: (302)-324-2500
http://www.delawareonline.com/
   newsjournal

**92. Knoxville News-Sentinel
(circ. 114,593)**
2332 News Sentinel Drive
Knoxville, TN 37921-5761
Phone: (865) 523-3131
http://www.knoxnews.com

93. The Columbia State (circ. 114,442)
P.O. Box 1333
Columbia, SC 29202
Phone: (803) 771-6161
http://www.thestate.com/mld/thestate

**94. Allentown Morning Call
(circ. 111,594)**
P.O. Box 1260
Allentown, PA 18105
Phone: (610) 820-6601
http://www.mcall.com

95. Albuquerque Journal (circ. 109,693)
Journal Center
7777 Jefferson NE
Albuquerque, NM 87109-4343
Phone: (505) 823-3800
http://www.abqjournal.com

**96. Lexington Herald Leader
(circ. 106,941)**
100 Midland Avenue
Lexington, KY 40508-1999
Phone: (859) 231-3104
http://www.kentucky.com/mld/kentucky

**97. Sarasota Herald-Tribune
(circ. 105,636)**
801 S Tamiami Trail
Sarasota, FL 34236
Phone: (941) 953-7755
http://www.heraldtribune.com/apps/pbcs.
   dll/frontpage

**98. Daytona Beach News-Journal (circ.
104,654)**
901 Sixth Street
Daytona Beach, FL 32117

Phone: (386) 252-1511
http://www.news-journalonline.com

**99. *Worcester Telegram & Gazette*
(circ. 102,592)**
20 Franklin Street
P.O.Box 15012
Worcester, MA 01615-0012

Phone: (508) 793-9100
http://www.telegram.com/apps/pbcs.
    dll/frontpage

**100. *The Washington Times*
(circ. 102,255)**
3600 New York Avenue NE
Washington, DC 20002

Phone: (800) 277-8500
http://www.washtimes.com

B. LARGEST MAGAZINES

Each year, *AdvertisingAge* magazine publishes a list known as the "Magazine 300." It represents the nation's top 300 magazines as measured by gross revenue from advertising and circulation. This section includes, in order, the top 100 U.S. magazines, as published in their September 2005 issue. The name of the magazine is listed first, followed by the publisher. For additional information, visit http://www.adage.com.

(Source: *Advertising Age,* Volume 76, Issue 39, 9/26/2005.)

1. *People*
Time Warner, Time Inc.
One Time Warner Center
New York, NY 10019-8016
Phone: (212) 522-6699
http://www.timewarner.com/corp/
    businesses/detail/time_inc/index.html;
    http://people.aol.com/people

2. *Sports Illustrated*
Time Warner, Time Inc.
One Time Warner Center
New York, NY 10019-8016
Phone: (212) 484-8000
http://www.timewarner.com/corp/
    businesses/detail/time_inc/index.html;
    http://sportsillustrated.cnn.com

3. *Time*
Time Warner, Time Inc.
One Time Warner Center
New York, NY 10019-8016
Phone: (212) 484-8000
http://www.timewarner.com/corp/
    businesses/detail/time_inc/index.html;
    http://www.time.com/time

4. *TV Guide*
Gemstar-TV Guide International
4 Radnor Corporate Center
Radnor, PA 19088
(this is the mailing address for the
    editorial office, but the magazine
    headquarters are in New York, NY)
http://www.gemstartvguide.com

5. *Better Homes & Gardens*
Meredith Corporation
125 Park Avenue
New York, NY 10017-5529

Phone: (212) 557-6600
Fax: (212) 551-7114
http://www.meredith.com/; http://www.
    bhg.com

6. *Newsweek*
The Washington Post Company
251 West 57th Street
New York, NY 10019-1894
Phone: (212) 445-4000
http://www.washpostco.com/; http://www.
    msnbc.msn.com/id/3032542/site/
    newsweek

7. *Parade*
Advance Publications–Parade Publications
711 Third Avenue
New York, NY 10017-4014
Fax: (212) 450-7284
http://www.parade.com

8. *Reader's Digest*
The Reader's Digest Association, Inc.
Reader's Digest Road
Pleasantville, NY 10570-7000
Phone: (914) 238-1000
http://www.rd.com

9. *Good Housekeeping*
The Hearst Corporation
250 West 55th Street
New York, NY 10019
Phone: (212) 649-2200
http://www.hearst.com/; http://www.
    goodhousekeeping.com

10. *Cosmopolitan*
The Hearst Corporation
224 West 57th Street
New York, NY 10019

Phone: (212) 649-3570
http://www.hearst.com/; http://www.
    cosmopolitan.com

11. *Woman's Day*
Lagardere, Hachette Filipacchi Media
    U.S.
1633 Broadway, 42nd Floor
New York, NY 10019
http://www.hfmus.com/HachetteUSA/
    Page.asp?Site=womansday; http://
    www.womansday.com

12. *BusinessWeek*
The McGraw-Hill Companies
1221 Avenue of the Americas, 43rd Floor
New York, NY 10020
Phone: (212) 512-2511
http://www.mcgrawhill.com/ims/default.
    shtml; http://www.businessweek.com

13. *InStyle*
Time Warner, Time Inc.
1271 Avenue of the Americas
New York, NY 10020
Phone: (212) 522-1212
http://www.timewarner.com/corp/
    businesses/detail/time_inc/index.html;
    http://www.instyle.com

14. *USA Weekend*
Gannett Co., Inc.
7950 Jones Branch Drive
McLean, VA 22107
(703) 854-6000
http://www.gannett.com; http://www.
    usatoday.com

15. *Family Circle*
Meredith Corporation

375 Lexington Avenue
New York, NY 10017-5514
http://www.meredith.com/; http://www.
    familycircle.com

16. *Fortune*
Time Warner, Time Inc.
One Time Warner Center
New York, NY 10019-8016
Phone: (212) 484-8000
http://www.timewarner.com/corp/
    businesses/detail/time_inc/index.html;
    http://money.cnn.com/magazines/
    fortune

17. *Forbes*
Forbes Inc.
90 5th Avenue
New York, NY 10011
Phone: (212) 366-8900
http://www.forbes.com

18. *Entertainment Weekly*
Time Warner, Time Inc.
One Time Warner Center
New York, NY 10019-8016
Phone: (212) 484-8000
http://www.timewarner.com/corp/
    businesses/detail/time_inc/index.html;
    http://www.ew.com/ew

19. *Ladies' Home Journal*
Meredith Corporation
125 Park Avenue
New York, NY 10017
http://www.meredith.com/mediakit/lhj/
    print/; http://www.lhj.com

20. *Vogue*
Advance Publications, Conde Nast
    Publications
4 Times Square
New York, NY 10036
Phone: (212) 286-2860
http://www.condenast.com/; http://www.
    style.com/vogue

21. *U.S. News & World Report*
Mortimer Zuckerman Publications
1050 Thomas Jefferson Street NW
Washington, DC 20007
Phone: (202) 955-2000
http://www.usnews.com

22. *Us Weekly*
Wenner Media/Walt Disney Co.
1290 Avenue of the Americas
New York, NY 10104-0298
http://www.usmagazine.com

23. *The New York Times Magazine*
The New York Times Company
229 West 43d Street
New York, NY 10036
Phone: (212) 556-1234
http://www.nytimes.com

24. *Glamour*
Advance Publications, Conde Nast
    Publications
4 Times Square
New York, NY 10036
Phone: (212) 286-2860
Fax: (212) 286-8336
http://www.condenast.com; http://www.
    glamour.com

25. *ESPN: The Magazine*
Walt Disney Co., ESPN Inc.
605 Third Avenue
New York, NY 10158-0180
Phone: (212) 916-9200
http://www.espn.com

26. *Vanity Fair*
Advance Publications, Conde Nast
    Publications
4 Times Square, 7th Floor
New York, NY 10036
Phone: (212) 286-2860
Fax: (212) 286-7036
http://www.condenast.com; http://www.
    vanityfair.com

27. *O, The Oprah Magazine*
The Hearst Corporation
1700 Broadway
New York, NY 10019
Phone: (212) 903-5366
http://www.hearst.com/magazines/
    property/mag_prop_o_2000.html;
    http://www.oprah.com

28. *Southern Living*
Time Warner, Time Inc., Southern
    Progress Corporation
2100 Lakeshore Drive
Birmingham, AL 35209
Phone: (205) 445-6000
http://www.timewarner.com/corp/
    businesses/detail/time_inc/index.
    html; http://www.southernliving.com/
    southern

29. *National Geographic*
National Geographic Society
P.O. Box 98199
Washington, DC 20090-8199
http://www.nationalgeographic.com/
    ngm/0602/index.html

30. *The New Yorker*
Advance Publications, Conde Nast
    Publications
4 Times Square
New York, NY 10036
http://www.condenast.com; http://www.
    newyorker.com

31. *Maxim*
Dennis Publishing
1040 Avenue of the Americas
New York, NY 10018
Fax: (212) 768-1319
http://www.maximonline.com

32. *Star Magazine*
American Media
1000 American Media Way
Boca Raton, FL 33464-1000
http://www.starmagazine.com

33. *Money*
Time Warner, Time Inc.
One Time Warner Center
New York, NY 10019-8016
Phone: (212) 484-8000
http://money.cnn.com

34. *National Enquirer*
American Media
1000 American Media Way
Boca Raton, FL 33464-1000
http://www.nationalenquirer.com

35. *Rolling Stone*
Wenner Media
1290 Avenue of the Americas
New York, NY 10104-0298
Phone: (212) 484-1616
http://www.rollingstone.com

36. *Golf Magazine*
Time Warner, Time Inc.
Time4 Media
2 Park Avenue, 10th Floor
New York, NY 10016
Phone: (212) 779-5000
Fax: (212) 779-5588
http://www.golfonline.com

37. *Elle*
Lagardere, Hachette Filipacchi Media U.S.
1633 Broadway, 43th Floor
New York, NY 10019
http://www.hfmus.com; http://www.elle.
    com

38. *Car and Driver*
Lagardere, Hachette Filipacchi Media U.S.
2002 Hogback Road
Ann Arbor, MI 48105

Phone: (734) 971-3600
http://www.hfmus.com; http://www.
caranddriver.com

39. *PC Magazine*
Ziff Davis Media
28 East 28th Street
New York, NY 10016-7930
Phone: (212) 503-3500
http://www.pcmag.com

40. *Parenting*
Time Warner, Time Inc./Parenting Group
One Time Warner Center
New York, NY 10019-8016
Phone: (212) 484-8000
http://www.parenting.com

41. *Parents Magazine*
Meredith Corporation
375 Lexington Avenue
New York, NY 10017
Phone: (212) 499-2000
http://www.meredith.com; http://www.
parents.com

42. *Real Simple*
Time Warner, Time Inc.
One Time Warner Center
New York, NY 10019-8016
Phone: (212) 484-8000
http://www.realsimple.com

43. *Prevention*
Rodale
733 Third Avenue, 15th Floor
New York, NY 10017-3204
Phone: (212) 697-2040
Fax: (212) 682-2237
http://www.rodale.com; http://www.
prevention.com

44. *Playboy*
Playboy Enterprises International
730 Fifth Avenue
New York, NY 10019
Phone: (212) 261-5000
Fax: (212) 957-2900
http://www.playboyenterprises.com

45. *Redbook*
The Hearst Corporation
224 West 57th Street
New York, NY 10019
Phone: (212) 649-3450
http://magazines.ivillage.com/redbook

46. *AARP: The Magazine*
AARP

601 E Street NW
Washington, DC 20049
http://www.aarpmagazine.org

47. *Golf Digest*
Advance Publications, Golf Digest Cos.
20 Westport Road
P.O. Box 850
Wilton, CT 06897
Phone: (203) 761-5100
http://www.golfdigest.com

48. *Shape Magazine*
American Media, Weider AMI
21100 Erwin Street
Woodland Hills, CA 91367
http://www.shape.com

49. *Country Living*
The Hearst Corporation
224 West 57th Street
New York, NY 10019
Phone: (212) 649-3500
http://www.hearst.com; http://magazines.
ivillage.com/countryliving

50. *Men's Health*
Rodale
733 Third Avenue, 15th Floor
New York, NY 10017-3204
Phone: (212) 697-2040
Fax: (212) 682-2237
http://www.rodale.com; http://www.
menshealth.com

51. *Architectural Digest*
Advance Publications, Conde Nast
Publications
4 Times Square
New York, NY 10036
Phone: (212) 286-2860
Fax: (212) 286-6905
http://www.condenast.com; http://www.
architecturaldigest.com

52. *Country Home*
Meredith Corporation
http://www.becreativebeyourself.com

53. *Travel & Leisure*
American Express Publishing
Corporation
1120 Avenue of the Americas, 10th Floor
New York, NY 10036
Phone: (212) 382-5600
http://www.amexpub.com/; http://www.
travelandleisure.com

54. *Endless Vacation*
Cendant, Resort Condiminiums
International

9998 North Michigan Road
Carmel, IN 46032
Fax: (317) 805-8229
http://www.rci.com/RCI/CDA/RCI_
EndlessVacation.jsp

55. *GQ*
Advance Publications, Conde Nast
Publications
4 Times Square
New York, NY 10036
Phone: (212) 286-6410
Fax: (212) 286-7969
http://www.condenast.com; http://men.
style.com/gq

56. *New York*
New York Magazine Holdings
444 Madison Avenue
New York, NY 10022
http://www.newyorkmetro.com

57. *Motor Trend*
Primedia, Consumer Magazines Group
260 Madison Avenue, 8th Floor
New York, NY 10016
Phone: (212) 726-4300
Fax: (917) 256-0025
http://www.primedia.com; http://www.
motortrend.com

58. *Brides Magazine*
Advance Publications, Fairchild
Publications
750 Third Avenue, 4th Floor
New York, NY 10017
http://www.fairchildpub.com/index.cfm;
http://www.brides.com

59. *Self*
Advance Publications, Conde Nast
Publications
4 Times Square
New York, NY 10036
Phone: (212) 286-2860
Fax: (212) 286-6174
http://www.condenast.com; http://www.
self.com

60. *Marie Claire*
Hearst Corporation/Comary
1790 Broadway
New York, NY 10019
Phone: (212) 649-5000
http://www.hearst.com; http://www.
marieclaire.com

61. *Cooking Light*
Time Warner, Time Inc., Southern
Progress Corporation

P.O. Box 62376
Tampa, FL 33662
http://corp.southernprogress.com/spc/;
    http://www.cookinglight.com

62. Fitness
Meredith Corporation
125 Park Avenue, 25th Floor
New York, NY 10017
http://www.meredith.com; http://www.
    fitnessmagazine.com

63. W
Advance Publications, Fairchild
    Publications
750 Third Avenue
New York, NY 10017
Phone: (212) 630-4900
Fax: (212) 630-4919
http://www.fairchildpub.com/index.cfm;
    http://www.style.com/w

64. Lucky
Advance Publications, Conde Nast
    Publications
4 Times Square, 6th Floor
New York, NY 10036
Phone: (212) 286-2860
Fax: (212) 286-4986
http://www.condenast.com; http://www.
    luckymag.com

65. Conde Nast Traveler
Advance Publications, Conde Nast
    Publications
4 Times Square, 14th Floor
New York, NY 10036-6561
Phone: (212) 286-2860
Fax: (212) 286-2094
http://www.condenast.com; http://www.
    concierge.com/cntraveler

66. Bon Appetit
Advance Publications, Conde Nast
    Publications
4 Times Square, 15th Floor
New York, NY 10036
Phone: (212) 286-2500
Fax: (212) 286-2536
http://www.condenast.com; http://www.
    epicurious.com/bonappetit

67. Harper's Bazaar
Hearst Corporation
1700 Broadway
New York, NY 10019
Phone: (212) 903-5000
http://www.hearst.com; http://www.
    harpersbazaar.com

68. Town & County
Hearst Corporation
1700 Broadway
New York, NY 10019
Phone: (212) 903-5000
http://www.hearst.com; http://www.
    townandcountrymag.com

69. Popular Photography
Lagardere, Hachette Filipacchi Media
    U.S.
1633 Broadway
New York, NY 10019
Phone: (212) 767-6000
Fax: (212) 767-5602
http://www.hfmus.com; http://www.
    popphoto.com

70. Woman's World
Bauer Publishing Company
270 Sylvan Avenue
Englewood Cliffs, NJ 07632-2521
Phone: (201) 569-6699
Fax: (201) 569-5303

71. Allure
Advance Publications, Conde Nast
    Publications
4 Times Square
New York, NY 10036
Phone: (212) 286-2458
Fax: (212) 286-4654
http://www.condenast.com; http://www.
    allure.com

72. The Economist
The Economist Group
1730 Rhode Island Avenue NW
Suite 1210
Washington, DC 20036
Phone: (202) 429-0890
Fax: (202) 429-0899
http://www.economistgroup.com; http://
    www.economist.com

73. Gourmet
Advance Publications, Conde Nast
    Publications
4 Times Square
New York, NY 10036
Phone: (212) 286-8050
Fax: (212) 286-2932
http://www.condenast.com; http://www.
    gourmet.com

74. Martha Stewart Living
Martha Stewart Omnimedia
11 West 42nd Street, 25th Floor
New York, NY 10036

Fax: (212) 827-8289
http://www.marthastewart.com

75. Road & Track
Lagardere, Hachette Filipacchi Media
    U.S.
1633 Broadway, 41st Floor
New York, NY 10019
Phone: (212) 767-6371
http://www.hfmus.com; http://www.
    roadandtrack.com

76. Seventeen
Hearst Corporation
1440 Broadway, 13th Floor
New York, NY 10018
Phone: (917) 934-6500
http://www.hearst.com; http://www.
    seventeen.com

77. Modern Bride
Advance Publications, Fairchild
    Publications
750 Third Avenue, 4th Floor
New York, NY 10017
http://www.fairchildpub.com; http://www.
    modernbride.com

78. Smithsonian
Smithsonian Institution
P.O. Box 37012
Washington, DC 20013-7012.
http://www.smithsonianmagazine.com

79. Sunset
Time Warner, Time Inc./Southern
    Progress Corporation
80 Willow Road
Menlo Park, CA 94025
http://www.southernprogress.com; http://
    www.sunset.com

80. Traditional Home
Meredith Corporation
125 Park Avenue
New York, NY 10017
Phone: (212) 557-6600
Fax: (212) 551-6914
http://www.meredith.com; http://www.
    traditionalhome.com

81. Information Week
United Business Media, CMP Media
600 Community Drive
Manhasset, NY 11030
Phone: (516) 562-5000
Fax: (516) 562-5036
http://www.cmp.com; http://www.
    informationweek.com

82. *Popular Mechanics*
Hearst Corporation
810 Seventh Avenue
New York, NY 10019
Phone: (212) 903-2853
http://www.hearst.com; http://www.
   popularmechanics.com

83. *Essence*
Time Warner, Time Inc.
135 West 50th Street, 4th Floor
New York, NY 10020
http://www.timewarner.com; http://www.
   essence.com

84. *InTouch Weekly*
Bauer Publishing Company
270 Sylvan Avenue
Englewood Cliffs, NJ 07632-2521
Phone: (201) 569-6699
Fax: (201) 569-5303
http://intouchweekly.hollywood.com

85. *Food & Wine*
American Express Publishing Company
1120 Avenue of the Americas
New York, NY 10036
Phone: (212) 382-5600
Fax: (212) 768-1568
http://www.amexpub.com; http://www.
   foodandwine.com

86. *Vibe*
Miller Publishing Group, Vibe/Spin
   Ventures
215 Lexington Avenue
New York, NY 10016
Phone: (212) 448-7300
Fax: (212) 448-7400
http://www.vibe.com

87. *PC World*
International Data Group
PC World Communications
501 Second Street
San Francisco, CA 94107
Phone: (415) 243-0500
Fax: (415) 442-1891
http://www.idg.com/www/home.nsf/Hom
   ePageForm!OpenForm&region=WW;

http://www.pcworld.com/magazine/
   login.asp

88. *Popular Science*
Time Warner, Time Inc./Time4 Media
2 Park Avenue, 9th Floor
New York, NY 10016
Phone: (212) 779-5000
Fax: (212) 779-5108
http://www.timewarner.com; http://www.
   popsci.com

89. *FHM*
Emap, Emap Metro
110 Fifth Avenue
New York, NY 10011
http://www.emap.com; http://www.fhmus.
   com

90. *House Beautiful*
Hearst Corporation
1700 Broadway
New York, NY 10019
Phone: (212) 903-5084
http://www.hearst.com; http://www.
   housebeautiful.com

91. *Consumer Reports*
Consumers Union of U.S.
101 Truman Avenue
Yonkers, NY 10703-1057
Phone: (914) 378-2000
http://www.consumersunion.org; http://
   www.consumerreports.org

92. *Esquire*
Hearst Corporation
250 West 55th Street
New York, NY 10019
Phone: (212) 649-4020
http://www.hearst.com; http://www.
   esquire.com

93. *Health*
Time Warner, Time Inc./Southern
   Progress Corp.
2100 Lakeshore Drive
Birmingham, AL 35209
http://www.southernprogress.com; http://
   www.health.com

94. *Field & Stream*
Time Warner, Time Inc./Time4 Media
2 Park Avenue, 10th Floor
New York, NY 10016
Phone: (212) 779-5316
Fax: (212) 686-6877
http://www.timewarner.com; http://www.
   fieldandstream.com

95. *American Profile*
Publishing Group of America
341 Cool Springs Boulevard
Suite 400
Franklin, TN 37067
Phone: (615) 468-6000; (800) 468-6000
Fax: (615) 468-6100
http://www.pubgroupofamerica.com;
   http://www.americanprofile.com

96. *The Sporting News*
Vulcan Ventures
475 Park Avenue South, 27th Floor
New York, NY 10016
Phone: (646) 424-2227
Fax: (646) 424-2232
http://www.sportingnews.com

97. *American Baby*
Meredith Corporation
125 Park Avenue
New York, NY 10017
Fax: (212) 455-1463
http://www.americanbaby.com

98. *FamilyFun*
Walt Disney Co., Buena Vista Magazines
http://familyfun.go.com/magazine

99. *Barron's*
Dow Jones & Co., Magazine Group
http://www.barrons.com

100. *eWeek*
Ziff Davis Media
500 Unicorn Drive
Woburn, MA 01801
Phone: (781) 938-2600
http://www.ziffdavis.com; http://www.
   eweek.com

C. LARGEST TELEVISION MARKETS

According to http://www.stationindex.com, the following are the top 50 United States television markets by Rank Designated Market Area (DMA) for 2005–2006. Also included are the major stations in each of these markets. By going to the individual Web sites of the stations, you can learn more about the station and access contact people, as well as employment information.

1. NEW YORK

WCBS (CBS 2)
http://www.cbsnewyork.com

WNBC (NBC 4)
http://www.wnbc.com

WNYW (FOX 5)
http://www.fox5ny.com

WABC (ABC 7)
http://www.wabctv.com

WWOR (UPN 9)
Secaucus, NJ
http://www.upn9.com

WPIX (WB 11)
http://www.wb11.com

WNET (PBS 13)
Newark, NJ
http://www.wnet.org

WLIW (PBS 21)
Garden City, NY
http://www.wliw.org

WNYE (PBS 25)
http://www.wnye.nycenet.edu

WNJU (Telemundo 47)
Newark, NJ
http://www.telemundo47.com

WRNN (ID: RNN 48)
Kingston, NY
http://www.mntv.com

WNJN (PBS 50)
Montclair, NJ
http://www.njn.net

WTBY (54)
Poughkeepsie, NY
http://www.tbn.org

WLNY (55)
Riverhead, NY
http://www.wlnytv.com

WNJB (ID: NJN 58)
New Brunswick, NJ
http://ww.njn.net

WMBC (63)
Newton, NJ
http://www.wmbctv.com

2. LOS ANGELES

KCBS (CBS 2)
http://www.cbs2.com

KNBC (NBC 4)
http://www.nbc4.tv

KTLA (WB 5)
http://www.ktla.com

KABC (ABC 7)
http://www.abc7.com

KCAL (9)
http://www.kcal9.com

KTTV (FOX 11)
http://www.fox11.com

KCOP (UPN 13)
http://www.kcop.com

KSCI (LA 18)
Long Beach, CA
http://www.kscitv.com

KWHY (22)
http://www.kwhy.com

KVMD (23)
Twentynine Palms, CA
http://www.kvmdtv.com

KVCR (PBS 24)
San Bernardino, CA
http://www.kvcr.org

KCET (PBS 28)
http://www.kcet.org

KPXN (30)
San Bernardino, CA
http://www.paxlosangeles.tv

KMEX (34)
http://www.kmex.com

KTBN (40)
Santa Ana, CA
http://www.tbn.org

KXLA (44)
Rancho Palos Verdes, CA
http://www.kxlatv.com

KOCE (PBS 50)
Huntington Beach, CA
http://www.koce.org

KVEA (Telemundo 52)
Corona, CA
http://www.telemundola.com

KDOC (56)
Anaheim, CA
http://www.kdoctv.net

KJLA (LA TV 57)
Ventura, CA
http://www.latv.com

KLCS (PBS 58)
http://www.klcs.org

KBEH (63)
Oxnard, CA
http://www.canal63.com

KHIZ (64)
Barstow, CA
http://www.khiztv.com

3. CHICAGO

WBBM (CBS 2)
http://www.cbs2chicago.com

WMAQ (NBC 5)
http://www.nbc5.com

WLS (ABC 7)
http://www.abc7chicago.com

WGN (WB 9)
http://www.wgntv.com

WTTW (PBS 11)
http://www.wttw.com

WYCC (PBS 20)
http://www.wycc.org

WWME-CA ("Me TV" 23)
http://www.wciu.com/metv.asp

WCIU (26)
http://www.wciu.com

WFLD (FOX Chicago 32)
http://www.foxchicago.com

WPWR (Power 50)
Gary, IN
http://www.upnchicago.com

4. PHILADELPHIA

KYW (CBS 3)
http://www.kywtv.com

WPVI (6 ABC)
http://www.wpvi.com

WCAU (NBC 10)
http://www.nbc10.com

WHYY (PBS 12)
Wilmington, DE
http://www.whyy.org

WPHL (WB 17)
http://www.wb17.com

WNJS (PBS 23)
Camden, NJ
http://www.njn.net

WTXF (FOX 29)
http://www.foxphiladelphia.com

WYBE (Public 35)
http://www.wybe.org

WLVT (PBS 39)
Allentown, PA
http://www.wlvt.org

WGTW (TBN 48)
Burlington, NJ
http://www.tbn.org

WNJT (PBS 52)
Trenton, NJ
http://www.njn.net

WPSG (UPN 57)
http://www.wpsg.com

WFMZ (69)
Allentown, PA
http://www.wfmz.com

5. BOSTON

WGBH (GBH 2) (PBS)
http://www.wgbh.org

WBZ (CBS 4)
http://www.cbs4boston.com

WCVB (5)
http://www.thebostonchannel.com

WHDH (7 NBC)
http://www.whdh.com

FXT (FOX 25)
http://www.fox25.com

WUNI (27)
Worcester, MA
http://www.wunitv.com

SBK (UPN 38)
http://www.upn38.com

GBX (GBH 44) (PBS)
http://www.wgbh.org

WYDN (48)
Worcester, MA
http://www.daystar.com

WZMY (MY TV 50)
Derry, NH
http://www.wzmy.tv

WLVI (Boston's WB/WB 56)
Cambridge, MA
http://www.wb56.com

6. SAN FRANCISCO– OAKLAND–SAN JOSE

KTVU (2)
Oakland, CA
http://www.ktvu.com

KRON (4)
San Francisco, CA
http://www.kron.com

KPIX (CBS 5)
San Francisco, CA
http://www.kpix.com

KGO (ABC 7)
San Francisco, CA
http://www.abc7news.com

KQED (PBS 9)
San Francisco, CA
http://www.kqed.org

KNTV (NBC 11)
San Jose, CA
http://www.nbc11.com

KBWB (WB 20)
San Francisco, CA
http://www.wb20.com

KRCB (PBS 22)
Cotati, CA
http://www.krcb.org

KTSF (26)
San Francisco, CA
http://www.ktsf.com

KMTP (32)
San Francisco, CA
http://www.kmtp.org

KICU (Action 36, Cable 6)
San Jose, CA
http://www.kicu.com

KCSM (PBS 43)
San Mateo, CA
http://www.kcsm.org

KBHK (UPN Bay Area 44)
San Francisco, CA
http://www.upn44.com

KSTS (Telemundo 48)
San Jose, CA
http://www.ksts.com

KFTY (TV 50)
Santa Rosa, CA
http://www.kfty.com

KTEH (PBS 54)
San Jose, CA
http://www.kteh.org

7. DALLAS–FORT WORTH

KDFW (FOX 4)
Dallas, TX
http://www.kdfwfox4.com

KXAS (NBC 5)
Fort Worth, TX
http://www.nbc5i.com

WFAA (8)
Dallas, TX
http://www.wfaa.com

KTVT (CBS 11)
Fort Worth, TX
http://www.cbs11tv.com

KERA (PBS 13)
Dallas, TX
http://www.kera.org

KTXA (UPN 21)
Fort Worth, TX
http://www.upn21.com

KDFI (27)
Dallas, TX
http://www.kdfi27.com

KDAF (WB 33)
Dallas, TX
http://www.wb33.com

KXTX (Telemundo 39)
Dallas, TX
http://www.telemundodallas.com

KFWD (52)
Fort Worth, TX
http://www.kfwd.tv

8. WASHINGTON, DC

WRC (NBC 4)
http://www.nbc4.com

WTTG (FOX 5)
http://www.fox5dc.com

WJLA (ABC 7)
http://www.wjla.com

WUSA (9)
http://www.wusatv9.com

WDCA (UPN 20)
http://www.upn20dc.com

WMPT (PBS 22)
Annapolis, MD
http://www.mpt.org

WETA (PBS 26)
http://www.weta.org

WNVT (30)
Goldvein, VA
http://www.mhznetworks.org

WBDC (WB 50)
http://www.wbdc.com

WNVC (56)
Fairfax, VA
http://www.mhznetworks.org

WWPX (60)
Martinsburg, WV
http://www.pax.tv

WFPT (PBS 62)
Frederick, MD
http://www.mpt.org

WJAL (68)
Hagerstown, MD
http://www.wjal.com

9. ATLANTA

WSB (Action News 2)
http://www.wsbtv.com

WAGA (FOX 5)
http://www.fox5atlanta.com

WGTV (PBS 8)
Athens, GA
http://www.gpb.org

WXIA (11 Alive)
http://www.11alive.com

WTBS (TBS 17)
http://www.tbs.com

WPBA (PBS 30)
http://www.wpba.org

WATL (WB 36)
http://www.wb36.com

WGCL (CBS 46)
Atlanta, GA
http://www.cbs46.com

WUPA (UPN Atlanta 69)
http://www.upn69.com

10. HOUSTON

KPRC (Local 2)
http://www.click2houston.com

KUHT (PBS 8)
http://www.houstonpbs.org

KHOU (11)
http://www.khou.com

KTRK (ABC 13)
http://www.abc13.com

KTXH (UPN 20)
http://www.ktxh.com

KLTJ (22)
http://www.kltj.org

KRIV (FOX 26)
http://www.fox26.com

KHWB (Houston's WB 39)
Houston, TX
http://www.khwbtv.com

KTMD (Telemundo 47)
http://www.ktmd.com

KNWS (51)
Katy, TX
http://www.knws51.com

KTBU (The Tube 55)
Conroe, TX
http://www.thetube.net

11. DETROIT

WJBK (FOX 2)
http://www.fox2detroit.com

WDIV (Local 4)
http://www.clickondetroit.com

WXYZ (7)
http://www.wxyz.com

WDWB (WB 20)
http://www.wb20detroit.com

WKPD (UPN Detroit 50)
http://www.upndetroit.com

WTVS (PBS 56)
http://www.wtvs.org

WWJ (CBS Detroit 62)
http://www.wwjtv.com

12. TAMPA–ST. PETERSBURG

WEDU (PBS 3)
Tampa, FL
http://www.wedu.org

WFLA (News Channel 8) (NBC)
Tampa, FL
http://www.wfla.com

WTSP (CBS 10)
Saint Petersburg, FL
http://www.tampabays10.com

WTVT (FOX 13)
Tampa, FL
http://www.wtvt.com

WUSF (PBS 16)
Tampa, FL
http://www.wusftv.usf.edu

WCLF (22)
Clearwater, FL
http://www.ctnonline.com

WFTS (ABC Action News 28)
Tampa, FL
http://www.wfts.com

WMOR (More TV 32)
Lakeland, FL
http://www.moretv32.com

WTTA (WB 38)
Saint Petersburg, FL
http://www.wtta38.com

WWSB (ABC 7 40)
Sarasota, FL
http://www.wwsb.com

WTOG (UPN 44)
Saint Petersburg, FL
http://www.upn44tv.com

13. SEATTLE-TACOMA

KOMO (KOMO 4 News) (ABC)
Seattle, WA
http://www.komotv.com

KING (KING 5) (NBC)
Seattle, WA
http://www.king5.com

KIRO (KIRO 7) (CBS)
Seattle, WA
http://www.kirotv.com

KCTS (PBS 9)
Seattle, WA
http://www.kcts.org

KSTW (UPN 11)
Tacoma, WA
http://www.kstw.com

KCPQ (Q13) (FOX)
Tacoma, WA
http://www.q13.com

KONG (16)
Everett, WA
http://www.kongtv.com

KTWB (WB 22)
Seattle, WA
http://www.ktwbtv.com

KBTC (PBS 28)
Tacoma, WA
http://www.kbtc.org

14. PHOENIX

KTVK (News Channel 3)
http://www.azfamily.com

KPHO (CBS 5)
http://www.kpho.com

KAZT (AZ TV 7)
Prescott, AZ
http://www.kaz.tv

KAET (PBS 8)
http://www.kaet.asu.edu

KSAZ (FOX 10)
http://www.fox10.com

KPNX (12 News) (NBC)
Mesa, AZ
http://www.azcentral.com/12news

KNXV (ABC 15)
http://www.abc15.com

KUTP (UPN 45)
http://www.upn45phoenix.com

KASW (WB 6)
http://www.azfamily.com/wb

15. MINNEAPOLIS–ST. PAUL

KTCA (Twin Cities Public TV 2)
St. Paul, MN
http://www.tpt.org

WCCO (WCCO 4 TV) (CBS)
Minneapolis, MN
http://www.wcco.com

KSTP (5 Eyewitness News) (ABC)
Saint Paul, MN
http://www.kstp.com

KMSP (FOX 9)
Minneapolis, MN
http://www.kmsp.tv

KARE (11) (NBC)
Minneapolis, MN
http://www.kare11.com

KTCI (PBS 17)
Saint Paul, MN
http://www.ktca.org

KMWB (The WB Minnesota 23)
Minneapolis, MN
http://www.kmwb23.com

WFTC (WFTC 29) (UPN)
Minneapolis, MN
http://www.upn29.com

KSTC (45)
Minneapolis, MN
http://www.kstc45.com

16. CLEVELAND-AKRON

WKYC (3) (NBC)
Cleveland, OH
http://www.wkyc.com

WEWS (News Channel 5) (ABC)
Cleveland, OH
http://www.newsnet5.com

WJW (FOX 8)
Cleveland, OH
http://www.fox8cleveland.com

WOIO (19 Action News) (CBS)
Shaker Heights, OH
http://www.actionnewsnow.com

WVPX (PAX 23)
Akron, OH
http://www.akron23.com

WVIZ (PBS 25)
Cleveland, OH
http://www.wviz.org

WUAB (43 The Block) (UPN)
Lorain, OH
http://www.43theblock.com

WEAO (PBS 49)
Akron, OH
http://www.ch4549.org

WBNX (Cleveland's WB 55)
Akron, OH
http://www.wbnx.com

17. MIAMI–FT. LAUDERDALE

WPBT (PBS 2)
Miami, FL
http://www.channel2.org

WFOR (CBS 4)
Miami, FL
http://www.cbs4.com

WTVJ (NBC 6)
Miami, FL
http://www.nbc6.net

WSVN (7)
Miami, FL
http://www.wsvn.com

WPLG (Local 10) (ABC)
Miami, FL
http://www.local10.com

WLRN (PBS 17)
Miami, FL
http://www.wlrn.org

WBFS (UPN 33)
Miami, FL
http://www.upn33.com

WBZL (WB 39)
Miami, FL
http://www.wb39.com

WSCV (Telemundo 51)
Fort Lauderdale, FL
http://www.telemundo51.com

18. DENVER

KWGN (WB 2)
http://www.wb2.com

KCNC (CBS 4)
http://www.news4colorado.com

KRMA (PBS 6)
http://www.krma.org

KMGH (ABC 7)
http://www.thedenverchannel.com

KUSA (9) (NBC)
http://www.9news.com

KBDI (PBS 12)
Broomfield, CO
http://www.kbdi.org

KTVD (UPN 20)
http://www.upn20.tv

KDVR (FOX 31)
http://www.fox31news.com

19. SACRAMENTO-STOCKTON-MODESTO

KCRA (3) (NBC)
Sacramento, CA
http://www.thekcrachannel.com

KVIE (PBS 6)
Sacramento, CA
http://www.kvie.org

KXTV (News 10) (ABC)
Sacramento, CA
http://www.news10.net

KOVR (CBS 13)
Stockton, CA
http://www.kovr13.com

KBSV (AssyriaVision 23)
Ceres, CA
http://www.betnahrain.org/KBSV/kbsv.htm

KMAX (UPN 31)
Sacramento, CA
http://www.upn31.com

KTXL (FOX 40)
Sacramento, CA
http://www.fox40.com

KQCA (WB 58)
Stockton, CA
http://www.kqca58.com

20. ORLANDO-DAYTONA BEACH-MELBOURNE

WESH (2) (NBC)
Daytona Beach, FL
http://www.wesh.com

WKMG (Local 6) (CBS)
Orlando, FL
http://www.local6.com

WFTV (9) (ABC)
Orlando, FL
http://www.wftv.com

WCEU (PBS 15)
New Smyrna Beach, FL
http://www.wceu.org

WKCF (WB 18)
Clermont, FL
http://www.wb18.com

WMFE (PBS 24)
Orlando, FL
http://www.wmfe.org

WRDQ (Action-TV 27)
Orlando, FL
http://www.wrdq.com

WOFL (FOX 35)
Orlando, FL
http://www.wofl.com

WTGL (52)
Cocoa, FL
http://www.tv52.org

WRBW (65) (UPN)
Orlando, FL
http://www.wrbw.com

21. ST. LOUIS

KTVI (FOX 2)
http://www.fox2ktvi.com

KMOV (News 4) (CBS)
http://www.kmov.com

KSDK (News Channel 5) (NBC)
http://www.ksdk.com

KETC (PBS 9)
http://www.ketc.org

KPLR (WB 11)
http://www.wb11tv.com

KDNL (ABC 30)
http://www.abcstlouis.com

WRBU (UPN 46)
East St. Louis, IL
http://www.upn46stl.com

22. PITTSBURGH

KDKA (2) (CBS)
http://www.kdka.com

WTAE (4) (ABC)
http://www.thepittsburghchannel.com

WPXI (11) (NBC)
http://www.wpxi.com

WQED (PBS 13)
http://www.wqed.org

WNPA (UPN Pittsburgh 19)
Jeannette, PA
http://www.wnpatv.com

WCWB (WB 22)
http://www.wcwb22.com

WPGH (FOX 53)
http://www.wpgh53.com

23. PORTLAND, OREGON

KATU (2) (ABC)
http://www.katu.com

KWBP-LP (5) (Portland's WB / KWBP)
http://www.wb32tv.com

KOIN (6) (CBS)
http://www.koin.com

KGW (8) (NBC)
http://www.kgw.com

KOPB (PBS 10)
http://www.opb.org

KPTV (FOX 12)
http://www.kptv.com

KWBP (Portland's WB 32)
Salem, OR
http://www.wb32tv.com

KPDX (UPN 49)
Vancouver, WA
http://www.kpdx.com

24. BALTIMORE

WMAR (2) (ABC)
http://www.wmar.com

WBAL (11) (NBC)
http://www.thewbalchannel.com

WJZ (13) (CBS)
http://www.wjz.com

WUTV (24) (UPN)
http://www.upn24.com

WBFF (FOX 45)
http://www.foxbaltimore.com

WNUV (WB 54)
http://www.wbbaltimore.com

WMPT (PBS 67)
http://www.mpt.org

25. INDIANAPOLIS

WTTV (WB 4)
Bloomington, IN
http://www.wb4.com

WRTV (rtv 6) (ABC)
http://www.theindychannel.com

WISH (8) (CBS)
http://www.wishtv.com

WTHR (13) (NBC)
http://www.wthr.com

WFYI (PBS 20)
http://www.wfyi.org

WNDY (UPN Indiana) (23)
Marion, IN
http://www.upn23.com

WTTK (WB 4 / WTTV) (29)
Kokomo, IN
http://www.wb4.com

WTIU (PBS 30)
Bloomington, IN
http://www.indiana.edu/~radiotv/wtiu

WIPB (PBS 49)
Munci, IN
http://www.bsu.edu/wipb

WXIN (FOX 59)
http://www.fox59.com

26. SAN DIEGO

XETV (FOX 6)
Tijuana, BN, MX
http://www.fox6.com

KFMB (Local 8) (CBS)
http://www.kfmb.com

KGTV (10) (ABC)
http://www.thesandiegochannel.com

KPBS (PBS 15)
http://www.kpbs.org

KBNT (Univision 17)
http://www.univision17.com

XHAS (Telemundo 33)
Tijuana, BN, MX
http://www.telemundo33.tv

KNSD (NBC 7 39)
http://www.nbcsandiego.com

XHUPN (UPN 13)
Tecate, BN, MX
http://www.upn13sandiego.com

KUSI (KUSI 9 51)
http://www.kusi.com

KSWB (KS WB 5) (69)
http://www.kswbtv.com

27. CHARLOTTE, NC

WBTV (3) (CBS)
http://www.wbtv.com

WSOC (9) (ABC)
http://www.wsoctv.com

WCCB (FOX Charlotte) (18)
http://www.fox18wccb.com

WNSC (ETV) (PBS 30)
Rock Hill, NC
http://www.wnsc.org

WCNC (36) (NBC)
http://www.wcnc.com

WTVI (PBS 42)
http://www.wtvi.org

WJZY (UPN 46)
Belmont, NC
http://www.upn46.com

WWWB (Charlotte's WB 55)
Rock Hill, NC
http://www.wb55.com

WUNG (UNC TV) (PBS 58)
Concord, NC
http://www.unctv.org

WAXN (Action 64)
Kannapolis, NC
http://www.action64.com

28. HARTFORD–NEW HAVEN

WSFB (3) (CBS)
Hartford, CT
http://www.wfsb.com

WTNH (8) (ABC)
New Haven, CT
http://www.wtnh.com

WTXX (WB 20)
Waterbury, CT
http://www.wtxx.com

WEDH (PBS 24)
Hartford, CT
http://www.cptv.org

WVIT (NBC 30)
New Britain, CT
http://www.nbc30.com

**WEDW (PBS 49), WEDN (PBS 53),
WEDY (PBS 65)**
Bridgeport, CT; Norwich; CT; New
Haven, CT
http://www.cptv.org

WCTX (59) (UPN)
New Haven, CT
http://www.wctx.com

WTIC (FOX 61)
Hartford, CT
http://www.fox61.com

29. RALEIGH-DURHAM

WUNC (UNC TV) (PBS 4)
Chapel Hill, NC
http://www.unctv.org

WRAL (5) (CBS)
Raleigh, NC
http://www.wral.com

WTVD (ABC 11)
Durham, NC
http://www.abc11tv.com

WNCN (NBC 17)
Goldsboro, NC
http://www.nbc17.com

WLFL (WB 22)
Raleigh, NC
http://www.wlfl22.com

WRDC (UPN 28)
Durham, NC
http://www.upn28tv.com

WRAZ (FOX 50)
Raleigh, NC
http://www.fox50.com

30. NASHVILLE

WKRN (News 2) (ABC)
http://www.wkrn.com

WSMV (4 News) (NBC)
http://www.wsmv.com

WTVF (News Channel 5) (CBS)
http://www.newschannel5.com

WNPT (PBS 8)
http://www.wnpt.net

WZTV (FOX 17)
http://www.fox17.com

WCTE (PBS 22)
Cookeville, TN
http://www.wcte.org

WNPX (28)
Cookeville, TN
http://www.paxnashville.tv

WUXP (UPN 30)
http://www.upn30.com

WNAB (WB 58)
http://www.wb58.net

31. KANSAS CITY

WDAF (FOX 4)
http://www.wdaftv4.com

KCTV (5) (CBS)
http://www.kctv5.com

KMOS (PBS 6)
Sedalia, MO
http://www.kmos.cmsu.edu/TV

KMBC (9) (ABC)
http://www.thekansascitychannel.com

KCPT (PBS 19)
http://www.kcpt.org

KCWE (UPN 29)
http://www.thekansascitychannel.com/
kcwetv

KMCI (38 The Spot)
Lawrence, KS
http://www.kmci.com

KSHB (Action News) (NBC 41)
http://www.nbcactionnews.com

KSMO (WB 62)
http://www.wb62.com

32. COLUMBUS, OH

WCMH (NBC 4)
http://www.nbc4i.com

WSYX (ABC 6)
http://www.wsyx6.com

WBNS (10) (CBS)
http://www.wbns10tv.com

WTTE (FOX 28)
http://www.wtte28.com

WOSU (PBS 34)
http://www.wosu.org

WSFJ (51)
Newark, OH
http://www.wsfj.com

WWHO (UPN Columbus 53)
Chillicothe, OH
http://www.upn53.com

33. MILWAUKEE

WTMJ (TMJ 4) (NBC)
http://www.touchtmj4.com

WITI (FOX 6)
http://www.fox6milwaukee.com

WMVS (MPTV) (PBS 10)
http://www.mptv.org

WISN (12) (ABC)
http://www.themilwaukeechannel.com

WVTV (WB 18)
http://www.wvtv18.com

WCGV (UPN 24)
http://www.wcgv24.com

WMVT (PBS 36)
http://www.mptv.org

WMLW-CA (41)
http://www.wmlw.com

WDJT (CBS 58)
http://www.cbs58.com

34. CINCINNATI

WLWT (5) (NBC)
http://www.channelcincinnati.com

WCPO (9) (ABC)
http://www.wcpo.com

WKRC (Local 12) (CBS)
http://www.wkrc.com

WPTO (PBS 14)
Oxford, OH
http://www.thinktv.org

WXIX (FOX 19)
Newport, KY
http://www.wxix.com

WOTH-LP (The Other Channel) (25)
http://www.wbqc.com/woth

WBQC-CA (UPN 38)
http://www.wbqc.com

WCET (PBS 48)
http://www.cetconnect.org

WCVN (PBS 54)
Covington, KY
http://www.ket.org

WSTR (WB 64)
http://www.wb64.net

35. GREENVILLE-SPARTANBURG-ASHEVILLE-ANDERSON

WYFF (4) (NBC)
Greenville, SC
http://www.thecarolinachannel.com

WSPA (News Channel 7) (CBS 2)
Spartanburg, SC
http://www.wspa.com

WLOS (13) (ABC)
Asheville, NC
http://www.wlos.com

WHNS (FOX Carolina) (21)
Asheville, NC
http://www.whns.com

WNTV (PBS 29), WNEH (PBS 38)
Greenville, SC; Greenwood, SC
http://www.scetv.org

WUNF (UNC TV) (PBS 33)
Asheville, NC
http://www.unctv.org

WBSC (WB 40)
Anderson, SC
http://www.wb40.com

WRET (PBS 49)
Spartanburg, GA
http://www.wret.org

WASV (UPN 62)
Asheville, NC
http://www.wasv.com

36. SALT LAKE CITY

KUTV (2) (CBS)
http://www.kutv.com

KTVX (ABC 4)
http://www.4utah.com

KSL (5) (NBC)
http://www.ksl.com

KUED (PBS 7)
http://www.kued.org

KUEN (UEN-TV) (9)
Ogden, UT
http://www.uen.org/tv

KBYU (PBS 11)
Provo, UT
http://www.kbyutv.org

KSTU (FOX 13)
http://www.fox13.com

KJZZ (14)
http://www.kjzz.com

KUPX (16)
Provo, UT
http://www.paxsaltlakecity.tv

KPNZ (Z 24) (UPN)
Ogden, UT
http://www.z24tv.com

KUWB (Utah's WB) (30)
Ogden, UT
http://www.wb30tv.com

37. SAN ANTONIO

WOAI (4) (NBC)
http://www.woai.com

KENS (5) (CBS)
http://www.mysanantonio.com

KLRN (PBS 9)
http://www.klrn.org

KSAT (12) (ABC)
http://www.ksat.com

KABB (FOX 29)
http://www.kabb.com

KRRT (WB 35)
Kerrville, TX
http://www.krrt.com

38. WEST PALM BEACH–FT. PIERCE

WPTV (5) (NBC)
West Palm Beach, FL
http://www.wptv.com

WPEC (News 12) (CBS)
West Palm Beach, FL
http://www.wpecnews12.com

WTCE (21)
Fort Pierce, FL
http://www.wjeb.org

WPBF (25) (ABC)
Tequesta, FL
http://www.thewpbfchannel.com

WFLX (FOX 29)
West Palm Beach, FL
http://www.wflxfox29.com

WTVX (WB/UPN TVX 34)
Fort Pierce, FL
http://www.upn34.com

WXEL (PBS 42)
West Palm Beach, FL
http://www.wxel.org

WPPB (63)
http://www.becon.tv

39. GRAND RAPIDS–KALAMAZOO–BATTLE CREEK

WWMT (3) (CBS)
Kalamazoo, MI
http://www.wwmt.com

WOOD (WOOD TV 8) (NBC)
Grand Rapids, MI
http://www.woodtv.com

WZZM (13) (ABC)
Grand Rapids, MI
http://www.wzzm13.com

WXSP-CA (15) (UPN)
Grand Rapids, MI
http://wxsp.tv/x

WXMI (FOX 17)
Grand Rapids, MI
http://www.wxmi.com

WGVU (PBS 35)
Grand Rapids, MI
http://www.wgvu.org

WOTV (ABC 4)
Battle Creek, MI
http://www.wotv.com

WGVK (PBS 52)
Kalamazoo. MI
http://www.wgvu.org

40. BIRMINGHAM

WBRC (FOX 6)
http://www.wbrc.com

WCIQ (PBS 7), WBIQ (PBS 10) (APT)
Mount Cheaha, AL; Birmingham, AL
http://www.aptv.org

WVTM (NBC 13)
http://www.nbc13.com

WDBB (WB 21)
Bessemer, AL; Homewood, AL
http://www.wtto21.com

WCFT (ABC 33 40)
Tuscaloosa, AL; Anniston, AL
http://www.abc3340.com

WIAT (42) (CBS)
http://www.wiat.com

WABM (UPN 68)
http://www.wabm68.com

41. HARRISBURG-LANCASTER-LEBANON-YORK

WGAL (News 8) (NBC)
Lancaster, PA
http://www.thewgalchannel.com

WLYH (UPN 15)
Lancaster, PA
http://www.upn15.com

WHP (21) (CBS)
Harrisburg, PA
http://www.whptv.com

WHTM (ABC 27)
Harrisburg, PA
http://www.abc27.com

WITF (PBS 33)
Harrisburg, PA
http://www.witf.org

WPMT (FOX 43)
York, PA
http://www.wpmt.com

42. NORFOLK–PORTSMOUTH–NEWPORT NEWS

WUND (UNC TV) (PBS 2)
Columbia, NC
http://www.unctv.org

WTKR (News Channel 3) (CBS)
http://www.wtkr.com

WSKY (SKY 4)
Manteo, NC
http://www.wsky4.com

WAVY (10) (NBC)
Portsmouth, VA
http://www.wavy.com

WVEC (13) (ABC)
Hampton, VA
http://www.wvec.com

WHRO (15) (PBS)
Hampton-Norfolk, VA
http://www.whro.org

WGNT (UPN 27)
Portsmouth, VA
http://www.upn27.com

WTVZ (WB 33)
Norfolk, VA
http://www.wtvz33.com

WUNP (PBS 36)
Roanoke Rapids, NC
http://www.unctv.org

WVBT (FOX 43)
Virginia Beach, VA
http://www.wvbt.com

43. NEW ORLEANS

WWL (4) (CBS)
http://www.wwltv.com

WDSU (6) (NBC)
http://www.theneworleanschannel.com

WVUE (FOX 8)
http://www.fox8live.com

WYES (PBS 12)
http://www.wyes.org

WGNO (ABC 26)
http://www.abc26.com

WLAE (PBS 32)
http://www.pbs.org/wlae

WNOL (WB 38)
http://www.wb38.com

WUPL (UPN New Orleans) (54)
Slidell, LA
http://www.upn54.com

44. MEMPHIS

WREG (News Channel 3) (CBS)
http://www.wreg.com

WMC (5) (NBC)
http://www.wmctv.com

WKNO (PBS 10)
http://www.wkno.org

WHBQ (FOX 13)
http://www.fox13whbq.com

WPTY (Eyewitness News ABC 30) (24)
http://www.abc24.com

WLMT (UPN 30)
http://www.upn30memphis.com

45. OKLAHOMA CITY

KFOR (News Channel 4) (NBC)
http://www.kfor.com

KOCO (5) (ABC)
http://www.channeloklahoma.com

KWTV (News 9) (CBS)
http://www.newsok.com

KETA (PBS 13)
http://www.oeta.onenet.net

KOKH (FOX 25)
http://www.kokh25.com

KOCB (WB 34)
http://www.kocb.com

KAUT (UPN 43)
http://www.upn43.com

KOCM (46)
Norman, OK
http://www.daystar.com

KSBI (52)
http://www.ksbitv.com

46. ALBUQUERQUE-SANTA FE

KASA (FOX) (2)
Santa Fe, NM
http://www.kasa.com

KOB (NBC) (4)
Albuquerque, NM
http://www.kobtv.com

KNME (PBS 5)
Albuquerque, NM
http://www.knmetv.org

KOAT (7) (ABC)
Albuquerque, NM
http://www.koat.com

KRQE (News 13) (CBS)
Albuquerque, NM
http://www.krqe.com

KWBQ (19) (WB)
Santa Fe, NM
http://www.wb19tv.com

KASY (UPN 50)
Albuquerque, NM
http://www.upn50tv.com

47. GREENSBORO–HIGH POINT–WINSTON-SALEM

WFMY (News 2) (CBS)
Greensboro, NC
http://www.wfmy.com

WGHP (FOX 8)
High Point, NC
http://www.fox8wghp.com

WXII (12) (NBC)
Winston-Salem, NC
http://www.wxii12.com

WTWB (20) (WB)
Lexington, NC
http://www.wtwb.com

WUNL (PBS 26)
Winston-Salem, NC
http://www.unctv.org

WXLV (ABC 45)
Winston-Salem, NC
http://www.abc45.com

WUPN (48) (UPN)
Greensboro, NC
http://www.upn48.com

48. LAS VEGAS

KVBC (3) (NBC)
http://www.kvbc.com

KVVU (FOX 5)
Henderson, NV
http://www.kvvutv.com

KLAS (8) (CBS)
http://www.klastv.com

KVLX (PBS 10)
http://www.klvx.org

KTVD (Action News) (ABC 13)
http://www.ktnv.com

KINC (15)
http://www.kinc-tv15.com

KVWB (WB Las Vegas) (12)
http://www.wblasvegas.com

KTUD-CA (UPN Las Vegas) (25)
http://www.ktudtv.com

KFBT (Gold 33)
http://www.kfbt33.com

KBLR (Telemundo 39)
Paradise, NV
http://www.kblr39.com

49. BUFFALO

WGRZ (2) (NBC)
http://www.wgrz.com

WIVB (4) (CBS)
http://www.wivb.com

WKBW (7) (ABC)
http://www.wkbw.com

WNED (PBS 17)
http://www.wned.org

WNLO (UPN 23)
http://www.wnlo.com

WUTV (FOX 29)
http://www.wutv.com

WNYO (WB 49)
http://www.wb49.net

WNGS (67)
Springville, NY
http://www.wngstv.com

50. LOUISVILLE

WAVE (3) (NBC)
http://www.wave3.com

WHAS (11) (ABC)
http://www.whas11.com

WKPC (KET) (PBS 15)
http://www.ket.org

WBNA (21)
http://www.wbna-21.com

WKLY (32) (CBS)
http://www.thelouisvillechannel.com

WBKI (WB 7) (34)
Campbellsville, KY
http://www.wbki.tv

WDRB (FOX 41)
http://www.fox41.com

WFTE (Great 58)
Salem, IN
http://www.great58.tv

WKMJ (KET2) (68)
http://www.ket.org

BIBLIOGRAPHY

GENERAL JOURNALISM

Ferguson, Donald L., and Jim Patten. *Opportunities in Journalism Careers.* New York: McGraw-Hill, 2001.

Goldberg, Jan. *Careers in Journalism.* 3rd Edition. New York: McGraw-Hill, 2005.

Kovach, Bill, and Tom Rosensteil. *The Elements of Journalism.* New York: Three Rivers Press, 2001.

Mills, Eleanor, ed, with Kira Cochrane. *Journalistas: 100 Years of the Best Writing and Reporting by Women Journalists.* New York: Carroll & Graf, 2005.

Morkes, Andrew, ed. *Preparing for a Career in Journalism. (What Can I Do Now?).* New York: Ferguson, 1998.

Seidman, David. *Exploring Careers in Journalism (Career Resource Library).* New York: Rosen Publishing Group, 2000.

Warley, Stephen. *Vault Career Guide to Journalism and Information Media.* New York: Vault, Inc., 2005.

Williams, Thomas A. *Publish Your Own Magazine, Guide Book, or Weekly Newspaper: How to Start, Manage, and Profit from a Homebased Publishing Company.* Boulder, Colo.: Sentient Publications, 2002.

Yager, Fred, and Jan Yager. *Career Opportunities in the Publishing Industry.* New York: Checkmark Books, 2005.

NEWSPAPERS

Mogel, Leonard. *The Newspaper: Everything You Need to Know to Make It in the Newspaper Business.* Sewickley, Pa.: GATF Press, 2000.

Woods, Kevin, ed. *Best Newspaper Writing 2002.* Chicago: Bonus Books, 2002.

MAGAZINES

American Society of Magazine Editors, ed. *Best American Magazine Writing of 2002.* New York: HarperCollins, 2002.

Bykofsky, Sheree, Jennifer Bayse Sander, and Lynne Rominger. *Complete Idiot's Guide to Publishing Magazine Articles.* Indianapolis, Ind.: Alpha Books, 2000.

Daly, Charles P., Patrick Henry, and Ellen Ryder. *The Magazine Publishing Industry.* Boston: Allyn & Bacon, 1996.

Johnson, Sammye, and Patricia Prijatel. *The Magazine: From Cover to Cover.* Lincolnwood, Ill.: NTC Publishing, 1999.

King, Stacey. *Magazine Design That Works.* Gloucester, Mass.: Rockport Publishers, 2001.

Mandell, Judy. *Magazine Editors Talk to Writers.* New York: Wiley, 1996.

Monti, Ralph. *Career Opportunities in Magazine Publishing.* Bloomfield, N.J.: Special Interest Media, 2003.

BROADCASTING

Arya, Bob. *Thirty Seconds to Air: A Field Reporter's Guide to Live Television Reporting.* Ames: Iowa State Press, 1999.

Block, Mervin. *Writing Broadcast News—Shorter, Sharper, Stronger.* Los Angeles: Bonus Books, 1997.

Crouse, Chuck. *Reporting for Radio.* Los Angeles: Bonus Books, 1992.

Dotson, Bob. *Make It Memorable: Writing and Packaging TV News with Style.* Los Angeles: Bonus Books, 2000.

Ellis, Elmo. *Opportunities in Broadcasting Careers.* New York: McGraw-Hill, 2004.

Freedman, Wayne. *It Takes More than Good Looks to Succeed at TV News Reporting.* Los Angeles: Bonus Books, 2003.

Gate, Linda, Lawrie Douglas, and Marie Kinsey. *A Guide to Commercial Radio Journalism.* 2nd ed. Burlington, Mass.: Focal Press, 1999.

Gormly, Eric K. *Writing and Producing Television News.* 2nd ed. Ames, Iowa: Blackwell Publishers, 2004.

Hedrick, Tom. *The Art of Sportscasting: How to Build a Successful Career.* Lanham, Md.: Diamond Communications, 2000.

Kalbfeld, Brad. *Associated Press Broadcast News Handbook.* New York: McGraw-Hill, 2000.

McCoy, Michelle, with Ann S. Utterback. *Sound and Look Professional on Television and the Internet: How to Improve Your On-Camera Presence.* Los Angeles: Bonus Books, 2000.

Mitchell, Leslie Scott. *Freelancing for Television And Radio.* 2nd ed. Oxford: Routledge, 2005.

Noronha, Shonan. *Opportunities in Television and Video Careers.* New York: McGraw-Hill, 2003.

Orlik, Peter B. *Career Perspectives in Electronic Media.* Ames, Iowa: Blackwell Publishers, 2004.

Redstone, Paul. *Broadcasting and the Media (The Insider Career Guides Series).* New York: Spiro Press, 2000.

Thompson, Robert. *The Broadcast Journalism Handbook: A Television News Survival Guide.* Lanham, Md.: Rowman & Littlefield Publishers, 2003.

Yehling, Carol, ed. *Broadcasting (Careers in Focus).* New York: Ferguson Publishing Company, 2001.

GENERAL WRITING

Banks, Michael A. *How to Become a Fulltime Freelance Writer: A Practical Guide to Setting up a Successful Writing Business at Home.* New York: Watson-Guptill Publications.

Bly, Robert. *Careers for Writers & Others Who Have a Way with Words.* 2nd ed. New York: McGraw-Hill, 2003.

Formichelli, Linda, and Diana Burrell. *The Renegade Writer: A Totally Innovative Guide to Freelance Writing Success.* Oak Park, Ill.: Marion Street Press, 2003.

Harper, Timothy, ed., and Samuel G. Freedman, foreword. *The ASJA Guide to Freelance Writing: A Professional Guide to the Business, for Nonfiction Writers of All Experience Levels.* New York: St. Martin's Griffin, 2003.

GENERAL REFERENCE

Career Information Center. 7th ed. 13 vols. New York: Macmillan, 1999.

Encyclopedia of Careers and Vocational Guidance. 11th ed. 4 vols. Chicago: Ferguson, 2000.

Farr, Michael, United States Department of Labor, Laverne L. Ludden, Laurence Shatkin, and Jist Publishing (Editor). *Enhanced Occupational Outlook Handbook.* Indianapolis, Ind.: JIST Publishing, 2002.

U.S. Department of Labor, Bureau of Labor Statistics. *Occupational Outlook Handbook. 2004–2005.* Indianapolis, Ind.: Jist Publishing, 2004.

CAREER EXPLORATION AND SELF-ASSESSMENT

Bernstein, Alan B., and Nicholas R. Schaffzin. *The Princeton Review Guide to Your Career.* 4th ed. New York: Princeton Review Publishing, 2000.

Boldt, Laurence G. *Zen and the Art of Making a Living: A Practical Guide to Creative Career Design.* New York: Penguin Books, 1999.

Bolles, Richard Nelson. *The 2004 What Color Is Your Parachute?* Berkeley: Ten Speed Press, 2004.

Edwards, Paul, and Sarah. *Finding Your Perfect Work.* Revised ed. New York: Jeremy P. Tarcher,2003.

Gurvis, Sandra. *Careers for Nonconformists: A Practical Guide to Finding and Developing a Career outside the Mainstream.* New York: Marlowe & Company, 2000.

Jansen, Julie. *I Don't Know What I Want, but I Know It's Not This: A Step-By-Step Guide to Finding Gratifying Work.* New York: Penguin Books, 2003.

Lore, Nicholas. *The Pathfinder: How to Choose or Change Your Career for a Lifetime of Satisfaction and Success.* New York: Fireside, 1998

Nemko, Marty, Paul Edwards, and Sarah Edwards. *Cool Careers for Dummies.* New York: Wiley Publishing, 2001.

Sher, Barbara. *Live the Life You Love: In Ten Easy Step-by-Step Lessons.* New York: Dell Publishing, 1997.

Tieger, Paul D., and Barbara Barron-Tieger. *Do What You Are: Discover the Perfect Career for You through the Secrets of Personality Type.* 3rd ed. Boston: Little, Brown 2001.

JOB SEARCH

Criscito, Pat. *Resumes in Cyberspace: Your Complete Guide to a Computerized Job Search.* Hauppauge, N.Y.: Barron's Educational Series, 2000.

Crispin, Gerry, and Mark Mehler. *CareerXroads 2000: The Directory of Job, Resume and Career Management Sites on the World Wide Web.* Indianapolis, Ind.: JIST Works, 2000

Dixon, Pam. *Job Searching Online for Dummies.* 2nd ed. Indianapolis, Ind.: IDG Books, 2000.

Figler, Howard. *The Complete Job-Search Handbook: Everything You Need to Know to Get the Job You Really Want.* 3rd ed. New York: Owl Books, 1999.

McKinney, Anne, ed. *Real-Resumes for Media, Newspaper, Broadcasting and Public Affairs Jobs: Including Real Resumes Used to Change Careers and Transfer Skills to Other Industries.* Fayetteville, N.C.: Prep Publishing, 2002.

Petras, Kathryn, and Ross Petras. *The Only Job Hunting Guide You'll Ever Need: The Most Comprehensive Guide for Job Hunters and Career Switchers.* New York: Simon & Schuster, 1995.

Yate, Martin. *Careersmarts: Jobs with a Future.* New York: Ballantine Books, 1997.

INDEX